SCHAUM'S OUTLINE OF

FRENCH GRAMMAR

Third Edition

•

by

MARY E. COFFMAN CROCKER

French Editor and Consultant
Toronto, Ontario

SCHAUM'S OUTLINE SERIES

McGRAW-HILL

New York   San Francisco   Washington, D.C.   Auckland   Bogotá   Caracus   Lisbon
London   Madrid   Mexico City   Milan   Montreal   New Dehli
San Juan   Singapore   Sydney   Tokyo   Toronto

MARY E. COFFMAN CROCKER is presently a French editor and consultant in Toronto, Ontario. She was previously Directrice des Éditions, Langues secondes, Centre Éducatif et Culturel, Montréal, Québec, and Sponsoring Editor, Foreign Language Department, McGraw-Hill Book Company, New York, New York. In addition to the *Schaum's Outline of French Vocabulary,* she is coauthor of *French: Language and Lifestyles.* She is a biographee in *Who's Who of American Women, Ninth Edition.*

Schaum's Outline of
FRENCH GRAMMAR

Copyright © 1990, 1981, 1973 by The McGraw-Hill Companies, Inc. All rights reserved. Printed in the United States of America. Except as permitted under the Copyright Act of 1976, no part of this publication may be reproduced or distributed in any form or by any means, or stored in a data base or retrieval system, without the prior written permission of the publisher.

14 15 16 17 18 19 20 PRS PRS 9 8 7

ISBN 0-07-013885-0

Sponsoring Editor, John Aliano
Production Supervisor, Louise Karam
Editing Supervisor, Meg Tobin

Library of Congress Cataloging-in-Publication Data

Coffman Crocker, Mary E.
   Schaum's outline of French grammar/
      Mary E. Coffman Crocker.—3rd ed.

   (Schaum's outline series)
   Includes index.
   1. French language—Grammar—1950- I. Title.
   II. Title: French grammar.

PC2112.C56   1990   88-39022
445—dc19   CIP

McGraw-Hill

A Division of The McGraw·Hill Companies

PREFACE

Like the first and second editions, the third edition of this review book has been designed and developed in order to facilitate the study of French grammar. The book is now divided into nine chapters. Each one concentrates on the basic problem areas of the language: nouns and articles, adjectives and adverbs; prepositions; numbers, dates, and time; verbs, interrogatives, negatives; pronouns; and special meanings of certain verbs. The chapter on prepositions is new to this edition.

Each grammatical or structural point is introduced by a simple explanation in English. The explanation is further clarified by many concrete examples. It is recommended that you first read the explanation and then study the illustrative examples. You should then write out the answers to the exercises that follow. You should rewrite the entire sentence in fill-in-the-blank exercises even though only one or two words are required. It is recommended that you correct yourself immediately before proceeding to the next exercise. An answer key appears at the end of the book.

In this edition, more exercises and review sections have been added to provide further practice. Many of the exercises have been put into authentic, meaningful contexts and involve practical, real-life situations to which students can relate. Some of the exercises will require you to understand meaning as well as form in order to successfully complete them. This will help you develop proficiency in French and prepare for communicative activities in your classroom.

One of the most difficult and tedious tasks in acquiring a second language is learning the many forms that exist in the language, whether they are noun, adjective, or verb forms. In *Schaum's Outline of French Grammar,* all forms have been logically grouped in order to make their acquisition as simple as possible and also to minimize what at first appear to be irregularities. In many texts, the verbs *courir, rire, rompre,* and *conclure* are treated as separate irregular verbs in the present tense. You will note, however, that these verbs have a lot in common. The same endings as those for regular **-re** verbs are added to the infinitive stem except in the third person singular:

> *courir—il court*, je cours, tu cours, nous cour**ons**, vous cour**ez**, ils cour**ent**
>
> *rire—il rit*, je ris, tu ris, nous ri**ons**, vous ri**ez**, ils ri**ent**
>
> *rompre—il rompt*, je romps, tu romps, nous romp**ons**, vous romp**ez**, ils romp**ent**
>
> *conclure—il conclut*, je conclus, tu conclus, nous conclu**ons**, vous conclu**ez**, ils conclu**ent**

This can be done with many verbs in all tenses. Making such groupings will greatly facilitate your task of mastering the many forms.

Schaum's Outline of French Grammar can be used as a review text, as a companion to any basic text, or as a reference book. In order to reinforce each point you are learning in your basic text, you may wish to get additional practice by doing the clear, logically organized exercises provided throughout this book.

Mary E. Coffman Crocker

CONTENTS

CONTENTS

Chapter 3 PREPOSITIONS

To Indicate Function, Result or Tendency. After Expressions of Duration,
Length of Time and Position of the Body.

Chapter 4 NUMBERS, DATES, TIME

Cardinal Numbers. Ordinal Numbers. Collective Numbers. Fractions.
Arithmetical Operations and Dimensions. Dimensions.

Chapter 5 VERBS

First Conjugation Verbs. Verbs Beginning with a Vowel. Verbs with
Spelling Changes: Verbs Ending in -cer and -ger; Verbs with -é- in the
Infinitive; Verbs with -e in the Infinitive; Verbs with -yer in the Infinitive.
Second Conjugation Verbs. Third Conjugation Verbs. Irregular Verbs:
Verbs like *ouvrir*; Verbs like *courir, rire, rompre, conclure*; *Battre* and
mettre; Verbs like *partir*; *Vaincre*; Verbs like *connaitre*; *Plaire* and *se taire*;
Verbs with infinitives ending in -ire: *Lire, dire, conduire, traduire*; *Ecrire,
vivre, suivre*; *Croire*; *voir* and *mourir*; Verbs like *craindre, peindre, joindre*;
Verbs like *prendre*; *Venir* and *tenir*; *Acquérir* and *conquérir*; *Pouvoir,
vouloir, pleuvoir*; *Boire, devoir, recevoir*; *Avoir*; *Etre*; *Aller*; *Faire*; *Savoir*;
Valoir and *Falloir*. Special Uses of the Present Tense: *Depuis, il y a ... que,
voilà ... que*, and *ça fait ... que* plus the present tense; *Venir de* plus the
present tense.

S'asseoir. Reflexive Verbs with Parts of the Body. Reflexive versus
Nonreflexive Verbs. Reflexive Verbs in the Infinitive.

Affirmative Imperatives. The Affirmative Imperative of Reflexive Verbs.
The Negative Imperative. The Negative Imperative of Reflexive Verbs.

Formation. Use.

Formation. Uses of the Imperfect Tense: Continuing action; With verbs
denoting mental activity or conditions; Descriptions in the past; *Si* and the
imperfect tense; *Depuis, il y avait ... que, voilà ... que, ça faisait ... que*
and the imperfect tense; *Venir de* plus the imperfect tense.

CONTENTS

Chapter 6   INTERROGATIVE WORDS AND CONSTRUCTIONS

Chapter 7   NEGATIVE WORDS AND CONSTRUCTIONS

CONTENTS

Chapter 1

Nouns and Articles

GENDER AND THE DEFINITE ARTICLE

Singular Forms

French nouns, unlike English nouns, have a gender. Every noun is either masculine or feminine. Nouns that refer specifically to males (people or animals), such as *father, son,* etc., are masculine. Those that refer to females (people or animals), such as *mother, daughter,* etc., are feminine. For most other nouns, gender is usually arbitrary and must be memorized.

The definite article (*the*) that accompanies masculine nouns is **le. La** accompanies feminine nouns. **L'** is used before masculine or feminine nouns beginning with a vowel or mute *h*.

Masculine		*Feminine*	
le garçon	*boy*	**la fille**	*girl*
le frère	*brother*	**la sœur**	*sister*
le père	*father*	**la mère**	*mother*
le chien	*dog*	**la chienne**	*dog*
le chat	*cat*	**la chatte**	*cat*
le musée	*museum*	**la plage**	*beach*
le marché	*market*	**la boutique**	*shop*
le salon	*living room*	**la chambre**	*bedroom*
l'ami	*(male) friend*	**l'amie**	*(female) friend*
l'homme	*man*	**l'épée**	*sword*

But:

le héros	*hero*
le haricot	*bean*
le hors-d'œuvre	*hors d'œuvre*

1

1 . Complete the following with the correct form of the definite article **le, la** or **l'**.

1. _____ garçon joue avec _____ chatte dans _____ salon.
2. _____ père prépare _____ dîner à _____ maison.
3. _____ professeur enseigne _____ histoire, _____ anglais, _____ géographie et _____ philosophie.
4. _____ arbre est plus grand que _____ fleur.
5. _____ chienne joue avec _____ chat sur _____ plage.
6. _____ artiste dessine _____ portrait.
7. _____ ami de Pierre joue avec _____ sœur de Marie.
8. _____ sœur regarde _____ statue dans _____ musée.
9. _____ enfant aime _____ bifteck et _____ fromage.
10. _____ mère laisse _____ lettre sur _____ bureau.

GENDER IDENTIFICATION BY WORD ENDINGS

Nouns ending in **-sion, -tion, -aison, -ance, -ence, -té, -ude, -ale, -ole** and **-ure** are usually feminine.

la version	*translation*
la nation	*nation*
la terminaison	*ending*
la connaissance	*knowledge*
la patience	*patience*
la beauté	*beauty*
la certitude	*certainty*
la plénitude	*plenitude*
la cathédrale	*cathedral*
la parole	*word*
la culture	*culture*
la facture	*bill*

Nouns ending in **-asme, -isme, -eau, -ment** and **-acle** are usually masculine.

l'enthousiasme	*enthusiasm*
le sarcasme	*sarcasm*
le classicisme	*classicism*
le couteau	*knife*
l'enseignement	*teaching, education*
le gouvernement	*government*
le spectacle	*show, performance*

2. Complete the following sentences with the definite article **le, la** or **l'**. For each word beginning with a vowel, indicate whether it is masculine or feminine by writing **l'(f.)** or **l'(m.)**.

1. _____ prononciation et _____ intonation sont importantes dans _____ étude des langues.
2. Elle étudie _____ classicisme, _____ romantisme, _____ symbolisme et _____ civilisation française.
3. Ils admirent _____ beauté de _____ peinture.
4. Elle étudie _____ impressionisme et _____ culture française.
5. Dès _____ naissance, il faut surveiller _____ nourriture du bébé.
6. _____ sarcasme sera évident dans _____ spectacle de ce soir.
7. _____ multitude exprime _____ certitude.
8. _____ parlement est dans _____ bâtiment en face.

WORDS WITH DIFFERENT MEANINGS IN
MASCULINE AND FEMININE FORMS

The following pairs of words have different meanings for masculine and feminine forms.

Masculine		Feminine	
l'aide	helper	l'aide	help
le critique	critic	la critique	criticism
le guide	guide	la guide	reins (of a horse)
le livre	book	la livre	pound
le manche	handle	la manche	sleeve
le mode	method, mode	la mode	fashion
l'office	office, duty	l'office	pantry
le pendule	pendulum	la pendule	clock
le poêle	stove	la poêle	frying pan
le poste	job	la poste	post office
le somme	nap	la somme	sum
le tour	turn, walk around	la tour	tower
le vase	vase	la vase	mud
le voile	veil	la voile	sail

3. Complete the following sentences with the correct form of the definite article **le** or **la.**

1. _____ critique fait _____ critique du roman.
2. On a offert _____ poste à _____ poste à M. Dupont.
3. On a fait _____ tour de _____ tour Eiffel.
4. _____ voile que la veuve porte est noir. _____ voile du bateau est jaune.
5. _____ guide explique comment tenir _____ guide du cheval.
6. Les pommes coûtent 2F _____ livre.
7. _____ mode détermine l'habit de l'homme.
8. L'homme se chauffe devant _____ poêle. Il met le bacon dans _____ poêle.
9. _____ manche de cette robe est déchirée. _____ manche de cette poêle est cassé.
10. Ne cassez pas _____ vase!

PLURAL FORMS OF NOUNS

Regular Plurals

Most nouns are made plural by adding **s** to the singular forms. **Les** is the definite article accompanying all plural nouns. Note the liaison between **les** and a word beginning with a vowel.

Masculine		Feminine	
Singular	Plural	Singular	Plural
le garçon	les garçons	la fille	les filles
le livre	les livres	la table	les tables
l'ami	les amis	l'amie	les amies

Nouns Ending in -s, -x or -z

Nouns ending in **-s, -x** or **-z** are alike in both the singular and plural forms.

Singular		*Plural*
le bras	*arm*	**les bras**
la fois	*time*	**les fois**
le vers	*verse*	**les vers**
le prix	*price*	**les prix**
le nez	*nose*	**les nez**
la voix	*voice*	**les voix**

Nouns Ending in -au, -eau, -eu or -œu

Nouns ending in **-au, -eau, -eu** or **-œu** add **x** to form the plural.

Singular		*Plural*
le noyau	*pit (of a fruit)*	**les noyaux**
le bateau	*boat*	**les bateaux**
le château	*castle*	**les châteaux**
la peau	*skin*	**les peaux**
le feu	*fire*	**les feux**
le jeu	*game*	**les jeux**
le vœu	*wish*	**les vœux**

Exceptions:

le landau	*carriage*	**les landaus**
le pneu	*tire*	**les pneus**

Nouns Ending in -ou

Nouns ending in **ou** add **s** to form the plural.

Singular		*Plural*
le clou	*nail*	**les clous**
le trou	*hole*	**les trous**
le sou	*penny*	**les sous**

Some nouns ending in **-ou** add **x** to form the plural.

Singular		*Plural*
le bijou	*jewel*	**les bijoux**
le caillou	*stone*	**les cailloux**
le chou	*cabbage*	**les choux**
le genou	*knee*	**les genoux**
le hibou	*owl*	**les hiboux**
le joujou	*toy*	**les joujoux**
le pou	*flea, louse*	**les poux**

Nouns Ending in -al

Many nouns ending in **-al** in the singular change **-al** to **-aux** to form the plural.

Singular		*Plural*
l'animal	*animal*	**les animaux**
le cheval	*horse*	**les chevaux**
l'hôpital	*hospital*	**les hôpitaux**
le journal	*newspaper*	**les journaux**

Exceptions:

le bal	*ball, dance*	**les bals**
le carnaval	*carnival*	**les carnavals**
le festival	*festival*	**les festivals**

Nouns Ending in -ail

Many nouns ending in **-ail** add **s** to form the plural.

le chandail	*sweater*	**les chandails**
le détail	*detail*	**les détails**
l'éventail	*fan*	**les éventails**

Exceptions:

le bail	*lease*	**les baux**
le travail	*work*	**les travaux**

Irregular Plurals

l'aïeul	*ancestor*	**les aïeux**
le bonhomme	*old fellow*	**les bonshommes**
le ciel	*sky*	**les cieux**
le gentilhomme	*gentleman*	**les gentilshommes**
l'œil	*eye*	**les yeux**
le monsieur	*gentleman*	**les messieurs**
madame	*Mrs.*	**mesdames**
mademoiselle	*Miss*	**mesdemoiselles**

Family names do not add **s** to form the plural.

les Dupont	*the Duponts*

4. Complete the following with the correct form of the indicated noun.

1. Les _____ sont petites. *table*
2. J'aime beaucoup les _____ de Baudelaire. *vers*
3. Ne mange pas les _____, ma petite. *noyau*
4. As-tu des _____? *sou*

5. Le chien est couvert de _____. *pou*
6. J'adore les _____. *festival*
7. _____ et _____, écoutez bien. *madame, mademoiselle*
8. Asseyez-vous sur les _____. *genou*
9. Les _____ de forêt sont destructifs. *feu*
10. Les _____ sont gentils. *ami*
11. Le Martien a deux _____. *nez*
12. Faites des _____ pour le retour du beau ciel bleu. *vœu*
13. Les éléphants sont de grands _____. *animal*
14. Regarde les jolis _____ de l'église. *vitrail*
15. J'aime beaucoup manger les _____. *chou*
16. Il fait très chaud. Voici des _____. *éventail*

5. Rewrite the following, changing all nouns to the plural. Make any other necessary changes.

1. La loi est juste.
2. La voix est jolie.
3. Regardez le feu!
4. Le trou est grand.
5. Le repas est bon.
6. Le journal explique le travail.
7. L'école est moderne.
8. Le château est joli.
9. Le détail du dessin sur le chandail est magnifique.
10. Le prix est élevé.
11. Le jeu est amusant.
12. Voilà le clou.
13. Le bijou est joli.
14. Le caillou est petit.
15. Le bateau est grand.
16. Le musée est grand.
17. L'œil est grand.
18. Le cheval est l'animal que vous aimez.
19. Le monsieur est grand.
20. Le bal a lieu samedi.
21. Le gentilhomme est grand.
22. Voici un bonhomme de neige.

6. Rewrite the following, changing the nouns to the singular. Make all necessary changes.

1. Les rois habitent dans les châteaux.
2. Les nez sont grands.
3. Les joujoux sont intéressants.
4. Les carnavals sont amusants.
5. Les cieux sont bleus.
6. Les amis sont aimables.
7. Les peaux de vison sont chères.
8. Les journaux sont intéressants.
9. Les aïeux sont célèbres.
10. Les yeux sont bruns.
11. Les bras sont forts.
12. Les clous sont longs.
13. Les vitraux sont jolis.

14. Les vœux sont compréhensibles.
15. Les chandails sont chauds.
16. Les hiboux sont noirs.
17. Les voix des chanteurs sont jolies.
18. Les jeux de cartes sont intéressants.

COMPOUND NOUNS

The plural of compound nouns is irregular.

1. If formed with two nouns in apposition, with a noun and an adjective, or with two adjectives, an **s** or **x** is added to both parts to form the plural.

Singular		*Plural*
le chou-fleur	*cauliflower*	**les choux-fleurs**
le wagon-restaurant	*dining car*	**les wagons-restaurants**
le beau-frère	*brother-in-law*	**les beaux-frères**
la belle-sœur	*sister-in-law*	**les belles-sœurs**
le coffre-fort	*safe*	**les coffres-forts**
la grand-mère	*grandmother*	**les grands-mères**
le grand-père	*grandfather*	**les grands-pères**
le sourd-muet	*deaf-mute*	**les sourds-muets**

2. If the compound noun is formed by a noun and its complement, only the first part is plural.

Singular		*Plural*
l'arc-en-ciel	*rainbow*	**les arcs-en-ciel**
le chef-d'œuvre	*masterpiece*	**les chefs-d'œuvre**
le timbre-poste	*stamp*	**les timbres-poste**

3. In rare cases, **s** is added only to the last part.

Singular		*Plural*
le pique-nique	*picnic*	**les pique-niques**

4. If the compound noun is formed by an invariable word plus a noun, only the noun is made plural.

Singular		*Plural*
l'avant-coureur	*forerunner, precursor*	**les avant-coureurs**
le bien-pensant	*right-thinking, orthodox person*	**les bien-pensants**

5. If the compound noun is formed by a verb and its complement, both parts are invariable.

Singular		*Plural*
l'abat-jour	*lampshade*	**les abat-jour**
le gratte-ciel	*skyscraper*	**les gratte-ciel**
le passe-partout	*passkey*	**les passe-partout**
le porte-plume	*pen-holder*	**les porte-plume**
le réveille-matin	*alarm clock*	**les réveille-matin**

But:

le cure-dent	*toothpick*	**les cure-dents**
le tire-bouchon	*corkscrew*	**les tire-bouchons**
le couvre-lit	*bedspread*	**les couvre-lits**

6. Other compound nouns that are the same in the singular and in the plural are as follows.

Singular		*Plural*
l'après-midi	*afternoon*	**les après-midi**
le hors-d'œuvre	*canapé*	**les hors-d'œuvre**
le tête-à-tête	*private talk*	**les tête-à-tête**

7. Rewrite the following sentences, putting the nouns in the plural.

1. L'après-midi le grand-père dort.
2. Le réveille-matin sonne à huit heures du matin.
3. La grand-mère met le chou-fleur dans le panier pour le pique-nique.
4. Il lit le chef-d'œuvre de Racine.
5. Il y a un gratte-ciel à New York.
6. Le timbre-poste est dans le coffre-fort.
7. Mets ta plume dans le porte-plume.
8. Pour ouvrir la bouteille de vin, prenez un tire-bouchon.
9. Le beau-frère mange le hors-d'œuvre.
10. La belle-sœur aime l'arc-en-ciel.

SPECIAL USES OF THE DEFINITE ARTICLE

With General or Abstract Nouns

Unlike English usage, in French the definite article must be used with all abstract nouns or nouns used in a general sense. Compare the French and English in the following examples.

L'homme est mortel.
Man is mortal.
Il aime les bananes.
He likes bananas.
La biologie est une science.
Biology is a science.
L'amour est divin.
Love is divine.
Les cigarettes ne sont pas bonnes pour la santé.
Cigarettes are not good for the health.

8. Complete the following with the appropriate definite article.

1. _____ Français sont fiers.
2. _____ vie est dure.
3. _____ patience est une vertu.
4. _____ chiens sont des animaux domestiques.
5. _____ diamants sont des bijoux.
6. _____ bananes sont des fruits.
7. _____ automne est une saison.
8. _____ charbon est noir.
9. Il aime _____ pommes frites.
10. Il n'aime pas _____ épinards.
11. _____ biologie est une science.
12. _____ femmes d'aujourd'hui sont conscientes de leurs droits.

With Titles

When talking about someone, the definite article must be used with titles. The article is omitted, however, in direct address.

Le docteur Martin est dentiste.
Doctor Martin is a dentist.

But:

Bonjour, docteur Martin.
Hello, Doctor Martin.

Le général Pierron est arrivé.
General Pierron has arrived.

But:

Comment allez-vous, général Pierron?
How are you, General Pierron?

The article is never used with **monsieur, madame** and **mademoiselle**.

Monsieur Le Blanc vient.
Mister Le Blanc is coming.
Comment allez-vous, Madame Le Blanc?
How are you, Mrs. Le Blanc?

In formal address, the article is used before the title.

Bonjour, madame la présidente.

9. Complete the following with the appropriate definite article, when it is necessary.

1. _____ docteur Merlier est un grand homme.
2. _____ comte de Deauville est ici.
3. Bonjour, _____ professeur Le Blanc.
4. _____ Mademoiselle Pierron habite à Roanne.
5. Où allez-vous, _____ Monsieur Péneau?
6. Savez-vous qui est _____ Madame Leclerc?
7. Comment allez-vous, _____ Madame Mercier?
8. Bonjour, monsieur _____ président.
9. _____ capitaine Andrieu va faire un discours.
10. _____ présidente préside l'assemblée.

With Languages and Academic Subjects

The definite article is used with languages unless the name of the language immediately follows the verb **parler** or the prepositions **de** or **en**.

Le français est une belle langue.
French is a beautiful language.
J'étudie le français et l'anglais.
I study French and English.
Je parle très bien (le) français.
I speak French very well.

But:

Je parle français.
I speak French.
J'ai un livre de français.
I have a French book.
Ce livre est écrit en français.
This book is written in French.

The definite article is also used with academic subjects.

J'étudie l'histoire et les mathématiques.
I study history and mathematics.

10. Complete the following with the definite article, when it is necessary.

   1. Parlez-vous _____ français?
   2. Il parle très couramment _____ français.
   3. J'apprends _____ biologie.
   4. _____ russe est une langue difficile.
   5. Est-ce que c'est un livre de _____ russe?
   6. Elle lui écrit en _____ allemand.
   7. Dites-vous cela en _____ anglais?

With Days of the Week, Seasons and Dates

The definite article is used with days of the weeks to indicate habitual occurrence. The definite article has the meaning of *every* or *on*. The definite article accompanying the days of the week is masculine.

J'ai ma classe de français le lundi.
I have my French class on Mondays (every Monday).
Le dimanche, je ne travaille pas.
On Sunday(s) I don't work.

The definite article is omitted when talking about a particular day.

Je suis allé au cinéma lundi.
I went to the movies (on) Monday.
Je viendrai vous voir samedi.
I will come to see you (on) Saturday.
Dimanche est le dernier jour de la semaine.
Sunday is the last day of the week.

The definite article is used with seasons when discussing the season in a general sense.

L'été est une saison agréable.
Summer is a nice season.
L'hiver est une saison froide.
Winter is a cold season.

But:

Je vais à la plage en été.
I go to the beach in summer.
Je fais du ski en hiver.
I ski in winter.
les robes d'hiver
winter dresses

The definite article is used with dates.

Le 15 septembre, les classes recommencent.
On the 15th of September (September 15) classes resume.
Il sera ici le 10 août.
He will be here on the 10th of August (August 10).

11. Complete the following with the definite article, when it is necessary.

1. _____ Mercredi est le troisième jour de la semaine.
2. Je vais toujours au cinéma _____ samedi.
3. _____automne est ma saison favorite.
4. Il n'y a pas de classes _____ dimanche.
5. Il fait beau en _____ automne.
6. Mes vacances commencent _____ vendredi.
7. J'ai mon cours de philosophie _____ lundi.
8. Je suis allé au musée _____ samedi dernier.
9. Il vous verra _____ mercredi prochain.
10. _____ 2 juin je vais en vacances.
11. Il viendra _____ 15 octobre.
12. Je pourrais vous voir _____ matin ou _____après-midi.

With Names of Continents, Countries, Provinces, Regions, Islands, Mountains and Rivers

The definite article is used with names of continents, countries, provinces, regions, islands, mountains and rivers.

La France n'est pas un grand pays.
France is not a large country.
La Bretagne est pittoresque.
Brittany is picturesque.
L'Amérique du Nord est un vaste continent.
North America is a vast continent.
La Corse est une île méditerranéenne.
Corsica is a Mediterranean island.
Les Pyrénées sont entre la France et l'Espagne.
The Pyrenees are between France and Spain.

But:

Je vais en France.
I am going to France.
l'histoire de France
the history of France

12. Complete the following with the appropriate definite article, when necessary.

1. _____ Seine divise Paris.
2. _____Europe est très diverse.
3. _____ Laurentides sont des montagnes du Québec.
4. _____ Midi est le sud de la France.
5. Je vais en _____ France en été.
6. _____ Corse est une île française.
7. Il traverse _____ lac Ontario.
8. _____Amérique du Sud est un vaste continent.

With Weights and Measures

The definite article is used with expressions of quantity when used in conjunction with a price to indicate **per.**

Les tomates coûtent deux francs le kilo.
Tomatoes cost two francs a (per) kilogram.
Les œufs coûtent quatre francs la douzaine.
Eggs cost four francs a dozen.

But:

Les bananes pèsent deux kilos.
The bananas weigh two kilograms.

13. Complete the following with the correct form of the definite article.

   1. _____ pommes coûtent deux francs _____ livre.
   2. J'ai payé cinq francs _____ kilo.
   3. _____ oranges coûtent six francs _____ douzaine.
   4. _____ lait coûte deux francs _____ litre.

With Parts of the Body or Clothing

The definite article is used instead of the possessive adjective with parts of the body or clothing, in order to avoid ambiguity.

Il se lave les mains.
He washes his hands.
Il s'en va les mains dans les poches.
He goes away with his hands in his pockets.

14. Complete the following sentences with the appropriate definite article.

   1. Il se brosse _____ dents.
   2. Il est rentré, _____ chemise déchirée.
   3. Il s'est cassé _____ jambe.
   4. Il a mal à _____ tête.
   5. Elle se lave _____ cheveux.

CONTRACTIONS OF THE DEFINITE ARTICLE

The definite article contracts with **à** (*to, at*) and **de** (*from, about, of*) in the following way:

à + le = au
à + les = aux
à + la do not contract
à + l' do not contract

Je vais **au musée.**	*I am going to the museum.*
Je parle **aux garçons.**	*I am speaking to the boys.*
Je parle **aux élèves.**	*I am speaking to the students.*
Je vais **à la pharmacie.**	*I am going to the pharmacy.*
Je parle **à l'étudiant.**	*I am speaking to the student.*
J'arrive **à l'hôpital.**	*I am arriving at the hospital.*

de + le = du
de + les = des
de + la do not contract
de + l' do not contract

Je parle **du garçon.**	*I am speaking about the boy.*
Je parle **des garçons.**	*I am speaking about the boys.*
Je parle **des étudiants.**	*I am speaking about the students.*
Je parle **de la fille.**	*I am speaking about the girl.*
Je parle **de l'élève.**	*I am speaking about the student.*

Note the liaison between **aux** and **des** and a noun that begins with a vowel.

>   Je parle **aux_élèves.**
>   Je parle **des_étudiants.**

15. Complete the following mini-dialogues with the appropriate contractions of the definite article.

    1. – Pierre va _____ restaurant.
      – Quel est le nom _____ restaurant?
      – C'est le restaurant *Chez Robert.*

    2. – Anne va _____ plage.
      – Quel est le nom _____ plage?
      – C'est la plage *Jones.*

    3. – André va _____ aéroport.
      – Quel est le nom _____ aéroport?
      – C'est l'aéroport Kennedy.

    4. – Anne va _____ bibliothèque.
      – Quel est le nom _____ bibliothèque et qu'est-ce qu'elle y fait?
      – C'est la bibliothèque Mercier et elle lit des livres _____ enfants.
      – Quels sont les noms _____ enfants?
      – Ce sont Anne, Marie, Claire, David, Jean et Pierre.

THE INDEFINITE ARTICLE

The indefinite articles (*a, an*) in French are **un** for masculine nouns and **une** for feminine nouns. The plural is **des** (*some, any*). Note the liaison between **des** and a word beginning with a vowel.

Masculine		*Feminine*	
Singular	*Plural*	*Singular*	*Plural*
un livre	**des livres**	**une peinture**	**des peintures**
un garçon	**des garçons**	**une fille**	**des filles**
un élève	**des_élèves**	**une élève**	**des_élèves**
un ami	**des_amis**	**une amie**	**des_amies**

Some nouns have two genders.

Masculine		*Feminine*	
un élève	*a student (male)*	**une élève**	*a student (female)*
un artiste	*an artist*	**une artiste**	*an artist*
un enfant	*a child*	**une enfant**	*a child*

16. Complete the following with the correct form of the indefinite article **un, une** or **des** to show what the people wear in various locations and situations.

    1. À la plage, je porte _____ maillot de bain, _____ chapeau de paille et _____ lunettes de soleil.
    2. Au lit, elle porte _____ pyjama ou _____ chemise de nuit.
    3. Au bureau, il porte _____ chemise, _____ costume, _____ cravate, et _____ chaussures.
    4. Au bal, Marie porte _____ jolie robe du soir et _____ bijoux et Jean porte _____ habit de cérémonie.
    5. Quand il pleut, on porte _____ imperméable et _____ parapluie.

6. En hiver, on porte _____ manteau, ____ foulard, _____ chapeau, _____ gants et ____ bottes.
7. Dans le jardin, il porte _____ jean et _____ tricot.
8. Au restaurant, elle porte _____ jupe, _____ blouse et _____ gilet.

OMISSION OF THE INDEFINITE ARTICLE

After the Verb *être*

Unlike English, the indefinite article is omitted after the verb **être** (*to be*) when the verb is followed by an unmodified noun indicating nationality, religion or profession.

Elle est médecin.
She is a doctor.
Il est catholique.
He is a Catholic.
Elle est canadienne.
She is a Canadian.

When **c'est** is used instead of **il est,** the indefinite article is used.

C'est un Français.
He is a Frenchman.
C'est un avocat.
He's a lawyer.

The indefinite article is also used when the noun that follows the verb **être** is modified.

Victor Hugo est un auteur célèbre.
Victor Hugo is a famous author.
Victor Hugo est un auteur que tous les Français connaissent.
Victor Hugo is an author whom all Frenchmen know.

17. What are the classmates doing ten years after graduation? Complete the following sentences with the appropriate indefinite article, when it is necessary.

1. Pierre est _____ chimiste. C'est _____ chimiste célèbre.
2. Anne est _____ avocate.
3. C'est _____ biologiste.
4. Lucille est _____ rédactrice qui voyage partout dans le monde.
5. Georges est _____ ingénieur.
6. Solange est _____ journaliste.
7. André est _____ professeur exigeant.
8. Jean est _____ avocat célèbre.

Other Omissions of the Indefinite Article

The indefinite article is not used:

1. after **quel** (*what a*).

Quelle belle vue!
What a beautiful view!

2. before nouns in apposition.

Paris, capitale de la France, est une grande ville.
Paris, the capital of France, is a big city.

3. after a noun that is a complement of another noun.

une robe de soie
a silk dress
un professeur d'histoire
a history professor

4. after the preposition **sans.**

Il travaille sans argent.
He works without money.

5. after **avec** when used with abstract nouns.

Travaillez avec soin.
Work with care.

But:

Travaillez avec des amis.
Work with some friends.

after **ni ... ni.**

Il n'a ni argent ni pain.
He has neither money nor bread.

18. Complete the following with the indefinite article, when it is necessary.

1. Quel _____ garçon!
2. *Le Cid,* _____ pièce de Corneille, est très célèbre.
3. *Les Misérables* est _____ roman de Victor Hugo.
4. Il achète une bague en _____ or.
5. Écoutez avec _____ enthousiasme.
6. Il travaille avec _____ copains.
7. Il reste sans _____ argent.
8. Il n'a ni _____ père ni _____ mère.

THE PARTITIVE

In English we use the words *some* or *any* or no article with nouns that cannot be counted, such as milk, coffee and tea. In French the partitive is used with these nouns and the partitive article cannot be omitted. The partitive is expressed by **de** plus the definite article. Note that **de** plus **le** = **du** and **de** plus **les** = **des.** The partitive articles are:

	Singular	*Plural*
Feminine	**de la**	**des**
Masculine	**du**	**des**
Masculine or feminine before a vowel	**de l'**	**des**

Study the following:

J'ai **de la soupe.**	*I have some soup.*
Elle veut **du sucre.**	*She wants some sugar.*
Il boit **de l'eau.**	*He is drinking (some) water.*
Voulez-vous **des oranges?**	*Do you want any oranges?*
Nous avons **des livres.**	*We have some books.*

Note that in general the partitive article is used in the singular. The plural **des** is the same as the plural indefinite article.

19. What does John eat and drink for each meal? Complete the following sentences with the appropriate form of the partitive.

Au petit déjeuner, il mange ____ pain, ____ confiture, ____ œufs brouillés ou ____
                             (1)   (2)   (3)   (4)

crêpes avec ____ sirop d'érable. Il boit ____ jus d'orange et ____ café avec ____
              (5)   (6)   (7)   (8)

sucre et ____ crème.
       (9)

Au déjeuner, il mange ____ soupe et ____ salade. Il boit ____ lait.
                        (10)   (11)   (12)

Au dîner, il mange ____ rosbif ou ____ poulet, ____ légumes et ____ riz. Il boit
                    (13)   (14)   (15)   (16)

____ eau minérale et ____ vin.
(17)   (18)

THE PARTITIVE VERSUS THE DEFINITE AND INDEFINITE ARTICLES

The definite article is used with nouns in a general sense. The partitive is used with an undetermined quantity of a noncountable item.

Il aime **le café.** (*all coffee*)
He likes coffee.
Il boit **du café.** (*some coffee*)
He drinks (some) coffee.

With nouns that can be counted, such as bananas (one banana), or items used in the plural (some bananas), the indefinite article is used.

Je voudrais **une poire.**
Je voudrais acheter **des tomates** et **des bananes.**

Certain nouns can be count or noncount nouns depending on the way in which they are used. The definite, indefinite or partitive article can be used depending on the meaning.

Voici **le gâteau.**
Here is the cake. (the cake I bought yesterday)
Voici **un gâteau.**
Here is a cake. (a whole cake).
Voici **du gâteau.**
Here is some cake. (part of the cake, a piece of cake)

20. Say that Pierre likes the following foods and drinks and is ordering them from a menu in a restaurant. Follow the model.

le fromage
Il aime beaucoup le fromage et il va prendre du fromage maintenant.

  1. l'eau minérale   4. la salade
  2. la soupe aux pois   5. le pain italien
  3. les artichauts   6. le thé

21. Complete the following conversations in a restaurant with the definite, indefinite or partitive article.

  1. – Aimez-vous ____ pain?
    – Il y a ____ pain sur le menu?
    – Oui, il y a ____ pain français sur le menu. ____ pain français est délicieux.

2. – _____ glace ici est délicieuse. J'aime beaucoup _____ glace. Je préfère _____ glace au chocolat à _____ glace à la vanille. Donc, je vais prendre _____ glace au chocolat.

3. – Regarde _____ gâteau. C'est _____ fameux gâteau qu'on fait à la pâtisserie Leclerc. C'est _____ gâteau formidable. Vas-y! Prends _____ gâteau.

4. – Il y a _____ fromage sur le menu?
   – Oui, je vais prendre _____ roquefort. J'aime _____ roquefort. Le roquefort est _____ fromage français.

EXCEPTIONS TO THE RULE FOR USING THE PARTITIVE

When the Sentence Is Negative

Normally, in negative sentences, the partitive article is replaced by **de.** Study the following. Note that **de** becomes **d'** before a word beginning with a vowel.

Affirmative	*Negative*
J'ai du pain.	**Je n'ai pas de pain.**
I have some bread.	*I don't have any bread.*
J'ai une robe.	**Je n'ai pas de robe.**
I have a dress.	*I don't have a dress.*
J'ai des livres.	**Je n'ai pas de livres.**
I have some books.	*I don't have any books.*
J'ai des amies.	**Je n'ai pas d'amies.**
I have some friends.	*I have no friends.*

If the sentence implies an affirmative idea or if you want to emphasize the noun, you may use the partitive forms in negative sentences.

N'avez-vous pas de la famille ici?
Don't you have any family here?
Je n'ai pas du respect pour lui, mais du mépris.
I don't have any respect for him, rather scorn.

22. Rewrite the following sentences in the negative.

   1. Il a du courage.
   2. Il y a de la soupe.
   3. J'ai des bonbons.
   4. Je bois de l'eau.
   5. Elle fume des cigarettes.

When an Adjective Precedes a Noun in the Plural

When an adjective precedes a noun in the plural, the partitive becomes **de.**

Singular	*Plural*
J'ai un bon livre.	**J'ai de bons livres.**
But:	
J'ai un livre intéressant.	**J'ai des livres intéressants.**

When an adjective is an integral part of the idea, the partitive is used.

des jeunes filles	*girls*
des jeunes gens	*young people*
des petits pains	*rolls*
des petits pois	*peas*

23. Rewrite the following sentences, putting the nouns in the plural.

1. Il y a une belle peinture ici.
2. Nous lisons un livre intéressant.
3. C'est une grande ville.
4. Elle mange un petit pain et un petit pois.
5. C'est une jeune fille.
6. Jai une grande armoire.

After Expressions of Quantity and Expressions with *de*

The partitive becomes **de** after expressions of quantity such as the following:

assez	*enough*	**une boîte**	*a box*
beaucoup	*a lot*	**une bouteille**	*a bottle*
peu	*a little*	**un verre**	*a glass*
trop	*too much*	**une tasse**	*a cup*
tant	*so many*	**un kilo**	*a kilogram*
autant	*as much*	**un litre**	*a liter*
moins	*less*	**une livre**	*a pound*
		une douzaine	*a dozen*
		une tranche	*a slice*

Elle veut **de** l'eau.	*But:*	Elle veut **un peu d'**eau.
She wants some water.		*She wants a little water.*
Il a **des** livres.	*But:*	Il a **beaucoup de** livres.
He has some books.		*He has many books.*
Je bois **du** vin.	*But:*	Je bois **un verre de** vin.
I am drinking some wine.		*I am drinking a glass of wine.*

La plupart (*most*) and **bien** (*many*) are exceptions to this rule.

La plupart du temps, je travaille.	**Bien des** fois, il fait des fautes.
Most of the time, I work.	*Many times, he makes mistakes.*

After expressions using **de**, such as **avoir besoin de** (*to need*), **se passer de** (*to get along without*), there is no partitive.

J'ai **de** l'argent.	*But:*	J'ai **besoin d'**argent.
I have some money.		*I need some money.*

Plusieurs (*several*) and **quelques** (*a few*) do not require the partitive. Study the following:

J'ai **beaucoup de** livres.	*But:*	J'ai **plusieurs** livres.
I have many books.		*I have several books.*
J'ai **assez de** livres.	*But:*	J'ai **quelques** livres.
I have enough books.		*I have some books.*

In expressions of quantity **de** cannot be used before a pronoun. **D'entre** is usually used.

Plusieurs **d'entre eux**	*Several of them*
Quelques-uns **d'entre nous**	*Some of us*

24. Complete the following sentences with the correct form of the partitive, when necessary.

1. Je voudrais un verre _____ eau.
2. Elle a beaucoup _____ amis.
3. Elle ne peut pas se passer _____ nourriture.
4. Il y a plusieurs _____ églises ici.
5. Elle achète une douzaine _____ pommes.
6. Il a quelques _____ amis.
7. Bien _____ gens aiment le cinéma.
8. Donne-moi une tranche _____ pain.
9. Il mange trop _____ bonbons.
10. Nous avons besoin _____ argent.
11. Elle achète une livre _____ beurre.
12. La plupart _____ temps, j'ai raison.

Review

25. Complete the following sentences with the appropriate definite article or contraction.

1. _____ père travaille _____ bureau.
2. C'est _____ ami de Pierre.
3. _____ qualité vaut mieux que _____ quantité.
4. _____ romans sont dans _____ bibliothèque.
5. _____ patience est une vertu.
6. _____ connaissance _____ langues est utile.
7. _____ femme achète des timbres _____ poste.
8. _____ homme se chauffe devant _____ poêle.
9. C'est _____ livre _____ professeur.
10. _____ enfants vont _____ école.
11. Ne donnez pas _____ bonbons _____ enfants.
12. _____ héros _____ histoire se lave _____ mains.

26. Rewrite the following sentences, changing the nouns to the plural. Make all other necessary changes.

1. Le repas est bon.
2. Le cheval est un animal.
3. J'aime le carnaval.
4. Ouvrez l'œil.
5. Le bateau est petit.
6. Le prix du clou n'est pas cher.
7. Le chou est dans le trou.
8. L'eau entoure le château.
9. Le jeu est intéressant.
10. L'après-midi, il prépare le hors-d'œuvre et le chou-fleur pour le pique-nique.
11. Monsieur, ne prenez pas ce bijou.
12. Le grand-père va acheter un abat-jour.

27. Tell what the people in various professions do. Complete the following with the correct form of the definite or indefinite article when necessary.

1. Madame Leclerc est _____ chirurgienne. C'est _____ chirurgienne célèbre. Elle aide _____ patiente qui s'est cassé _____ jambe. _____ chirurgiens font _____ travail délicat. Ils travaillent avec _____ soin.
2. Madame Dupont est _____ journaliste. Elle utilise _____ micro-ordinateur dans son travail. Quelle _____ journaliste! C'est _____ journaliste qui écrit bien.
3. Marie est _____ biologiste. Elle travaille dans _____ laboratoire avec _____ microscope. _____ biologie est _____ science intéressante.
4. Monsieur Fournier est _____ professeur à l'école secondaire. C'est _____ professeur dynamique. Il enseigne _____ anglais. Il parle _____ anglais, mais il comprend _____ français et _____ russe. Il donne ses cours _____ lundi, _____ mercredi et _____ vendredi. J'ai surtout aimé son cours _____ lundi dernier.

28. Monsieur Leclerc is doing the shopping. Show where he goes and what he buys. Complete the following sentences with the definite, indefinite or partitive articles and the contraction of the definite article when necessary.

1. _____ crémerie, il achète _____ crème, _____ beurre, _____ lait, _____ douzaine _____ œufs et _____ fromage. Il aime _____ brie. C'est _____ fromage délicieux.
2. Il sort _____ crémerie et il va _____ boucherie où il achète _____ viande: _____ bifteck, _____ veau et _____ agneau.
3. _____ charcuterie, il achète un kilo _____ porc et six tranches _____ jambon. _____ porc coûte 20 francs _____ kilo et _____ jambon coûte 15 francs.
4. _____ supermarché, il achète dix bouteilles _____ eau minérale, quelques _____ tomates, _____ petits pois, _____ farine, _____ sel, _____ poivre et _____ moutarde. Il n'y a pas _____ oranges; donc il achète _____ pommes.
5. Maintenant, il a assez _____ provisions et il peut rentrer chez lui. Ah! Il a oublié d'acheter _____ café et il n'y a pas _____ café chez lui. Donc, il s'arrête _____ épicerie pour acheter un peu _____ café. Il achète aussi _____ glace parce que _____ glace dans cette épicerie est délicieuse. Il achète _____ glace à la vanille pour lui, et _____ glace au chocolat pour sa femme. Il doit attendre un peu, car bien _____ gens font la queue pour acheter _____ glace.

29. Answer the following questions, using **le, la, l', les,** a contraction of the article with **à** or **de**, a partitive or a preposition.

Qu'est-ce qu'il regarde? *le livre / professeur*
Il regarde le livre du professeur.

1. Qu'est-ce qu'il attend? *arrivée / professeur*
2. Qu'est-ce qu'il entend? *cris / enfant*
3. À qui parle-t-il? *ami / Jean*
4. Qu'est-ce qu'elle aime? *voix / chanteur*
5. Qu'est-ce qu'il cherche? *jouets / enfants*
6. Où va-t-il? *supermarché / village*
7. Qu'est-ce qu'il aime? *vitrail / église*
8. Qu'est-ce qu'il regarde? *peintures / musée*
9. Où veut-elle aller? *bibliothèque / ville*
10. Qu'est-ce qu'il achète? *sucre / gâteaux / glace*

Chapter 2

Adjectives and Adverbs

FORMATION OF THE FEMININE OF ADJECTIVES

Regular Forms

Every adjective must agree in number and gender with the noun it modifies. Most adjectives add **-e** to the masculine form to form the feminine. The final consonant sound is heard in the feminine form but not in the masculine form.

Masculine	*Feminine*
Il est **grand**.	Elle est **grande**.

Below is a list of common regular adjectives. (The adjectives with an asterisk end in an **n** sound in the feminine in spoken French but have a nasalized ending in the masculine.)

Masculine	*Feminine*	
*américain	américaine	*American*
amusant	amusante	*amusing*
anglais	anglaise	*English*
chaud	chaude	*warm*
content	contente	*happy, contented*
court	courte	*short*
droit	droite	*right, straight*
étonnant	étonnante	*astonishing*
fort	forte	*strong*
français	française	*French*
froid	froide	*cold*
grand	grande	*tall, big*
gris	grise	*gray*
haut	haute	*high, tall*
*humain	humaine	*human*
intelligent	intelligente	*intelligent*

intéressant	**intéressante**	*interesting*
laid	**laide**	*ugly*
lent	**lente**	*slow*
lourd	**lourde**	*heavy*
mauvais	**mauvaise**	*bad*
méchant	**méchante**	*bad*
parfait	**parfaite**	*perfect*
petit	**petite**	*small, little*
***plein**	**pleine**	*full*
***prochain**	**prochaine**	*next*
puissant	**puissante**	*powerful*
sourd	**sourde**	*deaf*

Adjectives Ending in a Vowel, Pronounced Consonant or Mute *e*

Some adjectives sound the same in the masculine and feminine forms. If an adjective ends in a vowel or pronounced consonant (**r** or **l**), the feminine is formed by adding **-e.** Below is a list of the most common of these adjectives.

Masculine	*Feminine*	
bleu	**bleue**	*blue*
compliqué	**compliquée**	*complicated*
désolé	**désolée**	*sorry*
fatigué	**fatiguée**	*tired*
gai	**gaie**	*gay*
joli	**jolie**	*pretty*
poli	**polie**	*polite*
clair	**claire**	*clear*
dur	**dure**	*hard*
égal	**égale**	*equal*
noir	**noire**	*black*
sûr	**sûre**	*sure*

Il est **fatigué.**
Elle est **fatiguée.**

If the adjective ends in a mute **-e,** the oral and written forms are the same for both the masculine and the feminine forms. Below is a list of some of the most common of these adjectives.

Masculine	*Feminine*	
agréable	**agréable**	*nice, pleasant*
calme	**calme**	*calm*
célèbre	**célèbre**	*famous*
désagréable	**désagréable**	*disagreeable, unpleasant*
difficile	**difficile**	*difficult*
facile	**facile**	*easy*
fantastique	**fantastique**	*fantastic*

formidable	**formidable**	*fantastic*
gauche	**gauche**	*left*
honnête	**honnête**	*honest*
jaune	**jaune**	*yellow*
jeune	**jeune**	*young*
large	**large**	*wide*
libre	**libre**	*free*
magnifique	**magnifique**	*magnificent*
malade	**malade**	*sick*
mince	**mince**	*thin*
moderne	**moderne**	*modern*
nécessaire	**nécessaire**	*necessary*
pauvre	**pauvre**	*poor*
populaire	**populaire**	*popular*
rapide	**rapide**	*rapid*
riche	**riche**	*rich*
sale	**sale**	*dirty*

1. Follow the model.

Comment est la fille? *petit*
La fille est petite.

1. Comment est l'idée? *mauvais*
2. Comment est la cathédrale? *grand*
3. Comment est la tour? *haut*
4. Comment est la cuisine? *parfait*
5. Comment est la sorcière? *laid*
6. Comment est la peinture? *joli*
7. Comment est la femme? *honnête*
8. Comment est la chemise? *rouge*
9. Comment est la pierre? *dur*
10. Comment est la réponse? *clair*

2. Complete the following with the appropriate form of the indicated adjective.

1. Le jour est _____ . *mauvais*
2. Cette fille est _____ . *français*
3. L'écrivain est _____ . *grand*
4. L'homme est _____ . *poli*
5. Le charbon est _____ . *noir*
6. Le vieillard est _____ . *faible*
7. La robe est _____ . *noir*
8. La pièce est _____ . *fantastique*
9. Le film est _____ . *formidable*
10. La situation est _____ . *compliqué*

Adjectives Ending in *-el, -eil, -il, -en, -on, -et* and *-s*

Adjectives ending in **-el, -eil, -il, -en, -on, -et,** and some ending in **-s** double the final consonant before adding **-e.**

Masculine	*Feminine*	
cruel	**cruelle**	*cruel*
pareil	**pareille**	*similar*
gentil	**gentille**	*nice*
ancien	**ancienne**	*ancient, old*
parisien	**parisienne**	*Parisian*
bon	**bonne**	*good*
breton	**bretonne**	*Breton*

muet	muette	*silent*
net	nette	*clean*
bas	basse	*low*
épais	épaisse	*thick*
gras	grasse	*greasy*
las	lasse	*tired*
gros	grosse	*big, fat*

Some other adjectives that double the final consonant to form the feminine are:

Masculine	*Feminine*	
nul	nulle	*no*
paysan	paysanne	*peasant*
sot	sotte	*stupid*
tel	telle	*such a*

Some adjectives ending in **-et** change **-et** to **-ète** to form the feminine.

Masculine	*Feminine*	
complet	complète	*complete*
concret	concrète	*concrete*
discret	discrète	*discreet*
indiscret	indiscrète	*indiscreet*
inquiet	inquiète	*worried*
secret	secrète	*secret*

Exception:

| prêt | prête | *ready* |

Adjectives Ending in *-er*

Adjectives ending in **-er** change **-er** to **-ère** to form the feminine.

Masculine	*Feminine*	
amer	amère	*bitter*
cher	chère	*expensive, dear*
dernier	dernière	*last*
entier	entière	*entire*
étranger	étrangère	*foreign*
fier	fière	*proud*
léger	légère	*light*
premier	première	*first*

3. Complete the following with the appropriate form of the indicated adjective.

1. La sorcière est _____ . *cruel*
2. La femme est _____ . *parisien*
3. La pièce est _____ . *bon*
4. Cette dame est _____ de naissance. *muet*
5. La sauce est _____ . *épais*

6. Sa réponse était _____ . *discret*
7. La jeune fille est _____ à partir. *prêt*
8. La fille est _____ . *sot*
9. La peinture est _____ . *cher*
10. Cette dame est _____ de sa langue. *fier*

4. Follow the model.

La fille est cruelle. *Le garçon*
Le garçon est cruel.

1. La pièce est sensationnelle. *Le film*
2. Le monument est ancien. *La peinture*
3. Cette boîte est grosse. *Ce paquet*
4. Cet étudiant est las. *Cette étudiante*
5. Ce mot est secret. *Cette histoire*
6. La femme est inquiète. *L'homme*
7. Monsieur Le Blanc est étranger. *Madame Leclerc*
8. Marie est première en math. *Pierre*
9. Ce mot est pareil. *Cette phrase*

Adjectives Ending in -*x*

Most adjectives ending in **-x** change **-x** to **-se** to form the feminine.

Masculine	*Feminine*	
amoureux	amoureuse	*in love*
courageux	courageuse	*courageous*
curieux	curieuse	*curious*
ennuyeux	ennuyeuse	*boring*
furieux	furieuse	*furious*
heureux	heureuse	*happy*
jaloux	jalouse	*jealous*
merveilleux	merveilleuse	*marvelous*
peureux	peureuse	*fearful*
sérieux	sérieuse	*serious*

Exceptions:

doux	douce	*sweet*
roux	rousse	*reddish brown*
faux	fausse	*false*

Adjectives Ending in -*eur*

Adjectives ending in **-eur** form the feminine by changing **-eur** to **-euse** if the adjective is derived from a verb. Otherwise the feminine ends in **-rice.**

Masculine	*Feminine*	
flatteur	flatteuse	*flattering*
menteur	menteuse	*lying*

moqueur	moqueuse	*mocking*
trompeur	trompeuse	*tricking*
acteur	actrice	*acting*
conservateur	conservatrice	*conservative*
créateur	créatrice	*creative*
protecteur	protectrice	*protecting*

Exceptions:

antérieur	antérieure	*anterior*
extérieur	extérieure	*exterior*
inférieur	inférieure	*inferior*
intérieur	intérieure	*interior*
meilleur	meilleure	*best*
majeur	majeure	*major*
mineur	mineure	*minor*
postérieur	postérieure	*posterior*
supérieur	supérieure	*superior*

5. Complete the following with the correct form of the indicated adjective.

1. La fille est _____ . *heureux*
2. Son attitude est _____ . *sérieux*
3. L'homme est _____ . *furieux*
4. Le miel est _____ . *doux*
5. La chanson est _____ . *doux*
6. La chevelure est _____ . *roux*
7. La réponse est _____ . *faux*
8. La fille est _____ . *menteur*
9. La loi est _____ . *protecteur*
10. C'est la _____ chose. *meilleur*
11. C'est une femme _____ . *créateur*
12. C'est la cause _____ . *majeur*

Adjectives Ending in *-f*

Adjectives ending in **-f** in the masculine change **-f** to **-ve** to form the feminine.

Masculine	*Feminine*	
attentif	attentive	*attentive*
actif	active	*active*
bref	brève	*brief*
destructif	destructive	*destructive*
neuf	neuve	*new*
sportif	sportive	*athletic*
vif	vive	*alive, lively*

Note the grave accent on **brève.**

Adjectives Ending in -c

Adjectives ending in **-c** change **-c** to **-che** to form the feminine.

Masculine	Feminine	
blanc	**blanche**	white
franc	**franche**	frank
sec	**sèche**	dry

Note the grave accent on **sèche.**

Exceptions:

grec	**grecque**	Greek
public	**publique**	public

6. Complete the following with the appropriate form of the indicated adjective.

1. Le garçon est _____ . *actif*
2. La fille est _____ . *attentif*
3. Ce livre est _____ . *neuf*
4. Cette robe est _____ . *neuf*
5. La réponse était _____ . *bref*
6. La nappe est _____ . *blanc*
7. L'homme est _____ . *franc*
8. La robe est _____ . *sec*
9. L'actrice est _____ . *grec*
10. C'est une place _____ . *public*

Irregular Adjectives

Some adjectives are completely irregular in the feminine.

Masculine	Feminine	
aigu	**aiguë**	sharp
long	**longue**	long
favori	**favorite**	favorite
malin	**maligne**	sly
frais	**fraîche**	fresh

7. Complete the following with the appropriate form of the indicated adjective.

1. L'aiguille est _____ . *aigu*
2. La robe est _____ . *long*
3. C'est ma chemise _____ . *favori*
4. C'est une enfant _____ . *malin*
5. C'est un enfant _____ . *malin*
6. La viande est _____ . *frais*

The Adjectives *beau, nouveau, vieux*

The adjectives **beau, nouveau** and **vieux** have three forms. They have a special masculine singular form before words beginning with a vowel or silent **h**.

Masculine before a consonant	Masculine before a vowel	Feminine	
beau	bel	belle	*beautiful, handsome*
nouveau	nouvel	nouvelle	*new*
vieux	vieil	vieille	*old*

Two other adjectives that have special masculine singular forms are:

fou	fol	folle	*crazy*
mou	mol	molle	*soft*

Note that the masculine form before a vowel and the feminine form sound alike. When the masculine adjective follows a word beginning with a vowel, the regular masculine form is used.

C'est un **beau** garçon.
C'est un **bel** homme. *But:* Cet homme est **beau.**
C'est une **belle** femme.

C'est un **nouveau** livre.
C'est un **nouvel** appartment.   *But:* Cet appartment est **nouveau.**
C'est une **nouvelle** maison.

C'est un **vieux** livre.
C'est un **vieil** écrivain.   *But:* Cet écrivain est **vieux.**
C'est une **vieille** statue.

8. Complete the following with the correct form of the indicated adjective.

1. C'est un _____ livre. *nouveau*
2. C'est une _____ histoire. *beau*
3. C'est un _____ homme. *vieux*
4. C'est une _____ peinture. *nouveau*
5. C'est un _____ ami. *nouveau*
6. C'est un _____ tableau. *vieux*
7. C'est une _____ robe. *beau*
8. C'est une _____ dame. *vieux*
9. C'est un _____ artiste. *beau*
10. C'est un _____ garçon. *beau*
11. Cet artiste est _____ . *beau*
12. Cet arbre est _____ . *vieux*
13. Cet ami est _____ . *nouveau*

PLURAL OF ADJECTIVES

Regular Forms

Most adjectives form the plural by adding **-s** to the singular form.

Masculine		Feminine	
Singular	*Plural*	*Singular*	*Plural*
petit	petits	petite	petites
grand	grands	grande	grandes

Le garçon est **grand.**	La fille est **petite.**
The boy is tall.	*The girl is small.*
Les garçons sont **grands.**	Les filles sont **petites.**
The boys are tall.	*The girls are small.*

Adjectives Ending in -*s* or -*x*

Adjectives ending in **-s** or **-x** are the same in the masculine singular and plural forms.

Singular	*Plural*
frais	**frais**
gros	**gros**
heureux	**heureux**

un garçon **heureux**	des garçons **heureux**
a happy boy	*some happy boys*
un fruit **frais**	des fruits **frais**
a fresh fruit	*some fresh fruit*

The feminine plural is regular.

Singular	*Plural*
fraîche	**fraîches**
grosse	**grosses**
heureuse	**heureuses**

une pièce **merveilleuse**	des pièces **merveilleuses**
a marvelous play	*some marvelous plays*

Adjectives Ending in -*eu* or -*eau*

Adjectives ending in **-eu** or **-eau** add **-x** to form the plural.

Singular	*Plural*
hébreu	**hébreux**
beau	**beaux**
nouveau	**nouveaux**

Le livre est **beau.**	Les livres sont **beaux.**
The book is beautiful.	*The books are beautiful.*

Exception:

bleu	**bleus**

The feminine plural is regular.

Singular	Plural
belle	**belles**
nouvelle	**nouvelles**
bleue	**bleues**

La peinture est **belle.**
The painting is beautiful.

Les peintures sont **belles.**
The paintings are beautiful.

Adjectives Ending in *-al*

Adjectives ending in **-al** change **-al** to **-aux** to form the masculine plural.

Singular	Plural
légal	**légaux**
loyal	**loyaux**
médiéval	**médiévaux**
royal	**royaux**

L'ami est **loyal.**
The friend is loyal.

Les amis sont **loyaux.**
The friends are loyal.

Exceptions:

banal	**banals**
fatal	**fatals**
final	**finals**
natal	**natals**
naval	**navals**

The feminine plural is regular.

Singular	Plural
loyale	**loyales**
fatale	**fatales**

La loi est **légale.**
The law is legal.

Les lois sont **légales.**
The laws are legal.

9. Rewrite the following sentences in the plural.

1. Le film est incroyable.
2. Le film est merveilleux.

3. La robe est bleue.
4. La note est mauvaise.
5. La loi est légale.
6. Le château est beau.
7. Le chandail est bleu.
8. L'homme est gros.
9. Le coup est fatal.
10. La maison est nouvelle.
11. La tomate est parfaite.
12. Le mot est final.

10. Complete the following with the correct form of the indicated adjective.

1. Les romans sont _____ .
   intéressant
2. Les pièces sont _____ .
   merveilleux
3. Les châteaux sont _____ .
   médiéval
4. Les livres sont _____ .
   nouveau
5. Il passe les examens _____ .
   final
6. Les hommes sont _____ .
   grand
7. Les chandails sont _____ .
   bleu
8. Les poissons sont _____ . *frais*
9. Ce sont des accidents _____ .
   fatal
10. Les murs sont _____ . *épais*
11. Ce sont des décrets _____ .
    royal
12. Les peintures sont _____ . *beau*
13. Ces lois sont _____ . *légal*
14. Les questions sont _____ .
    intelligent
15. Les robes sont _____ . *bleu*
16. Les garçons sont _____ .
    heureux
17. Ces tableaux sont _____ . *beau*

AGREEMENT PROBLEMS OF CERTAIN ADJECTIVES

1. Certain adjectives placed before a noun are invariable and are attached to the noun with a hyphen.

une **demi**-heure	*a half hour*
des **demi**-frères	*half brothers*
la **mi**-septembre	*in mid-September*
les yeux **mi**-clos	*half-closed eyes*

But:

une heure et **demie**	*one and one-half hours*

2. The adjective **nu** is invariable when it precedes a noun without an article.

nu-pieds	*barefoot*

But:

les pieds **nus**	*bare feet*

3. **Ci-joint** and **ci-inclus** are invariable when placed before the noun.

> Vous trouverez **ci-joint** les documents que vous m'avez demandés.
> *You will find attached the documents you requested.*

> *But:*

> Vous trouverez deux documents **ci-joints.**
> *You will find two documents attached.*

4. **Haut** and **bas** are invariable before an article and a noun.

> **Haut** les mains.   *Hands high.*

5. When the adjective precedes the noun **gens,** it is feminine. When it follows, it is masculine.

> les **bonnes** gens   *good people*
> les gens **âgés**   *old people*

Adjectives of Color

1. Normally, the adjective of color agrees with the noun it modifies.

> une robe **blanche**   *a white dress*
> des yeux **bruns**   *brown eyes*

2. When the adjective of color is a compound adjective, it is invariable.

> des yeux **bleu clair**   *light blue eyes*
> des chaussures **noir et blanc**   *black and white shoes*
> une robe **vert foncé**   *a dark green dress*

3. If the adjective can also be a noun used as an adjective, it is invariable.

> des robes **orange**   *orange dresses*
> des joues **ivoire**   *ivory cheeks*

4. The adjective **marron** is invariable.

> une robe **marron**   *a maroon dress*

5. The adjective **châtain** agrees with a masculine plural noun.

> des cheveux **châtains**   *chestnut brown hair*

11. Complete the following sentences with the correct form of the indicated adjective.

1. Il est sorti _____ -pieds.   *nu*
2. Il y a beaucoup de _____ gens ici.   *vieux*

3. Elle va partir à onze heures et _____ . *demi*
4. Ce sont mes _____ -sœurs. *demi*
5. Il est sorti la tête _____ . *nu*
6. Les yeux _____ -clos, elle rêvait. *mi*
7. Vous trouverez deux pièces _____ . *ci-joint*
8. Restez une _____ -heure ici. *demi*
9. _____ les mains! *haut*
10. Ce sont des gens _____ . *âgé*
11. Donne-moi mes souliers _____ . *marron*
12. Elle a les yeux _____ . *brun foncé*

COMPOUND ADJECTIVES

1. When each of the two parts of the compound adjective modifies the noun, both adjectives agree with the noun.

      une fille **sourde-muette**   *a deaf-mute girl*

2. When the first part of the compound adjective ends in **-o** or **-i,** this part of the adjective is invariable.

      une pièce **tragi-comique**   *a tragic-comic play*
      des lois **anglo-saxonnes**   *Anglo-Saxon laws*

3. If the compound adjective is formed with an invariable word plus an adjective, only the adjective agrees with the noun.

      des pays **nord-africains**   *North African countries*
      l'avant-dernière fois   *the next-to-the-last time*
      des pays **sous-développés**   *underdeveloped countries*

4. If the first term of the compound adjective has an adverbial quality, it is invariable.

      des enfants **nouveau-nés**   *newborn children*

      But:

      les fenêtres **grandes ouvertes**   *wide-open windows*
      des fraises **fraîches cueillies**   *freshly picked strawberries*

12. Complete the following sentences with the correct form of the indicated compound adjective.

    1. C'est une histoire _____ . *tragi-comique*
    2. C'est une fille _____ . *sourd-muet*
    3. Ce sont des lapins _____ . *nouveau-né*
    4. Les gens _____ parlent espagnol. *sud-américain*
    5. Ce sont des pays _____ . *sous-développé*
    6. Gardez les fenêtres _____ . *grand ouvert*

POSITION OF ADJECTIVES

Normally, most adjectives follow the noun in French, particularly:

1. those indicating color or shape

une robe bleue	*a blue dress*
une maison carrée	*a square house*

2. adjectives of nationality, origin, religion, profession, or classification, or those that refer to the arts

une fille française	*a French girl*
une peinture parisienne	*a Parisian painting*
une église catholique	*a Catholic church*
une ville municipale	*a municipal city*
une école secondaire	*a secondary school*
le parti libéral	*the Liberal party*
l'art classique	*classical art*
le style roman	*Roman style*

3. those formed from a past or present participle

la porte ouverte	*the open door*
une vie animée	*a lively life*
la semaine passée	*last week*

4. those modified by an adverb

une conversation complètement bête
a completely stupid conversation

The following adjectives normally precede the noun.

autre	*other*	**vilain**	*villanous*
jeune	*young*	**bon**	*good*
même	*same*	**grand**	*big, great*
court*	*short*	**gros**	*fat*
haut	*high, tall*	**long**	*long*
joli	*pretty*	**gentil***	*nice*
mauvais	*bad*	**beau**	*beautiful, handsome*
méchant†	*bad, naughty*	**nouveau**	*new*
meilleur*	*best*	**vieux**	*old*
petit	*small*	**vrai**	*true*

*These adjectives can be placed before or after the noun.
†**Méchant** usually follows the noun, but it precedes sometimes.

When these adjectives are modified by short adverbs, they can either precede or follow the noun.

un homme très beau
un très bel homme

When the adjective precedes the noun, the **s** or **x** is pronounced **z** before a word beginning with a vowel.

de nouveaux_zétudiants

les autres_zamis

Grand is linked to a word beginning with a vowel with a **t** sound.

un grand_tami

Long is linked to a word beginning with a vowel with a **k** sound.

un long_kentretien

In the plural, **des** becomes **de** or **d'** before an adjective that precedes a noun.

un nouveau roman	*a new novel*
de nouveaux romans	*some new novels*

When an adjective is an integral part of the noun, the article is **des**.

des jeunes filles	*some young girls*
des petits pois	*some peas*
des jeunes gens	*young people*

When two adjectives are used together, they retain their usual position.

une jolie robe bleue	*a pretty blue dress*

When two adjectives have the same position, they can be joined by the conjunction **et**.

une femme intéressante et intelligente

If an adjective is an integral part of the noun, another adjective can precede without using the conjunction **et**.

un petit jeune homme
un parfait honnête homme

When an adjective that is pronounced differently in the feminine and in the masculine forms modifies one or more nouns of different genders, place the masculine nouns closest to the adjective.

des questions et des problèmes sociaux
social questions and problems

13. Describe the things in the room, using the indicated adjective, according to the model.

un chat *jeune*
Il y a un jeune chat.

un tapis *bleu*
Il y a un tapis bleu.

    1. un tableau *joli*
    2. une chaise *vieux*
    3. une peinture *intéressant*
    4. un livre *bon*
    5. un divan-lit *gros*

6. une lampe   *petit*
7. un fauteuil   *confortable*
8. une cheminée   *grand*
9. un tapis   *oriental*
10. une chaise   *rouge*

14. Rewrite the following sentences in the plural.

1. C'est un livre intéressant.
2. C'est un film formidable.
3. C'est une conférence importante.
4. C'est un bon ami.
5. C'est une autre histoire.
6. C'est une bonne école.
7. C'est un vieil ami.
8. C'est un bel écrivain.
9. C'est une vieille amie.
10. C'est une grande maison.
11. C'est un nouvel hôtel.
12. C'est une jeune fille.
13. C'est un petit pois.

15. Anne has just won the lottery and is going on a shopping spree. Tell what she buys. Follow the model.

une maison   *grand, blanc*
Elle achète une grande maison blanche.

1. un stéreo   *grand, japonais*
2. une robe   *long, bleu*
3. un chien   *gentil, petit, amusant*
4. des meubles   *beau, français*
5. des chaussures   *nouveau, italien*
6. des gants   *beau, noir*
7. un appareil photographique   *nouveau, fantastique*
8. un diamant   *gros, brillant*
9. un chat   *petit, jeune*
10. des peintures   *joli, vieux*

ADJECTIVES THAT CHANGE MEANING ACCORDING TO POSITION

Some adjectives have a different meaning depending on whether they precede or follow the noun.

ancien	un **ancien** professeur	*a former teacher*
	un professeur **ancien**	*an old (ancient) teacher*
bon	un homme **bon**	*a kind man*
	un **bon** homme	*a good man*
brave	un **brave** homme	*a good fellow, a kind man*
	un homme **brave**	*a courageous man*

certain	un **certain** risque	*a certain risk, some risk*
	un risque **certain**	*an unquestionable risk*
	une **certaine** élégance	*a particular elegance*
	une élégance **certaine**	*an indisputable elegance*
	un **certain** jour	*one day*
cher	un **cher** ami	*a dear friend*
	une robe **chère**	*an expensive dress*
dernier	la **dernière** semaine de l'année	*the last week of the year*
	la semaine **dernière**	*last week*
différent	**différentes** personnes	*various persons*
	des personnes **différentes**	*different persons*
divers	**diverses** circonstances	*several circumstances*
	des circonstances **diverses**	*various circumstances*
faux	une **fausse** note	*a note out of tune*
	une note **fausse**	*a wrong note*
grand	un **grand** écrivain	*a great writer*
	un écrivain **grand**	*a tall writer*
honnête	une **honnête** femme	*a virtuous woman*
	une femme **honnête**	*an honest woman*
jeune	un **jeune** homme	*a young man*
	un homme **jeune**	*a man still young*
malhonnête	un **malhonnête** homme	*a dishonest man*
	un homme **malhonnête**	*a rude man*
même	la **même** chose	*the same thing*
	la chose **même**	*the thing itself*
	le jour **même**	*that very day*
	même le professeur	*even the teacher*
moyen	le **Moyen** Âge	*The Middle Ages*
	l'âge **moyen**	*middle age*
nouveau	une **nouvelle** robe	*a new (different) dress*
	une robe **nouvelle**	*a new (style) dress*
pauvre	un **pauvre** garçon	*a poor (penniless) boy*
	un garçon **pauvre**	*a poor (unfortunate) boy*
prochain	la **prochaine** fois	*the next time*
	la semaine **prochaine**	*next week*
propre	sa **propre** chambre	*his (her) own room*
	une chambre **propre**	*a clean room*
	les **propres** termes	*the very, actual words*
	les termes **propres**	*the right terms*

sage	une **sage** femme	a midwife
	une femme **sage**	a wise woman
sale	un **sale** homme	a bad man
	un homme **sale**	a dirty (physically) man
seul	une **seule** personne	only one person
	une personne **seule**	a single person
triste	un **triste** livre	a poor, worthless book
	un livre **triste**	a sad book
vilain	un **vilain** personnage	a disagreeable character
	un personnage **vilain**	an ugly character

16. Follow the model.

pauvre Ce garçon n'a pas d'argent.
        C'est un garçon pauvre.

1. *ancien*   Ce monument est vieux.
                Monsieur Dupont est mon professeur.
2. *brave*   Cet homme est courageux.
                Cet homme est bon.
3. *cher*   Ce chandail coûte beaucoup.
                C'est un ami fidèle.
4. *dernier*   La semaine passée il est allé au cinéma.
                C'est la semaine finale du trimestre.
5. *différent* Diverses personnes sont venues.
                De nouvelles personnes sont venues.
6. *grand*   C'est un écrivain célèbre.
                C'est un écrivain de grande taille.
7. *pauvre* Ce garçon est pitoyable.
                Ce garçon n'a pas d'argent.
8. *propre* Cette chambre est nette.
                C'est ma chambre à moi.

17. Rewrite each of the following sentences, inserting the correct form of the indicated adjective in the correct position.

ancien Ce monument qui est vieux est un _____ monument _____ .
       Ce monument qui est vieux est un monument ancien.

1. *sage*   Cette femme qui assiste à l'accouchement est une _____ femme _____ .
           Une femme qui sait tout est une _____ femme _____ .
2. *certain* Tu vas sûrement tout perdre. C'est un _____ risque _____ .
           Si tu joues à la Bourse, tu vas courir un _____ risque _____ .
3. *même*   Elle est arrivée le _____ jour _____ comme prévu.
           _____ le professeur _____ va être d'accord avec vous.
           Marcher et *aller à pied* sont presque la _____ chose _____ .

4. *nouveau*   Je viens d'acheter cette robe; c'est une _____ robe _____ .
                Au printemps, les maisons de haute couture vont présenter une collection
                de _____ robes _____ .

5. *seul*   Une _____ personne _____ ne peut pas tout faire.
                Mon _____ souci _____ c'est ma famille.

6. *vilain*   Ce garçon est désagréable. C'est un _____ garçon _____ .
                Ce garçon n'est pas beau. C'est un _____ garçon _____ .

7. *faux*   Le piano ne marche pas bien. J'entends une _____ note
                _____ .
                Il faut chanter la note *b,* pas la note *c.* C'est une _____ note
                _____ .

8. *sale*   C'est un _____ manteau _____ .
                Cet homme n'est pas gentil. C'est un _____ homme _____ .

9. *triste*   Cette histoire ne vaut rien. C'est une _____ histoire _____ .
                Cette histoire me fait pleurer. C'est une _____ histoire
                _____ .

10. *malhonnête* Un homme qui extorque de l'argent aux autres est un _____
                  homme _____ .
                  Un homme qui dit des grossièretés est un _____ homme _____ .

11. *prochain* Je vous verrai la _____ semaine _____ .
                La _____ fois _____ , dites la vérité.

12. *divers*   _____ personnes _____ discutent des _____ circon-
                stances _____ .

FORMATION OF ADVERBS

Most adverbs are formed by adding **-ment** to the feminine form of the adjective. Adverbs modify a verb, an adjective, or another adverb, and they are invariable.

Regular Forms

Adjective		Adverb	
Masculine	*Feminine*		
final	finale	**finalement**	*finally*
fort	forte	**fortement**	*strongly*
parfait	parfaite	**parfaitement**	*perfectly*
extrême	extrême	**extrêmement**	*extremely*
facile	facile	**facilement**	*easily*
rapide	rapide	**rapidement**	*rapidly*
naturel	naturelle	**naturellement**	*naturally*
complet	complète	**complètement**	*completely*
amer	amère	**amèrement**	*bitterly*
heureux	heureuse	**heureusement**	*happily*
sérieux	sérieuse	**sérieusement**	*seriously*
doux	douce	**doucement**	*sweetly*
attentif	attentive	**attentivement**	*attentively*
franc	franche	**franchement**	*frankly*
long	longue	**longuement**	*at length*
frais	fraîche	**fraîchement**	*freshly*

18. Follow the model.

Comment travaille-t-il? *facile*
Il travaille facilement.

1. Comment chante-t-elle? *doux*
2. Comment a-t-il prononcé? *parfait*
3. Comment étudie-t-elle? *sérieux*
4. Comment danse-t-elle? *naturel*
5. Quand a-t-il compris? *final*
6. Comment est-il parti? *soudain*
7. Comment agit-il? *dangereux*
8. Comment parle-t-il? *rapide*
9. Comment répond-elle? *franc*
10. Comment écoute-t-il? *attentif*

Adverbs Formed from Adjectives Ending in a Vowel

If the masculine adjective ends in a vowel other than a mute **e,** the ending **-ment** is added to the masculine form of the adjective to form the adverb.

Masculine Adjective	*Adverb*	
hardi	**hardiment**	*boldly*
poli	**poliment**	*politely*
vrai	**vraiment**	*truly*
absolu	**absolument**	*absolutely*
résolu	**résolument**	*resolutely*

Exception:

gai	**gaîment** or **gaiement**	*gaily*

Some adjectives ending in **-u** in the masculine add a circumflex to the **u** when forming the adverb.

Masculine Adjective	*Adverb*	
assidu	**assidûment**	*attentively*
continu	**continûment**	*continually*
cru	**crûment**	*coarsely*
dû	**dûment**	*duly*

19. Follow the model.

Comment parle-t-il? *poli*
Il parle poliment.

1. Comment agit-il? *hardi*
2. Comment agit-elle? *résolu*
3. Comment chantent-elles? *gai*
4. Comment parle-t-il? *continu*
5. Comment parle-t-il? *cru*

Adverbs Ending in *-ément*

Some adjectives ending in a mute **e** change the **e** to **é** before adding **-ment** to form the adverb.

	Adjective	Adverb	
Masculine	*Feminine*		
aveugle	aveugle	**aveuglément**	*blindly*
commode	commode	**commodément**	*conveniently*
commun	commune	**communément**	*commonly*
confus	confuse	**confusément**	*confusingly*
énorme	énorme	**énormément**	*enormously*
exquis	exquise	**exquisément**	*exquisitely*
importun	importune	**importunément**	*importunely*
opportun	opportune	**opportunément**	*opportunely*
obscur	obscure	**obscurément**	*obscurely*
précis	précise	**précisément**	*precisely*
profond	profonde	**profondément**	*profoundly*
uniforme	uniforme	**uniformément**	*uniformly*

20. Complete the following sentences with the appropriate form of the adverb formed from the indicated adjective.

   1. Pierre explique _____ la situation. *confus*
   2. Le philosophe parle _____ . *profond*
   3. L'homme est _____ habillé. *exquis*
   4. L'homme entre _____ dans l'affaire. *aveugle*
   5. C'est _____ cela. *précis*
   6. Elle a fait cela _____ . *opportun*

Adverbs Ending in *-amment* and *-emment*

Adjectives ending in **-ant** and **-ent** in the masculine singular change **-ant** to **-amment** and **-ent** to **-emment** to form adverbs.

Masculine Adjective	Adverb	
abondant	**abondamment**	*abundantly*
brillant	**brillamment**	*brilliantly*
constant	**constamment**	*constantly*
courant	**couramment**	*fluently*
puissant	**puissamment**	*powerfully*
décent	**décemment**	*decently*
évident	**évidemment**	*evidently*
fréquent	**fréquemment**	*frequently*
patient	**patiemment**	*patiently*
prudent	**prudemment**	*wisely*

Exceptions:

Masculine Adjective	Adverb	
lent	**lentement**	*slowly*
présent	**présentement**	*presently*
véhément	**véhémentement**	*vehemently*

21. Complete the following sentences with the correct form of the adverb formed from the indicated adjective.

    1. Il parle _____ le français. *courant*
    2. Elle va à ce restaurant _____ . *fréquent*
    3. Le chimiste travaille _____ . *patient*
    4. Le conférencier parle _____ . *brillant*
    5. L'homme agit _____ . *décent*
    6. _____ , il est parti. *évident*
    7. La fille agit _____ . *prudent*
    8. Le professeur écoute _____ . *patient*
    9. Elle travaille _____ . *constant*
    10. Le garçon marche _____ . *lent*
    11. Le criminel agit _____ . *véhément*
    12. Ce livre est _____ illustré. *abondant*

Irregular Adverbs

Some adverbs have irregular stems.

Adjective		Adverb	
Masculine	Feminine		
bref	brève	**brièvement**	*briefly*
gentil	gentille	**gentiment**	*nicely*
impuni	impunie	**impunément**	*with impunity*

Some adverbs differ altogether from the corresponding adjective.

Adjective		Adverb	
Masculine	Feminine		
bon	bonne	**bien**	*well*
mauvais	mauvaise	**mal**	*badly*
meilleur	meilleure	**mieux**	*better*
petit	petite	**peu**	*little*
moindre	moindre	**moins**	*less*

Elle chante **bien.**	*She sings well.*
Il écrit **mal.**	*He writes badly.*
Il va **mieux.**	*He is better.*
Il travaille **peu.**	*He works a little.*

You can distinguish between **bon/mauvais** and **bien/mal** by remembering that the adjectives **bon** and **mauvais** modify nouns whereas the adverbs **bien** and **mal** modify verbs.

> Elle est **bonne (mauvaise)** en mathématiques.
> *She is good (bad) in mathematics.*

> Elle parle **bien (mal)** le français.
> *She speaks French well (badly).*

Some adjectives are identical to the masculine singular adjective.

Adjective and Adverb

bas   *low*
　Il parle **bas.**   *He speaks low.*
bon   *good*
　Ça sent **bon.**   *That smells good.*
chaud   *warm*
　Il fait **chaud.**   *It is warm (weather).*
cher   *expensive*
　Les robes coûtent **cher.**   *The dresses are expensive.*
clair   *clearly*
　Elle voit **clair.**   *She understands.*
court   *short*
　Il s'arrête **court.**   *He stops short.*
dur   *hard*
　Elle travaille **dur.**   *She works hard.*
faux   *false*
　Il chante **faux.**   *He sings out of tune.*
fort   *loudly, strongly*
　Il crie **fort.**   *He shouts loudly.*
haut   *loudly*
　Il parle **haut.**   *He speaks loudly.*
juste   *straight*
　Elle tire **juste.**   *She shoots straight.*
mauvais   *bad*
　Ça sent **mauvais.**   *That smells bad.*
net   *clean, short*
　Elle s'arrête **net.**   *She stops short.*

22. Complete the following sentences with the correct form of the adverb formed from the indicated adjective.

　　1. Le conférencier parle _____ .   *bref*
　　2. Il a agi _____ .   *gentil*
　　3. Elle parle _____ le français.   *bon*
　　4. L'élève écrit _____ .   *mauvais*
　　5. Cette fille parle _____ .   *petit*
　　6. Elle voit _____ .   *clair*
　　7. Le garçon parle _____ .   *bas*
　　8. Ces chandails coûtent _____ .   *cher*
　　9. Il travaille _____ .   *dur*
　　10. Elle chante _____ .   *bon*
　　11. Elle s'arrête _____ .   *court*
　　12. Il crie _____ .   *fort*

POSITION OF ADVERBS

In simple tenses, adverbs follow the verb.

Il parle **rapidement**.	*He speaks rapidly.*
Elle chante **bien**.	*She sings well.*

In compound tenses, short, common adverbs and some adverbs of manner are placed between the auxiliary verb and the past participle. Some of these are: **assez, bien, beaucoup, bientôt, déjà, encore, enfin, jamais, mal, mieux, moins, souvent, toujours, trop** and **vite**.

Elle veut voyager **partout**.	*She wants to travel everywhere.*
Elle a **beaucoup** parlé.	*She spoke a lot.*
Nous avons **bien** dormi.	*We slept well.*
Elle est **vite** descendue.	*She came down quickly.*
Elle a **trop** bu.	*She drank too much.*

Adverbs of place and certain adverbs of time such as **hier, aujourd'hui, demain, avant-hier, après demain, autrefois, tard** and adverbs ending in **-ment** usually follow the past participle.

Elle est arrivée **hier**.	*She arrived yesterday.*
Il est parti **tard**.	*He left late.*
On l'a rencontré **là-bas**.	*He was met there.*
Elle a compris **facilement**.	*She understood easily.*

The adverb that modifies an infinitive can be placed before or after it.

Je voudrais **toujours** garder mon sang-froid.
Je voudrais garder **toujours** mon sang-froid.
I always want to keep my cool.

Some adverbs may appear at the beginning of the sentence.

Finalement, elle est arrivée.	*Finally, she arrived.*
Elle est arrivée **finalement**.	*She arrived finally.*
Heureusement, il l'a bien fait.	*Happily, he did it well.*
Il l'a bien fait, **heureusement**.	*He did it well, happily.*

Many adverbs of time may also appear at the beginning of a sentence.

Enfin, il a fini.	*Finally, he finished.*
Aujourd'hui nous irons au cinéma.	*Today we will go the movies.*
Demain nous partirons.	*Tomorrow we will leave.*

23. Follow the model.

Vous avez parlé.   *bien*
Vous avez bien parlé.

1. Il court.   *rapidement*
2. La situation est impossible.   *absolument*
3. Elle a voyagé.   *beaucoup*

    4. Il a étudié. *bien*
    5. Nous avons mangé. *déjà*
    6. Nous y sommes allés. *souvent*
    7. Elle est arrivée. *hier*
    8. Elle a travaillé. *patiemment*
    9. Elle va travailler. *trop*
   10. J'ai mangé. *assez*

24. Follow the model.

A-t-elle fini? *heureusement*
Heureusement, elle a fini.

    1. Êtes-vous content? *naturellement*
    2. Va-t-il être à l'heure? *certainement*
    3. Est-il triste? *évidemment*
    4. Est-elle arrivée? *finalement*
    5. Est-elle arrivée à l'heure? *heureusement*

COMPARISON OF ADJECTIVES AND ADVERBS

Regular Comparisons

The comparative is formed by placing **plus, moins** or **aussi** before and **que** after the adjective or adverb.

Comparison of superiority

plus … que   *more … than*

Cette robe est **plus** belle **que** l'autre.
This dress is prettier than the other.
Il parle **plus** vite **que** moi.
He speaks more rapidly than I.

Comparison of equality

aussi … que   *as … as*

Elle est **aussi** intelligente **que** moi.
She is as intelligent as I am.
Il parle **aussi** couramment **que** Pierre.
He speaks as fluently as Peter.

Comparison of inferiority

moins … que   *less … than*

Ce tailleur est **moins** cher **que** l'autre.
This suit is less expensive than the other.
Ce garçon agit **moins** poliment **que** l'autre.
This boy acts less politely than the other.

Note that the disjunctive pronoun follows **que.**

Je suis **plus** intelligent **que lui.**
I am more intelligent than he.

In negative sentences, **aussi** can become **si.**

Affirmative

Elle parle **aussi** vite **que** son frère.
She speaks as quickly as her brother.

Negative

Elle ne parle pas **si** vite **que** son frère.
She does not speak as quickly as her brother.

Plus and **moins** do not change in negative sentences.

Elle ne parle pas **plus** vite **que** son frère.
She does not speak more quickly than her brother.
Elle ne parle pas **moins** vite **que** son frère.
She does not speak less quickly than her brother.

Plus and **moins** used as adverbs of quantity require **de** before a numeral.

Je travaille **plus de** soixante heures par semaine.
I work more than sixty hours per week.
Il y a **moins de** vingt personnes inscrites au cours.
There are less than twenty people enrolled in the course.

But:

Il peut porter **plus que** deux kilos.
He can carry more than two kilos.

When there is a clause depending on the comparative, **ne** must be used before the subordinate verb.

Il est **plus** intelligent **que** vous **ne** le pensez.
He is more intelligent than you think.
Elle est **plus** intelligente **qu'**elle **n'**en a l'air.
She is more intelligent than she appears.

25. Follow the model.

Marie est grande.   *less ... than*
Marie est moins grande que sa sœur.

1. Anne est intelligente.   *more ... than*
2. Cet enfant est poli.   *as ... as*
3. Elle est patiente.   *less ... than*
4. Annette est sérieuse.   *more ... than*
5. Il est gentil.   *as ... as*
6. Hélène parle intelligemment.   *more ... than*
7. Cet homme conduit dangereusement.   *as ... as*
8. Vous chantez doucement.   *less ... than*
9. Judith attend patiemment.   *more ... than*
10. Vous agissez poliment.   *as ... as*
11. Il a mangé des tartes.   *more ... than*
12. Elle a pris des livres.   *less ... than*

26. Follow the model.

Elle est petite. Hélène est plus petite.
Hélène est plus petite qu'elle.

    1. Il est grand. Georges est plus grand.
    2. Je suis intelligent. Pierre est plus intelligent.
    3. Nous travaillons patiemment. Les autres travaillent plus patiemment.
    4. Elle danse gaiement. Hélène danse aussi gaiement.
    5. Ils écoutent attentivement. Pierre écoute aussi attentivement.
    6. Elles sont intelligentes. Marc est moins intelligent.

27. Rewrite the following sentences in the negative.

    1. Il parle plus vite que moi.
    2. Il répond aussi intelligemment que Georges.
    3. Il chante moins doucement que Pierre.
    4. Elle est plus belle que Babeth.
    5. Elle est aussi gentille que sa sœur.

28. Combine the two sentences according to the model.

Vous croyez qu'elle est douée. Elle est plus douée.
Elle est plus douée que vous ne le croyez.

    1. Vous croyez qu'il est bête. Il est moins bête.
    2. Vous trouvez qu'elle est intelligente. Elle est plus intelligente.
    3. Vous pensez qu'il est drôle. Il est moins drôle.
    4. Il a l'air méchant. Il est plus méchant.
    5. Cette chanson a l'air compliquée. Elle est moins compliquée.

Comparative Followed by a Noun

    Followed by a noun, **plus ... que** becomes **plus de ... que, aussi ... que** becomes **autant de ... que** and **moins ... que** becomes **moins de ... que.**

    J'ai **plus de** livres **que** lui.
    I have more books than he does.
    Elle a **autant d'**argent **que** moi.
    She has as much money as I.
    Elle a **moins de** livres **que** moi.
    She has fewer books than I.

29. Follow the model.

Pierre a des livres.   *more*
Pierre a plus de livres que moi.

    1. Anne a de l'argent.   *as much*
    2. Elle a des robes.   *fewer*
    3. Il a des autos.   *more*
    4. Elle a des gâteaux.   *as many*
    5. Vous avez des peintures.   *more*
    6. Vous avez des disques.   *as many*

SUPERLATIVE OF ADJECTIVES AND ADVERBS

The superlative of an adjective is formed by adding the definite article **le, la** or **les** to the comparative form.

Marc est l'étudiant **le plus intelligent** de la classe.
Marc is the most intelligent boy in the class.
Cette peinture est **la plus belle** de toutes.
This painting is the most beautiful of all.
Ces peintures sont **les moins intéressantes** du musée.
These paintings are the least interesting in the museum.

If an adjective normally precedes the noun, the superlative will also precede the noun. If the adjective normally follows the noun, the superlative will normally follow.

Pierre est **un gentil garçon.**
Peter is a nice boy.
Pierre est **le plus gentil garçon** de la classe.
Peter is the nicest boy in the class.
Marie est **une fille intelligente.**
Mary is an intelligent girl.
Marie est **la fille la plus intelligente** de la classe.
Mary is the most intelligent girl in the class.

Note that the preposition **de** follows the superlative even when it means *in*.

When a verb follows the superlative, it is usually in the subjunctive.

C'est le film le plus intéressant que j'aie vu.
C'est la plus gentille fille que je connaisse.

The superlative of adverbs is formed by adding **le** to the comparative.

Ce garçon parle **le plus couramment.**
This boy speaks the most fluently.
Cette fille chante **le plus fort.**
This girl sings the loudest.

30. Follow the models.

Ce garçon est beau?
Oui, c'est le plus beau garçon du village.

Cette fille est intelligente?
Oui, c'est la fille la plus intelligente du village.

1. Cette fille est intéressante?
2. Cette rue est petite?
3. Ces enfants sont amusants?
4. Ce jardin est joli?
5. Ce garçon est honnête?
6. Ce professeur est exigeant?
7. Cette église est vieille?
8. Ces filles sont intelligentes?
9. Ce musée est grand?
10. Cette peinture est belle?

31. Follow the models.

Pierre parle vite?
Oui, il parle le plus vite de tous.

Anne parle vite?
Oui, elle parle le plus vite de toutes.

1. Georges chante fort?
2. Marie travaille sérieusement?
3. Hélène danse exquisément?
4. Le professeur parle profondément?
5. Anne chante brillamment?

IRREGULAR COMPARATIVES AND SUPERLATIVES

The adjective **bon** and the adverb **bien** are irregular in comparisons of superiority.

	Comparative	*Superlative*
bon(s), bonne(s)	**meilleur(s), meilleure(s)**	**le, la, les meilleur(e)(s)(es)**
	better	*the best*
bien	**mieux**	**le mieux**
	better	*the best*

Ce livre est **meilleur** que l'autre.
This book is better than the other.
Cette pomme est **meilleure** que l'autre.
This apple is better than the other.
Ces peintures sont **les meilleures** de toutes.
These paintings are the best of all.
Elle parle **mieux** que lui.
She speaks better than he.
Elle chante **le mieux** de toutes.
She sings the best of all.

Comparative and superlative forms of **bon** can be placed before or after the noun.

Il n'y a pas de **meilleures** méthodes.
Il est parmi les peintres **les meilleurs.**

Moins and **aussi** are used with **bon** and **bien.**

Ce livre est **moins (aussi) bon que** l'autre.
Elle parle **moins (aussi) bien que** lui.

Mauvais and **mal** have irregular as well as regular forms.

	Comparative	*Superlative*
mauvais(e)(es)	**plus mauvais(e)(es)**	**le, la, les plus mauvais(e)(es)**
	pire	**le, la, les pire(s)**
	worse	*the worst*
mal	**plus mal**	**le plus mal**
	pis	**le pis**
	worse	*the worst*

Cette note est **plus mauvaise que** l'autre.
Cette note est **pire que** l'autre.
This grade is worse than the other.
Cette note est **la plus mauvaise** de toutes.
Cette note est **la pire** de toutes.
This grade is the worst of all.
Il chante **plus mal que** Marie.
Il chante **pis que** Marie.
He sings worse than Mary.
Il chante **le plus mal** de tous.
He sings the worst of all.
Le pis de l'affaire c'est que vous avez échoué.
The worst of the matter is that you failed.

Note: **le pis** can only be used as a noun.

Plus mauvais and **le plus mauvais** are generally used in a concrete sense.

Cette automobile est **plus mauvaise que** l'autre.
This automobile is worse than the other.

Pire and **le pire** are generally used in a moral sense.

Il est **pire que** Pierre.
He is worse than Peter.

Petit has regular and irregular forms.

	Comparative	*Superlative*
petit(e)(s)(es)	**plus petit(e)(s)(es)**	**le, la, les plus petit(e)(s)(es)**
	moindre	**le, la, les moindre(s)**
	smaller	*the smallest*

Plus petit and **le plus petit** are used with things you can measure.

Mon auto est **plus petite que** la sienne.
My car is smaller than his (hers).

Moindre and **le moindre** are used in an abstract sense.

Je n'ai pas **la moindre** idée.
I don't have the slightest (least) idea.

The comparative of **beaucoup** is **plus** or **davantage.**

Pierre a **beaucoup de** livres.
Peter has many books.
Georges a **plus de** livres.
George has more books.
Georges en a **plus.**
George has more.

Davantage is used to indicate a comparison of superiority and is generally placed at the end of the sentence. It cannot modify a verb.

Cette femme est très intelligente mais sa fille l'est **davantage.**
This woman is very intelligent but her daughter is even more so.

The comparative of **peu** is **moins.**

André travaille **peu.**
Andrew works (a) little.
Pierre travaille **moins.**
Peter works less.

32. Complete the following with an appropriate comparison of superiority.
 1. Ce livre est bon mais celui-là est _____ .
 2. Ce garçon chante bien mais Pierre chante _____ .
 3. Cette peinture est bonne mais celle-là est _____ .
 4. Il parle bien mais Pierre parle _____ .
 5. Ce tableau est mauvais mais celui-là est _____ .
 6. Il chante mal mais Pierre chante _____ .
 7. André a beaucoup de disques. Georges en a _____ .
 8. Marie dessine un peu. Lisette dessine _____ .
 9. Ces écoles sont bonnes, mais celles-ci sont _____ de toutes.
10. Pierre travaille mal, mais André travaille _____ de tous.
11. Cette maison est petite. C'est _____ de toutes.
12. Je ne sais pas la réponse. Je n'ai pas _____ idée.

33. Follow the models.

Ce livre-ci est bon.
Ce livre-ci est aussi bon que ce livre-là.
Ce livre-ci est moins bon que ce livre-là.
Ce livre-ci est meilleur que ce livre-là.
Ce livre-ci est le meilleur de tous.

 1. Ce gâteau-ci est bon.
 2. Ces fromages-ci sont bons.
 3. Cette orange-ci est bonne.
 4. Ces tomates-ci sont bonnes.
 5. Ce beurre-ci est mauvais.
 6. Cette tarte-ci est mauvaise.

Il chante bien.
Il chante aussi bien que vous.
Il chante moins bien que vous.
Il chante mieux que vous.
Il chante le mieux de tous.

 7. Elle chante bien.
 8. Il écrit bien.
 9. Il travaille mal.

Adjectives without Comparative and Superlative Forms

Some adjectives introducing their complement by the preposition **à** have no comparative or superlative forms.

inférieur à	*inferior to*
supérieur à	*superior to*
antérieur à	*anterior to*
postérieur à	*posterior to*
intérieur à	*interior to*
extérieur à	*exterior to*

Les œufs bruns sont-ils **supérieurs** aux œufs blancs?
Are brown eggs superior to white eggs?

Some adjectives that already express comparisons of inferiority or superiority do not have special comparative forms.

aîné	*older, oldest*
cadet	*younger, youngest*
premier, première	*first*
dernier, dernière	*last*
principal, -e	*principal*

C'est mon frère **cadet.**
He's my younger brother.

Useful Phrases with Comparatives and Superlatives

plus ... plus	*the more ... the more*
moins ... moins	*the less ... the less*
plus ... moins	*the more ... the less*

Plus je lis ce livre, **plus** je l'aime.
The more I read this book, the more I like it.
Moins je lis, **moins** j'apprends.
The less I read, the less I learn.
Plus je fais le ménage, **moins** j'en ai envie.
The more I do housework, the less I want to.

de plus en plus	*more and more*
de moins en moins	*less and less*
de mieux en mieux	*better and better*

Ce travail devient **de plus en plus** difficile.
This work is becoming more and more difficult.
Le climat est **de moins en moins** agréable.
The climate is less and less agreeable.
Elle chante **de mieux en mieux.**
She sings better and better.

d'autant plus que	*all the more ... as, because*

Il est **d'autant plus** heureux ici **qu**'il a un jardin.
He is all the more happy here because he has a garden.

tant mieux	*so much the better*
tant pis	*so much the worse*
de mal en pis	*from bad to worse*

Les choses vont **de mal en pis.**
Things go from bad to worse.

34. Write the following sentences in French.

    1. The child talks more and more each day.
    2. The more he works, the more he understands.
    3. So much the better!
    4. The economy goes from bad to worse.
    5. He is all the more happy because he lives in the country.
    6. The sick person eats better and better.
    7. Mary is my older sister.

POSSESSIVE ADJECTIVES

In French **de** and the name of the person show possession.

le livre de Paul
Paul's book
la mère de Marie et de Georges
Mary and George's mother
les livres des garçons
the boys' books

Following are the forms for the possessive adjectives.

	Masculine singular	*Masculine or feminine singular before a vowel*	*Feminine singular*	*Plural*
my	**mon**	**mon**	**ma**	**mes**
your (fam.)	**ton**	**ton**	**ta**	**tes**
his, her, its	**son**	**son**	**sa**	**ses**
our	**notre**	**notre**	**notre**	**nos**
your	**votre**	**votre**	**votre**	**vos**
their	**leur**	**leur**	**leur**	**leurs**

The possessive adjective agrees in number and in gender with the noun modified, not with the possessor.

mon frère	*my brother*
ma sœur	*my sister*
mes frères	*my brothers*
Elle a **son livre.**	*She has her book.*
Il a **son livre.**	*He has his book.*

Note that **mon, ton** and **son** are used before feminine nouns or adjectives beginning with a vowel or silent **h.**

mon amie Hélène	*my friend Helen*
mon histoire préférée	*my favorite story*

The possessive adjective must be repeated before each noun.

Je dois écrire à **ma sœur**, à **mes parents** et à **mon oncle.**

Use of the Definite Article as a Possessive

Possessive adjectives are not used when referring to parts of the body, clothing, etc., when the possessor is clearly indicated. They are also not used with mental faculties.

Il a les mains dans les poches.
He has his hands in his pockets.
Elle lui a fait mal au bras.
She hurt his arm.
Lève la main.
Raise your hand.
Il a baissé la tête.
He lowered his head.
Il a perdu la mémoire.
He lost his memory.

When the possessor has not been mentioned, the possessive adjective can be used.

Ses yeux étaient d'un noir profond.
Elle avait **les yeux** d'un noir profond.

In the last sentence, the possessor **elle** is indicated and, therefore, the definite article is used.

However, after **regarder, montrer** or **voir** and when you want to emphasize the part of the body, the possessive adjectives are used with parts of the body.

Montre-moi tes mains.
Show me your hands.
Donne-moi ta main gauche.
Give me your left hand.
Elle regarde ses cheveux.
She looks at his hair.

With *on, personne, tout le monde*

When the object possessed is in the same clause as **on, personne** and **tout le monde,** the third person singular possessive adjectives **son, sa, ses** are used.

On aime son père et sa mère.
Tout le monde veut faire de son mieux.

However, if the object possessed is in a different clause from the one where **on** is used, the possessive adjectives **notre** and **votre** are used.

On n'est pas méchant par nature. Ce sont les circonstances qui nous forcent à l'être malgré notre désir.

With *chacun*

If **chacun** is a subject or object, **son, sa, ses** are used.

Chacun a son défaut.
Each one has his own faults.

If a plural subject is modified by **chacun,** the possessive adjective agrees with the subject.

Nous avons apporté chacun nos provisions.
Ils feront chacun son / leur devoir.
Ils sont partis chacun de son / leur côté.

The third person can be singular or plural.

The idea of possession can also be expressed by using **être à** plus a disjunctive pronoun.

Ce livre est à moi.
C'est mon propre livre.
This is my book.

It can also be expressed by a demonstrative pronoun plus **de** plus a noun.

mon auto et celle de mon père
my car and my father's (car)

To avoid ambiguity in translating *his* or *her*, a prepositional phrase **à lui** or **à elle** may be used.

Il parle à **son père à elle.**   *(her father)*
Il parle à **son père à lui.**   *(his father)*

35. Tell what the people are packing to go on vacation. Complete the following, choosing the correct form of the possessive adjective.

   1. *mon, ma, mes*   J'ai _____ robe, _____ blouses et _____ pantalon.
   2. *ton, ta, tes*   Voilà _____ appareil photographique, _____ cellule, et _____ filtres.
   3. *son, sa, ses*   Il a _____ chemise, _____ imperméable et _____ chaussures.
   4. *notre, nos*   Nous avons _____ sac de couchage et _____ provisions.
   5. *votre, vos*   Vous avez _____ gants et _____ chapeau.
   6. *leur, leurs*   Ils ont _____ cravates et _____ liste des adresses.

36. Follow the model.

C'est le livre de Paul.
C'est son livre.

   1. C'est le cahier de Pierre.
   2. C'est le livre de Marie.
   3. C'est la photo de Georges.
   4. Ce sont les amies de Marie.
   5. C'est l'amie de Paul.
   6. Ce sont les lettres du professeur.
   7. C'est l'école des garçons.
   8. C'est l'adresse de Babeth.
   9. Ce sont les livres de l'écrivain.
   10. C'est l'auto de Monsieur et de Madame Dupont.
   11. Ce sont les amis des garçons.
   12. Ce sont les livres des professeurs.

37. The following people are bringing friends and relatives to a party. Whom are the people bringing? Follow the model.

J'invite _____ cousin.
J'invite *mon* cousin.

   1. Nous invitons _____ cousines.
   2. Nicole invite _____ ami Pierre.
   3. J'invite _____ oncle Antoine.
   4. Monsieur et Madame Dupont invitent _____ voisins.
   5. Tu invites _____ mère.
   6. Paul invite _____ cousine Antoinette.
   7. Nous invitons _____ père.

8. Vous invitez _____ mère.
9. J'invite _____ amies.
10. Tu invites _____ professeurs.
11. David et Pierre invitent _____ tante.
12. J'invite _____ sœur Babeth.
13. Le professeur invite _____ élèves.
14. Tu invites _____ amie Anne.
15. Vous invitez _____ parents.

38. Complete the following sentences with the appropriate possessive adjective or definite article.

1. (My) _____ auto est en panne.
2. (Your, *fam.*) _____ livre est intéressant.
3. J'écris à (my) _____ mère.
4. J'aime (his) _____ cravate.
5. Il parle à (her) _____ père.
6. Ils lisent (their) _____ journal.
7. Paul parle à (his) _____ amie.
8. Ils ont (their) _____ billets.
9. Elle veut (her) _____ argent.
10. Il écrit à (his) _____ mère.
11. Elle adore (her) _____ père.
12. Nous écoutons (our) _____ professeurs.
13. Vous avez (your) _____ livres.
14. Tu as (your) _____ robe.
15. (Your, *formal*) _____ père m'a téléphoné hier soir.
16. (My) _____ amies viennent me voir souvent.
17. Elle écrit à (her) _____ parents.
18. Elle aime (his) _____ livres.
19. Nous aimons (our) _____ appartement.
20. Il a (his) _____ mains sur la table.
21. Elle a levé (her) _____ main.
22. Elle brosse (his) _____ cheveux.
23. Montre-moi (your, *fam.*) _____ mains.
24. On lui a rendu _____ liberté.
25. Vous avez apporté chacun _____ provisions.
26. Personne n'a oublié _____ livre.

39. Form sentences using a possessive adjective according to the model.

la maison ... de Pierre
C'est sa maison à lui.

1. le père ... de Marie
2. la sœur ... de Pierre
3. le livre ... à moi
4. la propriété ... de M. et de Mme Dupont
5. les stylos ... de Gisèle
6. le chien ... à toi
7. les enfants ... à nous
8. la bicyclette ... à vous

DEMONSTRATIVE ADJECTIVES

The demonstrative adjectives *this, that, these, those* are as follows:

Masculine singular		Feminine singular	Plural
Before a consonant	*Before a vowel*		
ce	**cet**	**cette**	**ces**

Ce garçon est beau.
Cet artiste est intelligent.
Cette fille est belle.
Ces livres sont intéressants.
Ces peintures sont belles.

To make a clear distinction between *this* and *that*, the suffix **-ci** (*this*) or **-là** (*that*) is added.

Je veux ce livre-ci.	*I want this book.*
Je ne veux pas ce livre-là.	*I don't want that book.*

40. Complete the following with the appropriate demonstrative adjective.

1. J'aime _____ roman.
2. Il a écrit _____ pièce.
3. _____ artiste travaille bien.
4. Je veux _____ livres d'art.
5. _____ animaux sont féroces.
6. Parlez à _____ enfant.
7. _____ église est vieille.
8. _____ peintures sont belles.
9. Nous allons déjeuner dans _____ restaurant.
10. _____ route va à Nice.

41. Madame Dupont is buying fruit for a fruit salad for her lunch. She is very particular about what she buys. Follow the model.

des pommes
Je voudrais ces pommes-ci, pas ces pommes-là.

1. une orange
2. un abricot
3. des cerises
4. une pomme
5. un pamplemousse
6. des raisins

INDEFINITE ADJECTIVES

Following are some of the most common indefinite adjectives.

1. **autre, autres**   *another, other, different*

Je voudrais essayer **une autre** robe.
I would like to try on another dress.
Avez-vous **d'autres** livres?
Do you have any other books?

Note that the plural of **un autre** is **d'autres.**

> **un autre** film
> *another film*
> **d'autres** films
> *other films*

In spoken language, **autre** is also used to reinforce a first or second person plural subject pronoun.

> **Nous autres,** nous viendrons.
> *As for us, we'll come.*

Autre is used without an article or demonstrative adjective in certain expressions.

> **Autres temps, autres mœurs.**
> *Other days, other ways.*
> **Ça c'est autre chose.**
> *That's another thing.*

2. **Aucun(e) ... ne, nul(le) ... ne, ne ... aucun(e)**   *no*

> **Aucun** travail **n'**est trop difficile.
> **Nul** travail **n'**est trop difficile.
> *No work is too difficult.*
> Il **n'**y a **aucun** homme ici.
> *There is no man here.*
> Il **n'**y a **aucune** peinture.
> *There is no painting.*

3. **certain(e), certain(e)s**   *certain, some*

Certain is placed before the noun. Sometimes **certain** can mean the same thing as **quelque.**

> Une **certaine** Madame Leroi vous attend.
> *A certain Mrs. Leroy is waiting for you.*
> **Certains** mots anglais se sont infiltrés dans la langue française.
> *Certain English words have infiltrated into the French language.*
> **Certaines** situations sont difficiles; d'autres ne le sont pas.
> *Certain situations are difficult; others are not.*

4. **chaque**   *each, every*

> **Chaque** personne a son pays.
> *Each person has his (her) country.*
> Il dit cela **chaque** fois.
> *He says that every time.*

5. **divers(es), différent(e)s, maint(e)s**   *several, various*

> **Divers** professeurs ont proposé **différents** projects.
> *Various teachers proposed various projects.*
> **Maintes** fois elle a proposé une solution.
> *Many times she proposed a solution.*

6. **même**   *same, itself, very, even*

After a noun, **même** means *itself.*

> Cet homme est l'honnêteté **même.**
> *This man is honesty itself.*

After a noun or a pronoun, it means *very, even, himself,* etc.

> Il a annoncé sa candidature ce jour **même.**
> *He announced his candidacy that very day.*
> **Même** son meilleur ami ne le croit pas.
> *Even his best friend does not believe him.*
> Ses parents **mêmes** ne le croient pas.
> *His parents themselves don't believe him.*
> **Lui-même** ne savait quoi dire.
> *He himself did not know what to say.*
> Écrivez-la **vous-même.**
> *Write it yourself.*

Before a noun and preceded by the article, it means *same.*

> C'est **le même livre.**
> *It's the same book.*
> Nous lisons **les mêmes journaux.**
> *We read the same newspapers.*

7. **n'importe**   *no matter*

N'importe combines with **quel, quelle, quels, quelles** to signify *no matter what (which).*

> Téléphonez-moi à **n'importe quelle** heure.
> *Telephone me at any hour.*

8. **plusieurs**   *several*

> Elle a **plusieurs** livres.
> *She has several books.*
> Il a **plusieurs** chemises.
> *He has several shirts.*

Plusieurs is invariable.

9. **quelque**   *a little, some, few*

In the singular, **quelque** means *a little.*

> Il me reste **quelque** temps.
> *I have a little time left.*

Or it may mean *some, any kind of.*

> Je voudrais trouver **quelque** poste.
> *I would like to find any (some) kind of job.*

In the plural, **quelque** means *a few, some* or *several.*

> Elle a acheté **quelques** livres.
> *She bought a few (some) books.*
> Il a **quelques** amis.
> *He has some (several) friends.*

Quelque can be an adverb and, therefore, invariable when it is used before a number and means **environ** (*about*).

> J'ai fait **quelque** cent mètres avant d'arriver à une route pavée.
> *I walked about one hundred meters before arriving at a paved road.*

10. **quelque ... que**   *whatever, however*
quel, quelle, quels, quelles ... que   *whatever*

Quelque and the interrogative adjective **quel** combine with the relative pronoun **que** to mean *whatever*. The verb that follows is always in the subjunctive. Before a noun **quelque** is an adjective and is variable.

>**Quelques** peurs **que** vous ayez, conquérez-les.
>*Whatever fears you have, conquer them.*

Before a descriptive adjective, **quelque** is an adverb and, therefore, invariable.

>**Quelque difficiles que** soient les problèmes, persévérez.
>*However difficult the problems are, persevere.*

Before an adverb, it is another adverb and, therefore, invariable.

>**Quelque bêtement** que vous agissiez, je vous aime toujours.
>*However stupidly you act, I always like you.*

Quel que is written as two words when it is followed by a verb (almost always the verb **être**). It agrees with the subject.

>**Quel que** soit votre métier, travaillez bien.
>*Whatever your profession, work well.*
>**Quelle que** soit la difficulté, surpassez-la.
>*Whatever the difficulty, surpass it.*
>**Quels que** soient les problèmes, ne vous inquiétez pas.
>*Whatever the problems, don't get upset.*

11. **quelconque**   *just any*

>Ce n'est pas une peinture **quelconque.** C'est une peinture de Picasso.
>*This is not just any painting. It's a painting by Picasso.*

12. **je ne sais quel(le)(s)(les)**   *I don't know*
   on ne sait quel(le)(s)(les)   *one doesn't know*
   Dieu sait quel(le)(s)(les)   *God only knows*
   etc.

These expressions are used to indicate an approximate resemblance. They are similar in meaning to **certain** in an undetermined sense.

>**Je ne sais quelle** personne a dit «Il n'y a pas de fumée sans feu.»
>*I don't know who said: "There is no smoke without fire."*
>Il le fera **Dieu sait quel jour.**
>*He'll do it some day or other. (God only knows when.)*
>Elle a **je ne sais quelles** idées.
>*She has some ideas or others.*

13. **tel** (*masc. sing.*), **tels** (*masc. pl.*), **telle** (*fem. sing.*), **telles** (*fem. pl.*)   *such, such a, like, as*

>**Tel** est mon avis.
>*Such is my opinion.*
>Je n'ai jamais vu **un tel** film.
>*I never saw such a film.*
>**Tel** père, **tel** fils.
>*Like father, like son.*
>Il faut parler français **tel que** les Français le parlent.
>*You must speak French as the French do.*
>Un homme **tel que** lui mérite des louanges.
>*A man such as he deserves praise.*

telle ou **telle** personne
such and such a person
Elle est partie **telle une flèche.**
She shot off like an arrow.

Use **si** instead of **tel** in expressions containing an adjective.

Avez-vous jamais vu une **si** belle peinture?
Have you ever seen such a beautiful painting?
Avez-vous jamais lu des livres **si** amusants?
Have you ever read such amusing books?

14. **tout** (*masc. sing.*), **tous** (*masc. pl.*), **toute** (*fem. sing.*), **toutes** (*fem. pl.*)   *all, every, the whole*

In the singular, **tout** means *each* or *every* when it is used without an article.

Tout homme a son pays.
Every man has his country.
Toute femme mérite cela.
Every woman deserves that.

When followed by an article, it means *the whole, the entire.*

Tout le pays est fertile.
The whole country is fertile.
Toute la montagne est couverte de neige.
The whole mountain is covered with snow.
Je serai honnête **toute ma** vie.
I will be honest my whole life.

In certain expressions, **tout** means *only.*

Pour **toute** réponse, il souriait.
His only answer was to smile.

In the plural, **tout** means *all* or *every.*

Tous les gens ont besoin de repos.
All people need rest.
Toutes les chemises sont chères.
All the shirts are expensive.
Elle y va **tous les** jours.
She goes there every day.

Tout is invariable when using the name of an author to mean the ensemble of his or her works.

J'ai lu **tout Simone de Beauvoir.**

Tout is an adverb and is invariable when used to mean *entirely.*

ma vie **tout entière**
my entire life
Nous sommes **tout seuls.**
We are all alone.

Tout is also invariable before a feminine word beginning with a vowel or silent **h.**

Elle est **tout agréable, tout heureuse.**
She is altogether agreeable, altogether happy.

However, the adverb **tout** must agree in gender and number before a feminine adjective beginning with a consonant or aspirate **h.**

     Elle est **toute surprise, toute honteuse.**
     She is altogether surprised, altogether ashamed.

42. Complete the following sentences with the correct French expression for the English words in parentheses.

   1. Je cherche _____ (some kind of) travail.
   2. Elle a acheté _____ (some) disques.
   3. Il y a _____ (several) livres sur la table.
   4. J'ai _____ (certain) choses à faire.
   5. J'ai discuté la situation avec _____ (various) personnes.
   6. _____ (Every) homme veut sa liberté.
   7. _____ (Every) fois qu'il ouvre la bouche, il m'ennuie.
   8. _____ (All) les hommes sont mortels.
   9. Avez-vous une _____ (other) idée?
  10. Je n'ai _____ (no) idée.
  11. _____ (Even) le professeur ne dira pas cela.
  12. Il est parti ce jour _____ (very).
  13. Il dit toujours la _____ (same) chose.
  14. Avez-vous jamais entendu _____ (such a) histoire?
  15. _____ (Like) mère, _____ (like) fille.
  16. _____ (Such) est mon but.
  17. _____ (Whatever) soit votre opinion, ne dites rien.
  18. Ce n'est pas une auto _____ (just any). C'est une Cadillac.
  19. _____ (Another) temps, _____ (other) endroits.
  20. Elle est _____ (altogether) surprise _____ (altogether) heureuse.
  21. _____ (Whatever) mesures que vous preniez, je vous appuie.
  22. Écoutez un disque _____ (any).
  23. Avez-vous jamais lu de _____ (such) beaux poèmes?
  24. Il a couru _____ (some) deux cents mètres.
  25. Elle est la bonté _____ (itself).
  26. Avez-vous _____ (other) livres?
  27. _____ (No) travail n'est trop difficile.

Review

43. Mary and John get along well since they are so much alike. Tell how Mary is like John. Follow the models.

Jean est toujours content.
Marie est toujours contente aussi.

Jean n'est jamais triste.
Marie n'est jamais triste non plus.

   1. Jean est intelligent.
   2. Jean est fort.
   3. Jean est sûr de lui-même.
   4. Jean est honnête.
   5. Jean est gentil.
   6. Jean est bon.
   7. Jean n'est pas sot.
   8. Jean n'est pas gros.

　　9. Jean est discret.
　10. Jean est fier.
　11. Jean est sérieux.
　12. Jean est roux.
　13. Jean est créateur.
　14. Jean est sportif.
　15. Jean est franc.
　16. Jean n'est pas malin.

44. Describe the house. Put the correct form of the adjective in parentheses in the correct place and use the conjunction **et** when necessary. Follow the models.

C'est une (petit, noir) _____ maison _____ .
C'est une *petite maison noire.*

C'est une (intéressant) _____ maison _____ .
C'est une *maison intéressante.*

　　1. C'est une (grand, blanc) _____ maison _____ aux (bleu foncé) _____
　　　volets _____ .
　　2. Derrière la maison il y a un (très joli) _____ jardin _____ avec des fleurs aux
　　　(vif) _____ couleurs _____ .
　　3. Dans le salon il y a de (beau, vieil) _____ meubles _____ , une (beau, noir et
　　　blanc) _____ chaise _____ , une (vieux, marron) _____ lampe _____
　　　avec un (vieux, marron) _____ abat-jour _____ .
　　4. Sur une table il y a des (frais cueilli) _____ fleurs _____ et une (beau,
　　　petit) _____ photo _____ .
　　5. Sur la photo, il y a une (petit, jeune, roux) _____ fille _____ , aux (bleu clair)
　　　_____ yeux _____ , et aux (ivoire) _____ joues _____ et un (beau, blond,
　　　sérieux) _____ homme _____ aux (châtain) _____ cheveux _____ . Ils ont l'air
　　　d'être des (royal) _____ gens _____ . C'est ma (favori) _____ photo _____ .
　　6. Sur une (autre) _____ table _____ il y a une (grand, merveilleux) _____
　　　statue _____ d'une (gros, malin) _____ chatte _____ aux (long) _____
　　　griffes _____ .
　　7. Au mur il y a de (gros) _____ peintures _____ de nos (natal, nord-africain) _____
　　　villages _____ .
　　8. Il y a une (grand) _____ cuisine _____ avec un (vieux) _____
　　　évier _____ , une (vieux) _____ poêle _____ et un (vieux) _____
　　　réfrigérateur _____ . On sent l'(doux) _____ odeur _____ des épices malgré
　　　les (grand-ouvert) _____ fenêtres _____ .
　　9. Dans la salle à manger, il y a une (grand, ancien) _____ table _____
　　　de (français) _____ style _____ .
　10. Dans la chambre, il y a de (nouveau, élégant) _____ meubles _____ , une
　　　(beau, nouveau) _____ armoire _____ , un (bon) _____ lit _____ , et
　　　une (grand, nouveau) _____ commode _____ .

45. Follow the model.

　　former　**C'est mon _____ professeur _____ .**
　　　　　　C'est mon *ancien professeur.*

　　1. *expensive*　C'est une _____ chaise _____ .
　　2. *courageous*　C'est un _____ homme _____ .
　　3. *poor (penniless)*　C'est une _____ fille _____ .
　　4. *clean*　C'est une _____ robe _____ .
　　5. *very*　Il est parti le _____ jour _____ .
　　6. *new, different*　Ce sont de _____ bottes _____ .

46. Follow the model.

Comment parle-t-il? *sérieux*
Il parle sérieusement.

1. Comment parle-t-il? *résolu*
2. Quand vient-il? *fréquent*
3. Comment parle-t-il? *courant*
4. Comment travaille-t-elle? *continu*
5. Comment a-t-il dormi? *bon*
6. Quand est-il-parti? *tard*
7. Quand a-t-il fini? *final*
8. A-t-il bien mangé? *heureux*
9. Quand a-t-elle fini? *hier*
10. Comment chante-t-elle? *bien*
11. Comment parle-t-il? *haut*
12. Comment voit-il? *clair*
13. Comment crie-t-il? *fort*

47. Show how the following people do things in a manner that reflects their personality. Follow the
models.

Robert / calme   Il parle...
Robert *est calme*.
Il parle *calmement*.

Marie et Solange / discret   Elles parlent...
Marie et Solange *sont discrètes*.
Elle parlent *discrètement*.

1. Pierre / sérieux.   Il travaille...
2. Anne / précis   Elle parle...
3. Yvette / attentif   Elle écoute...
4. Jean / franc   Il répond...
5. Jacques et Charles / intelligent   Ils répondent...
6. Marie et Jeanne / gentil   Elles agissent...
7. André et Marc / patient   Ils écoutent...
8. Diane / brillant   Elle résout le problème...
9. Paul et Philippe / véhément   Ils agissent...
10. David et Georges / loyal   Ils agissent...
11. Éric et Roger / lent   Ils marchent...
12. Nicole / naturel   Elle agit...

48. Compare the cities. You may substitute names of cities you know. Follow the models.

Les parcs de la ville A sont jolis.
Les parcs de la ville A sont aussi jolis que les parcs de la ville B.
Les parcs de la ville A sont moins jolis que les parcs de la ville C.
Les parcs de la ville A ne sont pas si jolis que les parcs de la ville C.
Les parcs de la ville A sont plus jolis que les parcs de la ville D.
Les parcs de la ville C sont les plus jolis de tous.

1. Les attractions de la ville A sont bonnes.
2. Les restaurants de la ville A sont bons.
3. Les magasins de la ville A sont chics.
4. La pollution de la ville A est mauvaise.
5. Les habitants de la ville A marchent vite.
6. Les habitants de la ville A vivent bien.

La ville A a des musées.
La ville A a plus de musées que la ville B.
La ville A a moins de musées que la ville C.
La ville A a autant de musées que la ville D.

7. La ville A a des théâtres.
8. La ville A a des cafés.

49. Describe the students in the classroom. Follow the model.

Pierre est un petit garçon.
Pierre est le plus petit garçon de la classe.

1. Marie est une fille intelligente.
2. Hélène est une jolie fille.
3. Pierre est un bel homme.
4. Henri est un garçon intéressant.

50. To whom do the following things belong? Complete the following sentences using the correct demonstrative and possessive adjectives. Follow the model.

_____ bracelet est à Marie; c'est _____ bracelet.
Ce bracelet est à Marie; c'est *son* bracelet.

1. _____ livre est à moi; c'est _____ livre.
2. _____ disques sont à Paul; ce sont _____ disques.
3. _____ raquette de tennis est à toi; c'est _____ raquette de tennis.
4. _____ auto est à Yvette; c'est _____ auto.
5. _____ bicyclette est à Charles; c'est _____ bicyclette.
6. _____ cassettes sont à vous; ce sont _____ cassettes.
7. _____ journaux sont à Solange et à moi; ce sont _____ journaux.
8. _____ skis sont à moi; ce sont _____ skis.
9. _____ appareil photographique est à toi; c'est _____ appareil photographique.
10. _____ micro-ordinateur est à Marc et à André; c'est _____ micro-ordinateur.
11. _____ dictionnaire est à vous; c'est _____ dictionnaire.
12. _____ voiture est à moi; c'est _____ voiture.
13. _____ billets sont à Nicole et à Anne; ce sont _____ billets.
14. _____ photos sont à toi; ce sont _____ photos.
15. _____ maison est à nous; c'est _____ maison.

51. Complete the following with the correct definite article or possessive adjective.

1. *his*   Il a _____ mains sur la table.
2. *your (formal)*   Regardez _____ mains.
3. *one's*   On a _____ responsabilité.
4. *your*   Lève _____ main.

52. You are in a department store. Tell what things you want to buy. Follow the model.

le livre
Je veux ce livre-ci, pas ce livre-là.

1. la robe
2. l'appareil photographique
3. le disque
4. les cravates

53. Change the sentences, using the indicated words. Make all necessary changes.

Pierre a des livres. *plusieurs*
Pierre a plusieurs livres.

1. Marie a des journaux. *quelque*
2. Hélène a beaucoup d'amis. *plusieurs*
3. Il a du temps. *quelque*
4. Des problèmes sont difficiles à résoudre. *certain*
5. Nous avons parlé à différentes personnes. *divers*
6. Tout homme veut réussir. *chaque*
7. Avez-vous des disques? *autre*
8. J'ai vu les maisons. *tout*
9. Il n'y a pas de livre ici. *aucun*
10. J'ai mangé les gâteaux. *tout*
11. Son ennemi le croit. *même*
12. Je n'ai jamais vu une pièce. *tel*
13. C'est mon choix. *tel*
14. L'homme veut être heureux. *tout*
15. Des livres sont intéressants. *autre*
16. Il a couru cent mètres. *quelque*
17. Elle est grande. *tout*
18. Prenez un livre. *quelconque*

Chapter 3

Prepositions

USES OF CERTAIN PREPOSITIONS

A preposition is an invariable word which introduces an element of a sentence that it unites or subordinates in a certain way to another element of the sentence. Prepositions can establish many kinds of connections or relationships between various parts of a sentence. They can indicate place, time, cause, goal, means, manner, possession, and so on.

> Il va **au** bureau.
> *He goes to the office.*
> Il habite ici **depuis** deux ans.
> *He has been living here for two years.*
> le livre **de** ma mère.
> *my mother's book (the book of my mother)*
> une machine **à** coudre
> *a sewing machine (a machine for sewing)*
> Il parle **d'**une voix basse.
> *He speaks in a low voice.*
> Il le fait **avec** hésitation.
> *He does it with hesitation.*

A prepositional locution is a group of words that have the same role as a preposition.

Prepositions	*Prepositional locution*
Il est **devant** l'école.	Il est **en face** de l'école.
Il travaille **pour** gagner de l'argent.	Il travaille **afin de** gagner de l'argent.

Prepositions and prepositional locutions are generally followed by a noun or noun group, a pronoun or an infinitive.

> Elle le fait **pour ses enfants.**
> Elle le fait **pour eux.**
> Elle le fait **pour gagner de l'argent.**

The difficulty for English-speakers is that often a preposition in English has several French counterparts, and the correct translation depends on the meaning in the sentence. For example, the preposition *with* in English can be translated in various ways in French, depending on the context.

Il va au cinéma **avec** moi.
He is going to the movies with me.
Il écrit **avec** un crayon.
He writes with a pencil.
Il écrit **de** la main gauche.
He writes with his left hand.
Il écrit **à** l'encre.
He writes with ink.
Elle embrasse son père **avec** joie.
She embraces her father with joy.
Elle danse **de** joie.
She danses with joy.
Elle parle **d'**une voix forte.
She speaks with a strong voice.
Le ciel est couvert **de** nuages.
The sky is covered with clouds.
Il marche la tête haute. (no preposition)
He walks with his head held high.

The correct uses of various prepositions are learned through practice. In most cases there are no rules. Each expression needs to be learned individually. The discussion here is not exhaustive. Please consult a good dictionary for further examples of the uses of various prepositions.

PREPOSITIONS TO INDICATE LOCATION OR DIRECTION TO OR FROM A PLACE

See also *Prepositions with geographical names*, pages 70–72.

à, de, dans, en, chez

à, *to, in, at*

With names of places, **à** can indicate location or direction in, at or to some place:

Jean est **à** l'école.
John is in (at) school.
J'allais souvent **à** Paris.
I went to Paris often.
Marie va **au** bureau tous les jours.
Mary goes to the office every day.
Il va **à** l'école à huit heures.
He goes to school at eight o'clock.
Il retourne **à la** maison à trois heures.
He returns home at three o'clock.

de, *from, about*

De indicates the place of origin with the verbs **venir, sortir, arriver, s'éloigner, partir,** etc.

Je reviens **du** bureau.
I am coming back from the office.

Elle est arrivée **de** Rome.
She arrived from Rome.

For contractions of the definite article with the prepositions **à** and **de,** see *Contractions of the definite article,* p. 12-13.

dans, en, *in, into*

Dans is always used with an article. **En** is rarely used with an article.

Dans la classe, on ne peut pas fumer.
Nous sommes **en** classe.
Nous allons **en** ville.

Dans is used to indicate place more precisely than **à** or **en** and often means **à l'intérieur de** (*inside*).

en ville	*in town, to town*
dans la ville	*in the town, inside the town*
en classe	*in class*
dans la classe de français	*in French class*
Est-ce qu'elle est **à** l'école?	*Is she in school?*
Oui, elle est **en** classe.	*Yes, she's in class.*
Oui, elle est **dans** la classe de chimie.	*Yes, she's in chemistry class.*
Il est **à** la maison?	*Is he at home?*
Oui, il est **dans** la cuisine.	*Yes, he's in the kitchen.*

Dans can indicate the place in which a thing can be found.

L'enfant met du chocolat **dans** la bouche.
Elle met l'argenterie **dans** les sacs et elle met les **sacs** dans le tiroir.
Il met ses clefs **dans** sa poche.

With the verb **prendre, dans** means *out of.*

Prenez deux dollars **dans** mon sac.
Take two dollars out of my bag.

Dans is used with the names of streets and avenues, but **sur** is used with the names of rural routes and boulevards.

Il habite **dans l'avenue Foch.**
Elle habite **dans la rue de Prony.**
Nous habitons **sur la route 11.**
L'école est **sur le boulevard Saint-Michel.**

chez, *to, at the house of, at someone's place*

Chez is used with a person, a person's name, a pronoun, a person's profession or business, a group or society.

Nous irons **chez Marie** vendredi soir.
We will go to Mary's house Friday night.
Il viendra **chez moi** samedi.
He will come to my home Saturday.

J'achète du pain **chez le boulanger.**
I buy bread at the baker's.
Je vais aller **chez le médecin** demain.
I am going to the doctor's tomorrow.
Chez les Français, on mange bien.
In French homes, one eats well.

Chez can also mean "in a person's work," figuratively speaking.

Chez cet auteur il y a beaucoup d'ironie.
In this author's work, there is a lot of irony.

Chez is also used in the following expressions.

Faites comme **chez vous.**
Make yourself at home. (Do as you do at home.)
Chez vous tout va bien.
Everything is well with you.

1. Complete the following sentences with the preposition **à, de, dans, en, chez** or **sur** plus the definite article when necessary.

   1. Pierre est _____ bureau. Il est _____ salle de conférence.
   2. Elle est _____ université. Elle est _____ classe. Elle est _____ classe de mathématiques.
   3. Il y a beaucoup de magasins _____ l'avenue des Champs-Elysées.
   4. Venez _____ nous demain soir.
   5. Il range les assiettes _____ le placard.
   6. Le matin, nous allons _____ supermarché; l'après-midi nous allons _____ le médecin.
   7. Prenez les stylos _____ le tiroir.
   8. Il sort _____ bureau à six heures et il retourne _____ maison à sept heures.
   9. Il y a beaucoup d'étudiants _____ le boulevard Saint-Michel.
   10. Nous irons _____ ville demain pour faire des courses.

PREPOSITIONS WITH GEOGRAPHICAL NAMES

à

The preposition **à** is used before the names of most cities.

Il va **à Paris.**
Elle est **à Genève.**

But:

Ils sont débarqué **au Havre.**

en

The preposition **en** is used with names of feminine countries or continents. Almost all names of countries ending in a mute **e** are feminine. (Exception: **le Mexique.**)

Je vais **en France.**
Nous irons **en Afrique.**
Nous sommes **en Europe.**

au

The preposition **au** is used with masculine countries.

> Elle va **au Mexique.**
> Nous sommes **au Canada.**
> Elle va **au Danemark.**
> Il va **au Portugal.**

The preposition **aux** is used with **États-Unis** since the word is plural.

> New York est **aux États-Unis.**

dans

The preposition **dans** is used before names of continents qualified by another expression.

> Nous irons **dans l'Amérique du Sud.**

In spoken language, **en** may be used with names of continents.

> Nous allons **en Amérique du Sud.**

When the name of a city or country is accompanied by a complement or an adjective, **dans le (l', la, les)** is used instead of **en.**

> J'aimerais vivre **dans la France du xixe siècle.**
> Nous allons voyager **dans toute la France.**
> Il vont **dans l'Italie du Nord.**

The preposition used before names of islands varies.

> **en Islande**
> **en Sardaigne**
> **en Haïti**
> **en Nouvelle-Guinée**

> **à la Réunion**
> **à la Martinique**
> **à la Guadeloupe**

> **à Chypre**
> **à Madagascar**
> **à Cuba**

With names of American states and Canadian provinces, **en** is used if the French form of the noun ends in **e** or **ie.**

> **en Californie**
> **en Pennsylvanie**
> **en Floride**
> **en Nouvelle-Écosse**
> **en Columbie-Britannique**

Otherwise, **dans le** or **dans l'État de** is used.

> **dans le Vermont**
> **dans le Colorado**
> **dans l'Ontario**
> **dans l'État de Vermont**

But:

au Nouveau-Mexique
au Nouveau-Brunswick
à Terre-Neuve *Newfoundland*

de

De is used to mean *from* or *of* and is used <u>without</u> the definite article before the names of cities, feminine countries and states and masculine <u>countries</u> beginning with a vowel.

Il est **de Paris.**
Elle revient **d'Angleterre.**
Il étudie l'histoire **de France.**
Je viens **de Californie.**

De is used to mean *from* or *of* and is used <u>with</u> the definite article before the names of masculine countries, provinces or states except those beginning with a vowel.

J'ai envoyé le paquet **du Canada.**
Elle vient **des États-Unis.**
Il vient **du Québec.**

One always says **partir pour, en route pour** or **passer par** with the name of a place.

Je **suis parti pour** la Martinique.
En route pour Marseille, elle s'est arrêtée à Lyon.
Elles **ont passé par** l'Allemagne et la France.

2. Complete the following sentences with the correct preposition plus the definite article.

1. Nous allons _____ France.
2. Elle est allée _____ Haïti et _____ Martinique.
3. Je suis _____ Paris et elle vient _____ Lyon.
4. Nous irons _____ Afrique et _____ Afrique du Nord.
5. Il demeure _____ Paris.
6. Il a voyagé _____ Mexique et _____ Amérique du Sud.
7. En route _____ l'Espagne, ils ont passé _____ la France.
8. L'action a lieu _____ Angleterre et _____ Italie.
9. J'ai demeuré _____ Californie, _____ Vermont et _____ Nouveau-Mexique.
10. San Francisco se trouve _____ États-Unis.
11. Il revient _____ Mexique, mais elle revient _____ Espagne.
12. Elle habite _____ Canada _____ Terre-Neuve.
13. Il va _____ San Francisco _____ Californie.
14. Il part _____ Haïti, et elle part _____ Cuba.

PREPOSITIONS WITH MODES OF TRANSPORTATION

The prepositions **à** and **en** and sometimes **par** are used with means of travel when you wish to describe by what means someone is traveling.

à	en	par
à bicyclette*	en auto	par le train
à cheval	en autobus	
à motocyclette	en avion	
à pied	en bateau	
à vélo*	en métro	
	en taxi	
	en voiture	

*You may also hear **en bicyclette** and **en vélo**.

Note that **à** and **en** are used without the definite article and **par** is used with the definite article.

To describe how someone enters or leaves a vehicle, use **monter dans** or **descendre de**, or **embarquer dans** or **débarquer de**.

monter **dans** un autobus	descendre **d'**un autobus
monter **dans** une voiture	descendre **d'**une voiture
monter **dans** un train	descendre **d'**un train
embarquer **dans** un bateau	débarquer **d'**un bateau

When referring to mailing a letter or a package, you use the preposition **par** with the means of transportation.

envoyer le paquet **par avion** ou **par bateau**

3. Complete the following sentences with the correct preposition to indicate how the people travel and mail things.

   1. Le cowboy voyage _____ cheval.
   2. Elle va au bureau _____ voiture ou _____ métro.
   3. Il va de New York à Paris _____ avion.
   4. Le petit va à l'école _____ pied.
   5. Le conducteur voyage _____ train.
   6. Le marin voyage _____ bateau.
   7. Elle va en ville _____ autobus.
   8. Elles vont au théâtre _____ taxi.
   9. Préfères-tu voyager _____ bicyclette ou _____ vélo?
   10. J'enverrai la lettre _____ avion et non _____ bateau.

PREPOSITIONS WITH EXPRESSIONS OF TIME

à, **at**

Il reviendra **à** cinq heures précises.
He'll return at exactly five o'clock.

dans, en, **in**

Dans can indicate the time after which a certain thing can be done. It can mean **après** (*after*) or **à la fin de** (*at the end of*).

Je le ferai **dans** une heure.
I'll do it in one hour.
(It is now two o'clock. I'll do it at three o'clock.)

L'avion arrive **dans** trois heures.
The plane arrives in three hours.
(It is now eight o'clock. The plane arrives at eleven o'clock.)
Il reviendra **dans** quatre heures.
He'll return in four hours.
Elle aura fini **dans** un mois.
She will have finished in a month.

En indicates the time necessary for the accomplishment of an action, the time in which something will be completed or accomplished (duration of an action).

Je le ferai **en** deux heures.
I can do it in two hours time.
(It will take me two hours to do it.)
Le bateau traverse l'Atlantique **en** cinq jours.
The boat crosses the Atlantic in five days.

---
avant, **before**

---
après, **after**

Avant is used to mean *before (in time)* and **après** is used to mean *after (in time)*.

Elle est arrivée **avant** les autres.
She arrived before the others.
Il est arrivé **après** Pierre.
He arrived after Peter.

Remember that the prepositions **devant** (*before*) and **derrière** (*after* or *behind*) are used with places.

Il est **devant** la maison.
He is in front of the house.
La table est **derrière** le divan.
The table is behind the couch.

4. Complete the following with the prepositions **à, dans, en, pendant, durant, avant** or **après**.

   1. Voyons! Il est une heure maintenant. Je l'aurai fini _____ trois heures. Donc, je l'aurai fini _____ quatre heures.
   2. Ce projet ne prendra pas beaucoup de temps. Je pourrai le terminer _____ une demi-heure.
   3. L'avion décolle _____ six heures précises.
   4. Marie est arrivée à trois heures. Hélène est arrivée à trois heures et quart. Marie est arrivée _____ Hélène et Hélène est arrivée _____ Marie.

5. Complete the following sentences with the preposition **dans** or **en**. Follow the models.

   Nous recevrons des invités _____ deux jours.
   Nous recevrons des invités *dans* deux jours.

   Elle finit l'exercice _____ dix minutes.
   Elle finit l'exercice *en* dix minutes.

   1. Le danseur a changé de costume _____ quinze minutes.
   2. Je suis occupé maintenant, mais je peux vous aider _____ une demi-heure.

3. Nos invités arriveront _____ une heure.
4. _____ cent ans le monde sera différent.
5. Le dîner sera prêt _____ deux heures.
6. Tu auras ma décision _____ dix jours ouvrables.
7. Il a couru dix kilomètres _____ trente minutes.
8. Le chien a très vite mangé son dîner. Il l'a mangé _____ trois minutes.

PREPOSITIONS USED TO JOIN TWO NOUNS

To Indicate Function or to Join a Noun that Modifies Another Noun

The prepositions **à** and **de** can introduce a noun that modifies or qualifies another noun and indicates the function of the preceding noun. In French a noun with a complement is often the same as an English expression composed of two nouns written either as two words or as a single compound word. The first noun in English is the complement in French. Study the following:

à	*de*
un verre à eau	**un verre d'eau**
a water glass (a glass for water)	*a glass of water*
une tasse à café	**une tasse de café**
a coffee cup (a cup for coffee)	*a cup of coffee*
une lime à ongles	**mon professeur de maths**
a nail file	*my math teacher*
une brosse à dents	**une agence de voyage**
a toothbrush	*a travel agency*
une cuiller à soupe	**une robe de chambre**
a soupspoon	*a dressing gown*
une cuiller à thé	**une salle de bains**
a teaspoon	*a bathroom*

To Mean *with*

Used with the article, **à** can mean *with*. **À** replaces **avec** when you wish to indicate that the second noun is a distinct part of the first one.

de la soupe aux pois
pea soup (soup with peas)
du café au lait
coffee with milk
la fille aux yeux bleus
the girl with blue eyes
la maison au toit rouge
the house with the red roof
la glace à la vanille
vanilla ice cream (ice cream made with vanilla)
l'homme à la barbe blanche
the man with the white beard
une tarte aux pommes
an apple pie (a pie made with apples)
une peinture à l'huile
an oil painting (a painting made with oil)

To Introduce the Material from Which an Object Is Made

De and **en** are used to introduce the material from which an object is made.

une robe **de** soie
des bas **de** nylon
un portefeuille **en** cuir
un bracelet **en** or

Usage determines whether you should use **de** or **en**. Often, either preposition is possible. **De** is usually used to indicate the type of object one is talking about and **en** emphasizes the material from which the object is made.

un sac **de** cuir
a leather bag

un sac **en** cuir
a bag made of leather

PREPOSITIONS OF CAUSE

De can also indicate a relationship of cause between the verb and the noun complement. It is translated by *with, of, for* or *from*.

Il danse **de** joie.
He dances for joy.
Je meurs **de** faim.
I'm dying of hunger.
Elle écrit **de** la main gauche.
She writes with her left hand.
La rue est couverte **de** neige.
The street is covered with snow.

PREPOSITIONS AFTER INDEFINITE PRONOUNS

When **quelque chose, rien, quelqu'un** and **personne** are modified by an adjective, the adjective is introduced by **de.**

Il mange quelque chose de bon.
He eats something good.
C'est quelqu'un de très adroit.
It's someone skillful.
Il n'y a eu personne de blessé dans la tempête.
No one was hurt in the storm.
Il ne dit rien d'intelligent.
He says nothing intelligent.

6. Complete the following sentences with the correct preposition **à, de** or **en.** Combine with the definite article when necessary.

   1. Il faut mettre du thé dans les tasses _____ thé.
   2. Je voudrais boire un verre _____ lait.
   3. Elle a pleuré _____ joie quand elle a appris qu'il n'y avait personne _____ blessé dans l'accident.

4. Je mets ma robe _____ chambre dans la salle _____ bains.

5. Il mange de la soupe _____ tomates, une tarte _____ bleuets et de la glace _____ chocolat.

6. Je fais ma toilette. Je me brosse les dents avec une brosse _____ dents. Je fais le soin des mains avec une lime _____ ongles.

7. Voilà mon professeur _____ histoire.

8. Je n'ai pas mangé depuis hier. Je meurs _____ faim.

9. L'homme _____ barbe noire parle à la fille _____ cheveux noirs.

10. Je vais acheter une bague _____ argent, un sac _____ cuir, et une robe _____ laine.

11. Il écrit _____ la main droite.

12. Ce professeur est quelqu'un _____ très intelligent.

PREPOSITIONS IN ADVERBIAL CLAUSES OF MANNER

In many adverbial phrases where *in, by* or *on* are used in English, **à** is used in French.

Il parle **à voix basse.**
He speaks in a low voice.
Il parle **à haute voix.**
He speaks aloud (with a loud voice, loudly)
Mettez les vêtements **au soleil** pour les faire sécher.
Put the clothes in the sun to make them dry.
Ce chandail est fait **à la main.**
This sweater is made by hand.
Il a les papiers **à la main.**
He has the papers in hand.
Le train est arrivé **à l'heure.**
The train arrived on time.
Ce bâtiment a été construit **au temps de** Louis XIV.
This building was constructed in the time of Louis XIV.
Les soldats marchent **à grands pas.**
The soldiers march in giant steps.

In an adverbial clause of manner, **de** introduces the noun modified by the indefinite article.

Il parle **d'une voix faible.**
He speaks with a weak voice.
Il me regarde **d'un air furieux.**
He looks at me with a furious expression (furiously).
Elle le fait **d'une manière adroite.**
She does this skillfully.

When the noun is not modified by an indefinite article, **avec** is used.

Il me parle **avec faiblesse.**
He speaks to me weakly.
Il me regarde **avec fureur.**
He looks at me furiously.
Il le fait **avec adresse.**
He does this skillfully.

7. Complete the following sentences with the prepositions **à, de** or **avec.**

1. Elle l'a regardé _____ curiosité.
2. Elle l'a regardé _____ un air curieux.
3. Je ne peux pas vous entendre. Parlez _____ haute voix.
4. Il me répond _____ un ton faible.
5. Il me répond _____ faiblesse.
6. Il a le document _____ la main.

PREPOSITIONS TO INTRODUCE AN INFINITIVE DEPENDING ON A NOUN OR ADJECTIVE

To Indicate Function, Result or Tendency

The preposition **à** can introduce an infinitive that indicates the function of the preceding noun or the use to which an object is destined. Often **à** has the meaning of *for*. The infinitive complement is often the equivalent of an expression with "ing" in English.

du papier à écrire
writing paper (paper for writing)
une machine à écrire / à laver / à coudre
a typewriter (a machine for writing) / a washing machine (a machine for washing) / a sewing machine (a machine for sewing)
une salle à manger
a dining room (a room for dining)
une chambre à coucher
a bedroom (a room for sleeping)
un fer à repasser
an iron
de l'eau à boire
drinking water (water for drinking)
une maison à vendre / à louer
a house for sale / for rent

À can introduce an infinitive phrase that describes a preceding noun in terms of a possible result.

C'est un bruit à réveiller tout le monde.
It's a noise that could wake everyone up.
C'est une tâche à rendre fou.
This is a task that can drive you crazy.
Ce sont des cris à rendre sourd.
These are shouts that can make you deaf.
Ce sont des larmes à faire pitié.
These are tears that can make you feel pity.
C'est un exercice à recopier.
This is an exercise to be recopied.

À can also introduce an infinitive phrase that intensifies the meaning of an adjective.

une histoire triste à en pleurer
a story sad enough to make you cry
un animal laid à faire peur
an animal ugly enough to make you afraid

After an adjective, **à** introduces an infinitive that indicates the action to which the adjective applies.

> **C'est facile à faire.**
> *It's easy to do.*
> **C'est difficile à comprendre.**
> *It's difficult to understand.*
> **C'est bon à manger.**
> *It's good to eat.*

After Expressions of Duration, Length of Time and Position of the Body

À introduces an infinitive after certain expressions indicating duration, length of time and position of the body. **À** plus the infinitive is used to describe what the subject does during this time or in this position.

> **Il passe son temps à travailler.** (duration)
> *He spends his time working.*
> **Elle reste assise à lire.** (position)
> *She remains seated while reading.*
> **Il met longtemps à apprendre cela.** (time)
> *He takes a long time to learn that.*
> **Elle est debout à travailler.**
> *She works standing up.*

Generally, infinitives following an adjective or noun are followed by **de.**

> **Je suis heureux d'être ici.**   *I am happy to be here.*
> **Je suis étonné d'apprendre cette nouvelle.**   *I am surprised to hear this news.*
> **J'ai peur de sortir la nuit.**   *I am afraid to go out at night.*
> **J'ai envie de partir.**   *I want to leave.*
> **Il avait raison de faire cela.**   *He was right to do that.*
> **J'ai la chance de faire cela.**   *I have the chance to do that.*

After the impersonal **il+être +** adjective, **de** precedes the infinitive.

> **Il est bon de se reposer.**   *It is good to rest.*
> **Il est nécessaire d'étudier.**   *It is necessary to study.*

When an infinitive depends on another verb, it is often introduced by **à** or **de.** For a detailed analysis, see *The Use of the prepositions* **à** *and* **de** *before an infinitive,* pp. 213–214.

8. Complete the following sentences with the correct preposition **à** or **de.**

1. Ce sont des devoirs _____ refaire.
2. Mets les vêtements sales dans la machine _____ laver.
3. Il est dangereux _____ ne pas faire attention.
4. Cet appartement _____ louer a une grande salle _____ manger.
5. Il a tort _____ dire cela.
6. Cet exercice est difficile _____ faire.
7. Il a honte _____ avoir volé la bicyclette.

8. C'est une histoire amusante _____ en rire aux éclats.
9. C'est un problème _____ rendre fou.
10. J'ai l'intention _____ partir demain.

Following is a list of some common prepositions.

à	*to, at, in, on*
après	*after, next to*
avant	*before (time)*
avec	*with*
chez	*at _____ 's house*
contre	*against*
dans	*in, inside, into*
de	*of, from, with, etc.*
depuis	*since, from*
derrière	*behind*
devant	*before*
durant	*during*
en	*in, to*
entre	*between, among*
envers	*toward (moral tendency)*
hors (de)	*outside (of)*
jusque	*until, up to*
malgré	*in spite of*
par	*by, through*
parmi	*among*
pendant	*during*
pour	*for, in order to (+infinitive)*
près	*near*
sans	*without*
sauf	*except*
selon	*according to*
sous	*under*
suivant	*following*
sur	*on, upon*
vers	*toward (direction)*

Following is a list of principal prepositional locutions.

à cause de	*because of*
à côté de	*beside*
afin de	*in order to*
à force de	*by means of*
à la mode de	*in the manner of*
à l'envie de	*to the envy of*
à l'exception de	*except*
à l'exclusion de	*to the exclusion of*
à moins de	*unless*
à raison de	*at the rate of*
au dedans	*inside, within*
au dehors de	*outside of*
au delà de	*above, beyond, past*

au-dessous de	*below*
au-dessus de	*above*
au lieu de	*instead of*
au milieu de	*in the middle of*
auprès de	*near*
autour de	*around*
au travers de	*through*
aux environs de	*in the vicinity of*
d'après	*according to*
de façon à	*so as to*
de manière à	*so as to*
de peur de	*for fear of*
en dedans de	*inside, on the inside of, within*
en dehors de	*outside of*
en dépit de	*in spite of*
en face de	*in front of, facing*
en haut de	*at the top of*
en bas de	*at the bottom of*
en raison de	*because of*
grâce à	*thanks to*
hors de	*outside of*
jusqu'à	*until, up to*
jusque dans	*up into*
loin de	*far from*
par dedans	*inside, through the inside*
par dehors	*by the outside*
par delà	*beyond*
par-dessous	*under*
par-dessus	*over, above, on top of*
par devant	*before, in front*
par rapport à	*with regard to, in relation to*
près de	*near*
proche de	*near*

For other uses of prepositions, see the following:

For the use of **après** with the past infinitive, see page 209.
For the use of **en** with the present participle, see pages 134 and 209.
For the use of **par** with an infinitive, see page 134.
For the use of **par** with the passive voice, see page 216.
For the use of prepositions with the year, months and seasons, see page 91.
For the use of **de** with measurements and age, see page 90.
For the use of the prepositions **à** and **de** before infinitives, see pages 213-215.
For the use of **à** and **de** to show possession, see pages 53-55.
For the use of **de** to introduce a complement of a superlative, see page 48.

Review

9. Translate the following sentences.

  1. a cup of tea
  2. a teacup

3. a glass of water
4. a water glass
5. a soupspoon
6. a cherry pie
7. chocolate ice cream
8. a bicycle for sale
9. the man with brown eyes
10. tomato soup
11. a travel agency
12. a geography teacher
13. a dress made of silk
14. a silk dress

10. Complete the following with the correct preposition or preposition plus definite article to show how and where people are traveling or where people live.

1. Il va _____ New York _____ Californie _____ avion.
2. Elle va _____ Paris _____ Lyon _____ train.
3. Il voyage _____ Japon _____ bateau.
4. Il va _____ école _____ pied.
5. Envoyez cette lettre _____ avion et non _____ bateau.
6. Il va _____ médecin _____ taxi.
7. Il habite _____ l'avenue Foch _____ Paris, _____ France.
8. Elle habite _____ le boulevard Métropolitain _____ Montréal, _____ Québec, _____ Canada.
9. Elle revient _____ bureau _____ métro.
10. Il va _____ Italie du Sud _____ Italie du Nord _____ autobus.
11. Elle va _____ boulanger _____ vélo.
12. Il va faire du ski _____ Colorado _____ États-Unis.
13. Il va prendre du soleil _____ Haïti ou _____ Martinique.
14. Il va _____ Buenos Aires _____ Argentine _____ l'Amérique du Sud.

11. Complete the following with the correct preposition or preposition plus the definite article.

D'habitude, Monsieur Leclerc va _____ usine _____ mardi _____ vendredi. Il y va ____
                                              (1)   (2)   (3)   (4)
auto. Il revient _____ bureau _____ six heures du soir d'habitude.
                      (5)   (6)

Mais aujourd'hui, c'est lundi et il ne travaille pas. Ses enfants sont _____ école. Ils sont
                                                                                      (7)
_____ classe, spécifiquement dans la classe _____ français. Sa femme est _____ bureau où
    (8)   (9)   (10)
elle travaille comme programmeuse dans l'industrie de l'informatique. Lui, il est _____ la
                                                                                          (11)
maison maintenant. Il est _____ la cuisine où il reste debout _____ travailler.
                              (12)   (13)

Et comme il travaille! Le matin, il passe son temps _____ faire le ménage. Il met les
                                                           (14)
vêtements sales dans la machine _____ laver; il range les verres _____ eau et les tasses
                                      (15)   (16)
_____ café, les cuillers _____ soupe, etc. _____ les placards. Il époussette les meubles et il
   (17)   (18)   (19)
passe l'aspirateur.

À midi il prend son déjeuner. Il mange de la soupe _____ légumes, un sandwich _____
                                                         (20)   (21)
jambon, et comme dessert une glace _____ fraises. Comme boisson il boit du café _____ lait.
                                         (22)   (23)
Maintenant il est _____ la cuisinière électrique en train de préparer le dîner. Il porte un
                      (24)
tablier _____ plastique. Le dîner qu'il prépare va être bon _____ manger. Il fait la cuisine
          (25)   (26)

_____ une manière professionnelle, _____ l'adresse d'un grand chef. Pendant qu'il prépare le
  (27)   (28)

dîner, il chante _____ haute voix. Il veut finir la préparation du dîner _____ l'arrivée des
                 (29)   (30)

autres. Il peut compléter cette tâche _____ deux heures. Il n'a pas le temps de se reposer
                                    (31)

maintenant. Il lira le journal _____ deux heures. Il aura fini ses tâches _____ deux heures. Il
                           (32)   (33)

est quatre heures maintenant; donc, il pourra lire _____ six heures.
                                                 (34)

_____ les Leclerc, tout est bien organisé grâce aux efforts de M. Leclerc. Lui, c'est
  (35)

quelqu'un _____ extraordinaire.
           (36)

Chapter 4

Numbers, Dates, Time

NUMBERS

Cardinal Numbers

The cardinal numbers in French are:

0 zéro	26 vingt-six	80 quatre-vingts
1 un	27 vingt-sept	81 quatre-vingt-un
2 deux	28 vingt-huit	82 quatre-vingt-deux
3 trois	29 vingt-neuf	90 quatre-vingt-dix
4 quatre	30 trente	91 quatre-vingt-onze
5 cinq	31 trente et un	92 quatre-vingt-douze
6 six	32 trente-deux	99 quatre-vingt-dix-neuf
7 sept	40 quarante	100 cent
8 huit	41 quarante et un	101 cent un
9 neuf	42 quarante-deux	102 cent deux
10 dix	50 cinquante	120 cent vingt
11 onze	51 cinquante et un	199 cent quatre-vingt-dix-neuf
12 douze	52 cinquante-deux	200 deux cents
13 treize	60 soixante	201 deux cent un
14 quatorze	61 soixante et un	202 deux cent deux
15 quinze	62 soixante-deux	300 trois cents
16 seize	70 soixante-dix	400 quatre cents
17 dix-sept	71 soixante et onze	500 cinq cents
18 dix-huit	72 soixante-douze	600 six cents
19 dix-neuf	73 soixante-treize	700 sept cents
20 vingt	74 soixante-quatorze	800 huit cents
21 vingt et un	75 soixante-quinze	900 neuf cents
22 vingt-deux	76 soixante-seize	1 000 mille
23 vingt-trois	77 soixante-dix-sept	1 001 mille un
24 vingt-quatre	78 soixante-dix-huit	1 100 mille cent
25 vingt-cinq	79 soixante-dix-neuf	onze cents

1 200	mille deux cents	2 000 deux mille
	douze cents	1 000 000 un million
1 900	mille neuf cents	1 000 000 000 un milliard
	dix-neuf cents	1 000 000 000 000 un billion
1972	mil (mille) neuf cent soixante-douze	
	dix-neuf cent soixante-douze	

Note that in numbers **21, 31, 41, 51, 61, 71,** the conjunction **et** is used. There is no hyphen.

vingt et un
quarante et un

Et is not used in **81, 91, 101.** Note the hyphens in **81** and **91.**

quatre-vingt-un
quatre-vingt-onze
cent un

When **vingt** and **cent** are multiplied, they become plural.

quatre vingts
deux cents

When **vingt** and **cent** are followed by another number, they are singular.

vingt-neuf
quatre-vingt-huit
cent quatre
deux cent douze

Mille is never plural.

cinq mille
deux mille cinquante

Million is preceded by the indefinite article.

un million de touristes

Note that **un million** is like a noun of quantity and takes **de** before a following noun.

un million d'hommes

In France, a period is used where the United States and Canada use a comma or a space, and a comma is used where the United States and Canada use a decimal point.

French	English	
1.121.000	1,121,000	1 121 000
3,50	3.50	3.50
1.350,50	1,350.50	1 350.50

Following are some expressions with cardinal numbers.

tous les trois ans	
une année sur trois	*every three years*
toutes les cinq minutes	*every five minutes*
dans huit jours	*in a week*
tous les quinze jours	*every two weeks*
tous les deux kilomètres	*every two kilometers*
une femme sur dix	*one woman in ten*
quatre-vingts pour cent de	*eighty percent of*
un à un	*one by one*

1. Write the following numbers and expressions in French.

1. 10
2. 19
3. 20
4. 21
5. 27
6. 31
7. 61
8. 70
9. 72
10. 80
11. 84
12. 90
13. 99
14. 100
15. 200
16. 565
17. 798
18. 1 124
19. 1 145 792
20. 2 954
21. two by two
22. every two weeks
23. one person in ten
24. every two years
25. every ten minutes

Ordinal Numbers

Most ordinal numbers are formed by adding the suffix **-ième** to the cardinal number. If the cardinal number ends in a mute **e,** the **e** is dropped.

deux	**deuxième**
sept	**septième**
quatorze	**quatorzième**
seize	**seizième**
cinquante et un	**cinquante et unième**
cent	**centième**
deux cent trois	**deux cent troisième**
mille	**millième**

Exceptions:

first	un, une	**premier, première**
fifth	cinq	**cinquième** (**u** is added)
ninth	neuf	**neuvième** (**f** becomes **v**)

Second, seconde can replace **deuxième.**

La première fois j'ai refusé; la **deuxième** fois j'ai accepté.
La première fois j'ai refusé; la **seconde** fois j'ai accepté.
la **deuxième** classe ou la **seconde** classe (avion, bateau, train)

But:

voyager en **seconde,** habiter au **second** (étage), une **seconde** fois

In titles of rulers, the cardinal numbers are used except for **premier, première** *(first)*.

François premier
Louis quatorze

In certain fixed expressions, **tiers** and **tierce** are used instead of **troisième.**

le **tiers** état
the third estate
une **tierce** personne
a third party

When cardinal and ordinal numbers are used together, the cardinal number precedes the ordinal.

les deux premières semaines
the first two weeks

2. Complete the following sentences with the correct ordinal number.

   1. Janvier est le (1) _____ mois de l'année.
   2. Septembre est le (9) _____ mois de l'année.
   3. Mai est le (5) _____ mois de l'année.
   4. La (1) _____ fois j'ai dit oui.
   5. Mardi est le (2) _____ jour de la semaine.
   6. C'est la (101) _____ fois que j'ai entendu cette chanson.
   7. C'est la (2) _____ fois qu'il a fait cela.
   8. Il faut demander l'avis d'une (3) _____ personne.

3. Write the following in French.

   1. Napoleon I
   2. Louis XV
   3. the first two years
   4. the last two days

Collective Numbers

To express an approximate quantity, the suffix **-aine** is added to the cardinal number. If the cardinal number ends in a mute **e,** the **e** is dropped before adding **-aine.** The **x** of **dix** becomes **z.**

Environ		
	10	**une dizaine**
	12	**une douzaine**
	15	**une quinzaine**
	20	**une vingtaine**
	40	**une quarantaine**
	50	**une cinquantaine**
	60	**une soixantaine**
	100	**une centaine**

Exceptions:

Environ		
	1 000	**un millier**
	1 000 000	**un million**
	1 000 000 000	**un milliard**
	1 000 000 000 000	**un billion**

When used before a noun, the preposition **de** is used.

Il y avait **une vingtaine de** personnes dans la salle.
Je voudrais **une douzaine de** poires.

Note that all collective numbers are feminine except for **un millier, un million, un milliard, un billion.**

Approximate quantity can also be expressed by using **à peu près, environ** and **dans les.**

Il y a **à peu près trente** élèves dans cette classe.
There are approximately thirty pupils in this class.
Il a **environ trente** ans.
He is around thirty years old.
Elle gagne **dans les trente mille** dollars par an.
She earns around thirty thousand dollars a year.

4. Follow the model.

Je voudrais des pommes. *12*
Je voudrais une douzaine de pommes.

1. Je voudrais des pêches. *10*
2. Je voudrais des poires. *20*
3. Je voudrais des pommes. *30*
4. Il y a des gens dans cette salle. *1 000 000*
5. Elle gagne 30 000$ par an. *dans les*

Fractions

Normally, the cardinal number and the ordinal number are used together to form fractions.

2/5   **deux cinquièmes**
3/8   **trois huitièmes**

Certain fractions have special forms.

1/2	**un demi, (une demie) la moitié**	6 1/2	**six et demi**
1/3	**un tiers**	5 1/3	**cinq et un tiers**
2/3	**deux tiers**		
1/4	**un quart**	9 1/4	**neuf et un quart**
3/4	**trois quarts**		

J'ai bu **la moitié de la bouteille.**
I drank half the bottle.
Je voudrais **une demi-bouteille** de vin.
I want a half-bottle of wine.

When a number with **demi** modifies a noun, **et demi** or **et demie** will follow the noun.

Il est quatre heures et demie.
It is half past four.
J'ai vingt ans et demi.
I am twenty and a half years old.

5. Write the following numbers in French.

1. 1/2
2. a half bottle
3. 21 1/2
4. 1/3
5. 3/4
6. 7/16
7. 10 1/4

Arithmetical Operations and Dimensions

Addition *(Addition)*
  3 et 3 font 6.
Soustraction *(Subtraction)*
  5 moins 1 font 4.
Multiplication *(Multiplication)*
  5 fois 10 font 50.
Division *(Division)*
  10 divisé par 2 fait 5.

Dimensions

Length, width, height and depth are expressed in the following ways.

Ce mur est long (haut) de cinq mètres (5 m).
Ce mur a cinq mètres (5 m) de long (de longueur) / de haut (de hauteur).
This wall is five meters (5 m) long/high.

Cette table est large d'un mètre cinquante (de 1 m 50).
Cette table a un mètre cinquante (1 m 50) de large (de largeur).
This table is one and one half meters (1 1/2 m) wide.

La piscine est profonde de trois mètres (3 m).
La piscine a trois mètres (3 m) de profondeur.
The swimming pool is three meters (3 m) deep.

Following is an example of how to measure something.

Cette boîte a trente centimètres (30 cm) de long (de longueur) sur vingt-quatre centimètres (24 cm) de large (de largeur) sur vingt-six centimètres (26 cm) de haut (de hauteur).
This box is thirty centimeters (30 cm) long by twenty-four centimeters (24 cm) wide by twenty-six centimeters (26 cm) high.

6. Write the following in French.

1. $10 + 5 = 15$
2. $18 - 6 = 12$
3. $8 \times 12 = 96$
4. $50 \div 5 = 10$
5. This box is 15 cm long by 10 cm wide by 8 cm high.

DATES

Days

lundi	*Monday*	**vendredi**	*Friday*
mardi	*Tuesday*	**samedi**	*Saturday*
mercredi	*Wednesday*	**dimanche**	*Sunday*
jeudi	*Thursday*		

Months

janvier	*January*
février	*February*
mars	*March*
avril	*April*
mai	*May*
juin	*June*
juillet	*July*
août	*August*
septembre	*September*
octobre	*October*
novembre	*November*
décembre	*December*

Note that the days of the week and the months of the year are not capitalized.

Dates are written as follows:

Quel jour est-ce aujourd'hui?
Quel jour sommes-nous aujourd'hui?
What day is it today?
C'est aujourd'hui le samedi cinq mai.
Today is Saturday, May 5.
C'est aujourd'hui le jeudi quatre août dix-neuf cent (mil [mille] neuf cent) quatre-vingt-huit.
Today is Thursday, August 4, 1988.

Note the following:

au mois de juin	*in the month of June*
en juin	*in June*
le premier juin	*June 1, the first of June*
le deux juin	*June 2*

Seasons

le printemps	*spring*
l'été	*summer*
l'automne	*fall*
l'hiver	*winter*

The seasons are all masculine. Note the prepositions that are used with the seasons:

au printemps	*in spring*
en été	*in summer*
en automne	*in fall*
en hiver	*in winter*

7. Write the following in French.

1. Monday, June 25
2. Tuesday, December 4
3. in the month of January
4. in June
5. April 1
6. What day is it today?
7. Today is Friday, August 11, 1989.
8. in spring
9. in summer
10. in winter

TIME

The expression for *What time is it?* is **Quelle heure est-il?** Time in French is expressed as follows:

1:00 a.m.	**une heure**	1 h	01:00
1:00 p.m.	**treize heures**	13 h	13:00
2:00 a.m.	**deux heures**	2 h	02:00
2:00 p.m.	**quatorze heures**	14 h	14:00
12:00 midnight	**minuit**	24 h (0 h)	24:00 (00:00)
12:00 noon	**midi**	12 h	12:00
12:30 a.m.	**minuit et demi**	0 h 30	00:30
12:30 p.m.	**midi et demi**	12 h 30	12:30
5:15 a.m.	**cinq heures et quart** **cinq heures quinze**	5 h 15	05:15
5:15 p.m.	**dix-sept heures et quart** **dix-sept heures quinze**	17 h 15	17:15
6:30 a.m.	**six heures et demie** **six heures trente**	6 h 30	06:30
6:30 p.m.	**dix-huit heures et demie** **dix-huit heures trente**	18 h 30	18:30
6:40 a.m.	**sept heures moins vingt**	6 h 40	06:40
6:40 p.m.	**dix-neuf heures moins vingt**	18 h 40	18:40
7:45 a.m.	**huit heures moins le quart** **huit heures moins un quart**	7 h 45	07:45
7:45 p.m.	**vingt heures moins le quart** **vingt heures moins un quart**	19 h 45	19:45

There are two ways of expressing the half hour or 15 minutes before or after the hour.

Il est deux heures et quart.
Il est deux heures quinze.
It is 2:15.

Il est huit heures et demie.
Il est huit heures trente.
It is 8:30.

Il est neuf heures moins le quart.
Il est neuf heures moins un quart.
It is 8:45.

When it is more than 30 minutes past the hour, the number of minutes is subtracted from the next hour.

Il est minuit moins vingt.
It is 11:40.
Il est six heures moins vingt-cinq.
It is 5:35.

The word **demi** agrees with the noun when it follows.

midi et demi
minuit et demi
une heure et demie
deux heures et demie

When **demi** precedes the noun, it is hyphenated and does not agree.

une demi-heure

Official time in France is based on the 24-hour system. Minutes are always added to the hour.

France		*Canada*
0 h	**zéro heure (minuit)**	00
08 h 40	**huit heures quarante (du matin)**	8:40
13 h	**treize heures (une heure de l'après-midi)**	13:00
20 h 50	**vingt heures cinquante (huit heures cinquante du soir)**	20:50

Le train part à 15 h 20 (15:20).
The train leaves at 3:20 p.m.

8. Write the following times in French.

   1. It is 1:00 a.m.   6. It is 9:15 p.m.
   2. It is 3:45 p.m.   7. It is 12:30 p.m.
   3. It is 8:30 a.m.   8. It is 12:30 a.m.
   4. It is noon.   9. It is 10:25 p.m.
   5. It is midnight.   10. It is 9:40 a.m.

9. Write the above exercise in the 24-hour system.

Review

10. Complete the following with the correct dates and seasons to show when the following holidays are celebrated. Follow the model.

la fête nationale du Québec
On célèbre la fête nationale du Québec le 24 juin en été.
Juin est le sixième mois de l'année.

   1. L'Hallowe'en
   2. Noël

3. la fête nationale en France
4. la fête du travail en France
5. le jour de l'An
6. le jour du Saint-Patrick

11. Write the following arithmetical problems in French.

1. $78 + 20 = 98$
2. $1/3 + 2/3 = 1$
3. $1\,000 + 1\,500 = 2\,500$
4. $3/4 - 1/2 = 1/4$
5. $1\,000 \times 1\,000 = 1\,000\,000$
6. $80\% \times 100 = 80$
7. $1\,200 \div 100 = 12$
8. $1\,000\,000\,000 \div 1\,000\,000 = 1\,000$
9. $2 \times 25 = 50$
10. $1955 - 1850 = 105$

12. Anne has a busy day. Tell what she does and at what time. Change the time in her schedule to conversational time, according to the model.

14 h   rencontrer une amie
Elle rencontre une amie à deux heures de l'après-midi.

1. 6 h 45   se lever
2. 7 h   prendre le petit déjeuner
3. 7 h 30   partir pour l'université
4. 8 h   avoir son cours de français
5. 8 h 50   prendre un café
6. 9 h 15   avoir son cours d'histoire
7. 12 h 15   prendre le déjeuner à la cafétéria
8. 13 h   travailler dans la bibliothèque
9. 16 h 45   rentrer chez elle
10. 18 h 30   prendre le dîner
11. 20 h 10   aller au cinéma
12. 24 h   se coucher

Chapter 5

Verbs

French verbs at first appear to be difficult to the native English-speaker. But they are really not as difficult as they appear. Fortunately, each verb is not unique; it does not function as an entity unto itself. Many verbs that are formed in the same way can be grouped together in classes or conjugations. This greatly facilitates learning verb forms. As you will observe in subsequent parts of this chapter, even many so-called irregular verbs have characteristics in common and thus can be grouped together.

FORMAL VERSUS FAMILIAR FORMS

In French there are three ways to express the pronoun *you*. To address a friend, relative or close associate, the pronoun **tu** is used. This is called the familiar singular form. To address someone whom you do not know well or someone older than yourself, the pronoun **vous** is used. This is called the formal singular form. To address two or more people, either friends or mere acquaintances, **vous** is also used. **Vous** is the plural for both the familiar **tu** singular form and the formal **vous** singular form.

The third person singular pronoun **on** is an indefinite pronoun meaning *one, they, we* or *people*.

THE PRESENT TENSE

First Conjugation Verbs

Regular first conjugation verbs are commonly referred to as **-er** verbs since their infinitives end in **-er.** Many of the most frequently used verbs belong to the first conjugation.

In order to form the present tense of **-er** verbs, the infinitive ending **-er** is dropped. To the root are added the personal endings **-e, -es, -e, -ons, -ez, -ent.**

parler

je parl**e**	nous parl**ons**
tu parl**es**	vous parl**ez**
il, elle, on parl**e**	ils, elles parl**ent**

travailler

je travaill**e**	nous travaill**ons**
tu travaill**es**	vous travaill**ez**
il, elle, on travaill**e**	ils, elles travaill**ent**

Il parle français.
Tu chantes bien.
Je porte un parapluie.
Elles traversent la rue.
Nous travaillons bien.
Vous regardez la télévision.

Below is a partial list of **-er** verbs.

briller	*to shine*	**louer**	*to rent*
cacher	*to hide*	**marcher**	*to walk*
casser	*to break*	**monter**	*to climb, to go up*
chanter	*to sing*	**montrer**	*to show*
chercher	*to look for*	**parler**	*to speak*
commander	*to order*	**porter**	*to carry, to wear*
compter	*to count*	**préparer**	*to prepare*
danser	*to dance*	**présenter**	*to present*
décider	*to decide*	**quitter**	*to leave*
déjeuner	*to have lunch*	**raconter**	*to tell (a story)*
demander	*to ask*	**refuser**	*to refuse*
dessiner	*to draw*	**regarder**	*to look at*
dîner	*to dine*	**rencontrer**	*to meet*
donner	*to give*	**rester**	*to stay*
fermer	*to close*	**retourner**	*to return*
fouiller	*to rummage through*	**sauter**	*to jump*
fréquenter	*to frequent*	**tomber**	*to fall*
gagner	*to win*	**toucher**	*to touch*
garder	*to keep*	**travailler**	*to work*
goûter	*to taste*	**traverser**	*to cross*
jouer	*to play*	**tromper**	*to deceive*
laisser	*to leave*	**visiter**	*to visit*
laver	*to wash*		

1. Complete the verbs in the following sentences with the appropriate ending.

1. Le soleil brill_____ .
2. L'enfant cass_____ le jouet.
3. On cherch_____ le cadeau.
4. Je gagn_____ le prix.
5. Je donn_____ le livre à Pierre.
6. Tu ferm_____ la porte.
7. Tu fréquent_____ ce restaurant.
8. Ils chant_____ une chanson.
9. Les femmes lav_____ les vêtements.
10. Nous march_____ dans le parc.
11. Nous mont_____ dans la tour.
12. Vous port_____ un bel habit.
13. Vous prépar_____ le dîner.
14. Vous rest_____ ici.

2. Complete the following sentences with the correct form of the indicated verb.

1. L'homme _____ un appartement. *louer*
2. Nous _____ français. *parler*

　　3. Elles _____ les peintures. *regarder*
　　4. Vous _____ à la maison. *rester*
　　5. Je _____ dans un bureau. *travailler*
　　6. Les enfants _____ dans l'escalier. *tomber*
　　7. Tu _____ la rue. *traverser*
　　8. La fille _____ une histoire. *raconter*
　　9. Ils _____ leurs amis au café. *rencontrer*
　10. Nous _____ beaucoup de questions. *poser*
　11. Vous _____ un poste dans le centre-ville. *chercher*
　12. Je _____ cette vue. *dessiner*
　13. Tu _____ des chansons populaires. *chanter*
　14. Nous _____ de la soupe, du poulet et une salade. *commander*
　15. Elles _____ souvent au restaurant. *dîner*

3. Choose the correct form of one of the verbs listed below to logically complete the following sentences.

fouiller / cacher / garder / fermer / fréquenter / déjeuner

　　1. Je _____ le cadeau de Noël.
　　2. Tu _____ ce quartier.
　　3. Nous _____ à midi.
　　4. Ils _____ le souvenir.
　　5. Vous _____ la porte.
　　6. Elle _____ dans le tiroir.

4. Form sentences by combining the elements of column A with the appropriate element of column B. Be sure to put the verb in the correct form.

A	B
1. Elle / danser	la fenêtre
2. Nous / louer	une histoire
3. Ils / jouer	le vin
4. Tu / goûter	un appartement
5. Je / raconter	dans le parc
6. Vous / fermer	à la discothèque

Verbs Beginning with a Vowel

　　Many verbs beginning with a vowel or silent **h** are **-er** verbs. They are conjugated like **-er** verbs, but a few special problems must be noted. The pronoun **je** becomes **j'**. This is called elision. In spoken French, in the **nous, vous, ils** and **elles** forms, a **z** sound is heard between the pronoun and a following verb. This is called liaison. The **n** of **on** is pronounced before words beginning with a vowel. Study the following:

aimer

j'aime	nous aimons
tu aimes	vous aimez
il, elle aime	ils aiment
on aime	elles aiment

Below is a partial list of some common **-er** verbs beginning with a vowel.

abandonner	*to abandon*		**embrasser**	*to kiss, to embrace*
accrocher	*to hang*		**emporter**	*to carry*
admirer	*to admire*		**enseigner**	*to teach*
aider	*to help*		**entourer**	*to surround*
aimer	*to like, to love*		**entrer**	*to enter*
allumer	*to light*		**épouser**	*to marry*
amuser	*to amuse*		**étudier**	*to study*
apporter	*to bring*		**expliquer**	*to explain*
arriver	*to arrive*		**exprimer**	*to express*
attacher	*to attach*		**habiter**	*to live (in)*
attirer	*to attract*		**imaginer**	*to imagine*
attraper	*to catch*		**inspirer**	*to inspire*
avaler	*to swallow*		**inviter**	*to invite*
avouer	*to admit*		**irriter**	*to irritate*
échapper	*to escape*		**opposer**	*to oppose*
échouer	*to fail*		**oser**	*to dare*
écouter	*to listen to*		**oublier**	*to forget*
écraser	*to break*		**utiliser**	*to use*

J'avale la pilule.
Nous arrivons à l'heure.
Vous osez le faire.
Elles admirent les statues.
Il échoue à l'examen.
Tu attrapes le ballon.

5. Rewrite the following sentences, putting the verbs in the singular.

1. Nous allumons la lampe.
2. Nous oublions son nom.
3. Nous attirons une foule.
4. Nous arrivons en retard.
5. Nous apportons le déjeuner.

6. Rewrite the following sentences, inserting the correct form of the indicated verb. Make all necessary changes.

1. Je _____ la peinture moderne.   *aimer*
2. Nous _____ à l'heure.   *arriver*
3. Tu _____ le livre.   *oublier*
4. Je _____ mes amis.   *aider*
5. Vous _____ le français.   *enseigner*
6. Ils _____ l'histoire.   *étudier*
7. Elles _____ à Paris.   *habiter*
8. Je _____ des disques.   *écouter*
9. Le garçon _____ le bifteck.   *apporter*
10. Nous _____ nos défauts.   *avouer*

Verbs with Spelling Changes

Verbs Ending in -cer and -ger

Verbs ending in **-cer** add a cedilla to the **c** before the letters **a** or **o** in order to retain the soft **c** sound.

avancer	**nous avançons**
commencer	**nous commençons**
lancer	**nous lançons**

Verbs ending in **-ger** add an **e** after the **g** before the letters **a** and **o** in order to maintain the soft **g** sound.

changer	**nous changeons**
manger	**nous mangeons**
nager	**nous nageons**

7. Complete the following sentences with the correct form of the indicated verb.

1. Nous _____ la leçon. *commencer*
2. Nous _____ le travail. *recommencer*
3. Nous _____ . *avancer*
4. Nous _____ beaucoup. *manger*
5. Nous _____ de place. *changer*
6. Nous _____ dans la rivière. *nager*

8. Complete the following sentences with the correct form of the indicated verb, according to the model.

Elle _____ le travail, mais nous ne le _____ pas. *commencer*
Elle *commence* le travail, mais nous ne le *commençons* pas.

1. Il _____ le travail, mais nous ne le _____ pas. *commencer*
2. Tu _____ seul, mais nous _____ en groupe. *voyager*
3. Elles _____ du pain, mais nous n'en _____ pas. *manger*
4. Je _____ la leçon, mais vous ne la _____ pas. *commencer*
5. Je _____ bien, mais vous ne _____ pas bien. *nager*
6. Il _____ la balle, mais elles ne la _____ pas. *lancer*

Verbs with -é- in the Infinitive

Verbs which have **-é-** in the next to the last syllable of the infinitive change **-é-** to **-è-** in all forms except the **nous** and **vous** forms.

compléter

je complète
tu complètes
il, elle, on complète
nous complétons
vous complétez
ils, elles complètent

Some of the most common of these verbs are:

céder	*to yield, to cede*	**posséder**	*to possess*
célébrer	*to celebrate*	**précéder**	*to precede*
compléter	*to complete*	**préférer**	*to prefer*
considérer	*to consider*	**protéger**	*to protect*
espérer	*to hope*	**répéter**	*to repeat*
interpréter	*to interpret*		

9. Rewrite the following sentences, putting the verbs in the singular.

1. Vous cédez votre place.
2. Nous considérons ce poste.
3. Nous célébrons la fête.
4. Vous répétez les exercices.
5. Vous préférez partir de bonne heure.

10. Rewrite the following sentences, putting the verbs in the plural.

1. J'espère le voir.
2. Je cède à ses demandes.
3. Tu préfères venir à huit heures.
4. Tu interprètes le poème.

11. Complete the following sentences with the correct form of the indicated verb.

1. Vous _____ le poème. *interpréter*
2. Elles _____ le travail. *compléter*
3. Nous _____ nos amis. *protéger*
4. Je _____ aller au cinéma. *préférer*
5. Ces hommes _____ cette profession. *considérer*
6. Tu _____ à ses demandes. *céder*

Verbs with -*e*- in the Infinitive

In some verbs which contain **-e-** in the next to the last syllable of the infinitive, the **-e-** changes to **-è-** in all forms except the **nous** and **vous** forms. Study the following.

lever

je l**è**ve
tu l**è**ves
il, elle, on l**è**ve
nous levons
vous levez
ils, elles l**è**vent

Some of the most common of these verbs are:

acheter	*to buy*
mener	*to lead*
amener	*to bring, to lead toward*
emmener	*to take, to lead away*

promener	to take a walk
lever	to raise
élever	to raise
enlever	to lift
geler	to freeze
peser	to weigh

In other verbs with **-e-** in the infinitive, the final consonant is doubled in all but the **nous** and **vous** forms.

jeter

je je**tt**e
tu je**tt**es
il, elle, on je**tt**e
nous jetons
vous jetez
ils, elles je**tt**ent

Two verbs belonging to this group are:

appeler	to call
jeter	to throw (away)

12. Rewrite the following sentences, putting the verbs in the singular.

1. Nous levons le rideau.
2. Vous pesez cinquante kilos.
3. Nous gelons en hiver.
4. Vous menez une vie tranquille.
5. Nous appelons un taxi.
6. Vous jetez la balle.

13. Rewrite the following sentences, putting the verbs in the plural.

1. J'achète des disques.
2. Tu lèves le rideau.
3. J'enlève les ordures.
4. Tu emmènes le chien dans de longues promenades.
5. J'appelle Pierre.
6. Tu jettes le livre.

14. Complete the following sentences with the correct form of the indicated verb.

1. Elle _____ une vie tranquille. *mener*
2. Les ouvriers _____ le papier dans la corbeille. *jeter*
3. Vous _____ le journal. *jeter*
4. Elles _____ un taxi. *appeler*
5. Nous _____ la tache. *enlever*
6. Ces paquets _____ deux kilos. *peser*
7. Tu _____ le garçon. *appeler*
8. Vous _____ vos enfants à l'exposition. *mener*
9. J' _____ une voiture. *acheter*
10. Nous _____ les copains. *appeler*

Verbs with -*yer* in the Infinitive

Verbs whose infinitive ends in **-oyer, -uyer** and **-ayer** change **-y-** to **-i-** in all but the **nous** and **vous** forms.

nettoyer

je nettoie	nous nettoyons
tu nettoies	vous nettoyez
il, elle, on nettoie	ils, elles nettoient

Verbs in **-ayer** can keep the **y** in all forms of the conjugation.

Some common **-yer** verbs are:

employer	*to use*
ennuyer	*to bore*
envoyer	*to send*
essayer	*to try*
essuyer	*to wipe*
nettoyer	*to clean*
payer	*to pay (for)*

15. Complete the following sentences with the correct form of the indicated verb.

    1. La femme de ménage _____ la salle. *nettoyer*
    2. Tu _____ la lettre par avion. *envoyer*
    3. Je _____ la facture. *payer*
    4. Ils _____ les fenêtres. *essuyer*
    5. Ces livres m'_____. *ennuyer*
    6. Nous _____ une bonne. *employer*
    7. Vous _____ l'addition. *payer*

16. Rewrite the following, putting the verbs in the singular.

    1. Nous payons ces dettes.
    2. Vous employez une femme de ménage.
    3. Vous essayer de réussir.
    4. Nous envoyons le cadeau.
    5. Ils nettoient les meubles.
    6. Elles essaient de le faire.

Second Conjugation Verbs

Verbs whose infinitive ends in **-ir** are second conjugation verbs. The endings **-is, -is, -it, -issons, -issez, -issent** are added to the stem.

finir	choisir
je fin**is**	je chois**is**
tu fin**is**	tu chois**is**
il, elle, on fin**it**	il, elle, on chois**it**
nous fin**issons**	nous chois**issons**
vous fin**issez**	vous chois**issez**
ils, elles fin**issent**	ils, elles chois**issent**

Je finis ma leçon.
Tu obéis aux lois.
Elle punit l'enfant.
Nous choisissons une peinture.
Vous remplissez la tasse.
Ils réussissent à l'examen.

Below is a list of the most common **-ir** verbs.

accomplir	*to accomplish*	**grandir**	*to become bigger*
agrandir	*to enlarge*	**obéir**	*to obey*
applaudir	*to applaud*	**punir**	*to punish*
bâtir	*to build*	**remplir**	*to fill*
choisir	*to choose*	**réunir**	*to reunite*
embellir	*to embellish*	**réfléchir**	*to think, to reflect*
envahir	*to invade*	**réussir**	*to succeed*
finir	*to finish*	**saisir**	*to seize*

17. Complete the following sentences with the correct verb ending.

1. Il chois_____ du poulet rôti.
2. L'artiste embell_____ la salle.
3. Je réuss_____ à l'examen.
4. Je sais_____ l'occasion.
5. Tu rempl_____ le verre.
6. Tu fin_____ ta leçon.

7. Les policiers pun_____ les criminels.
8. Ils obé_____ aux lois.
9. Nous applaud_____ beaucoup.
10. Nous bât_____ une maison.
11. Vous envah_____ la province.
12. Vous grand_____ beaucoup.

18. Complete the following sentences with the correct form of the indicated verb.

1. Je _____ la tasse de café.   *remplir*
2. Nous _____ les deux amis.   *réunir*
3. Ils _____ au professeur.   *obéir*
4. L'ami _____ un cadeau.   *choisir*
5. Tu _____ aux injustices.   *réfléchir*
6. Vous _____ la maison.   *agrandir*
7. Les soldats _____ le territoire.   *envahir*
8. On _____ les coupables.   *punir*
9. Nous _____ nos devoirs.   *finir*
10. Vous _____ tout.   *réussir*

19. Choose the correct form of one of the verbs listed below to logically complete the following sentences.

applaudir / réussir / remplir / accomplir / saisir / punir

1. Tu _____ l'occasion.
2. Il _____ le verre.
3. Vous _____ le méchant chat.
4. Elles _____ à la fin du concert.
5. Nous _____ la tâche.
6. Je _____ à l'examen.

20. Form sentences by combining the elements of column A with the appropriate element of column B. Be sure to put the verb in the correct form.

A

1. Nous / bâtir
2. Les enfants / grandir
3. Il / réussir
4. Vous / choisir
5. Je / finir
6. Tu / obéir

B

à l'examen
le travail
aux lois
une maison à la campagne
chaque année
votre programme d'études

Third Conjugation Verbs

Verbs whose infinitive ends in **-re** are third conjugation verbs. The endings **-s, -s, -, -ons, -ez, -ent** are added to the stem.

répondre	**entendre**
je répond**s**	j'entend**s**
tu répond**s**	tu entend**s**
il, elle, on répond	il, elle, on entend
nous répond**ons**	nous entend**ons**
vous répond**ez**	vous entend**ez**
ils, elles répond**ent**	ils, elles entend**ent**

Below is a list of some common **-re** verbs.

attendre	*to wait for*	**perdre**	*to lose*
défendre	*to defend*	**rendre**	*to give back*
descendre	*to go down, to descend*	**répandre**	*to spread*
entendre	*to hear*	**répondre**	*to answer*
fendre	*to split*	**tendre**	*to pull, to set (a trap)*
fondre	*to melt*	**vendre**	*to sell*
pendre	*to hang*		

Je réponds à la question.
Tu attends tes amis.
Il descend l'escalier.
Nous vendons la maison.
Vous entendez du bruit.
Elles perdent l'espoir.

21. Complete the following sentences with the correct form of the indicated verb.

1. L'avocat _____ son client. *défendre*
2. La glace _____ . *fondre*
3. Je _____ aux questions. *répondre*
4. Je _____ l'escalier. *descendre*
5. Tu _____ la peinture. *pendre*
6. Tu _____ du bruit. *entendre*

   7. Les charpentiers _____ du bois. *fendre*
   8. Elles _____ la nouvelle. *répandre*
   9. Nous _____ l'auto. *vendre*
 10. Nous _____ les devoirs au professeur. *rendre*
 11. Vous _____ la clef. *perdre*
 12. Vous _____ la corde. *tendre*

22. Rewrite the following sentences, putting the verbs in the plural.

   1. Elle vend l'auto.
   2. Tu descends sur la place.
   3. J'entends le professeur.
   4. Il fend du bois.

23. Rewrite the following sentences, putting the verbs in the singular.

   1. Ils entendent du bruit.
   2. Vous attendez le train.
   3. Elles perdent le match.
   4. Nous défendons cet homme.

24. Form sentences by combining the elements of column A with the appropriate element of column B. Be sure to put the verb in the correct form.

A	B
1. Vous / tendre	la maison
2. Je / entendre	l'espoir
3. Elles / descendre	à la question
4. Nous / perdre	les devoirs au professeur
5. Il / rendre	la rue
6. Je / attendre	un piège pour la souris
7. Tu / vendre	la chanson
8. Ils / répondre	un copain devant le cinéma

Irregular Verbs

Verbs like *ouvrir*

   Some verbs, although the infinitive ends in **-ir**, are conjugated like regular **-er** verbs. Some of the most common are **ouvrir** (*to open*), **couvrir** (*to cover*), **recouvrir** (*to cover again, cover completely*), **découvrir** (*to discover*), **offrir** (*to offer*), **souffrir (de)**, (*to suffer*), **cueillir** (*to pick, to gather*), **accueillir** (*to welcome*), and **recueillir** (*to collect, to pick, to gather*).

ouvrir	**cueillir**
j'ouvr**e**	je cueill**e**
tu ouvr**es**	tu cueill**es**
il, elle, on ouvr**e**	il, elle, on cueill**e**
nous ouvr**ons**	nous cueill**ons**
vous ouvr**ez**	vous cueill**ez**
ils, elles ouvr**ent**	ils, elles cueill**ent**

25. Complete the following sentences with the correct form of the indicated verb.

  1. Les paysannes _____ les fleurs. *cueillir*
  2. J' _____ la porte. *ouvrir*
  3. Elle _____ les invités. *accueillir*
  4. Vous _____ un cadeau. *offrir*
  5. Tu _____ beaucoup. *souffrir*
  6. Nous _____ la fenêtre. *ouvrir*
  7. L'enfant _____ un nouveau jouet. *découvrir*
  8. La neige _____ la terre. *recouvrir*
  9. Nous _____ la boîte. *recouvrir*
 10. Elles _____ d'une maladie étrange. *souffrir*

Verbs like *courir, rire, rompre, conclure*

  Some verbs whose infinitives end in **-ir** or **-re** are conjugated like regular **-re** verbs except in the **il, elle, on** form where a **t** is added to the stem. Some of the most common are **courir** (*to run*), **parcourir** (*to pass through, to pass over, to tour*), **secourir** (*to help, to assist*), **rire** (*to laugh*), **sourire** (*to smile*), **conclure** (*to conclude*), **rompre** (*to break*) and its derivatives **corrompre** (*to corrupt, to spoil*) and **interrompre** (*to interrupt*).

courir	**rire**
je cours	je ris
tu cours	tu ris
il, elle, on cour**t**	il, elle, on ri**t**
nous courons	nous rions
vous courez	vous riez
ils, elles courent	ils, elles rient

rompre	**conclure**
je romps	je conclus
tu romps	tu conclus
il, elle, on romp**t**	il, elle, on conclu**t**
nous rompons	nous concluons
vous rompez	vous concluez
ils, elles rompent	ils, elles concluent

26. Rewrite the following sentences, putting the verbs in the singular.

  1. Ils rient aux éclats.
  2. Elles courent vite.
  3. Ils concluent l'accord.
  4. Elles sourient beaucoup.
  5. Ils rompent les liens.
  6. Elles interrompent le professeur.

27. Complete the following sentences with the correct form of the indicated verb.

  1. L'enfant _____ vers son père. *courir*
  2. Elles _____ à haute voix. *rire*

3. La chaleur _____ la viande. *corrompre*
4. Vous _____ vos amis. *secourir*
5. Tu _____ le discours. *conclure*
6. Tu _____ les liens. *rompre*
7. Je _____ aux éclats. *rire*
8. Nous _____ le monde. *parcourir*
9. Il _____ beaucoup. *rire*
10. Nous _____ beaucoup. *sourire*
11. Nous _____ l'entretien. *interrompre*
12. Tu _____ très vite. *courir*
13. Les hommes d'affaires _____ l'accord. *conclure*
14. Ils _____ leur travail. *interrompre*
15. Vous _____ au spectacle. *rire*

Battre and *mettre*

The verbs **battre** (*to beat, to hit, to win*) and its derivatives **se battre** (*to fight*) and **combattre** (*to combat*), and **mettre** (*to put, to place, to wear* or *to put on* — clothes, *to turn on* — radio or T.V., *to set* — table) and its derivatives **admettre** (*to admit*), **permettre** (*to permit*), **promettre** (*to promise*), **remettre** (*to put back*), **soumettre** (*to overcome, to submit, to subjugate, to subject*), **se mettre à** (*to begin*) and **transmettre** (*to transmit*) are conjugated like regular **-re** verbs except that the double **t** becomes a single **t** in the singular forms.

battre	**mettre**
je bats	je mets
tu bats	tu mets
il, elle, on bat	il, elle, on met
nous battons	nous mettons
vous battez	vous mettez
ils, elles battent	ils, elles mettent

28. Rewrite the following sentences, putting the verbs in the singular.

1. Nous mettons les vêtements dans l'armoire.
2. Vous battez le tapis.
3. Ils remettent le travail à demain.
4. Elles promettent d'aller avec moi.

29. Rewrite the following sentences, putting the verbs in the plural.

1. Il admet le crime.
2. L'armée soumet les rebelles.
3. Tu mets la nappe sur la table.
4. Je bats le linge pour le nettoyer.

30. Complete the following sentences with the correct form of the indicated verb.

1. Elles _____ le record. *battre*
2. Tu _____ la question aux autres. *soumettre*
3. Elle _____ d'y aller. *promettre*
4. Nous _____ les livres sur l'étagère. *remettre*

  5. Vous _____ dans l'armée. *combattre*
  6. Je _____ le tapis. *battre*
  7. Tu _____ les livres sur la table. *mettre*
  8. Les soldats _____ les rebelles. *soumettre*
  9. Vous _____ que vous avez tort. *admettre*
 10. Il lui _____ d'y aller. *permettre*
 11. Nous _____ le message. *transmettre*
 12. Je lui _____ de venir. *promettre*

Verbs like *partir*

   Verbs like **partir** (*to leave*), **dormir** (*to sleep*), **s'endormir** (*to fall asleep*), **mentir** (*to tell a lie*), **servir** (*to serve*), **sentir** (*to feel, to smell*) and **sortir** (*to leave, to go out*) are conjugated like regular -**re** verbs in the plural. The regular -**re** endings are added to the stem of the first and second person singular forms after the final consonant has been dropped. A -**t**- is added to the third person singular form after the final consonant has been dropped. In the plural, note the consonant sounds **t** in **partir**, **mentir**, **sentir** and **sortir**; **m** in **dormir** and **v** in **servir**.

partir	**dormir**	**servir**
je **pars**	je **dors**	je **sers**
tu **pars**	tu **dors**	tu **sers**
il, elle, on **part**	il, elle, on **dort**	il, elle, on **sert**
nous partons	nous dormons	nous servons
vous partez	vous dormez	vous servez
ils, elles partent	ils, elles dorment	ils, elles servent

31. Complete the following sentences with the correct form of the indicated verb.

  1. Il _____ tout le temps. *mentir*
  2. Elle _____ de la salle. *sortir*
  3. Je _____ le dîner. *servir*
  4. Je _____ pour l'aéroport. *partir*
  5. Tu _____ huit heures. *dormir*
  6. Tu _____ les fleurs. *sentir*
  7. Ils _____ de bonne heure. *partir*
  8. Elles _____ souvent le samedi soir. *sortir*
  9. Nous _____ du thé. *servir*
 10. Nous ne _____ jamais. *mentir*
 11. Vous _____ ce soir. *sortir*
 12. Vous _____ bien. *dormir*

32. Rewrite the following sentences, putting the verbs in the singular.

  1. Nous partons à huit heures.   4. Elles servent un bon repas.
  2. Vous dormez bien.   5. Ils sentent l'odeur fraîche.
  3. Vous servez des apéritifs.   6. Elles dorment huit heures.

33. Rewrite the following sentences, puttings the verbs in the plural.

  1. Je sors de la classe.   3. Elle dort sur le divan.
  2. Il ment au professeur.   4. Tu pars de bonne heure.

Vaincre

Vaincre (*to conquer*) and **convaincre** (*to convince*) are conjugated like regular **-re** verbs except that the **c** changes to **qu** in the plural.

vaincre

je vaincs	nous vain**qu**ons
tu vaincs	vous vain**qu**ez
il, elle, on vainc	ils, elles vain**qu**ent

34. Rewrite the following sentences, putting the verbs in the plural.

1. Je vaincs le rival.
2. Tu vaincs la difficulté.
3. Il convainc le sceptique.
4. Elle convainc l'homme de sa culpabilité.

35. Rewrite the following sentences, using the cues provided.

Ils vainquent l'ennemi.
Je _____ .
Vous _____ .
Elles _____ .
Nous _____ .
Tu _____ .

Verbs like *connaître*

Connaître (*to know someone or to be acquainted with someone, some place or thing*) and similar verbs such as **apparaître** (to appear, to seem), **disparaître** (*to disappear*), **paraître** (*to seem, to appear*), **reconnaître** (*to recognize*) and **naître** (*to be born*) are conjugated alike. Note the circumflex over the **i** in the third person singular.

connaître

je connais
tu connais
il, elle, on connaît
nous connaissons
vous connaissez
ils, elles connaissent

Haïr (*to hate*) is conjugated like **connaître** in the singular, except that there is no circumflex on the **i** in the third person singular. Note the dieresis on the **i** in the plural.

haïr

je hais
tu hais
il, elle, on hait
nous haïssons
vous haïssez
ils, elles haïssent

36. Complete the following sentences with the correct form of the indicated verb.

1. Elles _____ les Dupont. *connaître*
2. Ils _____ cet homme. *reconnaître*
3. Une étoile _____ à l'horizon. *apparaître*
4. Un enfant _____ chaque minute. *naître*
5. Elle _____ dans le brouillard. *disparaître*
6. Il _____ l'injustice. *haïr*
7. Il _____ facile de le faire. *paraître*
8. Nous _____ nos amis. *reconnaître*
9. Nous _____ cette ville. *connaître*
10. Vous _____ la pauvreté. *haïr*
11. Vous _____ cette chanson. *reconnaître*
12. Je _____ cette femme. *connaître*
13. Je _____ dans la neige. *disparaître*
14. Tu _____ les menteurs. *haïr*
15. Tu _____ ces romans. *connaître*

37. Rewrite the following sentences, putting the verbs in the singular.

1. Les invités paraissent à la porte.
2. Nous connaissons les Leclerc.
3. Vous reconnaissez le criminel.
4. Ils haïssent la bureaucratie.
5. Ils disparaissent souvent.

38. Rewrite the following sentences, putting the verbs in the plural.

1. Je reconnais cet enfant.
2. Tu connais le poète.
3. Elle hait l'injustice.
4. Cet homme paraît malade.
5. Le chien disparaît derrière l'arbre.

Plaire and *se taire*

Plaire (*to be pleasing*), **déplaire** (*to displease*) and **se taire** (*to be quiet*) are conjugated like **connaître** except that there is only one **s** in the plural forms. There is no circumflex on the **i** in the third person singular of **se taire**.

plaire	se taire
je plais	je me tais
tu plais	tu te tais
il, elle, on plaît	il, elle, on se tait
nous plaisons	nous nous taisons
vous plaisez	vous vous taisez
ils, elles plaisent	ils, elles se taisent

39. Rewrite the following sentences, putting the verbs in the singular.

1. Ils plaisent à tout le monde.
2. Elles se taisent pendant le concert.
3. Nous plaisons à Marie.
4. Vous vous taisez pendant la conférence.

40. Rewrite the following sentences, putting the verbs in the plural.

1. Il plaît à cette femme.
2. Elle se tait pendant le spectacle.
3. Tu plais à tout le monde.
4. Je me tais maintenant.
5. Ce livre déplaît à Pierre.

Verbs with Infinitives Ending in -ire

Lire, dire, conduire, traduire

Many verbs whose infinitives end in **-ire** have a base ending in a **z** sound. Belonging to this group are **lire** (*to read*), **élire** (*to elect*), **dire** (*to speak, to tell, to say*), **interdire** (*to forbid*), **suffire** (*to be sufficient*), **conduire** (*to conduct, to drive*), **produire** (*to produce*), **traduire** (*to translate*), **construire** (*to build*), **reconstruire** (*to rebuild, to reconstruct*), **détruire** (*to destroy*), **cuire** (*to cook*) and **nuire** (*to do harm*). These verbs add the endings **-s, -s, -t, -sons, -sez, -sent** to the stem. The second person plural of **dire (vous dites)** is an exception.

lire	dire	conduire
je lis	je dis	je conduis
tu lis	tu dis	tu conduis
il, elle, on lit	il, elle, on dit	il, elle on conduit
nous lisons	nous disons	nous conduisons
vous lisez	vous di**tes**	vous conduisez
ils, elles lisent	ils, elles disent	ils, elles conduisent

41. Rewrite the following sentences, putting the verbs in the singular.

1. Les troupes détruisent la ville.
2. Ils élisent un président.
3. Vous dites la vérité.
4. Vous traduisez la phrase.
5. Nous lisons un roman.
6. Nous conduisons une Citroën.

42. Rewrite the following sentences, putting the verbs in the plural.

1. Elle lit *le Monde* tous les jours.
2. Il conduit une Renault.
3. Je dis la vérité.
4. Je détruis le livre.
5. Tu produis un nouveau jouet.
6. Tu dis bonjour.

43. Complete the following sentences with the correct form of the indicated verb.

1. Elle _____ un poème.   *lire*
2. Vous _____ au revoir.   *dire*
3. Ça _____ .   *suffire*
4. Je _____ bien.   *conduire*
5. Les ouvriers _____ le pont.   *reconstruire*

6. L'armée _____ la ville. *détruire*
7. Nous _____ les phrases. *traduire*
8. Ce panneau nous _____ de marcher sur le gazon. *interdire*
9. Tu _____ un hôtel. *reconstruire*
10. On _____ une maison. *construire*

Écrire, vivre, suivre

Écrire (*to write*), **décrire** (*to describe*), **vivre** (*to live*), **survivre** (*to survive*), **suivre** (*to follow, to take a course or class*), **poursuivre** (*to pursue, to follow up*) and **s'ensuivre** (*to come after, to follow*) are conjugated alike. Note the **v** in the plural forms.

écrire	vivre	suivre
j'écris	je vis	je suis
tu écris	tu vis	tu suis
il, elle, on écrit	il, elle, on vit	il, elle, on suit
nous écri**v**ons	nous vi**v**ons	nous sui**v**ons
vous écri**v**ez	vous vi**v**ez	vous sui**v**ez
ils, elles écri**v**ent	ils, elles vi**v**ent	ils, elles sui**v**ent

44. Complete the following sentences with the correct form of the indicated verb.

1. Elles _____ ce sentier. *suivre*
2. Les romanciers _____ des romans. *écrire*
3. Nous _____ la fête. *décrire*
4. Nous _____ un cours de français. *suivre*
5. Vous _____ une lettre. *écrire*
6. Vous _____ bien ici. *vivre*
7. Elle _____ un cours de chimie. *suivre*
8. Il _____ souvent à ses parents. *écrire*
9. Je _____ la scène. *décrire*
10. Je _____ cet homme. *poursuivre*
11. Tu _____ cette route. *suivre*
12. Tu _____ au xxe siècle. *vivre*

45. Rewrite the following sentences, putting the verbs in the plural.

1. Je vis bien ici.
2. Tu suis ce cours.
3. Elle écrit un poème.
4. Il décrit le match.

46. Rewrite the following sentences, putting the verbs in the singular.

1. Elles survivent à l'accident.
2. Ils écrivent les devoirs.
3. Nous vivons bien.
4. Vous suivez un cours de français.

Croire, voir and *mourir*

Like **-yer** verbs, **croire** (*to believe*) and **voir** (*to see*), **prévoir** (*to foresee*) and **revoir** (*to see again*) have an internal vowel change. The **i** changes to **y** in the **nous** and **vous** forms. The other forms are conjugated like regular **-re** verbs except in the third person singular, where a **t** is added to the stem.

croire

je crois
tu crois
il, elle, on croi**t**
nous cro**y**ons
vous cro**y**ez
ils, elles croient

voir

je vois
tu vois
il, elle, on voi**t**
nous vo**y**ons
vous vo**y**ez
ils, elles voient

Fuir (*to flee*) and **s'enfuir** (*to flee, run away*) have the same vowel change in the first and second person plural.

fuir

je fuis
tu fuis
il, elle, on fuit
nous fu**y**ons
vous fu**y**ez
ils, elles fuient

Mourir (*to die*) has an internal vowel change from **ou** to **eu** in the singular and the third person plural.

mourir

je m**eu**rs
tu m**eu**rs
il, elle, on m**eu**rt
nous mourons
vous mourez
ils, elles m**eu**rent

47. Complete the following sentences with the correct form of the indicated verb.

1. Nous _____ l'histoire. *croire*
2. Nous _____ clair. *voir*
3. Nous _____ de la salle. *s'enfuir*
4. Vous _____ qu'elle a raison. *croire*
5. Vous _____ votre ami. *croire*
6. Vous _____ la nouvelle dans le journal. *voir*

48. Change the sentence, using the cues given.

Nous mourons de faim.
Vous _____.
Il _____.
Je _____.
Tu _____.
Elles _____.

49. Rewrite the following sentences, putting the verbs in the singular.

1. Elles le voient.
2. Nous croyons en Dieu.
3. Vous fuyez sa présence.
4. Ils croient cette histoire.
5. Ils meurent de fatigue.
6. Nous mourons de peur.

50. Rewrite the following sentences, changing the first verb to the plural.

1. Je vois qu'il a tort.
2. Elle croit que vous êtes fatigué.
3. Il s'enfuit de la salle précipitamment.
4. Tu meurs de faim.
5. Tu crois l'histoire.

Verbs like *craindre, peindre, joindre*

Craindre (*to fear*), **plaindre** (*to pity, to feel sorry for*), **se plaindre** (*to complain*), **atteindre** (*to reach*), **éteindre** (*to put out, to extinguish*), **peindre** (*to paint*), **joindre** (*to join, to unite*) and **rejoindre** (*to rejoin, to reunite*) are conjugated similarly. They have an internal change from **n** to **gn** in the plural.

craindre	peindre	joindre
je crains	je peins	je joins
tu crains	tu peins	tu joins
il, elle, on craint	il, elle, on peint	il, elle, on joint
nous crai**gn**ons	nous pei**gn**ons	nous joi**gn**ons
vous crai**gn**ez	vous pei**gn**ez	vous joi**gn**ez
ils, elles crai**gn**ent	ils, elles pei**gn**ent	ils, elles joi**gn**ent

51. Complete the following sentences with the correct form of the indicated verb.

1. Elles _____ la pluie.   *craindre*
2. Ils _____ l'utile à l'agréable.   *joindre*
3. Nous _____ la lumière.   *éteindre*
4. Nous _____ le sommet.   *atteindre*
5. Vous me _____ trop.   *plaindre*
6. Vous _____ un portrait.   *peindre*
7. Elle _____ d'être en retard.   *craindre*
8. Il _____ un paysage.   *peindre*
9. Je vous _____ .   *plaindre*
10. Je _____ mes amis au café.   *rejoindre*
11. Tu _____ l'examen.   *craindre*
12. Tu _____ les murs de la maison.   *peindre*

52. Rewrite the following sentences, putting the verbs in the plural.

1. Je crains cet homme.
2. Tu rejoins Pierre à l'heure.
3. Il peint un paysage.

    4. Elle se plaint de tout.
    5. Elle joint les deux bouts.

53. Rewrite the following sentences, putting the verbs in the singular.

    1. Elles craignent de répondre.
    2. Nous peignons le mur.
    3. Vous éteignez la lumière.
    4. Ils vous plaignent.
    5. Nous joignons les deux bouts.

54. Follow the model.

Je crains le professeur, mais vous ne le _____ pas.
Je crains le professeur, mais vous ne le *craignez* pas.

    1. Je rejoins les copains, mais vous ne les _____ pas.
    2. Il craint l'examen, mais nous ne le _____ pas.
    3. Tu peins le mur, mais ils ne le _____ pas.
    4. Vous éteignez la lumière, mais je ne l' _____ pas.
    5. Nous plaignons les misérables, mais tu ne les _____ pas.
    6. Elles atteignent ce but, mais il ne l' _____ pas.

Verbs like *prendre*

    Prendre (*to take, to take* or *to eat* — food, a meal, *to drink* — beverage, *to buy* — a ticket), **apprendre** (*to learn*), **comprendre** (*to understand*), **reprendre** (*to take back*) and **surprendre** (*to surprise*) are conjugated like regular **-re** verbs in the singular. In the plural, the final **-d** is dropped from the stem and the regular endings are added. The consonant **n** is doubled in the third person plural.

prendre

je prends
tu prends
il, elle, on prend
nous pre**nons**
vous pre**nez**
ils, elles pre**nnent**

55. Rewrite the following sentences, putting the verbs in the plural.

    1. Je prends le déjeuner à midi.
    2. J'apprends les verbes.
    3. Tu reprends le disque.
    4. Tu surprends l'enfant.
    5. Il comprend le français.
    6. Cette nouvelle nous surprend.

56. Complete the following sentences with the correct form of the indicated verb.

    1. Je _____ la leçon.   *comprendre*
    2. Elle _____ son ami.   *surprendre*
    3. Nous _____ nos places.   *prendre*

4. Elles _____ les difficultés. *comprendre*
5. Tu _____ le poème. *apprendre*
6. Vous _____ l'autobus. *prendre*
7. Il _____ ses possessions. *reprendre*

Venir and *tenir*

Venir (*to come*) and its derivatives **revenir** (*to come back*), **convenir** (*to be convenient*), **devenir** (*to become*), **redevenir** (*to become again*), **parvenir** (to reach, to attain) and **se souvenir (de)** (*to remember*); **tenir** (*to have, to hold*) and its derivatives **appartenir** (*to belong to*), **contenir** (*to hold, to contain*), **maintenir** (*to maintain*), **obtenir** (*to obtain*) and **retenir** (*to retain*) are conjugated alike.

Note the vowel change from **-e-** to **-ie-** in the singular forms and the third person plural. Note the double consonant **nn** in the third person plural.

Tenir à plus an infinitive means *to be anxious to*. **Tenir à** plus a noun means *to like very much, to be attached to*.

venir	tenir
je v**ie**ns	je t**ie**ns
tu v**ie**ns	tu t**ie**ns
il, elle, on v**ie**nt	il, elle, on t**ie**nt
nous v**e**nons	nous t**e**nons
vous v**e**nez	vous t**e**nez
ils, elles v**ienn**ent	ils, elles t**ienn**ent

57. Complete the following sentences with the correct form of the indicated verb.

1. Ils _____ maintenant. *venir*
2. Elles _____ une chambre à l'hôtel. *retenir*
3. Cette robe vous _____ bien. *convenir*
4. Ce gant vous _____ . *appartenir*
5. Je _____ tout de suite. *revenir*
6. Je _____ fatigué. *devenir*
7. Tu _____ le prix. *obtenir*
8. Tu _____ à tes fins. *parvenir*
9. Nous _____ de ce voyage. *revenir*
10. Nous _____ à vous voir. *tenir*
11. Vous _____ votre opinion. *maintenir*
12. Vous _____ de bons résultats. *obtenir*

58. Rewrite the following sentences, putting the verbs in the singular.

1. Ils viennent tout de suite.
2. Vous devenez riches.
3. Nous maintenons notre position.
4. Les boîtes contiennent des papiers.
5. Nous parvenons à un âge avancé.

59. Rewrite the following sentences, putting the verbs in the plural.

1. Il tient à vous voir.
2. Elle vient tout de suite.
3. Ce livre vous appartient.

    4. Tu obtiens le prix.

    5. Je viens maintenant.

Acquérir and *conquérir*

    Acquérir (*to acquire, to buy, to gain*) and **conquérir** (*to conquer, to win*) have an internal vowel change from **é** to **ie** in all but the **nous** and **vous** forms. Study the following.

acquérir

j'acqu**ie**rs
tu acqu**ie**rs
il, elle, on acqu**ie**rt
nous acqu**é**rons
vous acqu**é**rez
ils, elles acqu**iè**rent

60. Rewrite the following sentences, putting the verbs in the singular.

    1. Nous acquérons de l'expérience.

    2. Nous conquérons son affection.

    3. Vous acquérez une maison.

    4. Vous conquérez l'ennemi.

61. Complete the following sentences with the correct form of the indicated verb.

    1. J' _____ une auto. *acquérir*

    2. Elles _____ son estime. *conquérir*

    3. Tu _____ une maison. *acquérir*

    4. Vous _____ beaucoup de livres. *acquérir*

    5. Il _____ l'ennemi. *conquérir*

    6. Nous _____ son affection. *conquérir*

Pouvoir, vouloir, pleuvoir

    Pouvoir (*to be able to*), **vouloir** (*to want, to wish*) and **pleuvoir** (*to rain*) are conjugated similarly. Note the change from **ou** to **eu** in the stem of **vouloir** and **pouvoir** in all but the first and second person plural forms. **Pleuvoir** has only a third person singular form.

pouvoir	**vouloir**	**pleuvoir**
je p**eu**x	je v**eu**x	
tu p**eu**x	tu v**eu**x	
il, elle, on p**eu**t	il, elle, on v**eu**t	il pl**eu**t
nous pouvons	nous voulons	
vous pouvez	vous voulez	
ils, elles p**eu**vent	ils, elles v**eu**lent	

62. Complete the following sentences with the correct form of the indicated verb.

    1. Les garçons _____ jouer au football. *pouvoir*

    2. Je _____ de l'argent. *vouloir*

    3. Tu _____ partir. *pouvoir*

4. Elle _____ m'accompagner. *vouloir*
5. Nous _____ attendre. *vouloir*
6. Vous _____ voir le film. *pouvoir*

63. Rewrite the following sentences, putting the verbs in the singular.

1. Nous pouvons partir maintenant.
2. Nous voulons revenir demain.
3. Vous pouvez sortir maintenant.
4. Vous voulez rester ici.
5. Ils peuvent venir ce soir.
6. Elles veulent savoir la réponse.

64. Rewrite the following sentences in the plural.

1. Je peux attendre une minute.
2. Je veux sortir maintenant.
3. Il veut jouer au football samedi.
4. Elle peut rester ici si elle le veut.

Boire, devoir, recevoir

Boire (*to drink*), **devoir** (*to owe, to have to*), **recevoir** (*to receive*), **apercevoir** (*to perceive*) and **décevoir** (*to disappoint, to deceive*) are conjugated similarly. Note the cedilla on the **c** in the singular and third person plural forms of **recevoir** and its derivatives. Note the internal vowel change in the first and second person plural forms. Note also the **v** in all plural forms.

boire	devoir	recevoir
je b**ois**	je d**ois**	je re**çois**
tu b**ois**	tu d**ois**	tu re**çois**
il, elle, on b**oit**	il, elle, on d**oit**	il, elle, on re**çoit**
nous b**uv**ons	nous d**ev**ons	nous re**cev**ons
vous b**uv**ez	vous d**ev**ez	vous re**cev**ez
ils, elles b**oiv**ent	ils, elles d**oiv**ent	ils, elles re**çoiv**ent

65. Complete the following sentences with the correct form of the indicated verb.

1. Les enfants _____ beaucoup de lait. *boire*
2. Elles _____ beaucoup de cadeaux. *recevoir*
3. Ils _____ de l'argent à Pierre. *devoir*
4. Marie _____ un coup de téléphone. *recevoir*
5. Elle _____ partir de bonne heure. *devoir*
6. Il vous _____ . *décevoir*
7. Je _____ du café. *boire*
8. Je _____ des paquets. *recevoir*
9. Tu _____ une tache sur la robe. *apercevoir*
10. Tu _____ une lettre. *recevoir*
11. Nous _____ du vin. *boire*
12. Nous _____ beaucoup de lettres. *recevoir*
13. Vous _____ vos amis. *décevoir*
14. Vous _____ de l'eau. *boire*

66. Follow the model.

> **Je _____ partir, mais vous ne _____ pas partir. *devoir***
> **Je *dois* partir, mais vous ne *devez* pas partir.**

1. Je _____ de l'eau, mais vous n'en _____ pas. *boire*
2. Tu _____ un cadeau, mais nous n'en _____ pas. *recevoir*
3. Je _____ de l'argent, mais vous n'en _____ pas. *devoir*
4. Vous _____ du vin, mais ils n'en _____ pas. *boire*
5. Nous _____ cent francs, mais elles ne _____ rien. *devoir*

67. Rewrite the following sentences, putting the verbs in the plural.

1. Je dois de l'argent.
2. Je reçois une carte postale.
3. Tu bois du vin.
4. Tu reçois la lettre.
5. Il déçoit le professeur.
6. Elle reçoit de l'argent.

Avoir

The verb **avoir** (*to have*) is completely irregular. Study the following.

j'**ai**	nous **avons**
tu **as**	vous **avez**
il, elle, on **a**	ils, elles **ont**

68. Complete the following sentences with the correct form of the verb **avoir**.

1. Il _____ sommeil.
2. Elle _____ faim.
3. Tu _____ beaucoup d'amis.
4. Tu _____ tort.
5. J' _____ froid.
6. J' _____ chaud.
7. Nous _____ une Renault.
8. Nous _____ de la chance.
9. Vous _____ honte.
10. Vous _____ peur.
11. Ils _____ soif.
12. Elles _____ raison.

69. Some friends are getting ready to go on a trip and are checking to be sure no one has forgotten anything. Follow the model.

> **Il a ses valises. Et vous?**
> **Nous avons nos valises aussi.**

1. Il a les billets. Et les amis?
2. Nous avons de l'argent. Et toi?
3. Tu as ton passeport. Et nous?
4. Ils ont les billets. Et les autres?
5. J'ai des cartes de crédit. Et Pierre?
6. Ils ont leurs visas. Et vous, Marie et Anne?

70. Mary and her friends are getting ready to go on a picnic. Who is bringing the provisions? Follow the model.

> **Qui a les pommes? *Tu***
> **Tu as les pommes.**

1. Qui a les sandwichs? *Je*
2. Qui a le couvert? *Vous*

3. Qui a le dessert? *Nous*
4. Qui a le panier? *Anne*
5. Qui a les boissons? *Michel et André*
6. Qui a les serviettes? *Pierre*
7. Qui a le tire-bouchon? *Tu*

Être

The verb **être** (*to be*) is completely irregular. Study the following.

<table>
<tr><td>je suis</td><td>nous sommes</td></tr>
<tr><td>tu es</td><td>vous êtes</td></tr>
<tr><td>il, elle, on est</td><td>ils, elles sont</td></tr>
</table>

71. Complete the following sentences with the correct form of the verb **être.**

1. Il _____ français.
2. Elle _____ petite.
3. Tu _____ fatigué.
4. Tu _____ gentil.
5. Je _____ en retard.
6. Je _____ à l'heure.
7. Ils _____ malades.
8. Elles _____ heureuses.
9. Nous _____ contents.
10. Nous _____ fatiguées.
11. Vous _____ américain.
12. Vous _____ françaises.

72. Rewrite the following sentences, changing the singular pronouns and verbs to the plural and the plural pronouns and verbs to the singular. Make all necessary changes.

1. Nous sommes françaises.
2. Il est heureux.
3. Elles sont malades.
4. Vous êtes loyaux.
5. Je suis fort.
6. Tu es grand.

73. What are the nationalities of the following people? Follow the model.

Elle / le Canada
Elle est du Canada. Elle est canadienne.

1. Je / la France
2. Il / l'Italie
3. Tu / les États-Unis
4. Nous / l'Allemagne
5. Elles / la Russie
6. Vous / la Chine

74. What are the following people's professions? Follow the model.

Je / médecin
Je suis médecin.

1. Elle / journaliste
2. Il / avocat
3. Elles / dentistes
4. Nous / ingénieurs

5. Tu / chirurgien
6. Je / professeur

Aller

The verb **aller** (*to go*) is completely irregular. Study the following.

je **vais**	nous **allons**
tu **vas**	vous **allez**
il, elle, on **va**	ils, elles **vont**

75. Complete the following sentences with the correct form of the verb **aller**.

1. Il _____ à Paris en voiture.
2. Elle _____ à la boutique.
3. Tu _____ à l'école.
4. Tu _____ en ville.
5. Je _____ à pied.
6. Je _____ au cinéma.
7. Ils _____ à la chasse.
8. Elles _____ au musée.
9. Nous _____ à Paris.
10. Nous _____ au théâtre.
11. Vous y _____ par le train.
12. Vous _____ à la plage.

76. Say how the people are feeling. Follow the model.

Je / bien
Je vais bien.

1. Nous / très bien
2. Vous / bien
3. Ils / très mal
4. Tu / assez bien
5. Elle / mieux
6. Je / mal

77. Say where the following people are going, based on what they want to do. Choose from the list below. Follow the model.

au restaurant / au cinéma / à la discothèque / à la boulangerie / à la piscine / à la bibliothèque / au théâtre

Il veut voir une pièce de théâtre.
Il va au théâtre.

1. Elle veut danser.
2. Tu veux lire.
3. Nous voulons regarder un film.
4. Je veux nager.
5. Vous voulez manger.
6. Anne et Michèle veulent acheter du pain.

Faire

The verb **faire** (*to do, to make*) is completely irregular. Study the following.

je **fais**	nous **faisons**
tu **fais**	vous **faites**
il, elle, on **fait**	ils, elles **font**

78. Complete the following sentences with the correct form of the verb **faire.**

1. Il _____ froid.
2. Elle _____ la salade.
3. Je _____ la leçon.
4. Je _____ un gâteau.
5. Tu _____ du golf.
6. Tu _____ ton droit.

7. Elles _____ du bien.
8. Ils _____ du ski.
9. Nous _____ du bruit.
10. Nous _____ du piano.
11. Vous _____ du sport.
12. Vous _____ votre possible.

79. Change the sentence, using the cue provided.

Je fais fortune.
Tu _____.
Nous _____.
Ils _____.
Elle _____.
Vous _____.

80. What do the people do in the following places? Complete the sentences choosing from the list below. Put the verb **faire** in the correct form.

faire la vaisselle
faire le ménage
faire attention

faire des réparations à l'auto
faire du ski
faire une promenade

1. Elle _____ dans le garage.
2. Nous _____ dans la cuisine.
3. Tu _____ dans le salon.
4. Les enfants _____ dans le parc.
5. Vous _____ en classe.
6. Je _____ dans les Alpes.

Savoir

The verb **savoir** (*to know a fact, to know how to*) is completely irregular. Study the following.

je **sais**	nous **savons**
tu **sais**	vous **savez**
il, elle, on **sait**	ils, elles **savent**

81. Complete the following sentences with the correct form of the verb **savoir.**

1. Il _____ la vérité.
2. Elle _____ la réponse.
3. Je _____ parler français.
4. Je _____ la date de sa naissance.
5. Tu _____ son nom.
6. Tu _____ qu'il arrive.
7. Elles _____ jouer du piano.
8. Ils _____ son adresse.
9. Nous _____ où elle va.
10. Nous _____ conduire une voiture.

11. Vous _____ quand l'avion va partir.
12. Vous _____ qu'elles sont contentes.

82. Rewrite the following sentences, putting **savoir** in the plural.

1. Je sais qu'elle est malade.   3. Il sait faire du ski.
2. Tu sais où elle habite.   4. Elle sait faire la cuisine.

83. Tell what the people know how to do based on the information given. Choose from the list below. Follow the model.

bien écrire   réparer les autos
parler espagnol   faire la cuisine
jouer du piano   bien conduire
guérir les maladies

Il est journaliste.
Il sait bien écrire.

1. Nous sommes médecins.
2. Elle est mécanicienne.
3. Je suis musicien.
4. Vous êtes un grand chef.
5. Ils habitent en Espagne.
6. Tu es chauffeur de taxi.

Valoir *and* falloir

The verbs **valoir** (*to be worth*) and **falloir** (*to be necessary*) are irregular. Study the following.

valoir	**falloir**
je **vaux**	
tu **vaux**	
il, elle, on **vaut**	il **faut**
nous **valons**	
vous **valez**	
ils, elles **valent**	

Il vaut mieux means *it is better*.

84. Complete the following sentences with the correct form of the indicated verb.

1. Il _____ la peine de le faire. *valoir*
2. Il _____ partir de bonne heure. *falloir*
3. Ces robes _____ le prix. *valoir*
4. Vous _____ la peine. *valoir*

85. Rewrite the following, substituting the words provided.

Il faut rentrer de bonne heure.
_____ arriver _____ .
Il vaut mieux _____ .
_____ venir _____ .

Special Uses of the Present Tense

The present tense in French is used the same as in English to express an action which is going on in the present. Note, however, that special helping verbs such as *am, are, is* in English are not used in French. The present tense is also used, as in English, to express habitual actions taking place in the present or a permanent situation.

Elle dort maintenant.
She is sleeping now.
Tous les matins, ils vont à l'école.
Every morning they go to school.
La neige est blanche.
Snow is white.

To insist on the duration of an action, use **être en train de** plus an infinitive.

Il est en train de s'habiller.
He's getting dressed.

The present tense can be used to express the immediate future.

J'arrive dans cinq minutes.
I'll come in five minutes.

Depuis, il y a ... que, voilà ... que, and *ça fait ... que* plus the present tense

A special use of the present tense is with the time expressions **depuis, il y a ... que, voilà ... que,** and **ça fait ... que** to express an action which began in the past but continues into the present.

Depuis quand attend-elle?	*How long has she been waiting?*
Elle attend depuis une semaine. **Voilà une semaine qu'elle attend.** **Il y a une semaine qu'elle attend.** **Ça fait une semaine qu'elle attend.**	*She has been waiting for a week.*

Depuis can mean *for* or *since*. Study the following.

Depuis quand habite-t-elle ici?	*Since when has she been living here?*
Elle habite ici depuis novembre.	*She has been living here since November.*
Depuis combien de temps habitez-vous ici?	*For how long have you been living here?*
Nous habitons ici depuis trois ans.	*We have been living here for three years.*

You will note that in English the past tense (present perfect) is used. Since the action continues into the present, the present tense must be used in French.

Note that **une heure** may mean *one o'clock*. To say *since one o'clock* use **depuis.** To say *for an hour,* use **il y a ... que, voilà ... que** or **ça fait ... que.**

J'attends depuis deux heures.	*I have been waiting since two o'clock.*
Il y a deux heures que j'attends.	*I have been waiting for two hours.*

Venir de **plus the Present Tense**

Venir de plus the present tense means *to have just done something*.

Elle **vient d**'arriver.   *She has just arrived.*

86. Complete the following sentences with the appropriate form of the indicated verb.

   1. Nous _____ Pierre depuis cinq ans. *connaître*
   2. Elle _____ ici depuis deux ans. *être*
   3. Il y a un an que je _____ ici. *demeurer*
   4. Ça fait deux mois que nous _____ le français. *apprendre*
   5. Il y a longtemps que vous _____ ce poème. *écrire*

87. Change the sentence according to the model.

Je travaille depuis une heure.
Il y a une heure que je travaille.
Ça fait une heure que je travaille.
Voilà une heure que je travaille.

   1. Je lis ce poème depuis une heure.
   2. J'attends l'autobus depuis cinq minutes.
   3. Elle cherche ce livre depuis deux semaines.
   4. Ils dorment depuis cinq heures.

88. Answer the following questions, using the cue provided.

   1. Depuis quand travaillez-vous? *depuis une heure*
   2. Depuis quand habite-t-il ici? *Il y a deux ans*
   3. Depuis quand attends-tu le train? *Ça fait 15 minutes*
   4. Depuis quand conduisez-vous une auto? *depuis l'âge de 18 ans*
   5. Depuis quand attendez-vous un taxi? *Voilà dix minutes*
   6. Depuis quand étudie-t-il le français? *Il y a longtemps*
   7. Depuis quand lisent-ils? *depuis une heure*
   8. Depuis quand jouez-vous de la guitare? *Il y a un mois*
   9. Quand vient-elle d'arriver? *il y a deux minutes*
  10. Quand venez-vous de finir le travail? *il y a une heure*

Review

89. Complete the following sentences with the appropriate form of the present tense of the indicated verb.

   1. Je _____ voyager en avion. *préférer*
   2. Tu _____ une carte à tes parents. *envoyer*
   3. Nous _____ le travail. *commencer*
   4. Elle _____ le garçon. *appeler*
   5. Vous _____ une nouvelle robe. *choisir*
   6. Tu _____ un cadeau à Pierre. *offrir*
   7. Elle _____ aux éclats. *rire*
   8. Ils _____ leurs passions. *vaincre*
   9. Nous _____ cette histoire. *croire*
  10. Il _____ de faim. *mourir*

11. Elle _____ cet homme. *connaître*
12. Cela me _____ . *plaire*
13. Je _____ le couvert. *mettre*
14. Vous _____ beaucoup de voyages. *faire*
15. Elle _____ huit heures. *dormir*
16. Nous _____ la phrase. *traduire*
17. Elle _____ ce boulevard. *suivre*
18. Vous _____ sa réponse. *craindre*
19. Elle _____ un portrait. *peindre*
20. Nous _____ la leçon. *comprendre*
21. Ils _____ tout de suite. *revenir*
22. Elles _____ le faire. *pouvoir*
23. Vous _____ partir. *vouloir*
24. Marie _____ une lettre. *recevoir*
25. Vous _____ travailler. *devoir*
26. Nous _____ du vin. *boire*
27. Elle _____ qu'il _____ . *savoir, venir*
28. Nous _____ beaucoup d'amis. *avoir*
29. Vous _____ contents. *être*
30. Je _____ à l'école. *aller*
31. Il _____ arriver de bonne heure. *falloir*

90. Form sentences using the subjects and verbs given and choosing a logical completion from the list below. Follow the model.

les liens
les fenêtres quand il fait chaud
au restaurant
dans une usine
cet homme de partir
un bon film au cinéma
beaucoup de journaux
mon ami devant le cinéma
aux examens
du sel dans le ragoût
leur maison

cette chanson
sa leçon
ici souvent
une vie tranquille
dans le lac
la police quand nous voyons un crime
toujours les réponses
le faire
beaucoup de lettres
tout le temps

Je / travailler
Je travaille dans une usine.

1. Vous / manger
2. Les garçons / nager
3. Nous / appeler
4. Je / réussir
5. Les hommes / rompre
6. Ils / vendre
7. Nous / ouvrir
8. Les chefs / mettre
9. Je / attendre
10. Les bébés / dormir

11. Marie / mener
12. Georges / convaincre
13. Nous / connaître
14. Vous / lire
15. Angèle / apprendre
16. Les Pierron / venir
17. Les enfants / voir
18. Je / pouvoir
19. David / recevoir
20. Nous / savoir

REFLEXIVE VERBS

The action of a reflexive verb is both executed and received by the subject. Since the subject also receives the action, an additional pronoun is needed. This is called the reflexive pronoun. Study the following.

se réveiller	**s'habiller**
je **me** réveille	je **m'**habille
tu **te** réveilles	tu **t'**habilles
il, elle, on **se** réveille	il, elle, on **s'**habille
nous **nous** réveillons	nous **nous** habillons
vous **vous** réveillez	vous **vous** habillez
ils, elles **se** réveillent	ils, elles **s'**habillent

Note that **me** becomes **m'**, **te** becomes **t'** and **se** becomes **s'** before a vowel or a mute **h.**

Je **m'**habille.
Tu **t'**arrêtes.
Il **s'**amuse bien.

Reflexive verbs may be used with a strictly reflexive meaning as well as in other ways where the English equivalent does not use a reflexive verb.

Je me lave.	*I wash myself.*
Je me trompe.	*I am mistaken.*

Many reflexive verbs are conjugated like regular **-er** verbs or **-er** verbs with spelling changes. Below is a partial list.

-er *verbs*

s'amuser	*to amuse oneself*	**se moquer de**	*to make fun of*
s'arrêter	*to stop*	**s'occuper de**	*to be busy with,*
se blesser	*to hurt onself*		*to take care of*
se brosser	*to brush oneself*	**se passer**	*to happen*
se coucher	*to go to bed*	**se passer de**	*to do without*
se débrouiller	*to get along, to manage,*	**se peigner**	*to comb*
	to handle a situation	**se porter**	*to feel*
se demander	*to wonder*	**se presser**	*to hurry*
se dépêcher	*to hurry*	**se raser**	*to shave*
se fâcher	*to become angry*	**se reposer**	*to rest*
s'habiller	*to get dressed*	**se retrouver**	*to meet each other*
s'intéresser à	*to be interested in*	**se réveiller**	*to wake up*
se laver	*to wash*	**se tromper**	*to be mistaken*
se marier	*to get married*	**se trouver**	*to be located, to be found*

Spelling change verbs

s'acheter	*to buy for oneself*	**s'ennuyer**	*to become bored*
s'appeler	*to be named*	**se lever**	*to get up*
se rappeler	*to remember*	**se promener**	*to take a walk*

Below is a list of irregular reflexive verbs with references to similarly conjugated nonreflexive verbs.

s'en aller	*to go away*	aller (p. 121.)
s'endormir	*to fall asleep*	partir (p. 108.)
s'entendre (avec)	*to get along (with)*	-re verbs (p. 104.)
se plaindre	*to complain*	craindre (p. 114.)
se sentir	*to feel*	partir (p. 108.)
se souvenir de	*to remember*	venir (p. 116.)
se taire	*to be quiet*	plaire (p. 110.)

91. Complete the following with an appropriate reflexive pronoun.

1. Elle _____ endort à onze heures du soir.
2. Je _____ peigne dans la salle de bains.
3. Ils _____ trompent souvent.
4. Tu _____ habilles bien.
5. Nous _____ couchons de bonne heure.
6. Vous _____ dépêchez pour ne pas manquer le commencement du spectacle.
7. Je _____ arrête devant le cinéma.
8. Tu _____ débrouilles bien.
9. Il _____ rase chaque matin.
10. Nous _____ levons de bonne heure.

92. Complete the following sentences with the correct form of the indicated verb.

1. Il _____ à sept heures. *se réveiller*
2. Je _____ pour arriver à l'heure. *se dépêcher*
3. Tu _____ dans la salle de bains. *se laver*
4. Nous _____ au café. *se retrouver*
5. Vous _____ bien. *se débrouiller*
6. Les hommes _____ le matin. *se raser*
7. Elles _____ en blanc. *s'habiller*
8. Je _____ Marie. *s'appeler*
9. Tu _____ bien. *s'amuser*
10. Elle _____ avec Jean. *se marier*
11. Nous _____ dans le jardin. *se promener*
12. Vous _____ de moi. *se moquer*

93. Answer the following questions, choosing from the cues provided. Follow the model.

à dix heures	de mes vacances
parce qu'il est fatigué	si nous recevons une bonne note
sur le divan	dans une rue déserte
bien	parce que la conférence commence
Oui, ... souvent	parce que le film n'est pas intéressant
Marie	à côté du bureau de poste
dans la salle de bains	

Où est-ce qu'il se peigne?
Il se peigne dans la salle de bains.

1. Comment vous appelez-vous?
2. Où se passe l'action?

3. Où se trouve la pharmacie?
4. Qu'est-ce que vous vous demandez?
5. Pourquoi vous ennuyez-vous?
6. Pourquoi s'en va-t-il?
7. À quelle heure se couchent-elles?
8. Se fâchent-ils?
9. Comment vous portez-vous?
10. De quoi vous souvenez-vous?
11. Pourquoi se tait-il?
12. Où est-ce que l'enfant s'endort?

S'asseoir

A common, completely irregular reflexive verb is **s'asseoir** (*to sit down*). Study the following forms.

s'asseoir

je **m'assieds**	nous **nous** asseyons
tu **t'assieds**	vous **vous** asseyez
il, elle, on **s'assied**	ils, elles **s'asseyent**

94. Complete the following sentences with the correct form of the verb **s'asseoir**.

1. Il _____ à table.
2. Elle _____ devant le bureau.
3. Je _____ à ma place.
4. Je _____ en face du professeur.
5. Tu _____ au premier rang.
6. Tu _____ sur le balcon.
7. Ils _____ dans les fauteuils.
8. Elles _____ au théâtre.
9. Nous _____ parce que nous sommes fatigués.
10. Nous _____ à table.
11. Vous _____ devant le feu.
12. Vous _____ sur la chaise.

95. Rewrite the following sentences in the plural.

1. Il s'assied devant vous.
2. Je m'assieds devant le feu.
3. Tu t'assieds dans le fauteuil.
4. Elle s'assied au premier rang.

96. Rewrite the following sentences in the singular.

1. Nous nous asseyons.
2. Vous vous asseyez à table.
3. Ils s'asseyent devant le bureau.
4. Elles s'asseyent sur le balcon.

Reflexive Verbs with Parts of the Body

You will note that when a part of the body is used with reflexive verbs, the definite article rather than the possessive adjective is used.

Je me lave **la** figure.	*I wash* **my** *face.*
Je me lave **les** mains.	*I wash* **my** *hands.*

You will also note that when the noun is ordinarily plural in English, it is singular in French.

Elles se lavent | **la figure.** | *They wash* | *their faces.* |

97. Complete the following sentences with the appropriate definite article.

1. La fille se lave _____ figure.   3. Ils se brossent _____ dents.
2. Elles se lavent _____ mains.   4. Ils se lavent _____ figure.

Reflexive versus Non-reflexive Verbs

Many verbs function both reflexively and nonreflexively. If the action reverts to the subject, the verb is reflexive. If, however, the action is performed on another person or object, the verb is not reflexive.

Reflexive:	Je me lave.	*I wash myself.*
Nonreflexive:	Je lave la voiture.	*I wash the car.*
Reflexive:	Je me lève.	*I get up.*
Nonreflexive:	Je lève la main.	*I raise my hand.*

The reflexive verb is also used to indicate reciprocal action.

Reflexive:	Nous nous aimons.	*We like each other.*
Nonreflexive:	Nous aimons nos amies.	*We like our friends.*

98. Complete the following sentences with the appropriate reflexive pronoun, when it is necessary.

1. Je _____ lave dans la salle de bains.   5. Nous _____ couchons tôt.
2. Je _____ lave la voiture.   6. Nous _____ couchons les enfants.
3. Elle _____ lève la main.   7. Tu _____ habilles le bébé.
4. Elle _____ lève de bonne heure.   8. Tu _____ habilles en noir.

99. Follow the model.

Nous aimons nos amis.
Nous nous aimons.

1. Nous écrivons à nos parents.
2. Ils aiment leurs amis.
3. Ils regardent leurs copains.
4. Nous cherchons nos amis.

Reflexive Verbs in the Infinitive

The reflexive pronoun always immediately precedes the reflexive verb in the infinitive. Note that the pronoun agrees with the subject.

Je vais **me promener.**	*I am going to take a walk.*
Tu vas **te peigner.**	*You are going to comb your hair.*
Il va **se raser.**	*He is going to shave.*

Nous allons **nous dépêcher.**	*We are going to hurry.*
Vous allez **vous amuser.**	*You are going to amuse yourself.*
Elles vont **s'asseoir.**	*They are going to sit down.*

See pages 229–231 for reflexive verbs in the negative.

100. Complete the following sentences with the correct form of the indicated reflexive verb.

1. Je vais _____. *s'asseoir*
2. Tu vas _____. *se raser*
3. Nous allons _____. *se peigner*
4. Ils vont _____. *se réveiller*
5. Elle va _____. *s'habiller*
6. Vous allez _____. *s'endormir*

IMPERATIVES

Affirmative Imperatives

The imperative or command is the same form as the second person singular and the first and second person plural forms of the verb without the pronoun. For **-er** verbs, the **s** is dropped from the second person singular to form the imperative.

parler		**finir**		**attendre**	
Parle!	*Speak!*	Finis!	*Finish!*	Attends!	*Wait!*
Parlons!	*Let's speak!*	Finissons!	*Let's finish!*	Attendons!	*Let's wait!*
Parlez!	*Speak!*	Finissez!	*Finish!*	Attendez!	*Wait!*

The imperative forms of **aller** are **va, allons, allez. Va** becomes **vas** and the familiar imperative of **-er** verbs adds **s** before the pronouns **y** and **en.**

Vas-y!   **Parles-en!**

The imperatives of **être, avoir** and **savoir** are irregular.

être	**avoir**	**savoir**
Sois!	Aie!	Sache!
Soyons!	Ayons!	Sachons!
Soyez!	Ayez!	Sachez!

The imperative forms for these verbs are the subjunctive forms.

101. Write the imperative forms for each of the following.

1. parler français
2. écouter le professeur
3. choisir un livre
4. réfléchir à ces idées
5. attendre le train
6. vendre l'auto
7. prendre le déjeuner
8. ouvrir la porte
9. boire du lait
10. écrire la lettre
11. partir maintenant
12. venir tout de suite

102. Follow the model.

> **Tu es à l'heure.**
> **Sois toujours à l'heure!**

1. Tu es honnête.
2. Nous sommes en avance.
3. Vous êtes heureux.
4. Tu as de la patience.
5. Nous avons du courage.
6. Vous avez de la pitié.
7. Tu sais la vérité.
8. Nous savons la réponse.
9. Vous savez le poème par cœur.

The Affirmative Imperative of Reflexive Verbs

In the affirmative imperative, the reflexive pronoun follows the verb and is joined to it by a hyphen. Note that **te** changes to **toi** in the affirmative imperative.

> **Lève-toi!**   *Get up!*
> **Levons-nous!**   *Let's get up!*
> **Levez-vous!**   *Get up!*

103. Follow the model.

> **se coucher / vous**
> **Couchez-vous!**

1. se lever / tu
2. s'amuser / vous
3. s'habiller vite / tu
4. se dépêcher / nous

The Negative Imperative

The imperative is made negative by placing **ne** or **n'** before the imperative form of the verb and **pas** after it.

Affirmative	*Negative*
Travaille!	**Ne** travaille **pas!**
Écoute!	**N'**écoute **pas!**

104. Rewrite the following imperatives in the negative.

1. Parlez!
2. Travaille!
3. Soyez en retard!
4. Restons ici!
5. Aie du courage!
6. Écoutez la conversation!
7. Arrivons à l'heure!

The Negative Imperative of Reflexive Verbs

In the negative imperative of reflexive verbs, the reflexive pronoun precedes the verb.

Affirmative	*Negative*
Réveille-toi!	Ne te réveille pas!
Réveillons-nous!	Ne nous réveillons pas!
Réveillez-vous!	Ne vous réveillez pas!

Note that the reflexive pronoun **te** does not change in the negative imperative.

105. Rewrite the following imperatives in the negative.

1. Couche-toi!
2. Habille-toi!
3. Dépêchez-vous!
4. Amusez-vous bien!
5. Réveillons-nous!

THE PRESENT PARTICIPLE

Formation

The present participle is formed by dropping the ending **-ons** from the first person plural of the present tense and adding **-ant**.

nous parlons	**parlant**
nous finissons	**finissant**
nous répondons	**répondant**
nous dormons	**dormant**
nous craignons	**craignant**

Only **avoir, être** and **savoir** are irregular.

avoir	**ayant**
être	**étant**
savoir	**sachant**

Use

When the present participle is used as an adjective, it agrees with the noun it modifies.

une fille **souriante**	*a smiling girl*
Il parle d'une voix **menaçante**.	*He speaks with a menacing voice.*

The present participle is invariable when it is used to express an action that takes place at the same time as the action of the principal verb.

Je vois mon père **faisant** la cuisine.
I see my father cooking.

The present participle can be replaced by **qui** plus a verb.

Je vois mon père **faisant (qui fait)** la cuisine.
I see my father cooking (who is cooking).

The present participle is often used after the preposition **en. En** means *by, while, upon, although.*

On apprend le français **en étudiant.**
One learns French by studying.
En me promenant, j'ai rencontré mon ami.
While taking a walk, I met my friend.
En arrivant, j'ai vu Marie.
Upon arriving, I saw Mary.
Tout **en** vous **aimant,** je reconnais vos défauts.
Although I like you, I recognize your faults.

By doing something is expressed in French by **en** plus the present participle except after the verbs **commencer** and **finir. Par** with the infinitive is used with these verbs.

Il a fini **par travailler.**   *He finally started working.*
Elle a commencé **par faire** l'appel.   *She began by calling the roll.*

With prepositions other than **en,** the infinitive is used rather than the present participle. (See Uses of the Infinitive, pp. 208–209.)
The present participle can also express cause.

Étant professeur, il veut enseigner.
Since he is a teacher, he wants to teach.

106. Say that the following people do two things at the same time. Follow the model.

Il écoute la musique quand il travaille.
Il écoute la musique en travaillant.

1. J'écoute la radio quand je fais mes devoirs.
2. Pierre regarde la télévision quand il mange.
3. Anne écoute la musique quand elle s'habille.
4. Nous écoutons les nouvelles à la radio quand nous conduisons.
5. Vous lisez quand vous attendez l'autobus.
6. Le chef chante quand il prépare le repas.

107. Say that something else happens while the following people do things.

Quand il sort, il tombe.
En sortant, il tombe.

1. Quand il se promène, il rencontre son ami Paul.
2. Pendant qu'elle descend la rue, elle tombe.
3. Pendant qu'elle raconte une histoire amusante, elle rit.
4. Quand il regarde la télévision, il s'endort.
5. Pendant que les spectateurs se lèvent, ils crient bravo.

108. Change the sentences to show how people can accomplish things.

On travaille et on apprend.
C'est en travaillant qu'on apprend.

1. On étudie et on reçoit de bonnes notes.
2. On joue du piano tous les jours et on apprend à bien jouer.

3. On a de l'ambition et on devient chef de l'entreprise.
4. On court tous les jours et on reste en forme.
5. On est généreux et on a de bons amis.
6. On sait les verbes et on réussit à l'examen de français.
7. On mange moins et on maigrit.
8. On travaille et on gagne de l'argent.

109. Say what the people are doing. Follow the model.

Que fait-il?   *étudier / manger*
Il étudie en mangeant.

1. Que fait-il?   *se brûler la main / faire la cuisine*
2. Que fait-elle?   *s'ennuyer / faire ce travail*
3. Que faites-vous?   *s'amuser / nager*
4. Que font-elles?   *entrer / courir*
5. Que fait-il?   *parler / dormir*
6. Que fait-elle?   *finir / dormir*
7. Que fait-il?   *commencer / remercier les invités*

110. Follow the model.

Il est professeur et il veut enseigner.
Étant professeur, il veut enseigner.

1. Il est chirurgien et il veut travailler à l'hôpital.
2. Elle a de l'argent et elle peut voyager partout.
3. Nous voulons réussir et nous travaillons.
4. Il dit au revoir et il part.
5. Je sais la leçon et maintenant je peux jouer avec mes amis.

THE IMPERFECT TENSE

Formation

The imperfect tense is formed by dropping the **-ons** ending from the first person plural of the present tense and adding the endings **-ais, -ais, -ait, -ions, -iez, -aient.** The singular and the third person plural forms all sound alike although they are spelled differently.

parler (base: **parlons**)	**finir** (base: **finissons**)
je parl**ais**	je finiss**ais**
tu parl**ais**	tu finiss**ais**
il, elle, on parl**ait**	il, elle, on finiss**ait**
nous parl**ions**	nous finiss**ions**
vous parl**iez**	vous finiss**iez**
ils, elles parl**aient**	ils, elles finiss**aient**

The imperfect tense of the verb **être** has an irregular stem to which the regular endings are added.

> j'**étais**
> tu **étais**
> il, elle, on **était**
> nous **étions**
> vous **étiez**
> ils, elles **étaient**

111. Rewrite the following sentences in the imperfect tense.

1. Nous travaillons beaucoup.
2. Nous prenons le déjeuner à huit heures.
3. Nous pouvons le faire.
4. Nous attendons longtemps.
5. Nous écrivons beaucoup de lettres.
6. Nous lisons des romans policiers.
7. Nous voyons clair.
8. Nous rions souvent.
9. Nous craignons de partir.
10. Nous venons souvent.
11. Nous nous débrouillons.
12. Nous nous couchons de bonne heure.

112. Complete the following sentences with the correct form of the imperfect tense of the indicated verb.

1. Je _____ de place. *changer*
2. Je _____ des livres d'occasion. *vendre*
3. Tu _____ à haute voix. *parler*
4. Tu _____ la musique classique. *préférer*
5. Elle _____ une femme de ménage. *employer*
6. Il _____ ce cours. *suivre*
7. Elles _____ le petit déjeuner à sept heures. *prendre*
8. Ils _____ réussir. *vouloir*
9. Nous _____ la vérité. *dire*
10. Nous _____ du vin. *boire*
11. Vous _____ vos devoirs. *faire*
12. Vous _____ des histoires. *lire*

113. Rewrite the following sentences in the imperfect tense.

1. Je suis content.
2. Tu es heureux.
3. Elle est fatiguée.
4. Nous sommes malades.
5. Vous êtes triste.
6. Ils sont enfants.

114. Rewrite the following sentences in the imperfect tense.

1. Ils peuvent chanter.
2. Nous apprenons le français.
3. Je sors souvent.
4. Tu as beaucoup de temps.

5. Elle vient nous voir.
6. Vous buvez du lait.
7. Il ment souvent.
8. Elle croit ses amis.
9. Nous sommes heureuses.
10. Elle se dépêche.
11. Vous vous habillez bien.
12. Ils se promènent dans le parc.

Uses of the Imperfect Tense

Continuing Action

The imperfect tense is used less in English than in French. The imperfect tense is used to describe activities in the past. The imperfect tense is used to indicate actions begun in the past but not necessarily completed. It is used to express those past actions which are habitual or customary. Some common adverbial expressions which would indicate continuance and thus frequently use the imperfect are:

toujours	*always*
fréquemment	*frequently*
d'habitude	*usually*
souvent	*often*
bien des fois	*often, many times*
quelquefois	*sometimes*
parfois	*sometimes*
de temps en temps	*sometimes, from time to time*
tous les jours (lundis)	*every day (Monday)*
en ce temps-là	*at that time*
chaque année (jour, mois)	*every year (day, month)*
le lundi (le mardi, etc.)	*on Mondays (on Tuesdays, etc.)*

Study the following examples.

Elles **mangeaient toujours** dans ce restaurant.	*They always used to eat at this restaurant.*
Il **venait** me voir **fréquemment**.	*He came to see me frequently.*
Chaque été, j'**allais** à la plage.	*Every summer I went to the beach.*
Je **jouais** au football **souvent**.	*I played football often.*
Nous **allions bien des fois** à Paris.	*We went to Paris many times.*
Il **travaillait tous les jours**.	*He worked every day.*
En ce temps-là, je **chantais** bien.	*At that time, I sang well.*

The imperfect tense is used to describe what people were doing rather than report what people did.

Ils chantaient pendant que les filles bavardaient.
They were singing while the girls were talking.

115. Say that the following people used to do the same things they do now. Rewrite the following sentences in the imperfect tense.

1. Chaque année, elle va en vacances.
2. Nous lisons souvent.

3. Nous rentrons toujours à la même heure.
4. Elle fait des courses tous les jours.
5. Chaque matin, elles achètent des baguettes.
6. D'habitude, je mange des croissants au petit déjeuner.
7. Bien des fois, vous savez vous débrouiller.
8. Tu voyages fréquemment.
9. Elle va en Europe chaque été.
10. Il craint le tonnerre.
11. Il fait du ski quelquefois.
12. De temps en temps, vous dites des bêtises.

116. Say that you used to do the following. Follow the model.

Joues-tu au football? *quand j'étais jeune*
Pas maintenant, mais quand j'étais jeune, je jouais au football.

1. Lis-tu souvent? *en ce temps-là*
2. Riez-vous? *quand j'étais jeune*
3. Chantes-tu bien? *autrefois*
4. Vous couchez-vous de bonne heure? *quand j'étais jeune*

With Verbs Denoting Mental Activity or Conditions

Since most mental processes involve duration or continuance, verbs which deal with mental activities or conditions are often expressed in the imperfect when used in the past. The most common of these verbs are:

aimer	*to like*
avoir	*to have*
croire	*to believe*
désirer	*to desire, to want*
espérer	*to hope*
être	*to be*
penser	*to think*
préférer	*to prefer*
pouvoir	*to be able to*
regretter	*to be sorry*
savoir	*to know*
vouloir	*to want*

117. Rewrite the following sentences in the past.

1. Je ne veux pas partir.
2. Vous regrettez les jours passés.
3. Nous pouvons venir tous les samedis.
4. Il ne sait pas les réponses.
5. Elles croient que vous avez raison.
6. Nous espérons recevoir de bonnes notes.
7. À quoi penses-tu?
8. Nous sommes désolés de ne pas pouvoir venir.
9. Elle préfère voyager en auto.
10. Je le désire beaucoup.

Descriptions in the Past

The imperfect tense is used to describe conditions or circumstances that accompanied a past action or to designate a condition in the past that no longer exists.

Il faisait beau.
The weather was nice.
Il avait de la chance.
He was lucky.
Il portait une chemise blanche.
He wore a white shirt.
Le Louvre était le palais des rois de France.
The Louvre was the palace of the kings of France.
Louis XIV était roi de France.
Louis XIV was king of France.

118. Rewrite the following sentences in the past. Describe the setting and the people at the skating rink.

1. Il est huit heures du soir.
2. Il fait froid.
3. Les étoiles brillent dans le ciel.
4. Il y a beaucoup de monde sur la patinoire.
5. Il y a un homme qui a à peu près soixante ans.
6. Une fille fait du patinage avec son ami.
7. Elle est blonde et lui, il est brun.
8. Ils portent de beaux patins.
9. Ils sont heureux.

Si and the Imperfect Tense

Si and the **on** or **nous** form of the verb in the imperfect tense can be used as a kind of imperative to make a wish or suggestion.

Si on jouait au tennis?   *How about playing tennis?*
Si nous jouions au tennis?   *Suppose we play tennis?*

Il a une nouvelle voiture.   *He has a new car.*
Si j'avais une nouvelle voiture aussi!   *If only I had a new car, too!*

119. Jean complains that she and her husband never do or buy things. Her husband proposes to do the following.

Nous ne jouons jamais au golf!
Si on jouait au golf?
Si nous jouions au golf?

1. Nous ne jouons jamais aux cartes.
2. Nous ne faisons jamais de ski.
3. Nous n'allons jamais au cinéma.
4. Nous ne dînons jamais au restaurant.
5. Nous n'achetons jamais une nouvelle voiture.

Depuis, il y avait ... que, voilà ... que, ça faisait ... que **and the Imperfect Tense**

Depuis, il y avait ... que, voilà ... que and **ça faisait ... que** are used with the imperfect tense to mean *had been.*

Depuis quand attendait-il?	*How long had he been waiting?*

Il attendait depuis dix minutes.	
Voilà dix minutes qu'il attendait.	*He had been waiting for ten minutes.*
Il y avait dix minutes qu'il attendait.	
Ça faisait dix minutes qu'il attendait.	

Venir de **plus the Imperfect Tense**

Venir de and the imperfect tense are used to mean *to had just done something.*

Il **venait d'**arriver.	*He had just arrived.*

120. Complete the following sentences with the appropriate form of the imperfect tense of the indicated verb.

1. Depuis quand _____ -vous? *travailler*
2. Elle _____ ce livre depuis deux ans. *écrire*
3. Voilà longtemps que mon grand-père _____ aller au cinéma. *vouloir*
4. Il y avait deux mois que Jean _____ Marie. *connaître*
5. Voilà deux ans que j' _____ la médecine. *étudier*
6. Depuis quand _____ -ils ce bâtiment? *construire*
7. Nous _____ la vérité depuis longtemps. *savoir*
8. Vous _____ ici depuis trois mois. *habiter*
9. Vous _____ partir. *venir de*
10. Elle _____ téléphoner. *venir de*

THE CONVERSATIONAL PAST TENSE (*PASSÉ COMPOSÉ*) OF VERBS CONJUGATED WITH *AVOIR*

The *Passé Composé* of *-er* Verbs

The *passé composé* or conversational past tense of most verbs is formed by adding the present tense of the helping verb **avoir** to the past participle. The past participle of **-er** verbs is formed by adding **-é** to the infinitive stem.

Infinitive: parler
Past participle: **parlé**

j'ai parl**é**
tu as parl**é**
il, elle, on a parl**é**
nous avons parl**é**
vous avez parl**é**
ils, elles ont parl**é**

Short adverbs precede the past participle.

Elle a **bien** chanté.   *She sang well.*

But:

Elle a chanté **lentement.**   *She sang slowly.*

121. Rewrite the following sentences in the *passé composé*.

1. J'oublie ma valise.
2. Elle prépare un bon repas.
3. Nous ramassons les papiers.
4. Vous sautez de joie.
5. Elles goûtent le vin.
6. Tu portes une nouvelle robe.
7. Le petit frappe à la porte.
8. Ils appellent leurs amis.
9. Je paie l'addition.
10. Je mange vite.
11. Elle garde toujours le secret.
12. Elle achète déjà des cadeaux pour Noël.
13. Je travaille vite.
14. Le conférencier quitte la salle.
15. Il jette les ordures.
16. Tu cherches partout.
17. Je chasse le gibier.
18. Nous dînons au restaurant.
19. Vous fermez la porte.
20. Elles louent l'appartement.

The *Passé Composé* of *-ir* Verbs

The past participle of **-ir** verbs is formed by adding **-i** to the infinitive stem. Some verbs whose infinitive ends in **-ir** have regular past participles even though they are irregular in the present tense.

finir	**fini**
choisir	**choisi**
dormir	**dormi**
mentir	**menti**
servir	**servi**
accueillir	**accueilli**
cueillir	**cueilli**

122. Rewrite the following sentences in the *passé composé*.

1. Ils applaudissent le concert.
2. Je choisis un beau tapis.
3. Elle remplit la tasse de café.
4. Nous réfléchissons aux problèmes.
5. La police saisit le criminel.
6. Vous dormez bien.
7. Tu obéis aux lois.
8. Vous accomplissez déjà la tâche.

9. Les écoliers finissent leurs devoirs.
10. Les ouvriers bâtissent une maison.

The *Passé Composé* of *-re* Verbs

The past participle of **-re** verbs is formed by adding **-u** to the infinitive stem. Some **-re** verbs that are irregular in the present tense have regular past participles.

vendre	**vendu**
répondre	**répondu**
battre	**battu**
rompre	**rompu**
vaincre	**vaincu**

123. Rewrite the following sentences in the passé composé.

1. Le bûcheron fend du bois.
2. Nous entendons du bruit.
3. Ils rompent les liens.
4. Vous vainquez le problème.
5. Il bat le tapis.
6. Elle répond vite.
7. La marchande vend des légumes.
8. La glace fond.
9. Tu attends tes amis.
10. L'avocat défend son client.

Irregular Past Participles

Past Participles Ending in *-é*

être	**été**

Past Participles Ending in *-i*, *-is*, *-it*

-i
rire	**ri**
sourire	**souri**
suffire	**suffi**
suivre	**suivi**

-is
acquérir	**acquis**
conquérir	**conquis**
mettre	**mis**
prendre	**pris**
apprendre	**appris**

comprendre	**compris**
surprendre	**surpris**
reprendre	**repris**

-it

dire	**dit**
écrire	**écrit**
décrire	**décrit**
conduire	**conduit**
construire	**construit**
cuire	**cuit**
détruire	**détruit**
produire	**produit**
reconstruire	**reconstruit**
traduire	**traduit**

Past Participles Ending in *-ait*

faire	**fait**

124. Complete the following sentences with the correct form of the past participle of the indicated verb.

1. Elle a _____ à l'heure. *être*
2. Il a _____ un bon voyage. *faire*
3. Vous avez _____ en disant cela. *sourire*
4. Ces réponses ont _____. *suffire*
5. Nous avons _____ un cours de français. *suivre*
6. Ils ont _____ une collection de peintures. *acquérir*
7. J'ai _____ les livres sur l'étagère. *mettre*
8. Tu as _____ le dîner à sept heures. *prendre*
9. Nous avons _____ la leçon. *comprendre*
10. La police a _____ le voleur. *surprendre*
11. Il a _____ une Renault. *conduire*
12. L'architecte a _____ une belle maison. *construire*
13. Ils ont _____ des œufs. *cuire*
14. Les bombes ont _____ la ville. *détruire*
15. Le traducteur a _____ le roman. *traduire*
16. Elles vous ont _____ cela. *dire*
17. Vous avez _____ beaucoup de cartes postales. *écrire*
18. Il a _____ la scène. *décrire*

125. Rewrite the following sentences in the *passé composé*.

1. Elle suit un cours d'histoire.
2. L'élève apprend l'alphabet.
3. Vous écrivez vos devoirs.
4. Nous faisons des progrès.
5. Je dis la vérité.
6. Ils surprennent leurs amis.
7. Tu ris aux éclats.
8. Elle suit ce boulevard.
9. Ils construisent un pont.
10. Elle met le couvert.

Past Participles Ending in *-u*

Verbs with infinitives in **-aître, tenir** and its derivatives and **courir** and its derivatives add **-u** to the infinitive stem to form the past participle.

connaître	**connu**
reconnaître	**reconnu**
paraître	**paru**
apparaître	**apparu**
disparaître	**disparu**
tenir	**tenu**
convenir	**convenu**
courir	**couru**
secourir	**secouru**

Verbs with infinitives in **-aire** and **-oir** and some other verbs are completely irregular since their past participles are not formed on the infinitive stem.

plaire	**plu**
déplaire	**déplu**
se taire	**tu**
devoir	**dû**
décevoir	**déçu**
apercevoir	**aperçu**
concevoir	**conçu**
recevoir	**reçu**
avoir	**eu**
boire	**bu**
croire	**cru**
pouvoir	**pu**
savoir	**su**
voir	**vu**
falloir	**fallu**
valoir	**valu**
vouloir	**voulu**
lire	**lu**
élire	**élu**
vivre	**vécu**
survivre	**survécu**

Note the circumflex on the **u** of **dû**. Note the cedilla on the **ç** of past participles ending in **çu**.
See Chapter 9 for special meanings of **pouvoir, savoir** and **vouloir** in the *passé composé*.

126. Complete the following sentences with the correct form of the past participle of the indicated verb.

1. Une étoile a _____ à l'horizon. *apparaître*
2. J'ai _____ cet homme. *reconnaître*
3. Elles ont _____ deux places. *retenir*
4. Vous avez _____ vers votre ami. *courir*
5. Ce film m'a _____. *déplaire*
6. Vous avez _____ travailler dur. *devoir*

7. Elle a _____ un cadeau. *recevoir*
8. Nous avons _____ du café. *boire*
9. Elle a _____ la réponse. *avoir*
10. Tu as _____ cette histoire. *croire*
11. Elle a _____ la vérité. *savoir*
12. Nous avons _____ le faire. *pouvoir*
13. Vous avez _____ ce film. *voir*
14. Elle a _____ aller à la pêche. *vouloir*
15. Cette robe a _____ le prix. *valoir*
16. Vous avez _____ ce roman. *lire*
17. Elle a _____ au XIXe siècle. *vivre*

127. Rewrite the following sentences in the *passé composé*.

1. Je connais les LeBlanc.
2. Cette décision déplaît à ces gens.
3. Elle croit le professeur.
4. Il survit à ses parents.
5. Tu vois tes amis.
6. Elles reçoivent le prix.
7. Elle retient une chambre à l'hôtel.
8. Nous courons vite.
9. Ils maintiennent un air calme.
10. Vous apercevez quelque chose d'étrange.
11. Tu dois répondre.
12. Cet homme paraît étrange.
13. Elle lit les romans de Proust.
14. Cette conférence plaît à tout le monde.
15. Il a de l'argent.
16. Vous tenez votre promesse.
17. Ils élisent un président.
18. Nous reconnaissons cette peinture.
19. Nous buvons du lait.
20. Il veut faire ce devoir.

Past Participles Ending in *-ert*

Some verbs whose infinitives end in **-rir** have past participles ending in **-ert.**

ouvrir	**ouvert**
couvrir	**couvert**
découvrir	**découvert**
offrir	**offert**
souffrir	**souffert**

128. Rewrite the following sentences in the *passé composé*.

1. Il ouvre la fenêtre.
2. Le biologiste découvre un microbe.
3. Vous souffrez d'un rhume.
4. Nous ouvrons les cadeaux.
5. La mère couvre l'enfant.

6. Il offre un cadeau à son ami.
7. Tu couvres le mur de peintures.
8. Je souffre de maux de tête.

Past Participles of Verbs Ending in *-indre*

The past participles of verbs ending in **-indre** are irregular.

craindre	**craint**
plaindre	**plaint**
atteindre	**atteint**
éteindre	**éteint**
peindre	**peint**
joindre	**joint**

129. Rewrite the following sentences in the *passé composé*.

1. Il atteint son but.
2. Elle craint cet homme.
3. Nous rejoignons nos amis.
4. Vous éteignez la lumière.
5. L'artiste peint un portrait.
6. Nous plaignons cet homme.
7. Vous craignez les rues désertes.
8. Nous joignons nos amis par téléphone.

Agreement of the Past Participle with Verbs Conjugated with *avoir*

The past participle of verbs using **avoir** in the *passé composé* agree in number and in gender with a preceding direct object.

Voilà **la lettre** que j'ai **écrite**.
Voilà **les photos** que j'ai **prises**.
Voilà **l'homme** que j'ai **craint**.
Voilà **les disques** que j'ai **achetés**.

Most past participles sound alike in the masculine and feminine except for those ending in a consonant.

les hommes que j'ai **vus**
la femme que j'ai **vue**

But:

la lettre que j'ai **écrite**
le poème que j'ai **écrit**

Compare the masculine and feminine of the following past participles.

Masculine	*Feminine*
pris	**prise**
mis	**mise**
dit	**dite**

offert   **offerte**
écrit   **écrite**
craint   **crainte**

Note that there is no oral or written change for the masculine singular and plural when the past participle ends in **s.**

le disque que j'ai **pris**
les disques que j'ai **pris**

The past participle of verbs conjugated with **avoir** is invariable.

1. when it is used with an impersonal verb:

la pluie qu'**il y a eu**

2. when the past participle is followed by a complementary infinitive and it is the infinitive that agrees with the preceding direct object:

les tâches qu'elle a **dû compléter**

See also pages 211–213.

The past participle of certain intransitively used verbs accompanied by a unit of price, weight, distance, length, time, etc., is invariable.

les deux heures que j'ai **couru** (intransitive)

But:

les dangers que j'ai **courus** (transitive)

les cent kilos que j'ai **pesé**

But:

les paquets que j'ai **pesés**

130. Complete the following sentences with the correct form of the past participle of the indicated verb.

1. Voilà la place que j'ai _____ . *prendre*
2. Voilà le billet que j'ai _____ . *prendre*
3. Voilà la ville qu'il a _____ . *peindre*
4. Voilà le tableau qu'il a _____ . *peindre*
5. Voilà les dames que j'ai _____ . *craindre*
6. Voilà les hommes que j'ai _____ . *craindre*
7. Voilà les peines que j'ai _____ . *endurer*
8. Voilà les maux que j'ai _____ . *endurer*
9. Voilà la photo que j'ai _____ . *voir*
10. Voilà le film que j'ai _____ . *voir*

131. Rewrite the following sentences according to the model.

J'ai écrit la lettre.
Quelle lettre avez-vous écrite?

1. J'ai appris la leçon.
2. J'ai compris le livre.
3. J'ai mis les disques.
4. J'ai couvert les murs.

5. J'ai dit la phrase.
6. J'ai conduit cette auto.
7. J'ai pris ces blouses.
8. J'ai ouvert les fenêtres.
9. J'ai lu le poème.
10. J'ai craint le criminel.
11. J'ai vu ces pièces.
12. J'ai cru l'histoire.

132. Add the correct ending to the past participle if necessary.

1. Les pommes que j'ai pesé _____ sont dans le panier.
2. Les deux cents dollars que ces robes m'ont coûté _____ .
3. Les deux cents kilos que j'ai pesé _____ .
4. Les livres qu'elle n'a pas pu _____ terminer.
5. Les vingt ans que j'ai fait _____ ce travail.
6. Les larmes que cette situation m'a coûté _____ .

THE *PASSÉ COMPOSÉ* OF VERBS CONJUGATED WITH *ÊTRE*

The following verbs use **être** as the helping verb in the *passé composé*. Study the following past participles.

aller	**allé**	*to go*
venir	**venu**	*to come*
entrer	**entré**	*to enter*
sortir	**sorti**	*to leave, to go out*
arriver	**arrivé**	*to arrive*
partir	**parti**	*to leave*
monter	**monté**	*to go up*
descendre	**descendu**	*to go down*
naître	**né**	*to be born*
mourir	**mort**	*to die*
revenir	**revenu**	*to come back*
retourner	**retourné**	*to go back*
tomber	**tombé**	*to fall*
rester	**resté**	*to stay*
rentrer	**rentré**	*to return*
devenir	**devenu**	*to become*

It is helpful to think of the first 12 of these verbs as opposite pairs.

With verbs conjugated with **être,** the past participle agrees in number and in gender with the subject.

aller

je suis **allé(e)**	nous sommes **allé(e)s**
tu es **allé(e)**	vous êtes **allé(e)(s)(es)**
il, on est **allé**	ils sont **allés**
elle est **allée**	elles sont **allées**

133. Complete the following sentences with the correct form of the *passé composé* of the indicated verb.

    1. Elle _____ au théâtre. *aller*
    2. Il _____ dans la salle. *entrer*
    3. Elles _____ à l'heure. *arriver*
    4. Ils _____ dans le taxi. *monter*
    5. Elle _____ à huit heures du soir. *naître*
    6. Il _____ chez lui. *retourner*
    7. Elles _____ sur le trottoir. *tomber*
    8. Ils _____ chez eux. *rester*
    9. Elle _____ à minuit. *rentrer*
    10. Il _____ ce soir. *sortir*
    11. Elles _____ de bonne heure. *partir*
    12. Ils _____ nous voir. *venir*
    13. Elle _____ du train. *descendre*
    14. Il _____ tard hier. *revenir*
    15. Elles _____ riches. *devenir*
    16. Ils _____ dans l'accident. *mourir*

134. Rewrite the following sentences in the *passé composé*.

    1. Elle monte dans le wagon.
    2. Nous (f.) arrivons de bonne heure.
    3. Monsieur, vous rentrez tard.
    4. Pierre et Georges, vous devenez ennuyeux.
    5. Marie et Lucille, vous revenez trop tard.
    6. Nous (m.) restons chez nous.
    7. Vous (f. sing). mourez de faim.
    8. Nous (f.) partons de bonne heure.
    9. Je (f.) rentre chez moi.
    10. Tu (m.) descends dans la rue.
    11. Vous (f. pl.) entrez dans l'atelier.
    12. Les bonnes viennent à l'heure.
    13. Les enfants tombent dans l'escalier.
    14. Je (m.) vais au bureau.
    15. Tu (f.) vas au restaurant.
    16. Il part à l'heure.

Monter, descendre, sortir with *être* and *avoir* in the *Passé Composé*

When **monter, descendre** and **sortir** have direct objects, they use **avoir** rather than **être** as the auxiliary verb in the *passé composé*.

Elle est montée.	*She went up.*
Elle a monté l'escalier.	*She went up the stairs.*
Elle est descendue.	*She came down.*
Elle a descendu les valises.	*She brought the suitcases down.*
Elle est sortie.	*She went out.*
Elle a sorti de l'argent.	*She got out some money.*

135. Rewrite the following sentences in the *passé composé*.

1. Elle monte vite.
2. Elle monte l'escalier.
3. Nous (f.) descendons du train.
4. Nous descendons la valise.
5. Elles sortent samedi.
6. Elles sortent l'argenterie du tiroir.
7. Il monte dans sa chambre.
8. Ils descendent les valises.
9. Nous sortons de l'argent.
10. Elles descendent de l'autobus.

The *Passé Composé* of Reflexive Verbs

All reflexive verbs are conjugated with **être** in the *passé composé*.

se lever

je me suis levé(e)	nous nous sommes levé(e)s
tu t'es levé(e)	vous vous êtes levé(e)(s)(es)
il, on s'est levé	ils se sont levés
elle s'est levée	elles se sont levées

The past participle of **s'asseoir** is **assis**.

Agreement of the Past Participle with Reflexive Pronouns

The past participle of a reflexive verb agrees in number and in gender with the reflexive pronoun when it is used as a direct object.

Elle s'est lavée.   *She washed herself.*

Se is the direct object and therefore, the past participle agrees.

When the direct object is not the reflexive pronoun, there is no agreement.

Elle s'est lavé les mains.   *She washed her hands.*

Les mains is the direct object and therefore, there is no agreement. But if **les mains** is replaced by the object pronoun **les,** the participle will agree with the preceding direct object **les.**

Elle se **les** est **lavées.**   *She washed them.*

136. Complete the following sentences with the correct form of the *passé composé* of the indicated verb.

1. Elle _____ hier.   *se dépêcher*
2. Il _____ ce matin.   *se raser*
3. Elles _____ hier.   *s'ennuyer*
4. Ils _____ du voyage.   *se souvenir*
5. Je (m.) _____ immédiatement.   *s'asseoir*
6. Je (f.) _____ hier soir.   *se tromper*

7. Tu (m.) _____ à sept heures. *se réveiller*
8. Tu (f.) _____ les mains. *se laver*
9. Vous (m. pl.) _____ dans le parc. *s'amuser*
10. Vous (f. pl.) _____ en bleu. *s'habiller*
11. Nous (m. pl.) _____ hier soir. *se reposer*
12. Nous (f. pl.) _____ tout de suite. *s'endormir*

137. Rewrite the following sentences in the *passé composé*.

1. Il se débrouille bien.
2. Elle se lève de bonne heure.
3. Nous (f.) nous amusons bien.
4. Hélène et Marie, vous vous trompez.
5. Elles se retrouvent devant le musée.
6. Elle se lave les mains.
7. Ils se brossent les dents.
8. Je (f.) m'assieds devant le feu.
9. Elles se couchent dans le lit.
10. Tu (m.) te réveilles à huit heures.
11. Vous (f. sing.) vous peignez.
12. Je (m.) me trompe.
13. Nous (m.) nous dépêchons.
14. Pierre et Jean, vous vous rasez.

Uses of the *Passé Composé*

Past Action

The *passé composé* is used to express an action that was completed at a definite time in the past. Some common adverbial expressions that are used with the *passé composé* are:

hier	*yesterday*
avant-hier	*the day before yesterday*
hier soir	*last night*
l'autre jour	*the other day*
la semaine dernière (passée)	*last week*
l'année passée (dernière)	*last year*

138. Complete the following sentences with the appropriate form of the *passé composé* of the indicated verb.

1. Hier, nous _____ au cinéma. *aller*
2. On _____ la cathédrale au neuvième siècle. *bâtir*
3. Elle _____ son ami l'autre jour. *voir*
4. Ils _____ me voir hier soir. *venir*
5. Vous _____ en Europe l'année dernière. *voyager*
6. Elle _____ de bonne heure hier soir. *se coucher*
7. Nous _____ la maison la semaine dernière. *louer*
8. Christophe Colomb _____ les Antilles. *découvrir*
9. Elle _____ cela avant-hier. *dire*
10. Il _____ ce matin. *se raser*

Differences between the *Passé Composé* and the Imperfect Tense

Specific Action versus Habitual or Continuing Action

You have already learned the basic uses of the imperfect tense and the *passé composé*. The imperfect tense is used to describe continuing action, habitual action or past action of long duration. The *passé composé* is used to express an action which definitely began and was completed in the past. Even though the action may have taken place in the past for an extended period of time, the *passé composé* is used if the action has been terminated.

Il **a joué** au football **hier.**
Il **jouait** au football **tous les samedis.**

Elle **a parlé une fois** au professeur.
Elle **parlait souvent** au professeur.

139. Rewrite the following, changing **l'autre jour** to **bien des fois.** Make all necessary changes.

1. Elle est venue me voir l'autre jour.
2. Tu l'as vu l'autre jour.
3. Pierre a dit cela l'autre jour.
4. Nous avons reçu des lettres l'autre jour.
5. Vous l'avez appelé l'autre jour.

140. Rewrite the following, changing **tous les ans** to **l'année passée.**

1. Elle venait me voir tous les ans.
2. J'allais à Paris tous les ans.
3. Je voyais Marie tous les ans.
4. Nous voyagions en Europe tous les ans.
5. Elle jouait ce rôle tous les ans.

141. Rewrite the following in either the *passé composé* or the imperfect tense according to the indicated time expression.

1. Ils ont regardé la télévision hier soir.
   _____ chaque soir.

2. En ce temps-là, il jouait au tennis.
   L'autre jour _____ .

3. Elle répétait cette phrase bien des fois.
   _____ une fois.

4. Pierre est venu ici hier.
   _____ tous les dimanches.

5. Nous allions à ce restaurant tous les samedis.
   _____ samedi dernier.

6. Hier soir, nous avons discuté politique.
   Souvent _____ .

7. Ta mère était toujours malade.
   _____ pendant deux ans.

8. Pendant son dernier voyage, elle a payé avec des chèques de voyage.
   Pendant tous ses voyages, _____ .

9. Nous y sommes allés l'année dernière.
_____ de temps en temps.

10. D'habitude, il dormait jusqu'à sept heures.
Ce matin, _____ .

142. Answer the following according to the model. Use the *passé composé* or the imperfect tense.

Lire le journal?   Oui, hier
Oui, j'ai lu le journal *hier*.

1. Recevoir la carte?   *Oui, hier*
2. Habiter à New York?   *Oui, l'année dernière*
3. Aller au concert?   *Oui, tous les dimanches*
4. Travailler beaucoup?   *Oui, en ce temps-là*
5. Dormir beaucoup?   *Oui, hier soir*
6. Conduire cette auto?   *Oui, toujours*
7. Nager beaucoup?   *Oui, l'été dernier*
8. Aller à la plage?   *Oui, la semaine dernière*

Specific Action versus Ongoing Action

The imperfect tense is used to describe what was taking place and continuing to take place in the past when something else happened. The latter action is expressed in the *passé composé*. If the actions occurred simultaneously, the two actions are in the same tense.

Quand je suis arrivé, ils dansaient.
When I arrived, they were dancing.
Elle mangeait quand le téléphone a sonné.
She was eating when the telephone rang.
Pendant que nous dormions, il a neigé.
While we were sleeping, it snowed.

Paul est venu et Marie est partie.
Paul came and Mary left.
Les enfants jouaient pendant que leurs parents les regardaient.
The children were playing while their parents were watching them.

Sometimes the tense will change, depending upon whether the speaker wishes to portray the event as a background condition or something that happened.

Un homme a vendu la peinture et l'autre l'a achetée.
One man sold the painting and the other bought it.
(Here the speaker is merely reporting what took place.)

Un homme vendait la peinture et l'autre l'achetait.
One man was selling the painting and the other was buying it.
(Here the speaker wishes to describe the background, what was taking place.)

J'ai eu peur quand le voleur est entré dans la maison.
I became afraid when the thief entered the house.
(change in state of mind)
J'avais peur quand le voleur est entré dans la maison.
I was afraid when the thief entered the house.
(description of state of mind)

143. Complete the following sentences with the appropriate form of either the *passé composé* or the imperfect tense of the indicated verbs to show what the people were doing when something else happened.

    1. Je _____ quand elle _____ à la porte. *lire, frapper*
    2. Elle _____ une promenade quand elle _____ un billet de mille francs sur le trottoir. *faire, découvrir*
    3. Elles _____ quand tu _____. *manger, téléphoner*
    4. Nous _____ sa connaissance quand nous _____ en Europe. *faire, être*
    5. Marie _____ avec sa mère quand je _____. *parler, entrer*
    6. Je vous _____ quand vous _____ du théâtre. *voir, sortir*
    7. Pendant qu'il _____ son déjeuner, il _____ la mauvaise nouvelle à la radio. *prendre, entendre*
    8. Je _____ quand le téléphone _____. *dormir, sonner*
    9. Elles _____ des élections quand il _____ les résultats. *discuter, annoncer*
    10. Pendant que nous _____ en vacances, des cambrioleurs _____ dans notre maison. *être, entrer*

144. Complete the following sentences as if you were telling someone what happened.

    1. Un homme _____ et un autre _____ du vin. *manger, boire*
    2. La police _____ et le voleur _____. *entrer, partir*
    3. Pierre _____ les valises et Marie _____ les billets. *faire, prendre*
    4. Le bébé _____ et le chien _____. *pleurer, aboyer*
    5. Ma mère _____ le repas pendant que je (j') _____ le couvert. *préparer, mettre*

145. Rewrite the sentences of the previous exercise as if you were describing to someone what was happening.

Events versus Background

    The imperfect tense is used to describe the background conditions to an event in the *passé composé*. In other words, the imperfect tense relates the conditions, state of mind or actions that were going on and the *passé composé* relates what happened or what happened next.

Event	*Background or Conditions*
J'ai fait une promenade hier.	**Il faisait beau.**
	J'étais de bonne humeur.
J'ai mangé très vite	**parce que j'avais très faim.**

146. Tell why the following people did certain things. Follow the model.

Roland / aller à la plage / faire beau
Roland est allé à la plage parce qu'il faisait beau.

    1. Pierre / aller chez le médecin / être malade
    2. Monsieur et Madame Dupont / aller en vacances / avoir besoin de repos
    3. Nicole / manger / avoir faim
    4. Nous / se dépêcher / être en retard
    5. Vous / mettre un imperméable / pleuvoir
    6. Tu / nager / vouloir être en forme

147. Rewrite the following story in the past.

C'est le sept juillet. Il est quatre heures de l'après-midi. Il fait très chaud. Je fais des courses. Pendant que je me promène le long du boulevard, je rencontre mon amie. Nous décidons d'aller chez le bijoutier. Pendant que nous regardons les bracelets et les colliers, un homme entre dans le magasin. Il a à peu près 25 ans. Il a les cheveux noirs. Il porte un pantalon noir, une chemise verte et un masque au visage. Il tire un révolver et demande de l'argent au caissier. Le caissier a peur et il lui donne de l'argent. Mais heureusement, un autre employé voit le vol et appelle la police. La police arrive et arrête le voleur.

Review

148. Rewrite the following sentences in the *passé composé*.

1. Tu parles beaucoup.
2. Elles dorment bien.
3. Ils répondent à la question.
4. Elles suivent les instructions.
5. Elle descend l'escalier.
6. Nous (f.) nous levons de bonne heure.
7. Nous (m.) allons au musée.
8. Elle monte dans le wagon.
9. Nous prenons les billets.
10. Il fait la leçon.
11. Elles montent les bagages.
12. Je reconnais cet homme.
13. Il revient tout de suite.
14. Elles écrivent les devoirs.
15. Elles se promènent dans le parc.
16. Cette peinture me plaît.
17. Vous recevez la lettre.
18. Tu lis le roman.
19. Ils vivent bien ici.
20. Vous peignez ce paysage.
21. Elle ouvre la fenêtre.
22. Voilà les photos que je vous offre.
23. Voilà les pièces que je lis.
24. Elles se débrouillent bien.

149. Answer the questions according to the model.

Te rases-tu aujourd'hui?
Non, mais je me suis rasé hier.

1. Apprends-tu cette leçon aujourd'hui?
2. Veut-il aller au cinéma aujourd'hui?
3. La comprenez-vous aujourd'hui?
4. Vous souvenez-vous de la réponse aujourd'hui?
5. Vaut-il le prix aujourd'hui?
6. Rit-elle aujourd'hui?
7. Souffrez-vous d'un rhume aujourd'hui?
8. Disons-nous la vérité aujourd'hui?
9. Revient-elle à huit heures aujourd'hui?

    10. Mettez-vous un imperméable aujourd'hui?
    11. Reste-t-il jusqu'à dix heures aujourd'hui?
    12. Vois-tu Pierre aujourd'hui?

150. Complete the following sentences with the correct form of the *passé composé* or imperfect
tense of the indicated verb.

    1. Chaque jour, Pierre _____ à la Faculté de Médecine où il _____ aux cours
    d'anatomie et où il _____ ses amis. *aller, assister, voir*
    2. Samedi dernier, nous _____ de bonne heure. Nous _____ et ensuite, nous
    _____ le reste de la journée à nous amuser. *se lever, travailler, passer*
    3. D'habitude, Monsieur Leroi _____ au bureau en métro. Il _____ huit
    heures par jour et ensuite, il _____ à la maison pour revoir sa famille. *aller,
    travailler, rentrer*
    4. Hier soir, ils _____ aux cartes, ils _____ la télévision, ils _____ des
    disques et ensuite, ils _____ . *jouer, regarder, écouter, se coucher*
    5. Bien des fois, nous _____ notre temps pour aller à l'école et nous _____ en
    route. *prendre, s'amuser*
    6. L'année passée, nous _____ un voyage en Europe où nous _____ des
    musées et des monuments et où nous _____ . *faire, voir, s'amuser*

151. Complete the following paragraph, putting the verbs in the imperfect or *passé composé.*

    Il est sept heures du matin. Je vais dans les montagnes parce que je veux faire du ski. Il fait
froid et il fait du vent mais le soleil brille. Je porte un beau costume de ski. J'arrive au chalet.
J'achète mon billet pour les remonte-pentes et je fais la queue pour monter la montagne. Je
remarque qu'il y a beaucoup de monde sur les pistes de ski. Je monte. Je descends. Je suis très
content(e). Je sais bien faire du ski. Mais malheureusement, à la quatrième descente, je tombe.
Je me casse la jambe. On m'emmène à l'hôpital où on met ma jambe dans du plâtre. La journée
qui commence bien finit mal.

THE LITERARY PAST TENSE (*PASSÉ SIMPLE*)

    The *passé simple* or literary past tense is a past tense that designates a completed action in the
past with no relation to the present tense. The *passé simple* is used in literary contexts whereas the
passé composé is used in conversation.

The *Passé Simple* of *-er* Verbs

    The *passé simple* of regular **-er** verbs is formed by dropping the **-er** ending from the infinitive
and adding the endings **-ai, -as, -a, -âmes, -âtes, -èrent.** Note that some **-er** verbs that are irregular
in the present tense are regular in the *passé simple.*

parler	**aller**
je parl**ai**	j'all**ai**
tu parl**as**	tu all**as**
il, elle, on parl**a**	il, elle, on all**a**
nous parl**âmes**	nous all**âmes**
vous parl**âtes**	vous all**âtes**
ils, elles parl**èrent**	ils, elles all**èrent**

Remember that **-cer** verbs add a cedilla to the **c** before the vowels **a** or **o** and that **-ger** verbs add **e** before the vowels **a** or **o**.

commencer	**il commença**
manger	**il mangea**

152. Rewrite the following sentences in the *passé simple*.

1. On a publié le livre en 1973.
2. On a brûlé Jeanne d'Arc en 1431 à Rouen.
3. Tu as acheté ce disque.
4. Tu as appelé ton père.
5. J'ai emmené mes amis avec moi.
6. J'ai envoyé le télégramme.
7. Nous sommes allés à Paris.
8. Nous avons trouvé ce livre.
9. Vous avez célébré la fête.
10. Vous êtes arrivées à l'heure.
11. Les Américains ont débarqué en Normandie en 1944.
12. Ils ont commencé la construction de la cathédrale en 1150.

153. Rewrite the following sentences in the *passé composé*.

1. Il chercha son père.
2. Nous donnâmes de l'argent à nos amis.
3. Elles méditèrent sur l'avenir.
4. Je frappai à la porte.
5. Vous devinâtes les résultats.
6. Tu montas vite.
7. Nous comptâmes notre argent.
8. Ils marchèrent dans les rues désertes.
9. Je retournai chez moi.
10. Elle alla à l'église.

The *Passé Simple* of *-ir* and *-re* Verbs

To form the *passé simple* of **-ir** and **-re** verbs, the endings **-is, -is, -it, -îmes, -îtes, -irent** are added to the infinitive stem.

finir	attendre
je fin**is**	j'attend**is**
tu fin**is**	tu attend**is**
il, elle, on fin**it**	il, elle, on attend**it**
nous fin**îmes**	nous attend**îmes**
vous fin**îtes**	vous attend**îtes**
ils, elles fin**irent**	ils, elles attend**irent**

Note that the singular forms of the present tense and the *passé simple* are identical for regular **-ir** verbs.

154. Complete the following sentences with the correct form of the *passé simple* of the indicated verb.

1. Christophe Colomb _____ le Nouveau Monde.   *découvrir*
2. Elle _____ sa mère.   *attendre*
3. Tu _____ la salle.   *embellir*
4. Tu _____ tes amis.   *défendre*

5. J'_____ les acteurs. *applaudir*
6. Je _____ tout de suite. *partir*
7. Nous _____ le fil. *perdre*
8. Nous _____ la lecture. *finir*
9. Vous _____ à l'examen. *réussir*
10. Vous _____ des fleurs. *vendre*
11. Ils _____ des chemises. *choisir*
12. Elles _____ aux questions. *répondre*

155. Rewrite the following sentences in the *passé composé*.

1. Ils découvrirent la vérité.
2. Nous réfléchîmes aux problèmes.
3. Il agrandit le palais.
4. Vous répandîtes la nouvelle.
5. Je vendis des timbres.
6. Tu rendis tes devoirs.
7. Elles finirent leurs devoirs.
8. Vous descendîtes le boulevard.

Irregular Verbs Building the *Passé Simple* upon the Past Participle

For most irregular verbs, the stem for the *passé simple* is the past participle. The endings **-s, -s, -t, -ˆmes, -ˆtes, -rent** are added to this stem.

Verbs with Past Participles Ending in *-i*

The *passé simple* of many irregular verbs whose infinitive ends in **-ir** or **-re** is formed by adding the endings **-s, -s, -t, -ˆmes, -ˆtes, -rent** to the past participle. Note that they are like **finir** in the *passé simple*.

Infinitive	Past participle	Passé simple
dormir	dormi	**je dormis, nous dormîmes**
mentir	menti	**je mentis, nous mentîmes**
partir	parti	**je partis, nous partîmes**
sentir	senti	**je sentis, nous sentîmes**
servir	servi	**je servis, nous servîmes**
sortir	sorti	**je sortis, nous sortîmes**
rire	ri	**je ris, nous rîmes**
sourire	souri	**je souris, nous sourîmes**
suffire	suffi	**je suffis, nous suffîmes**
suivre	suivi	**je suivis, nous suivîmes**

Verbs with Past Participles Ending in *-i* Plus a Consonant

The final consonant of the past participle of these verbs is replaced by the endings **-s, -s, -t, -ˆmes, -ˆtes, -rent.**

Infinitive	Past participle	Passé simple
acquérir	acquis	**j'acquis, nous acquîmes**
dire	dit	**je dis, nous dîmes**
mettre	mis	**je mis, nous mîmes**
prendre (and its derivatives)	pris	**je pris, nous prîmes**

156. Rewrite the following sentences in the *passé simple*.

1. Elle a suivi la route.
2. Tu es parti.
3. Je suis sortie.
4. Nous avons menti.
5. Vous avez dormi huit heures.
6. Ils ont ri aux éclats.
7. Elle a acquis les peintures.
8. J'ai mis le couvert.
9. Tu as dit la vérité.
10. Nous avons pris le déjeuner.
11. Vous avez appris la vérité.
12. Ils ont compris la situation.

157. Rewrite the following sentences in the *passé composé*.

1. Nous sortîmes ce soir-là.
2. Elle suivit la route pour Dijon.
3. Elles prirent les livres.
4. Vous mîtes votre manteau.
5. Tu servis un bon repas.
6. Je souris en entrant.

Verbs with Past Participles Ending in -*u*

pouvoir

je **pus**	nous **pûmes**
tu **pus**	vous **pûtes**
il, elle, on **put**	ils, elles **purent**

avoir

j'**eus**	nous **eûmes**
tu **eus**	vous **eûtes**
il, elle, on **eut**	ils, elles **eurent**

Pouvoir and **avoir** can be used as a pattern for the following verbs.

Infinitive	Past participle	Passé simple
avoir	eu	j'eus, nous eûmes
boire	bu	je bus, nous bûmes
connaître	connu	je connus, nous connûmes
courir	couru	je courus, nous courûmes
croire	cru	je crus, nous crûmes
devoir	dû	je dus, nous dûmes
lire	lu	je lus, nous lûmes
paraître	paru	je parus, nous parûmes
plaire	plu	je plus, nous plûmes
pouvoir	pu	je pus, nous pûmes
recevoir	reçu	je reçus, nous reçûmes
savoir	su	je sus, nous sûmes
se taire	tu	je me tus, nous nous tûmes
valoir	valu	je valus, nous valûmes
vivre	vécu	je vécus, nous vécûmes
vouloir	voulu	je voulus, nous voulûmes

158. Rewrite the following sentences in the *passé simple*.

1. Elle a bu trop de vin.
2. Il a vite couru.
3. Tu as voulu venir.
4. Tu as pu le faire.
5. J'ai cru l'histoire.
6. J'ai reconnu cet homme.
7. Nous avons lu *les Misérables*.
8. Nous avons reçu la lettre.
9. Vous avez dû travailler.
10. Vous avez eu des difficultés.
11. Les étoiles ont apparu à l'horizon.
12. Ils ont vécu à Londres.

159. Complete the following sentences with the correct form of the *passé simple* of the indicated verb.

1. Nous _____ trop de café. *boire*
2. Elles nous _____ . *reconnaître*
3. Tu _____ la carte. *recevoir*
4. Je _____ à New York. *vivre*
5. Vous _____ l'histoire. *lire*
6. Ils _____ venir. *pouvoir*
7. Elle _____ à tout le monde. *plaire*
8. Nous _____ le professeur. *croire*

Irregular Verbs not Building the *Passé Simple* upon the Past Participle

Some verbs add the endings **-s, -s, -t, -̂mes, -̂tes, -rent** to an irregular stem. Note that all contain the vowel **i** except **mourir, être, venir** and **tenir.**

Infinitive	Past participle	Passé simple
battre	battu	**je battis, nous battîmes**
rompre	rompu	**je rompis, nous rompîmes**
offrir	offert	**j'offris, nous offrîmes**
ouvrir	ouvert	**j'ouvris, nous ouvrîmes**
couvrir	couvert	**je couvris, nous couvrîmes**
souffrir	souffert	**je souffris, nous souffrîmes**
vaincre	vaincu	**je vainquis, nous vainquîmes**
écrire	écrit	**j'écrivis, nous écrivîmes**
conduire	conduit	**je conduisis, nous conduisîmes**
traduire	traduit	**je traduisis, nous traduisîmes**
naître	né	**je naquis, nous naquîmes**
voir	vu	**je vis, nous vîmes**
craindre	craint	**je craignis, nous craignîmes**
joindre	joint	**je joignis, nous joignîmes**
peindre	peint	**je peignis, nous peignîmes**
faire	fait	**je fis, nous fîmes**
mourir	mort	**je mourus, nous mourûmes**

être	été	**je fus, nous fûmes**
tenir	tenu	**je tins, nous tînmes**
venir	venu	**je vins, nous vînmes**

160. Complete the following sentences with the correct form of the *passé simple* of the indicated verb.

   1. Elle _____ les liens. *rompre*
   2. Nous _____ le tapis. *battre*
   3. Vous _____ du vin. *offrir*
   4. Il _____ à la gare. *conduire*
   5. Ils _____ le roman. *traduire*
   6. Tu _____ tes amis. *convaincre*
   7. Nous _____ une lettre. *écrire*
   8. Victor Hugo _____ en 1802. *naître*
   9. Vous _____ vos copains. *voir*
 10. L'artiste _____ le portrait. *peindre*
 11. Vous _____ l'examen final. *craindre*
 12. Nous _____ nos amis. *rejoindre*
 13. Il _____ de son mieux. *faire*
 14. Nous _____ du tennis. *faire*
 15. Je _____ content. *être*
 16. Ils _____ malades. *être*
 17. Albert Camus _____ dans un accident. *mourir*
 18. Il _____ de Paris. *venir*
 19. Nous _____ une chambre à l'hôtel. *retenir*
 20. Elles _____ ce soir. *revenir*

161. Rewrite the following sentences in the *passé composé*.

   1. Il traduisit le livre.
   2. Ils écrivirent des romans.
   3. Il fut roi de France.
   4. Je vins te voir.
   5. Elles rejoignirent leurs amis.
   6. Ils vinrent de Paris.
   7. Nous ouvrîmes la porte.
   8. Vous souffrîtes beaucoup.
   9. Elle naquit à Paris.
 10. Nous vîmes le film.

Review

162. What did the following people do? Rewrite the following sentences in the *passé composé*.

   1. Samuel de Champlain fonda Québec en 1608.
   2. Pierre et Marie Curie découvrirent le radium.
   3. Edgar Degas peignit des portraits et des scènes de danse.
   4. Napoléon vainquit l'ennemi dans beaucoup de batailles.
   5. Albert Camus mourut dans un accident de voiture.
   6. Le peuple de Paris détruisit la Bastille.
   7. Charles de Gaulle fut président de la Cinquième République.

8. Le Corbusier fit bâtir beaucoup de bâtiments célèbres.
9. Jean Anouilh écrivit *Antigone*.
10. Louis XIV devint roi de France en 1643.

THE FUTURE

Aller with an Infinitive

The immediate future can be expressed by using the verb **aller** with an infinitive. This is the equivalent of the English *to be going to*.

> **Je vais travailler ici.**
> *I am going to work here.*
> **Nous allons aller au cinéma.**
> *We are going to go to the movies.*
> **Ils vont venir à sept heures.**
> *They are going to come at seven o'clock.*

163. Complete the following sentences with the appropriate form of the verb **aller.**

1. Je _____ partir demain.
2. Nous _____ faire du ski.
3. Qui _____ mettre le couvert?
4. Vous _____ nager dans la mer.
5. Elles _____ faire le repas.
6. Tu _____ voyager en avion.

164. Rewrite the following sentences in the future, using **aller** with the infinitive.

1. Nous faisons les valises.
2. Je regarde la télévision.
3. Elle parle au professeur.
4. Vous sortez de bonne heure.
5. Ils habitent à New York.
6. Tu viens tout de suite.
7. Nous buvons du café.
8. Vous lisez le journal.
9. Il sait les résultats.
10. Vous finissez le travail.

Regular Forms of the Future Tense

The future tense of most verbs is formed by adding **-ai, -as, -a, -ons, -ez, -ont** to the infinitive. The final **-e** of **-re** verbs is dropped before adding the future endings. The future tense is used as in English to express an event or describe a condition that will take place in the future.

parler	finir	attendre
je parler**ai**	je finir**ai**	j'attendr**ai**
tu parler**as**	tu finir**as**	tu attendr**as**
il, elle, on parler**a**	il, elle, on finir**a**	il, elle, on attendr**a**
nous parler**ons**	nous finir**ons**	nous attendr**ons**
vous parler**ez**	vous finir**ez**	vous attendr**ez**
ils, elles parler**ont**	ils, elles finir**ont**	ils, elles attendr**ont**

Note that the second and third person singular forms sound alike; the first person singular and the second person plural sound alike, and the first and third person plurals sound alike. The forms are all spelled differently, however.

For **-er** verbs, if the stem ends in two pronounced consonants, the **e** is pronounced.

> je parlerai

If the stem ends in one pronounced consonant, the **e** is not pronounced.

> je dînerai

165. Complete the following sentences with the correct form of the future tense of the indicated verb.

1. Il _____ du problème avec nous. *discuter*
2. Elle _____ à l'heure. *finir*
3. Tu _____ les livres. *vendre*
4. Tu _____ de cela plus tard. *parler*
5. Je _____ du bifteck ce soir. *manger*
6. Je _____ la tasse de café. *remplir*
7. Vous _____ aux lois. *obéir*
8. Vous _____ à la question demain. *répondre*
9. Nous _____ tous par hélicoptère dans cinquante ans. *voyager*
10. Nous _____ les instructions. *suivre*
11. Ils _____ de bonne heure. *se réveiller*
12. Elles _____ leurs devoirs demain. *rendre*

166. Rewrite the following sentences in the future tense.

1. Nous allons regarder la télévision.
2. Vous allez étudier davantage.
3. Je vais écrire des cartes postales.
4. Il va plaire à cette fille.
5. Elles vont dormir huit heures.
6. L'artiste va peindre un portrait.
7. Tu vas conduire prudemment.
8. Elle va dire la vérité.
9. Elles vont rejoindre leurs amis.
10. Vous allez suivre les instructions.
11. Je vais prendre le déjeuner à midi.
12. Elle va se coucher à dix heures.

Verbs Using the Third Person Singular Form of the Present Tense as the Future Stem

Some verbs use the third person singular form of the present tense rather than the infinitive as the future stem.

Verbs ending in *-yer*

Infinitive	Base	Future
employer	il emploie	**j'emploierai, nous emploierons**
ennuyer	il ennuie	**j'ennuierai, nous ennuierons**
essayer	il essaie	**j'essaierai, nous essaierons**
essuyer	il essuie	**j'essuierai, nous essuierons**
nettoyer	il nettoie	**je nettoierai, nous nettoierons**
payer	il paie	**je paierai, nous paierons**

Verbs with -e- in the infinitive

Infinitive	Base	Future
acheter	il achète	**j'achèterai, nous achèterons**
lever	il lève	**je lèverai, nous lèverons**
mener	il mène	**je mènerai, nous mènerons**
peser	il pèse	**je pèserai, nous pèserons**
appeler	il appelle	**j'appellerai, nous appellerons**
jeter	il jette	**je jetterai, nous jetterons**

167. Rewrite the following sentences in the future tense.

1. Elle nettoie sa chambre.
2. Il paie ses dettes.
3. Elle essaie de partir.
4. Il ennuie ses amis.
5. On achète des bonbons.
6. Elle mène une vie tranquille.
7. Elle lève le rideau.
8. Il appelle ses amis.
9. Elle jette la lettre dans la corbeille.

168. Complete the following sentences with the correct form of the future tense of the indicated verb.

1. Nous _____ la salle. *nettoyer*
2. Vous _____ vos amis au téléphone. *appeler*
3. Ils _____ les enfants au cinéma. *emmener*
4. Je _____ les fruits. *peser*
5. Tu _____ la tache. *enlever*
6. Elle _____ cette viande. *jeter*
7. Il _____ du pain. *acheter*
8. Nous _____ de faire ce travail. *essayer*

Verbs with Irregular Future Stems

Some verbs have completely irregular future stems to which the regular future endings are added.

Infinitive	Future
cueillir	**je cueillerai, nous cueillerons**
s'asseoir	**je m'assiérai, nous nous assiérons**
aller	**j'irai, nous irons**
avoir	**j'aurai, nous aurons**
être	**je serai, nous serons**
faire	**je ferai, nous ferons**
savoir	**je saurai, nous saurons**
falloir	**il faudra**
valoir	**je vaudrai, il vaudra**
vouloir	**je voudrai, nous voudrons**

apercevoir	**j'apercevrai, nous apercevrons**
décevoir	**je décevrai, nous décevrons**
devoir	**je devrai, nous devrons**
pleuvoir	**il pleuvra**
recevoir	**je recevrai, nous recevrons**
courir	**je courrai, nous courrons**
secourir	**je secourrai, nous secourrons**
mourir	**je mourrai, nous mourrons**
pouvoir	**je pourrai, nous pourrons**
voir	**je verrai, nous verrons**
envoyer	**j'enverrai, nous enverrons**
tenir (and its derivatives)	**je tiendrai, nous tiendrons**
venir (and its derivatives)	**je viendrai, nous viendrons**

169. Complete the following sentences with the correct form of the future tense of the indicated verb.

1. Elles _____ des fleurs. *cueillir*
2. Ils _____ à table. *s'asseoir*
3. Nous _____ à Paris. *aller*
4. Il _____ besoin d'une voiture. *avoir*
5. Vous _____ à l'heure. *être*
6. Nous le _____ exprès. *faire*
7. Vous _____ le poème par cœur. *savoir*
8. Il _____ le faire. *falloir*
9. Il _____ mieux vous coucher maintenant. *valoir*
10. Nous _____ lire ce livre. *vouloir*
11. Nous _____ quelque chose d'étrange ici. *apercevoir*
12. Il _____ ses amis. *décevoir*
13. Tu _____ partir. *devoir*
14. Il _____ à verse. *pleuvoir*
15. Elle _____ une lettre demain. *recevoir*
16. Tu _____ à la maison. *courir*
17. Elles _____ les pauvres. *secourir*
18. Il _____ à l'hôpital. *mourir*
19. Elle _____ jouer ce rôle. *pouvoir*
20. Ils _____ leurs amis ce soir. *voir*
21. Tu _____ la lettre par avion. *envoyer*
22. Elles _____ avec nous. *venir*
23. Il _____ sa place. *retenir*
24. Nous _____ demain. *revenir*

170. Follow the model.

A-t-elle reçu une invitation?
Non, mais la prochaine fois, elle recevra une invitation.

1. Ont-ils pu finir à l'heure?
2. Avez-vous fait le voyage en avion?
3. Ont-ils su la vérité?
4. Êtes-vous allé voir ce film?

5. A-t-il eu confiance en son ami?
6. As-tu envoyé la lettre par avion?
7. A-t-elle vu Pierre?
8. Avez-vous retenu une chambre?
9. Est-elle venue avec André?
10. A-t-il reçu une bonne note?
11. Avez-vous secouru les pauvres?
12. A-t-il valu la peine d'y aller?
13. Avez-vous fait de votre mieux?
14. As-tu cueilli des fleurs?
15. Ont-ils été à l'heure?
16. As-tu voulu sortir?
17. A-t-il fallu le faire?
18. As-tu dû le faire?
19. Avez-vous aperçu l'incendie?
20. Vous êtes-vous assis au premier rang?
21. A-t-il plu?
22. Est-il mort hier?
23. Avez-vous couru?

Special Uses of the Future Tense

After Certain Conjunctions

The future tense is used after the following conjunctions when the verb of the main clause is in the future tense. The future time is implied in the dependent clause. Note that the present tense is often used in English.

quand
lorsque   } *when*
au moment où

dès que
aussitôt que   } *as soon as*

pendant que }
tandis que }   *while (at the same time as)*

Quand
Lorsque   } **Pierre arrivera, je le verrai.**
Au moment où

When Peter arrives, I will see him.

Je le verrai { **quand**
                   lorsqu'   } **il arrivera.**
                   au moment où }

I will see him when he arrives.

Dès que
Aussitôt que   } **vous viendrez, nous dînerons.**

As soon as you come, we will eat dinner.

Nous dînerons $\left\{ \begin{array}{l} \textbf{dès que} \\ \textbf{aussitôt que} \end{array} \right\}$ **vous viendrez.**

We will eat as soon as you come.

$\left. \begin{array}{l} \textbf{Pendant que} \\ \textbf{Tandis que} \end{array} \right\}$ **le garçon jouera de la guitare, les filles chanteront.**

While the boy plays the guitar, the girls will sing.

Le garçon jouera de la guitare $\left\{ \begin{array}{l} \textbf{pendant que} \\ \textbf{tandis que} \end{array} \right\}$ **les filles chanteront.**

The boy will play the guitar while the girls will sing.

The verb will also be in the future tense after these conjunctions with an imperative that refers to an action that will take place in the future.

Dites-moi quand il arrivera.
Tell me when he will arrive.
Parlez à Jean dès qu'il arrivera.
Speak to John when he arrives.

If the action is habitual, the present tense is used after these conjunctions.

Tous les jours je le vois quand il part pour l'école.
Every day I see him when he leaves for school.

171. Complete the following sentences with the correct form of the future tense of the indicated verb.

1. Quand il _____ , nous _____ . *arriver, manger*
2. Lorsque je _____ Paul, je lui _____ le livre. *voir, donner*
3. Dès qu'il _____ le travail, je le _____ . *finir, payer*
4. Aussitôt que nous _____ , nous _____ . *terminer, sortir*
5. Tandis que l'enfant _____ , je _____ le journal. *dormir, lire*
6. Pendant que les garçons _____ la cuisine, les filles _____ le couvert. *faire, mettre*
7. Téléphonez-moi quand vous _____ venir. *pouvoir*
8. Payez quand vous _____ . *vouloir*
9. Écrivez-moi une carte quand vous _____ en Europe. *voyager*
10. Nous _____ au moment où nos amis _____ . *partir, arriver*

After *penser que, savoir que, espérer que, ne pas savoir si* and in Indirect Discourse

The present or future tense can be used after **penser que, savoir que, espérer que, ne pas savoir si** and in indirect discourse when the main clause is in the present.

Je pense qu'il viendra.
Je pense qu'il vient.

Je sais qu'il viendra.
Je sais qu'il vient.

J'espère qu'il viendra.
J'espère qu'il vient.

Je ne sais s'il viendra.
Je ne sais s'il vient.

The future tense is also used in indirect discourse to express a future action when the main clause is in the present tense.

Il dit qu'il viendra.
He says he will come.

Il me demande si nous irons au théâtre.
He asks me whether we will go to the theater.

172. Rewrite the following sentences, putting the second verb in the future tense.

    1. Je pense qu'elle étudie.
    2. Je sais qu'il vient.
    3. J'espère que nous arrivons à l'heure.
    4. Je crois qu'ils viennent.
    5. Je ne sais s'il veut y aller.
    6. Je ne sais si elle peut venir.

173. Follow the model.

Elle dit qu'elle va venir.
Elle dit qu'elle viendra.

    1. Il dit qu'il va sortir.
    2. Elle dit qu'elle va pouvoir le faire.
    3. Elles disent qu'elles vont travailler.
    4. Ils disent qu'ils vont savoir le poème par cœur.

To Express Probability

In familiar conversational French, the future is sometimes used to express supposition or probability, particularly with **avoir** or **être**. Since these forms are used in conversation, the meaning is often conveyed by intonation. The future of probability is never used out of context.

J'entends la radio. Il **sera** à la maison.
I hear the radio. He must be at home.
Il court vite. Il **aura** froid.
He is running fast. He must be cold.
Elle ne mange pas. Elle **sera** malade.
She does not eat. She must be sick.

174. Complete the following sentences with the correct form of the future tense of the indicated verb.

    1. Il _____ à la maison. Je vois de la lumière. *être*
    2. Il n'est pas au bureau aujourd'hui. Il _____ malade. *être*
    3. Il _____ faim. Il en a l'air. *avoir*
    4. Ils courent. Ils _____ peur. *avoir*

175. Rewrite the following sentences, using the future of probability.

    1. Elle n'est pas dans sa chambre. Elle est (probablement) avec Pierre.
    2. Regardez ce qu'ils achètent. Ils ont (probablement) de l'argent à jeter.
    3. Comme elle court! Elle a (probablement) peur.
    4. Elles viennent me voir. Elles ont (probablement) besoin de moi.
    5. Elle ne mange pas. Elle est (probablement) malade.

176. Translate the following sentences, using the future tense.

    1. He must be afraid.
    2. He is probably home.
    3. He must be sick.
    4. She must be cold.

Review

177. Complete the following sentences with the correct form of the future tense of the indicated verb.

    1. Elles _____ devant le cinéma. *attendre*
    2. Il _____ trois heures. *être*
    3. Quand il _____ , nous _____ le travail. *venir, faire*
    4. Aussitôt qu'elles _____ , nous _____ au cinéma. *venir, aller*
    5. Quand elle _____ la chambre, je la _____ . *nettoyer, payer*
    6. Vous _____ une vie tranquille ici. *mener*
    7. Tu _____ à cette question. *réfléchir*
    8. Elle _____ vous aider. *savoir*
    9. Ils _____ leurs amis samedi prochain. *voir*
    10. Nous _____ le faire. *pouvoir*
    11. Elle _____ besoin de ce livre. *avoir*
    12. Il _____ le faire. *falloir*
    13. Nous _____ à table. *s'asseoir*
    14. Ils _____ de faim. *mourir*
    15. Vous _____ voir ce film. *vouloir*

178. Form sentences in the future to show the predictions about the students in the yearbook.

Marie / être pilote / aller partout dans le monde.
Marie sera pilote. Elle ira partout dans le monde.

    1. Pierre / gagner à la loterie / acheter une villa
    2. Anne / devenir millionnaire / faire le tour du monde
    3. Nicole / être chirurgienne / savoir guérir les gens malades
    4. Martine et Sylvie / découvrir un remède contre le cancer / obtenir le prix Nobel
    5. Monique / se marier / avoir trois enfants
    6. Georges et Nicole / être astronautes / pouvoir voyager en fusée
    7. Tu / courir dans le marathon / recevoir une médaille d'or
    8. Nous / pouvoir voyager partout / voir beaucoup de sites historiques
    9. Vous / être écrivain / écrire un roman
    10. Paul / aller habiter à la campagne / mener une vie tranquille

THE CONDITIONAL TENSE

Formation

The conditional tense is formed by adding the endings **-ais, -ais, -ait, -ions, -iez, -aient** to the future stem of the verb. Note that the endings are the same as those for the imperfect tense.

parler	finir	attendre
je parler**ais**	je finir**ais**	j'attendr**ais**
tu parler**ais**	tu finir**ais**	tu attendr**ais**
il, elle, on parler**ait**	il, elle, on finir**ait**	il, elle, on attendr**ait**
nous parler**ions**	nous finir**ions**	nous attendr**ions**
vous parler**iez**	vous finir**iez**	vous attendr**iez**
ils, elles parler**aient**	ils, elles finir**aient**	ils, elles attendr**aient**

Verbs that have irregular stems in the future tense have the same irregular stem in the conditional tense.

Infinitive	*Conditional*
employer	**j'emploierais, nous emploierions**
acheter	**j'achèterais, nous achèterions**
appeler	**j'appellerais, nous appellerions**
cueillir	**je cueillerais, nous cueillerions**
s'asseoir	**je m'assiérais, nous nous assiérions**
aller	**j'irais, nous irions**
avoir	**j'aurais, nous aurions**
être	**je serais, nous serions**
faire	**je ferais, nous ferions**
savoir	**je saurais, nous saurions**
falloir	**il faudrait**
valoir	**je vaudrais, il vaudrait**
vouloir	**je voudrais, nous voudrions**
apercevoir	**j'apercevrais, nous apercevrions**
décevoir	**je décevrais, nous décevrions**
devoir	**je devrais, nous devrions**
pleuvoir	**il pleuvrait**
recevoir	**je recevrais, nous recevrions**
courir	**je courrais, nous courrions**
secourir	**je secourrais, nous secourrions**
mourir	**je mourrais, nous mourrions**
pouvoir	**je pourrais, nous pourrions**
voir	**je verrais, nous verrions**
envoyer	**j'enverrais, nous enverrions**
tenir (and its derivatives)	**je tiendrais, nous tiendrions**
venir (and its derivatives)	**je viendrais, nous viendrions**

179. Rewrite the following sentences in the conditional tense.

1. Je dînerai en ville.
2. Tu resteras à la maison.
3. Elle prendra l'avion.
4. Nous paierons nos dettes.
5. Vous viendrez à trois heures.
6. Il sera de retour à huit heures.
7. Elle aura faim.
8. Nous le ferons.
9. Elle enverra la lettre par avion.
10. Il mourra de remords.
11. Elles verront leurs amis.
12. Vous pourrez voir ce film.
13. Ils secourront les pauvres.
14. Nous nous assiérons devant le feu.

180. Complete the following sentences with the correct form of the conditional tense of the indicated verb.

1. Elles _____ dans la mer, mais l'eau est trop froide. *nager*
2. J'_____ un sonnet, mais je ne suis pas poète. *écrire*
3. Il me _____ , mais il n'a pas d'argent. *payer*
4. Pourquoi n'_____ -vous pas en avion? *aller*
5. Elles _____ tout de suite, mais il n'y a pas de vol jusqu'à mardi. *venir*
6. Nous _____ à New York, mais nous avions autre chose à faire. *être*
7. Il le _____ tout de suite. *faire*
8. Il _____ la lettre par avion. *envoyer*
9. Nous _____ tous les détails. *savoir*
10. Vous _____ de bonne heure. *se coucher*
11. Je _____ à table. *s'asseoir*
12. Tu _____ tes amis. *recevoir*
13. Vous _____ le faire. *pouvoir*
14. Nous _____ travailler. *devoir*
15. Ils _____ les billets s'ils avaient le temps. *acheter*
16. J'_____ un stylo si j'en avais un. *employer*
17. Il _____ les pierres de Carnac en Bretagne. *voir*
18. Je _____ vous voir. *vouloir*
19. Nous _____ soif. *avoir*
20. Il _____ de faim. *mourir*

Uses of the Conditional Tense

To Express the Idea *would*

The conditional tense describes an action that would happen if it were not for some other circumstances. It is translated by *would* in English.

Dans ce cas-là, je viendrais.
In that case, I would come.
À votre place, nous lui en parlerions.
In your situation, we would speak to him about it.

Do not confuse the meaning of the conditional with the verb **devoir**.

Je devrais travailler.   *I should study.*
Je travaillerais.   *I would study.*

181. Follow the model.

Qu'est-ce que je devrais faire—accepter ou refuser? *À votre place*
À votre place, j'accepterais.

1. Qu'est-ce que je devrais faire—étudier ou sortir? *À votre place*
2. Qu'est-ce que je devrais faire—venir ou rester à la maison? *À votre place*
3. Qu-est-ce que je devrais faire—aller à Paris ou aller à Marseille? *Dans ce cas-là*
4. Qu'est-ce que je devrais faire—écrire ou téléphoner? *Dans ce cas-là*

After Certain Conjunctions

The conditional tense is used after **quand, lorsque, dès que, aussitôt que** and **tant que** when the main verb is in the conditional tense.

Il mangerait quand il arriverait.
He would eat when he arrived.
Il ferait le travail dès qu'il reviendrait.
He would do the work as soon as he returned.

It is also used after **au cas où.**

J'attendrai encore une heure au cas où elle viendrait.
I will wait another hour in case she comes.

182. Complete the following sentences with the correct form of the conditional tense of the indicated verb.

1. Il _____ dès qu'il _____ . *finir, revenir*
2. Il _____ quand il _____ le temps. *lire, avoir*
3. Elle _____ aussitôt que vous _____ . *comprendre, expliquer*
4. Elle _____ le faire lorsque vous lui _____ les instructions. *pouvoir, donner*
5. Je ne sortirai pas au cas où il _____ . *rentrer*
6. Nous rentrons à la maison au cas où nos invités _____ . *revenir*

To Soften a Request, Command or Desire

The conditional tense is used to soften a request, command, or desire.

Je voudrais vous dire quelque chose.
I would like to tell you something.
J'aimerais aller à Paris.
I would like to go to Paris.
Pourriez-vous m'aider?
Could you help me?
Voudriez-vous aller au cinéma?
Would you like to go to the movies?

183. Soften the following requests. Follow the models.

Attendez-moi.
Pourriez-vous m'attendre?

1. Venez tout de suite.   3. Donnez-moi ce livre.
2. Conduisez-moi à l'aéroport.   4. Aidez-moi.

Allons au cinéma!
Voudriez-vous aller au cinéma?

5. Dînons en ville!   7. Allons voir ce film!
6. Assistons à la conférence!   8. Prenons le train!

du café
Je voudrais du café.

9. du vin rouge   11. ce livre
10. deux billets aller et retour   12. ces chaussures

To Express Possibility or Unsure Action

The conditional tense is used to express a possible action or condition in the present. It is often used with exclamations or questions.

Quelle heure **serait**-il? Il **serait** trois heures.
What time could it be? It could be three o'clock already.

It is also used to describe an action that is unsure or not known to be true. It is often used by journalists and reporters.

Il **serait** à New York aujourd'hui.
He is rumored to be in New York today.
Il **aurait** une peinture de Braque.
He allegedly has a Braque painting.
Quel accident! Il y **aurait** trois morts.
What an accident! It is said there are three deaths.

184. Rewrite the following sentences, using the conditional tense of possibility.

1. (Peut-être) est-il huit heures? Ils sont arrivés.
2. Elle a (peut-être) bien 50 ans!
3. Comme il court! (Peut-être) sait-il les résultats.
4. (On dit qu') il fait sa médecine à Paris maintenant.

185. Translate the following sentences into French, using the conditional tense.

1. He is rumored to live in Paris.   3. The president is rumored to be in New York.
2. She allegedly has a Picasso painting.   4. It could be two o'clock already.

In Indirect Discourse

The conditional tense is used to express a future action in indirect discourse when the main verb is in the past tense. The present conditional can be equivalent to a simple future in the past.

Il m'a dit qu'il viendrait.
He told me he would come.
Il m'a demandé si je voyagerais en France.
He asked me if I would travel in France.
Je croyais qu'elle voudrait venir.
I thought she would want to come.

Remember that the future tense is used when the verb in the main clause is in the present tense.

Il dit qu'il viendra.
He says he will come.

186. Rewrite the following sentences, putting the verb in the main clause in the past tense. Make all necessary changes.

    1. Il me dit qu'il sortira ce soir.
    2. Elle m'assure qu'elle sera heureuse.
    3. Il me demande si je mènerai une vie tranquille.
    4. Elle dit qu'elle m'écrira.

187. Complete the following sentences with the correct form of the future or conditional tense of the indicated verb.

    1. Elle dit qu'elle _____ la lettre. *écrire*
    2. Il m'a demandé si je _____ . *venir*
    3. Il décide qu'il _____ le voyage en avion. *faire*
    4. Elles ont dit qu'elles _____ peur. *avoir*
    5. Nous avons dit que nous _____ le couvert. *mettre*
    6. Elle dit qu'elle _____ le faire. *pouvoir*
    7. Elle m'a assuré qu'elle _____ heureuse. *être*
    8. Je dis que je ne _____ pas ici. *être*

Review

188. What would the following people do with a lot of money? Complete the following with the correct form of the conditional tense.

Avec beaucoup d'argent,

    1. il _____ ses dettes. *payer*
    2. nous _____ au Japon. *aller*
    3. tu _____ le meilleur champagne. *boire*
    4. il _____ le dépenser sagement. *falloir*
    5. je _____ quand même. *mourir*
    6. elle _____ le tour du monde. *faire*
    7. vous _____ beaucoup de liberté. *avoir*
    8. elles _____ quoi faire. *savoir*
    9. nous _____ tous les pays du monde. *voir*
    10. tu _____ des cadeaux à tous vos amis. *envoyer*
    11. elle _____ acheter une nouvelle maison. *pouvoir*
    12. il _____ plus ou moins heureux. *être*
    13. ils _____ chez nous en avion. *venir*
    14. vous _____ une nouvelle voiture. *acheter*

COMPOUND TENSES

    The compound tenses are formed by using the appropriate tense of the auxiliary verb **avoir** or **être** and the past participle. Review the formation of the past participles on pages 140–150.

Pluperfect Tense (*Plus-que-parfait*)

    The pluperfect tense (*plus-que-parfait*) is formed by using the imperfect tense of the verb **avoir** or **être** with the past participle.

parler	entrer	se lever
j'avais parlé	j'étais entré(e)	je m'étais levé(e)
tu avais parlé	tu étais entré(e)	tu t'étais levé(e)
il, elle, on avait parlé	il, on était entré	il, on s'était levé
nous avions parlé	elle était entrée	elle s'était levée
vous aviez parlé	nous étions entré(e)s	nous nous étions levé(e)s
ils, elles avaient parlé	vous étiez entré(e)(s)(es)	vous vous étiez levé(e)(s)(es)
	ils étaient entrés	ils s'étaient levés
	elles étaient entrées	elles s'étaient levées

The pluperfect tense is used the same in French as in English to express a past action completed prior to another past action.

Elle avait parlé et ensuite nous sommes partis.
She had spoken and then we left.
Ils avaient déjà terminé quand je suis parti.
They had already finished when I left.
Elles étaient déjà descendues quand je suis entré.
They had already come down when I came in.

It can also be used to express a habitual action when used after a conjunction of time.

Quand j'avais fini mes devoirs, j'allais jouer avec mes amis.
When I had finished my homework, I went to play with my friends.

189. Complete the following sentences with the appropriate form of the pluperfect tense of the indicated verb.

1. Nous (f.) _____ déjà _____ . *arriver*
2. Elle _____ ce roman. *lire*
3. Tu _____ la valise. *faire*
4. Le petit _____ le disque. *casser*
5. Nous (m.) _____ déjà _____ . *descendre*
6. Ils _____ . *manger*
7. J'(f.) _____ déjà _____ . *partir*
8. Vous (m. pl.) _____ du voyage. *revenir*
9. Elle _____ de bonne heure. *se coucher*
10. Nous (f.) _____ tard. *se lever*

190. Rewrite the following sentences according to the model to show what had already happened when something else took place.

Je suis partie et ensuite il est entré.
J'étais déjà partie quand il est entré.

1. Je suis revenu et ensuite elle est entrée.
2. Elles ont déjeuné et ensuite je suis arrivé.
3. J'ai fini mes devoirs et ensuite le téléphone a sonné.
4. Elle a écrit la lettre et ensuite son ami a frappé à la porte.
5. Les voleurs sont partis et ensuite la femme a crié.
6. Nous nous sommes couchés et ensuite il est revenu.

191. Follow the model.

Mangeaient-ils quand vous êtes arrivé?
Non, ils avaient déjà mangé quand je suis arrivé.

1. Regardais-tu la télévision quand on a annoncé le dîner?
2. Les étudiants faisaient-ils leurs devoirs quand le professeur est entré?
3. Sortiez-vous quand elles sont arrivées?
4. Rentraient-elles quand il a commencé à pleuvoir?
5. Lisait-elle le journal quand il est arrivé?
6. Ton père se raisait-il quand tu es parti?
7. Nous moquions-nous du politicien quand il est arrivé sur la scène?

Future Perfect Tense (*Futur Antérieur*)

The future perfect tense (*futur antérieur*) is formed by using the future tense of the auxiliary verb **avoir** or **être** with the past participle.

finir	venir	se réveiller
j'aurai fini	je serai venu(e)	je me serai réveillé(e)
tu auras fini	tu seras venu(e)	tu te seras réveillé(e)
il, elle, on aura fini	il, on sera venu	il, on se sera réveillé
nous aurons fini	elle sera venue	elle se sera réveillée
vous aurez fini	nous serons venu(e)s	nous nous serons réveillé(e)s
ils, elles auront fini	vous serez venu(e)(s)(es)	vous vous serez réveillé(e)(s)(es)
	ils seront venus	ils se seront réveillés
	elles seront venues	elles se seront réveillées

The future perfect tense is used to express a future action that will be completed prior to another future action.

Elles auront mangé avant mon arrivée.
They will have eaten before my arrival.
Il sera déjà parti quand vous arriverez.
He will have already left when you arrive.
Nous nous serons couchés quand vous reviendrez.
We will have already gone to bed when you return.
Demain à cette heure, nous serons arrivés en France.
Tomorrow at this time, we will have arrived in France.

The future perfect tense is used especially after the conjunctions **quand, après que, aussitôt que, dès que** and **tant que** with the future or future perfect in the main clause.

Après qu'elle sera partie, nous nous coucherons.
After she has left, we'll go to bed.

Like the future tense, the future perfect tense is often used to express probability. It is often used in this way with all verbs. See page 168.

Il n'est pas ici. Il **sera parti.**
He is not here. He must have left.
Qu'est-ce que j'ai fait de mon journal? Je l'**aurai jeté!**
What did I do with my newspaper? I must have thrown it away!

192. Complete the following sentences with the appropriate form of the future perfect of the indicated verb.

1. Nous _____ déjà _____ avec le directeur.   *parler*

2. Vous _____ avant minuit. *rentrer*
3. Elles _____ le travail avant notre arrivée. *faire*
4. Tu _____ cela avant lundi. *apprendre*
5. Elle _____ ces disques avant la soirée. *acheter*
6. Elle _____ de Paris avant samedi. *rentrer*
7. Je _____ déjà _____ quand vous reviendrez. *partir*
8. Nous _____ cette exposition avant votre départ. *voir*
9. Vous _____ votre composition avant la fin de juin. *écrire*
10. Vous _____ quand ils reviendront. *se coucher*
11. Téléphonez-moi dès que vous _____ l'histoire. *lire*
12. Je vous le dirai aussitôt que j'_____ la voiture. *acheter*

193. Say what the people have to do first before they can do something else. Follow the model.

Je ne peux pas sortir. Il faut d'abord que je finisse le travail.
Je sortirai quand j'aurai fini le travail.

1. Je ne peux pas partir. Il faut d'abord qu'ils rentrent.
2. Ils ne peuvent pas aller mieux. Il faut d'abord qu'ils prennent le médicamment.
3. Vous ne pouvez pas vous coucher. Il faut d'abord que vous éteigniez les lumières.
4. Tu ne peux pas avoir un diplôme. Il faut d'abord que tu étudies pendant quatre ans.
5. Nous ne pouvons pas résoudre le problème. Il faut d'abord que le professeur explique une chose.
6. Elle ne peut pas manger. Il faut d'abord qu'elle aille au supermarché.

Conditional Past Tense (*Passé du Conditionnel*)

The conditional past tense (*passé du conditionnel*) is formed by using the conditional tense of the auxiliary verb **avoir** or **être** and the past participle.

attendre	**partir**	**se laver**
j'aurais attendu	je serais parti(e)	je me serais lavé(e)
tu aurais attendu	tu serais parti(e)	tu te serais lavé(e)
il, elle, on aurait attendu	il, on serait parti	il, on se serait lavé
nous aurions attendu	elle serait partie	elle se serait lavée
vous auriez attendu	nous serions parti(e)s	nous nous serions lavé(e)s
ils, elles auraient attendu	vous seriez parti(e)(s)(es)	vous vous seriez lavé(e)(s)(es)
	ils seraient partis	ils se seraient lavés
	elles seraient parties	elles se seraient lavées

The conditional past tense is used to describe what would have taken place if something else had not interfered.

Dans ce cas-là, j'aurais refusé.
In that case, I would have refused.
Ils auraient fait le voyage, mais ils n'avaient pas assez d'argent.
They would have taken the trip, but they didn't have enough money.
Elle serait venue, mais elle n'avait pas d'auto.
She would have come, but she didn't have a car.
Il se serait rasé, mais il n'avait pas de rasoir.
He would have shaved, but he didn't have a razor.

Like the conditional, the conditional perfect is used to express a possible action in the past.

> J'ai trouvé sa lettre. **Serait**-il **venu** en mon absence?
> *I found his letter. Could it be that he came in my absence?*

It is also used to describe an action that is unsure. Like the present conditional, it is used by journalists and reporters.

> Dix avions **auraient été abbatus** hier.
> *It is reported that ten planes were brought down yesterday.*

See page 173.

194. Complete the following sentences with the correct form of the conditional past tense of the indicated verb.

    1. Ils _____ , mais il a commencé à pleuvoir. *finir*
    2. Nous _____ , mais nous n'avions pas faim. *manger*
    3. Nous _____ hier, mais il n'y avait pas de vol. *rentrer*
    4. Elle _____ le petit, mais elle ne pouvait pas. *accompagner*
    5. Tu _____ tes amis, mais ils ne sont pas venus. *voir*
    6. Vous _____ de l'eau, mais vous n'avez pas eu soif. *boire*
    7. Elle _____ le médicament, mais elle n'était pas malade. *prendre*
    8. Dans ce cas-là, elle _____ venir. *pouvoir*
    9. Dans ce cas-là, je _____ . *se coucher*
  10. Tu _____ en noir. *s'habiller*

195. Follow the model to show what the people would have done had they had certain things.

> **Elle / venir / auto**
> **Elle serait venue, mais elle n'avait pas d'auto.**

    1. Il / se raser / rasoir
    2. Elles / manger au restaurant / argent
    3. Vous / faire un voyage / temps
    4. Nous / écrire la lettre / papier
    5. Je / partir / parapluie
    6. Tu / ouvrir le paquet / couteau

The Past Anterior (*Passé Antérieur*) and the *Passé Surcomposé*

The *passé antérieur* is formed by using the *passé simple* of the auxiliary verb **avoir** or **être** and the past participle.

finir	venir
j'eus fini	je fus venu(e)
tu eus fini	tu fus venu(e)
il, elle, on eut fini	il, on fut venu
nous eûmes fini	elle fut venue
vous eûtes fini	nous fûmes venu(e)s
ils, elles eurent fini	vous fûtes venu(e)(s)(es)
	ils furent venus
	elles furent venues

The *passé surcomposé* is a double compound tense formed by using the *passé composé* of the auxiliary verb **avoir** and the past participle. It is rarely used with verbs conjugated with **être** except when these verbs imply result, not action.

finir	**arriver**
j'ai eu fini	j'ai été arrivé(e)
tu as eu fini	tu as été arrivé(e)
il, elle, on a eu fini	il, on a été arrivé
nous avons eu fini	elle a été arrivée
vous avez eu fini	nous avons été arrivé(e)s
ils, elles ont eu fini	vous avez été arrivé(e)(s)(es)
	ils ont été arrivés
	elles ont été arrivées

Like the *plus-que-parfait*, the *passé antérieur* expresses a past action that occurred before another past action. It is usually used in subordinate clauses after **quand, lorsque, après que, aussitôt que, dès que** or **à peine** which indicate a past action immediately preceding another.

> **Quand il eut fini, il partit.**
> *When he had finished, he left.*
> **Lorsqu'elle fut arrivée, nous partîmes.**
> *When she had arrived, we left.*

Note that the subject and verb are inverted after **à peine**.

> **À peine eut-elle fini qu'elle partit.**
> *She had hardly finished when she left.*

The *passé antérieur* is only used in written language. In spoken language, it is replaced by the *passé surcomposé*.

> **Quand il a eu fini, il est parti.**
> *When he had finished, he left.*

196. Rewrite the following sentences in spoken language.

1. Quand il eut mangé, il partit.
2. Lorsqu'elles furent réunies, elles élurent un président.
3. Lorsque le professeur eut fini le discours, il descendit de l'estrade.
4. À peine eut-il fini que nous arrivâmes.
5. Après qu'ils furent guéris, ils retournèrent au travail.
6. Quand il fut arrivé, la conférence commença.

197. Rewrite the following sentences in written language.

1. Dès qu'elle a eu appris la nouvelle, elle a décidé de partir.
2. À peine a-t-elle eu reçu l'invitation qu'elle y a répondu.
3. À peine a-t-elle été entrée qu'elle a compris la situation.
4. Aussitôt qu'ils ont été partis, ils ont soupiré.

SI CLAUSES

Si (*if*) clauses are used to express conditions contrary to fact. For such clauses, there is a definite sequence of tenses to be followed.

Si *clause*	Result clause
Present indicative or passé composé	Future or imperative
Imperfect	Conditional
Pluperfect	Past Conditional

Study the following examples.

Si vous n'avez pas <u>compris</u>, dites-le-moi.
If you didn't understand, tell me.
Si vous n'avez pas <u>compris</u>, vous me le <u>direz</u>.
If you didn't understand, you will tell me.
Si j'<u>ai</u> assez d'argent, je <u>ferai</u> le voyage.
If I have enough money, I will take the trip.
Si j'<u>avais</u> assez d'argent, je <u>ferais</u> le voyage.
If I had enough money, I would take the trip.
Si j'<u>avais eu</u> assez d'argent, j'<u>aurais fait</u> le voyage.
If I had had enough money, I would have taken the trip.

Si vous <u>venez</u>, nous <u>resterons</u>.
If you come, we will stay.
Si vous <u>veniez</u>, nous <u>resterions</u>.
If you came, we would stay.
Si vous <u>étiez venu</u>, nous <u>serions restés</u>.
If you had come, we would have stayed.

In sentences expressing general rules or conditions, the present tense can be used in both clauses.

Si j'ai faim, je mange.
If I am hungry, I eat.
Si on étudie, on reçoit de bonnes notes.
If one studies, one gets good grades.

Si becomes **s'** before the pronouns **il** and **ils,** but not before the pronouns **elle** and **elles.** The **si** clause can come first or second.

S'il a le temps, il viendra nous voir.
Elles viendront nous voir, si elles ont le temps.

198. Complete the following sentences with the appropriate form of the indicated verb.

1. Elles y iront si elles _____ le temps. *avoir*
2. Si vous _____ à l'heure, je vous attendrai. *être*
3. Je _____ s'il ne pleut pas. *partir*
4. S'il fait beau, nous _____ une promenade. *faire*
5. S'ils _____ assez de temps, ils viendraient. *avoir*
6. Il paierait ses dettes s'il _____ de l'argent. *avoir*
7. Si j'avais le temps, je le _____ . *faire*
8. Nous _____ chez nous s'il pleuvait. *rester*
9. S'il _____ des billets, il serait allé au théâtre. *prendre*
10. J'aurais été content si vous _____ . *venir*
11. S'il avait fait froid, il _____ son manteau. *mettre*
12. Vous _____ à l'heure si vous étiez parti de bonne heure. *arriver*

199. Answer the following questions: **Que feront les gens s'ils ont de l'argent? Que feraient les gens s'ils avaient de l'argent? Qu'est-ce que les gens auraient fait s'ils avaient eu de l'argent?** Follow the model.

Pierre / faire le tour du monde
Si Pierre a de l'argent, il fera le tour du monde.
Si Pierre avait de l'argent, il ferait le tour du monde.
Si Pierre avait eu de l'argent, il aurait fait le tour du monde.

1. Anne / acheter une Mercedes
2. Nous / aller en Europe
3. Tu / s'habiller bien
4. Marie et Nicole / venir nous voir plus souvent
5. Georges / ne pas travailler
6. Je / faire un long voyage
7. Les Dupont / vivre bien
8. Vous / avoir une grande maison

200. Find the result clause by combining an element from the first column with an element from the second column. Then form sentences with three **si** clauses as in the model.

1. S'il (pleuvoir), ils	voir les Pyramides
2. Si elle (se casser) la jambe, elle	dormir
3. S'il (accepter) ce poste, il	mettre un imperméable
4. Si nous (rentrer) trop tard, nos parents	jouer dans le parc
5. Si tu (aller) en Egypte, tu	aller à la salle d'urgence à l'hôpital
6. S'il (faire) beau, les enfants	gagner beaucoup d'argent
7. Si vous (arriver) à l'aéroport à temps, vous	se dépêcher
8. Si les étudiants (étudier), ils	pouvoir prendre l'avion de 10 heures
9. Si je (avoir) sommeil, je	réussir à l'examen
10. Si nous (être) en retard, nous	se fâcher

Continue.

1. S'il pleut, ils mettront un imperméable.
   S'il pleuvait, ils mettraient un imperméable.
   S'il avait plu, ils auraient mis un imperméable.

SUBJUNCTIVE

The indicative mood is used to report an action which is taking, has taken or will take place. The action is not dependent upon an opinion or condition. When the statement implies a truth, fact or probability, the indicative mood is used.

Marie mange beaucoup.
Mary eats a lot.
Je sais qu'il est parti.
I know he left.
Il est probable qu'il ira à New York.
It is probable that he will go to New York.
Il est vrai que la terre est ronde.
It is true that the earth is round.

The subjunctive is used to express an action which is dependent upon a subjective idea, opinion or condition. The idea in the dependent clause is either contrary to fact, or possible but not probable.

Le père veut que son fils devienne médecin.
The father wants his son to become a doctor.
Il faut qu'elle se réveille tôt.
It is necessary for her to wake up early.
Je doute qu'il vienne.
I doubt that he is coming.

In the first example, even though the father wants his son to become a doctor, it is not certain that the boy will carry out the father's desire. Therefore, the action is expressed in the subjunctive. In English an infinitive, rather than the subjunctive, is used.

The father wants his son to become a doctor.

In French, however, a clause must be used.

(See *Uses of the Subjunctive*, beginning on page 187.)

PRESENT SUBJUNCTIVE

Regular Forms

The present subjunctive is formed by dropping the **-ent** ending from the third person plural of the present indicative and adding the endings **-e, -es, -e, -ions, -iez, -ent.**

	parler	**finir**	**attendre**
Base:	**ils parlent**	**ils finissent**	**ils attendent**
	je parl**e**	je finiss**e**	j'attend**e**
	tu parl**es**	tu finiss**es**	tu attend**es**
	il, elle, on parl**e**	il, elle, on finiss**e**	il, elle, on attend**e**
	nous parl**ions**	nous finiss**ions**	nous attend**ions**
	vous parl**iez**	vous finiss**iez**	vous attend**iez**
	ils, elles parl**ent**	ils, elles finiss**ent**	ils, elles attend**ent**

Note that for **-er** verbs, there is no difference between the subjunctive and the present indicative in the **je, tu, il, elle, on, ils, elles** forms. The same is true for the third person plural of all regular subjunctive forms. Note that unlike the present indicative of regular **-ir** and **-re** verbs, there is no audible difference between the third person plural and the singular forms.

Present indicative	*Subjunctive*
il finit	**il finisse**
ils finissent	**ils finissent**
il attend	**il attende**
ils attendent	**ils attendent**

Note that verbs ending in **-ier,** such as **étudier** and **oublier,** and the verbs **rire** and **sourire** have a double **i** in the **nous** and **vous** forms since the base ends in **-i.**

Base	*Subjunctive*
ils étudient	**nous étudiions**
	vous étudiiez

Other verbs that are regular in the subjunctive are:

	Verb	Base
Verbs like	ouvrir	**ils ouvrent**
Verbs like	courir	**ils courent**
	rire	**ils rient**
	conclure	**ils concluent**
	rompre	**ils rompent**
	battre	**ils battent**
	mettre	**ils mettent**
	partir	**ils partent**
Verbs like	connaître	**ils connaissent**
	plaire	**ils plaisent**
	se taire	**ils se taisent**
	lire	**ils lisent**
	dire	**ils disent**
	conduire	**ils conduisent**
	traduire	**ils traduisent**
	dormir	**ils dorment**
	servir	**ils servent**
	suivre	**ils suivent**
	vivre	**ils vivent**
	vaincre	**ils vainquent**
	craindre	**ils craignent**
	joindre	**ils joignent**
	peindre	**ils peignent**
	s'asseoir	**ils s'asseyent**

201. Complete the following sentences with the correct form of the subjunctive of each indicated verb.

1. Il faut qu'elles _____ .
   (parler, entrer, finir, réussir, attendre, répondre)
2. Il ne veut pas qu'elle _____ .
   (partir, sortir, mentir, se repentir, dormir)
3. Il veut que je _____ .
   (rompre les liens, vaincre mes passions, craindre cet homme, peindre ce portrait)
4. Il est nécessaire que tu _____ .
   (écrire la lettre, suivre la route, vivre ici, décrire la vue, servir le déjeuner)
5. Elle désire que nous _____ .
   (parler, lire, dormir, disparaître, s'asseoir)
6. Il veut que vous _____ .
   (sourire, étudier, rire, oublier ceci)

Spelling Changes in the Present Subjunctive

Verbs ending in **-yer,** such as **employer, envoyer, nettoyer, essayer, payer,** etc., and **croire** and **voir** change the **i** of the third person plural base to **y** in the **nous** and **vous** forms. The vowel changes are the same as those for the present indicative.

envoyer	croire
Base: **ils envoient**	**ils croient**
j'envoie	je croie
tu envoies	tu croies
il, elle, on envoie	il, elle, on croie
ils, elles envoient	ils, elles croient
nous envo**y**ions	nous cro**y**ions
vous envo**y**iez	vous cro**y**iez

Verbs with Internal Vowel Changes in the Present Subjunctive

Verbs with -*é*- in the Infinitive

Verbs with **-é-** in the infinitive, such as **céder, compléter, considérer, espérer, préférer, répéter,** etc., change the **è** of the third person plural stem to **-é-** in the **nous** and **vous** forms.

	céder		
Base:	**ils cèdent**		
	je cède		
	tu cèdes	*But:*	**nous cédions**
il, elle, on cède			**vous cédiez**
ils, elles cèdent			

Verbs with -*e*- in the Infinitive

Verbs with **-e-** in the infinitive, such as **acheter, appeler, jeter, lever, mener,** etc., change the base in the **nous** and **vous** forms. Verbs which in the present indicative change **-e-** to **-è-** in the singular and the third person plural forms retain the **e** in the **nous** and **vous** forms.

acheter

Base:	**ils achètent**
But:	**nous achetions**
	vous achetiez

Verbs which double the consonant in the third person plural have only one consonant in the **nous** and **vous** forms.

jeter

Base:	**ils jettent**
But:	**nous jetions**
	vous jetiez

In other words, the spelling changes are the same as those for the present indicative.

202. Complete the following sentences with the correct form of the present subjunctive of the indicated verb.

1. Il est essentiel qu'ils _____ le paquet. *envoyer*
2. Il est nécessaire que nous _____ la salle. *nettoyer*
3. Je veux qu'elles _____ l'histoire. *croire*

  4. Elle veut que vous _____ ce film.   *voir*
  5. Il faut qu'ils _____ ce problème.   *considérer*
  6. Il faut que nous _____ nos places.   *céder*
  7. Il est important qu'ils _____ ce livre.   *acheter*
  8. Il est important que nous _____ le rideau.   *lever*
  9. Il faut qu'ils _____ leurs amis.   *appeler*
 10. Il est nécessaire que vous _____ ce papier.   *jeter*

Prendre, tenir, venir

Prendre, tenir and **venir** also undergo an internal vowel change in the present subjunctive.

prendre

Base: **ils prennent**
But: **nous prenions**
         vous preniez

tenir

Base: **ils tiennent**
But: **nous tenions**
         vous teniez

venir

Base: **ils viennent**
But: **nous venions**
         vous veniez

One way to remember the subjunctive forms for spelling-change verbs and verbs with internal vowel changes is the following:

1. Add the endings to the third person present indicative base for the singular and third person plural forms.
2. Drop the ending **-ant** from the present participle before adding the endings to the **nous** and **vous** forms.

Example: **prendre**

Singular and third person plural

Base form	Subjunctive
ils prenn / ent	**je prenne**
	tu prennes
	il / elle / on prenne
	ils / elles prennent

Nous and *vous*

Base form	Subjunctive
pren / ant	**nous prenions**
	vous preniez

Verbs with Variable Bases in the Present Subjunctive

The following verbs have variable bases in the present subjunctive.

mourir

Base: **ils meurent**
But: **nous mourions**
       vous mouriez

recevoir (décevoir, concevoir), devoir

recevoir

Base: **ils reçoivent**
But: **nous recevions**
       vous receviez

devoir

Base: **ils doivent**
But: **nous devions**
       vous deviez

boire

Base: **ils boivent**
But: **nous buvions**
       vous buviez

Note that the base changes are the same for these verbs in the present indicative and the present subjunctive.

Present indicative	*Subjunctive*
nous mourons	**nous mourions**
nous recevons	**nous recevions**
nous buvons	**nous buvions**

203 . Complete the following sentences with the correct form of the present subjunctive of the indicated verb.

1. Il faut qu'ils _____ leur temps. *prendre*
2. Il est important que vous _____ l'autobus. *prendre*
3. Il est possible qu'elle _____ à l'heure. *venir*
4. Il est important que vous _____ les places maintenant. *retenir*
5. Il est possible que le malade _____ . *mourir*
6. Il est possible que vous _____ de fatigue. *mourir*
7. Il faut qu'ils _____ de l'argent. *recevoir*
8. Il est possible que nous _____ de l'argent. *recevoir*
9. Il faut que tu _____ le médicament. *boire*
10. Il vaut mieux que nous _____ du lait. *boire*

Verbs with Irregular Bases in the Present Subjunctive

The following verbs have irregular bases in the present subjunctive.

avoir	**être**
j'aie	je sois
tu aies	tu sois
il, elle, on ait	il, elle, on soit
ils, elles aient	ils, elles soient
nous ayons	nous soyons
vous ayez	vous soyez

pouvoir

je puisse
tu puisses
il, elle, on puisse
ils, elles puissent
nous puissions
vous puissiez

faire

je fasse
tu fasses
il, elle, on fasse
ils, elles fassent
nous fassions
vous fassiez

savoir

je sache
tu saches
il, elle, on sache
ils, elles sachent
nous sachions
vous sachiez

vouloir

je veuille
tu veuilles
il, elle, on veuille
ils, elles veuillent
nous voulions
vous vouliez

aller

j'aille
tu ailles
il, elle, on aille
ils, elles aillent
nous allions
vous alliez

valoir

je vaille
tu vailles
il, elle on vaille
ils, elles vaillent
nous valions
vous valiez

falloir

il faille

pleuvoir

il pleuve

204. Change the following sentences, substituting the words given.

1. Il est nécessaire que nous soyons à l'heure.　(vous, ils, elle, tu, je)
2. Il faut que tu aies de la patience. (je, il, elles, nous, vous)
3. Il est bon que je puisse venir. (nous, vous, ils, tu, elle)
4. Il est important que tu fasses le travail. (je, il, elles, nous, vous)
5. Il faut que tu saches la vérité. (vous, nous, ils, elle, je)
6. Il est possible qu'il veuille partir. (nous, vous, tu, elles, je)
7. Il faut que j'aille au supermarché. (tu, ils, elle, nous, vous)
8. Il est important que ça vaille la peine. (elle, nous, vous, tu, ils)

Uses of the Subjunctive

Subjunctive in Noun Clauses

　　The subjunctive is required in clauses following verbs which denote desire, doubt, denial, necessity, fear, etc. The subjunctive verb usually appears in a clause introduced by **que**.

　　Some common expressions requiring the subjunctive are:

1. wish, preference or desire

vouloir	*to want*
bien vouloir	*to agree, to be willing*
désirer	*to wish, to desire*

préférer   *to prefer*
aimer mieux   *to prefer*
souhaiter   *to wish*

Je veux qu'il parte.
I want him to leave.

Note that **espérer** (*to hope*) is followed by the indicative.

J'espère qu'il viendra.
I hope he will come.

2. doubt

douter   *to doubt*

Je doute qu'il vienne.
I doubt he is coming (will come).

3. denial

nier   *to deny*

Elle nie qu'elle vous connaisse.
She denies that she knows you.

4. emotions and feelings

être content   *to be happy*
être heureux   *to be happy*
être triste   *to be sad*
être fâché   *to be angry*
être fier   *to be proud*
être désolé   *to be sorry*
être surpris   *to be surprised*
avoir peur   *to be afraid*
avoir crainte   *to be afraid*
craindre   *to fear*
regretter   *to be sorry*
être furieux   *to be mad, furious*
se fâcher   *to be angry*
se réjouir   *to rejoice, to be happy*

Je suis heureux que vous puissiez venir.
I am happy that you can come.
Elle est triste que nous partions.
She is sad that we are leaving.
Elle craint que nous n'attendions pas.
She is afraid that we will not wait.

5. an order, command or requirement (See page 199.)

commander   *to ask, to order*
exiger   *to demand*
ordonner   *to command, to order*

Il exige que nous soyons à l'heure.
He demands that we be on time.

6. permission or refusal of permission (See page 199.)

permettre	*to permit*
consentir	*to consent*
défendre	*to forbid*
empêcher	*to prevent*

Il permet que nous fassions cela.
He permits us to do that.
Il défend que nous fumions en classe.
He forbids us to smoke in class.

205. Complete the following sentences with the correct form of the present subjunctive of each indicated verb.

1. Je veux qu'ils _____ .
   (parler, manger, écrire, dormir, venir, sortir, conduire)

2. Elle préfère que nous _____ .
   (payer, céder, appeler le garçon, venir, boire, aller, être, ici)

3. Pourquoi commandes-tu que je _____ ?
   (travailler, lire, venir, finir, sortir)

4. Elle craint que vous ne _____ .
   (venir, comprendre, manger, attendre)

206. Say what the following people's wishes or feelings are. Follow the model.

Il veut que: Vous travaillez.
Il veut que vous travailliez.

A. Le professeur veut que:

1. Tu lis le livre.
2. Vous étudiez la leçon.
3. Nous complétons nos devoirs.
4. Elles savent les réponses.
5. Je fais attention en classe.
6. Il est à l'heure.

B. Je doute que:

1. Le politicien dit la vérité.
2. Tu pars à l'heure.
3. Il pleut demain.
4. Vous achetez cette maison.
5. Ils meurent de faim.
6. Nous prenons nos vacances sur la lune.

C. Pierre est heureux que:

1. Ses amis peuvent aller en Europe en été.
2. Babeth vient le voir.
3. Jeanne et Anne reçoivent de bonne notes.
4. Claire peint un beau portrait.
5. Nous considérons son offre.
6. Vous recevez le prix.

D. Le médecin ordonne que:

1. Vous prenez les pilules quatre fois par jour.
2. Tu as de la patience.
3. La patiente se repose.
4. Nous buvons huit verres d'eau par jour.
5. Je suis un régime.
6. Vous êtes calme.

E. Anne regrette que:

1. Vous ne voulez pas venir à la surprise-partie.
2. Tu ne veux pas le faire.
3. Son amie n'obtient pas la médaille d'or.
4. Nous ne pouvons pas aller au cinéma avec elle.
5. Sa sœur n'est pas à la maison.

207. Complete the following sentences with the appropriate form of the indicated verb.

1. Je préfère que tu _____ l'auto. *conduire*
2. Elle craint que vous _____ en retard. *arriver*
3. Mes parents défendent que je _____ . *fumer*
4. Il nie qu'il la _____ . *connaître*
5. Je suis triste que vous _____ malade. *être*
6. Il ordonne que je _____ le travail. *faire*
7. Il permet que nous y _____ . *aller*
8. Elle doute que vous le _____ . *savoir*
9. Nous sommes contents qu'elles _____ venir. *vouloir*
10. Il veut que nous _____ son œuvre. *traduire*
11. Ils commandent que je _____ de bonne heure. *rentrer*
12. Nous sommes désolés qu'il ne _____ pas ce soir. *venir*
13. Il désire que je _____ la leçon. *comprendre*
14. Nous voulons que tout _____ bien. *aller*
15. Je préfère que vous ne _____ pas ce soir. *sortir*

Subjunctive with Impersonal Expressions that Express Opinion or Emotions

The subjunctive is also required after many impersonal expressions that denote an element of subjectivity.

il est temps que	*it is time that*
il vaut mieux que	*it is better that*
il est préférable que	*it is better that*
il faut que	*it is necessary that*
il est nécessaire que	*it is necessary that*
il est essentiel que	*it is essential that*
il importe que	*it is important that*
il est important que	*it is important that*
il suffit que	*it is enough that, it suffices that*
il est indispensable que	*it is indispensable that*

il convient que	*it is fitting that, it is proper that*
il est convenable que	*it is fitting that, it is proper that*

il est possible que	*it is possible that*
il se peut que	*it is possible that*
il est impossible que	*it is impossible that*
il est utile que	*it is useful that*
il est inutile que	*it is useless that*

il est douteux que	*it is doubtful that*
il est peu probable que	*it is unlikely that*
il n'est pas certain que	*it is uncertain that*
il est heureux que	*it is fortunate that*
il est bon que	*it is good that*
c'est (il est) dommage que	*it is a pity that*
il semble que	*it seems that*
il est honteux que	*it is shameful that*
il est triste que	*it is sad that*
il est surprenant que	*it is surprising that*
il est étonnant que	*it is surprising that*
il est urgent que	*it is urgent that*

Il est temps que vous veniez.
It is time for you to come.
Il faut que vous étudiez.
It is necessary for you to study.
Il est douteux qu'il réussisse.
It is doubtful that he will succeed.
C'est dommage qu'elle ne vienne pas.
It's a pity that she is not coming.

If the opinion is a general one, then the impersonal expression is followed by the infinitive.

Il vaut mieux ne pas sortir par un temps pareil.
One shouldn't go out in such weather.
Il faut étudier pour réussir.
It is necessary to study to succeed.

The indicative is used with the following expressions.

il est certain que	*it is certain that*
il est sûr que	*it is sure that*
il est probable que	*it is probable that*
il est évident que	*it is evident that*
il est exact que	*it is exact that*
il est clair que	*it is clear that*
il est vrai que	*it is true that*
il est vraisemblable que	*it is conceivable that*
il paraît que	*it seems that*

Although **il semble que** is followed by the subjunctive, **il me semble que** is followed by the indicative.

Il semble qu'il maigrisse.
It seems he is getting thin.

Il me semble que je fais votre connaissance pour la première fois.
It seems to me that I am meeting you for the first time.

208. Complete the following sentences with the correct form of the present subjunctive of each indicated verb.

    1. Il est possible qu'il le _____ .
       (préparer, lire, recevoir, faire, savoir, perdre)

    2. Il est nécessaire que nous le _____ .
       (finir, manger, comprendre, suivre, faire, répéter, retenir)

    3. Il est douteux que vous _____ .
       (comprendre, venir, finir, sortir, savoir la réponse)

    4. Il n'est pas certain qu'il _____ .
       (réussir, comprendre, arriver, finir, répondre)

209. Introduce each of the following by the indicated expression.

    1. Nous recevons ces lettres. *Il est essentiel*
    2. Je te le dis. *Il suffit*
    3. Tu es ici. *Il vaut mieux*
    4. Vous voulez venir. *Il est bon*
    5. Elle écrit ses devoirs. *Il est important*
    6. Ils vont au marché. *Il faut*
    7. Vous venez. *Il est temps*
    8. Vous êtes malade. *C'est dommage*
    9. Elles partent tout de suite. *Il vaut mieux*
   10. Tu réussis à l'examen. *Il est heureux*
   11. Paul peut venir. *Il est douteux*
   12. Tu mens. *Il est honteux*
   13. Ils savent la vérité. *Il est bon*
   14. On le craint. *Il est possible*
   15. Ils viendront demain. *Il convient*

Subjunctive with Expressions of Doubt

The indicative is used with expressions that denote certainty in the affirmative.

il est sûr que	*it is sure that*
il est certain que	*it is certain that*
il est probable que	*it is probable that*

The subjunctive is used in the negative and interrogative forms of the above expressions, since uncertainty is implied.

Indicative	*Subjunctive*
Il est sûr qu'il viendra.	**Il n'est pas sûr qu'il vienne.** **Est-il sûr qu'il vienne?**
Il est certain qu'elle comprend.	**Il n'est pas certain qu'elle comprenne.** **Est-il certain qu'elle comprenne?**

Il est probable qu'il le fera.   **Il n'est pas probable qu'il le fasse.**
                                          Est-il probable qu'il le fasse?

The indicative is used with affirmative forms of **croire** and **penser** since there is no uncertainty.

Je pense qu'il vient.
Je crois qu'elle comprend.

The subjunctive is used with the negative and interrogative forms of **croire** and **penser** when they express doubt or uncertainty.

Je ne crois pas qu'il vienne.
I don't believe he is coming. (But I don't know for sure.)
Croyez-vous qu'il vienne?
Do you think he is coming? (The answer is unknown for sure.)

You will note that many expressions that take the indicative are followed by a future tense.

Indicative   *Subjunctive*

Il est certain qu'il viendra.   **Il n'est pas certain qu'il vienne.**
Je crois qu'elles seront ici.   **Je ne crois pas qu'elles soient ici.**

Note that the conditional can also be used if the clause expresses a supposition or eventuality.

Je ne crois pas qu'il pourrait le faire.
I don't think he could do it.

210. Complete the following sentences with the correct form of the indicated verb.

1. Il est sûr qu'il _____ ici demain. *être*
2. Il n'est pas sûr qu'elle le _____ . *faire*
3. Est-il sûr qu'ils _____ ? *venir*
4. Il est certain qu'elles _____ demain. *venir*
5. Il n'est pas certain que nous _____ les résultats aujourd'hui. *savoir*
6. Est-il certain que vous y _____ ? *aller*
7. Il est probable qu'elle le _____ . *faire*
8. Il n'est pas probable qu'il _____ les billets. *obtenir*
9. Est-il probable que nous _____ le travail? *finir*
10. Je pense qu'elle _____ raison *avoir*
11. Je ne pense pas qu'elle _____ la réponse. *savoir*
12. Pensez-vous qu'il le _____ ? *croire*
13. Je crois qu'elle _____ venir. *vouloir*
14. Je ne crois pas qu'elles _____ le faire. *vouloir*
15. Croyez-vous que nous _____ le faire? *pouvoir*

211. Answer the following questions, according to the indicated cue.

1. Crois-tu que Jean le sache? *Non*
2. Êtes-vous certain que Pierre le sache? *Non*
3. Est-il probable qu'il conduise une auto? *Non*
4. Est-il sûr qu'ils viennent? *Non*
5. Croyez-vous qu'elles arrivent demain? *Non*
6. Est-il sûr qu'elle parte tout de suite? *Non*
7. Est-il probable qu'il vienne? *Non*
8. Êtes-vous certain que Jean vienne? *Non*

Subjunctive with subordinate conjunctions

The following conjunctions require the subjunctive.

1. Of time

avant que	*before*
en attendant que	*until*
jusqu'à ce que	*until*
aussi (de si) loin que	*far from*

On lui dira au revoir avant qu'il (ne) parte.
We will tell him good-bye before he leaves.

2. Of cause or negation

non que	*not that*
non pas que	*not that*
sans que	*without*

Elle est partie sans que je la voie.
She left without my seeing her.

3. Of purpose or result

afin que	*in order that*
pour que	*in order that*
de manière que	*so that*
de façon que	*so that*
de sorte que	*so that*
de crainte que	*for fear that*
de peur que	*for fear that*

Elle ne vous parle pas de peur que vous la réprimandiez.
She does not speak to you for fear that you will scold her.

In certain cases, **de manière que, de façon que** and **de sorte que** are followed by the indicative, particularly when the result is an accomplished and presumably irreversible deed or fact.

Les étudiants se taisaient de sorte que personne ne **pouvait** entendre le moindre bruit.
The students were so quiet you couldn't hear the slightest noise.

4. Of concession

bien que	*although*
quoique	*although*
encore que	*although*
malgré que	*although*

Bien qu'il soit chez lui, il ne répond pas au téléphone.
Although he is at home, he does not answer the telephone.

5. Of condition

à condition que	*on condition that*
en cas que	*in case*
pourvu que	*provided that*

supposé que	supposing that
à moins que	unless
soit que ... soit que	whether ... or

Ils iront à la plage à moins qu'il (ne) pleuve.
They will go to the beach unless it rains.

Ne is usually used after **à moins que, avant que, de peur que, de crainte que, de manière que, de sorte que** when the verb in the dependent clause is affirmative. When the verb is negative, **ne ... pas** is used.

Nous nous réveillons tôt de peur qu'elle ne parte sans nous.
We are getting up early for fear that she will leave without us.
Nous nous réveillons tôt de peur qu'elle ne nous attende pas.
We are getting up early for fear that she will not wait for us.

The following conjunctions do not take the subjunctive.

aussitôt que	as soon as
dès que	as soon as
après que	after
pendant que	while
parce que	because

Review the use of conjunctions with the future and conditional tenses on pages 166–167 and 172.

212. Complete the following sentences with the correct form of each indicated expression.

1. À moins que tu ne _____ , le professeur se fâchera.
(savoir la leçon, faire tes devoirs, lire le roman, écrire la composition)

2. Quoiqu'il _____ , je m'en irai.
(neiger, faire froid, pleuvoir)

3. Il se couchera aussitôt qu'il _____ .
(être fatigué, arriver, rentrer, revenir)

213. Complete the following sentences with the correct form of the subjunctive of the indicated verb.

1. Je le verrai avant qu'il ne _____ . *partir*
2. Je lui répondrai avant qu'elle ne _____ . *sortir*
3. Je lirai en attendant qu'elle _____ . *venir*
4. Il m'aidera jusqu'à ce que je _____ une meilleure note. *recevoir*
5. Je les attendrai jusqu'à ce qu'ils _____ . *revenir*
6. Elle part sans qu'on lui _____ au revoir. *dire*
7. Je parlerai lentement pour que vous _____ . *comprendre*
8. Je partirai tôt afin que je _____ arriver à l'heure. *pouvoir*
9. Il fera cela de sorte que nous _____ contents. *être*
10. De peur qu'il ne _____ , je prendrai un parapluie. *pleuvoir*
11. Je resterai ici de crainte que mes amis n' _____ . *arriver*
12. Quoiqu'il _____ riche, je ne l'aime pas. *être*
13. Bien qu'elles _____ , elles ne réussissent pas. *étudier*
14. Nous sortirons ce soir à moins qu'il ne _____ . *neiger*

15. Je vous attendrai pourvu que vous n' _____ pas trop en retard. *arriver*
16. À moins qu'il ne _____ beau, je ne sortirai pas. *faire*
17. À moins que tu ne _____ la leçon, il se fâchera. *savoir*

214. Complete the following sentences with the correct form of the indicated verb.

1. Aussitôt qu'il _____ , nous partirons. *arriver*
2. Je me dépêche de peur qu'elle ne m' _____ pas. *attendre*
3. Dès qu'elle _____ , nous mangerons. *venir*
4. Je vous l'expliquerai afin que vous le _____ mieux. *comprendre*
5. Ils chantaient pendant que je _____ de la guitare. *jouer*
6. Elle me verra avant que je ne _____ . *partir*

The Subjunctive as an Imperative

The subjunctive may be used as an imperative when not talking to the person to whom the command is directed.

Qu'il parte tout de suite!
Let him leave immediately!
Qu'elle ne revienne jamais!
May she never return!
Vive le roi!
Long live the king!
Ainsi soit-il!
So be it!

The Subjunctive after an Affirmation

The subjunctive is used after the following expressions of affirmation.

que je sache   *that I know*
pas que je sache   *not that I know*
autant que je sache   *as much as I know*

Personne n'est à la porte que je sache.
No one is at the door so far as I know.

215. Change the sentence according to the model.

Il part maintenant.
Qu'il parte maintenant!

1. Elle vient tout de suite.
2. Il conduit sagement.
3. Il répond au professeur.
4. Ils obéissent à leurs parents.
5. Elle apprend la leçon.
6. Elles disent la vérité.
7. Il sait la réponse.
8. Elles finissent leurs devoirs.

Subjunctive in Relative Clauses

Indefinite antecedent

The subjunctive is used in relative clauses when the antecedent (the word the clause modifies) is indefinite. In other words, it is used after a noun or pronoun representing someone or something that is not yet identified or found. If the antecedent is definite, the indicative is used.

Je connais un médecin qui peut m'aider.
I know a doctor who can help me.
Je cherche un médecin qui puisse m'aider.
I am looking for a doctor who can help me. (But I haven't found one yet.)

Je connais un homme qui sait parler français.
I know a man who knows how to speak French.
Je cherche un homme qui sache parler français.
I am looking for a man who knows how to speak French. (But I haven't found him yet.)

216. Complete the following sentences with the correct form of each indicated expression.

    1. Je connais une dactylographe qui _____ .
      (parler français, écrire bien, savoir taper à la machine)

    2. J'ai besoin d'une dactylographe qui _____ .
      (parler français, écrire bien, savoir taper à la machine)

217. Rewrite the following sentences according to the model.

Je connais une fille. Elle sait parler français.
Je connais une fille qui sait parler français.

    1. Je cherche un homme. Il connaît la route.
    2. J'ai trouvé un homme. Il connaît cette chanson.
    3. Je veux acheter une blouse. Elle me va bien.
    4. J'ai une blouse. Elle me va bien.
    5. Je cherche un poste. Il est intéressant.
    6. J'ai un poste. Il est intéressant.

After rien, personne, quelqu'un

The subjunctive is also used after **rien, personne** or **quelqu'un** when doubt is implied.

Il n'y a personne qui puisse m'aider.
Il n'y a rien qu'il puisse faire.
Y a-t-il quelqu'un qui puisse le faire?

But:

Il y a quelqu'un qui peut le faire.

218. Complete the following sentences with the correct form of the indicated verb.

    1. Y a-t-il quelqu'un qui _____ la réponse? *savoir*
    2. Il n'y a personne qui _____ le faire. *vouloir*
    3. Il n'y a rien qui _____ m'aider. *pouvoir*
    4. Il y a quelqu'un qui _____ le français. *lire*
    5. Il n'y a personne qui _____ aider cet enfant. *pouvoir*

With the superlative and seul, unique

The subjunctive is used in a relative clause after a superlative expression, and after **seul** and **unique** when the superlative expression implies judgment or is considered to be an exaggeration.

C'est le plus beau poème qu'il connaisse.
It is the most beautiful poem that he knows.
C'est le seul livre que je comprenne.
It is the only book that I understand.

219. Complete the following sentences with the appropriate form of the indicated verb.

1. C'est le meilleur livre que j' _____ .   *avoir*
2. C'est le seul livre que je _____ .   *vouloir*
3. Pierre est le garçon le plus gentil que je _____ .   *connaître*
4. C'est la ville la plus cosmopolite qui _____ dans le monde.   *exister*
5. C'est la seule chose que je _____ .   *comprendre*

The Subjunctive after Indefinite Words such as *si ... que, quelque ... que, quel ... que, qui que ... , etc.*

The subjunctive is used after certain indefinite words.

Si ... que	*However*
Quelque	*However*
Quel que	*Whatever*
Qui que	*Whoever*
Quoi que	*Whatever*
Où que	*Wherever*
Soit que ... soit que	*Whether ... or*
De quelque manière que	*However*

Si intelligent qu'il soit, il ne pourra pas comprendre.
However intelligent he may be, he will not understand.
Quelque fort qu'il soit, il ne pourra pas le faire.
However strong he is, he won't be able to do it.
Quelques fautes que les élèves fassent, il faut les encourager.
Whatever mistakes the students make, you must encourage them.
Quels que soient vos problèmes, vous pourrez les résoudre.
Whatever your problems are, you can resolve them.
Qui que vous soyez, je ne vous connais pas.
Whoever you may be, I don't know you.
Quoi que tu dises, je te croirai.
Whatever you say, I'll believe you.
Où que vous alliez, je vous suivrai.
Wherever you go, I'll follow.
Soit qu'il vienne, soit qu'il ne vienne pas, j'irai quand même.
Whether he comes or not, I'll go.
De quelque manière qu'elle agisse, vous l'aimerez.
However she acts, you will like her.

220. Complete the following sentences with the appropriate form of the indicated verb.

    1. Quelque difficulté que vous _____ , perséverez. *avoir*
    2. Qui que vous _____ , travaillez bien. *être*
    3. Quoi qu'il _____ , il le fait bien. *faire*
    4. Où que nous _____ , nous vous téléphonerons. *aller*
    5. Quels que _____ vos problèmes, je vous aiderai. *être*
    6. Quoi qu'on _____ , vous êtes gentille. *dire*
    7. Si bon que je _____ , elle ne m'aime pas. *être*
    8. Quelque méchamment qu'il _____ , il a beaucoup d'amis. *agir*
    9. De quelque manière qu'il _____ , on ne le comprend pas. *parler*
    10. Soit qu'elle _____ , soit qu'elle ne _____ pas, nous commencerons la conférence. *venir*

Avoiding the Subjunctive

When there is no change of subject in the relative clause, the infinitive is usually used.

Il est heureux qu'il vienne.
Il est heureux de venir.

Verbs indicating a command, permission or refusal of permission (see pages 188-189) are usually not used with a subjunctive clause. The clause is normally replaced by an indirect object introduced by **à** and followed by an infinitive introduced by **de**.

Il permet que son fils parte.
Il permet à son fils de partir.
He permits his son to leave.

You can also avoid the subjunctive by replacing a clause with a noun.

Je vais le voir **avant qu'il ne parte.**
I'm going to see him before he leaves.
Je vais le voir **avant son départ.**
I'm going to see him before his departure.

221. Rewrite the following sentences using an infinitive construction or a noun instead of the subjunctive.

    1. Il se dépêche afin qu'il arrive à l'heure.
    2. Il est content qu'il soit ici.
    3. Il ordonne que son fils parte.
    4. Il permet que l'avocat parle.
    5. J'attends jusqu'à ce qu'il arrive.
    6. Nous ferons cela avant que nous partions.

Review

222. Complete the following sentences with the appropriate form of the indicated verb.

    1. Je veux que vous y _____ aussi. *aller*
    2. Je n'ai rien qui leur _____ . *plaire*
    3. Je crois qu'il _____ . *venir*
    4. Il va attendre jusqu'à ce que nous _____ . *revenir*

5. Je connais quelqu'un qui _____ le faire. *pouvoir*
6. Il permet que je _____ du vin. *boire*
7. Il regrette que je ne _____ pas le faire. *pouvoir*
8. Il vaut mieux qu'il _____ de bonne heure. *partir*
9. Il est probable qu'il _____ la réponse. *savoir*
10. C'est le plus beau livre que je _____ . *connaître*
11. Il faut que nous _____ le travail. *faire*
12. Il est certain qu'il _____ la vérité. *dire*
13. Croyez-vous qu'il _____ demain? *pleuvoir*
14. Si malades que nous _____ , nous travaillerons. *être*
15. Je le ferai à moins que vous n' _____ le temps de le faire. *avoir*
16. Il se dépêche afin d' _____ à l'heure. *arriver*

THE PAST SUBJUNCTIVE

The past subjunctive is formed by using the subjunctive of the verb **avoir** or **être** and the past participle.

parler	**venir**
j'aie parlé	je sois venu(e)
tu aies parlé	tu sois venu(e)
il, elle, on ait parlé	il, on soit venu
nous ayons parlé	elle soit venue
vous ayez parlé	nous soyons venu(e)s
ils, elles aient parlé	vous soyez venu(e)(s)(es)
	ils soient venus
	elles soient venues

Je regrette qu'il n'ait pas attendu.
I am sorry that he didn't wait.
Je suis content qu'elle soit venue.
I am happy that she came.

223. Complete the following sentences with the correct form of the past subjunctive of the indicated verb.

1. Elle est contente que tu _____ . *arriver*
2. Elle a peur que nous _____ cela à tout le monde. *dire*
3. Il est possible qu'elles vous _____ . *reconnaître*
4. Je ne crois pas qu'elle _____ . *venir*
5. Il est possible que vous _____ . *rester*
6. Nous doutons qu'elle _____ . *souffrir*
7. Je ne crois pas qu'ils _____ leurs devoirs. *faire*
8. Bien qu'il _____ , il n'a pas réussi. *étudier*
9. Nous sommes heureux qu'elle _____ . *s'amuser*
10. Quoique les enfants _____ de bonne heure, ils étaient fatigués le matin. *se coucher*

224. Rewrite the following sentences, putting the action of the dependent clause in the past.

1. Elle doute que nous comprenions.
2. Je regrette que tu arrives.
3. Il est possible que vous finissiez à l'heure.

4. Je ne crois pas qu'elles viennent.
5. Je doute qu'elle fasse le travail.
6. Pensez-vous qu'il se rase?

225. Comment on the following, using the indicated expression. Follow the model.

Elle est arrivée à l'heure.   *Je doute que*
Je doute qu'elle soit arrivée à l'heure.

1. Nous avons reconnu cet homme. *Il doute que*
2. Ils sont partis. *Je ne crois pas que*
3. Vous avez fait vos devoirs. *Il est important que*
4. Elle est revenue de bonne heure. *Il se peut que*
5. Il a su la réponse. *Je doute que*

THE IMPERFECT SUBJUNCTIVE

The imperfect subjunctive is formed by dropping the **s** from the second person singular form of the *passé simple* (literary past tense) and adding the endings **-sse, -sses, -ˆt, -ssions, -ssiez, -ssent.**

	parler	finir	attendre
Base:	**tu parlas**	**tu finis**	**tu attendis**
	je parla**sse**	je fini**sse**	j'attendi**sse**
	tu parla**sses**	tu fini**sses**	tu attendi**sses**
	il, elle on parl**ât**	il, elle, on fin**ît**	il, elle, on attend**ît**
	nous parla**ssions**	nous fini**ssions**	nous attendi**ssions**
	vous parla**ssiez**	vous fini**ssiez**	vous attendi**ssiez**
	ils, elles parla**ssent**	ils, elles fini**ssent**	ils, elles attendi**ssent**

	avoir	être
Base:	**tu eus**	**tu fus**
	j'eu**sse**	je fu**sse**
	tu eu**sses**	tu fu**sses**
	il, elle, on e**ût**	il, elle, on f**ût**
	nous eu**ssions**	nous fu**ssions**
	vous eu**ssiez**	vous fu**ssiez**
	ils, elles eu**ssent**	ils, elles fu**ssent**

Study the following. For other verbs which have irregular forms in the *passé simple*, see pages 158–161.

Infinitive	*Passé simple*	*Imperfect subjunctive*
partir	tu partis	**je partisse, il partît**
rire	tu ris	**je risse, il rît**
dire	tu dis	**je disse, il dît**
prendre	tu pris	**je prisse, il prît**
avoir	tu eus	**j'eusse, il eût**
boire	tu bus	**je busse, il bût**
connaître	tu connus	**je connusse, il connût**

courir	tu courus	**je courusse, il courût**
croire	tu crus	**je crusse, il crût**
devoir	tu dus	**je dusse, il dût**
lire	tu lus	**je lusse, il lût**
paraître	tu parus	**je parusse, il parût**
plaire	tu plus	**je plusse, il plût**
pouvoir	tu pus	**je pusse, il pût**
recevoir	tu reçus	**je reçusse, il reçût**
savoir	tu sus	**je susse, il sût**
se taire	tu te tus	**je me tusse, il se tût**
vivre	tu vécus	**je vécusse, il vécût**
vouloir	tu voulus	**je voulusse, il voulût**
battre	tu battis	**je battisse, il battît**
rompre	tu rompis	**je rompisse, il rompît**
offrir	tu offris	**j'offrisse, il offrît**
ouvrir	tu ouvris	**j'ouvrisse, il ouvrît**
couvrir	tu couvris	**je couvrisse, il couvrît**
souffrir	tu souffris	**je souffrisse, il souffrît**
vaincre	tu vainquis	**je vainquisse, il vainquît**
écrire	tu écrivis	**j'écrivisse, il écrivît**
conduire	tu conduisis	**je conduisisse, il conduisît**
traduire	tu traduisis	**je traduisisse, il traduisît**
naître	tu naquis	**je naquisse, il naquît**
voir	tu vis	**je visse, il vît**
craindre	tu craignis	**je craignisse, il craignît**
joindre	tu joignis	**je joignisse, il joignît**
peindre	tu peignis	**je peignisse, il peignît**
faire	tu fis	**je fisse, il fît**
mourir	tu mourus	**je mourusse, il mourût**
être	tu fus	**je fusse, il fût**
tenir	tu tins	**je tinsse, il tînt**
venir	tu vins	**je vinsse, il vînt**

Use of the Imperfect Subjunctive

The imperfect subjunctive is used only in written language when the verb in the main clause is in the past of the indicative or in the conditional. In spoken language, the present subjunctive replaces the imperfect subjunctive.

Spoken and written: **Je veux qu'il vienne me voir.**
                        I want him to come to see me.

Written: **Je voulais qu'il vînt me voir.**
Spoken: **Je voulais qu'il vienne me voir.**
                        I wanted him to come to see me.

226. Complete the following sentences with the correct form of the imperfect subjunctive of the indicated verb.

1. Je doutais qu'il _____ me voir.   *venir*
2. Elle cherchait quelqu'un qui _____ le faire.   *pouvoir*

3. Je voudrais qu'il _____ à l'heure. *être*
4. Je ne croyais pas qu'ils _____ à l'heure. *finir*
5. Il doutait que nous _____ malades. *être*
6. Elle était heureuse que vous _____ la vérité. *savoir*
7. Il était content que nous _____ le travail. *faire*
8. Elle était heureuse qu'il _____ la lettre. *écrire*
9. Elle voulait que vous _____ tout de suite. *venir*
10. On craignait que les enfants ne _____ pas à l'heure. *rentrer*
11. Il avait peur que tu ne _____ fâché. *devenir*
12. Il fallait que les enfants _____ de bonne heure. *se coucher*

227. Rewrite the following sentences in spoken language.

1. Il voulait que nous vinssions.
2. J'étais heureux qu'elles fussent à l'heure.
3. Il fallait qu'elle le fît.
4. Elle était trop fatiguée pour que la soirée fût agréable.
5. Je cherchais quelqu'un qui pût le faire.
6. Je craignais que l'équipe ne gagnât pas le prix.

THE PLUPERFECT SUBJUNCTIVE

The pluperfect subjunctive is formed by using the imperfect subjunctive of **avoir** or **être** and the past participle.

parler	**partir**
j'eusse parlé	je fusse parti(e)
tu eusses parlé	tu fusses parti(e)
il, elle, on eût parlé	il, on fût parti
nous eussions parlé	elle fût partie
vous eussiez parlé	nous fussions parti(e)s
ils, elles eussent parlé	vous fussiez parti(e)(s)(es)
	ils fussent partis
	elles fussent parties

Use of the Pluperfect Subjunctive

The pluperfect subjunctive is a literary tense. In conversation, the past subjunctive replaces the pluperfect subjunctive.

Spoken and Written: **Il regrette que nous ne soyons pas venus.**
He is sorry we didn't come.

Written: **Il regrettait que nous ne fussions pas venus.**
Spoken: **Il regrettait que nous ne soyons pas venus.**
He was sorry we didn't come.

If the subjunctive is obligatory, the sentence can usually be rewritten to avoid it.

Bien qu'il eût déjà mangé, il alla au restaurant.
Il avait déjà mangé, mais il est allé au restaurant.

228. Complete the following sentences with the correct form of the pluperfect subjunctive of the indicated verb.

    1. Il doutait qu'elle _____ malade. *être*
    2. Je regrettais qu'elles ne _____ pas _____ . *venir*
    3. Elle était heureuse que vous _____ la vérité. *savoir*
    4. Elle était triste qu'il _____ . *partir*
    5. J'étais heureux qu'il _____ la lettre. *écrire*
    6. Il était content que tu _____ . *réussir*
    7. Il était possible qu'elles _____ cela. *savoir*
    8. Elles ne croyaient pas que j' _____ tant de chance. *avoir*
    9. Nous préférions attendre jusqu'à ce qu'ils _____ . *revenir*
    10. Elle avait peur qu'il n' _____ pas _____ le travail. *finir*
    11. Il semblait que nous _____ des efforts inutiles. *faire*
    12. Elle était contente que nous _____ . *se débrouiller*

229. Rewrite the following sentences in spoken language.

    1. Je regrettais qu'elle ne fût pas venue à l'heure.
    2. Bien qu'elles eussent déjà compris, ils continuaient à leur expliquer.
    3. J'étais contente qu'il eût connu mon ami.
    4. Il fallait que vous eussiez dit cela.
    5. Il semblait que nous eussions fait des efforts.
    6. Il avait peur que le pain ne fût devenu trop dur.

SI CLAUSES IN THE SUBJUNCTIVE

The subjunctive is used in *if* clauses in literary style. The pluperfect subjunctive can be used in the *if* clause to replace the pluperfect indicative and in the main clause to replace the past conditional. It is in reality "a literary past conditional."

Spoken:	**S'il l'avait cru, il serait parti.**
Written:	**S'il l'eût cru, il fût parti.**
	S'il l'avait cru, il fût parti.
	S'il l'eût cru, il serait parti.

230. Rewrite the following sentences, putting all verbs in literary style.

    1. S'il avait eu assez d'argent, il serait allé au cinéma.
    2. Si vous étiez venu, vous auriez vu Paul.
    3. S'il avait été prêt, il serait parti.
    4. Si vous étiez venu, vous auriez appris la nouvelle.
    5. S'il avait fait beau, nous serions partis.
    6. Si elle était revenue, elle serait venue nous revoir.

231. Rewrite the following sentences in spoken language.

    1. Le nez de Cléopâtre s'il eût été plus court, toute la face de la terre eût changé.
    2. Si elle eût eu assez d'argent, elle fût venue nous voir.
    3. Si nous eussions su cela, nous l'eussions dit.
    4. S'il eût fait beau, elle fût partie.
    5. S'il eût plu, elles ne fussent pas venues.
    6. Si j'eusse su cela, je ne vous eusse pas répondu.

SEQUENCE OF TENSES IN INDIRECT DISCOURSE

Direct discourse *directly cites* someone's words.

Il me dit: « Viens chez moi samedi. »
Il me dit: « Je le ferai dans une heure. »

Indirect discourse *indirectly reports* someone's words.

Il me dit de venir chez lui samedi.
Il me dit qu'il le fera dans une heure.

When the verb in the principal introductory phrase is in the present or the future tense, there is no tense change in indirect discourse. When the principal verb is in the past tense, the following changes of tense occur.

	Direct discourse		*Indirect discourse*
	imperfect		imperfect
	present		imperfect
	passé composé		plus-que-parfait
il	future	**il a dit**	present conditional
dit	present conditional		past conditional
il dira	futur antérieur		past conditional
	imperative		infinitive or subjunctive
	subjunctive		subjunctive

Pierre dit: « **Il faisait** beau hier. »
Pierre **dit** qu'**il faisait** beau hier.
Pierre **a dit** qu'**il faisait** beau hier.

Elle dit: « Je **pars** tout de suite. »
Elle **dit** qu'**elle part** tout de suite.
Elle **a dit** qu'**elle partait** tout de suite.

Anne répond: « **J'ai vu** le film hier. »
Anne **répond** qu'**elle a vu** le film hier.
Anne **a répondu** qu'**elle avait vu** le film hier.

Il déclare: « **Je viendrai** ici demain. »
Il **déclare** qu'**il viendra** ici demain.
Il **a déclaré** qu'**il viendrait** ici demain.

André dit: « **Je voudrais** faire sa connaissance. »
André **dit** qu'**il voudrait** faire sa connaissance.
André **a dit** qu'**il aurait voulu** faire sa connaissance.

Marie dit: « **Pierre aura fini** à trois heures. »
Marie **dit** que **Pierre aura fini** à trois heures.
Marie **a dit** que **Pierre aurait fini** à trois heures.

Elle lui dit: « **Attends** un moment. »
Elle lui **dit d'attendre** un moment.
Elle lui **a dit d'attendre** un moment.

Il lui suggère: « **Allons** au cinéma. »
Il lui **suggère** qu'**ils aillent** au cinéma.
Il lui **a suggéré** qu'**ils aillent** au cinéma.

Le professeur dit: « **Je veux que vous fassiez** le travail. »
Le professeur **dit** qu'il **veut que** nous **fassions** le travail.
Le professeur **a dit** qu'il **voulait que nous fassions** le travail.

Note that the first and second persons are generally replaced by the third person in indirect discourse.

Indirect Discourse in Sentences with an Interrogative Word

After the verbs **demander, se demander, ignorer, savoir, comprendre** and **chercher,** certain interrogative words change in form and in order.

A direct question related to a verb and **est-ce que** becomes **si** in indirect discourse. **Si** means *whether* or *if.*

Direct discourse

Il demande: « **Les Leblanc seront ici bientôt? »**
                 « **Est-ce que les Leblanc seront ici bientôt? »**
                 « **Les Leblanc seront-ils ici bientôt? »**

Indirect discourse

Il demande si les Leblanc seront ici bientôt.
He asks whether the Leblancs will be here soon.

Interrogative Pronouns in Indirect Discourse

Qui is used in all cases for people.

Direct discourse	*Indirect discourse*
Il demande: « Qui est-ce que tu vois? »	**Il demande qui tu vois.**
Il demande: « Qui vois-tu? »	**Il demande qui est-ce que tu vois.** (*spoken*)
Il demande: « Avec qui va-t-elle à la partie? »	**Il demande avec qui elle va à la partie.**
	Il demande avec qui est-ce qu'elle va à la partie. (*spoken*)

For things, the subject pronoun **ce qui** and the object pronoun **ce que** are used. **Quoi** is the object of the preposition.

Je me demande **ce qui** se passe, **ce que** vous dites, **avec quoi** elle peint.

In spoken language, the long forms of **ce qui** and **ce que, qu'est-ce qui** and **qu'est-ce que** and **avec quoi est-ce que** are used.

See Interrogative pronouns, pages 223–224.

Inversion of the Subject in Indirect Discourse

In indirect discourse, there is never inversion of the pronoun subject and the verb but there can be simple inversion of the noun subject and the verb.

Direct discourse	*Indirect discourse*
Je me demande: « Quand se mariera-t-il? »	**Je me demande quand il se mariera.**
Je lui demande: « Où travaille ta femme? »	**Je lui demande où travaille sa femme (où sa femme travaille).**

Inversion can be used only if the verb stands alone without a direct object.

There can never be inversion with **pourquoi.**

   Elle demande pourquoi ils sont toujours en retard.

Inversion is used with **ce que, avec qui, avec quoi.**

   Je ne sais pas ce que fait son enfant.

There is never inversion after **qui** as a direct object.

   J'ignore qui Marie va épouser.

232. Put the following sentences in indirect discourse. Then put the answers in the past tense. Follow the model.

   Pierre dit: « Je veux acheter une bicyclette. »
   Pierre *dit* qu'*il veut* acheter une bicyclette.
   Pierre *a dit* qu'*il voulait* acheter une bicyclette.

   1. André dit: « Je ne peux pas le faire. »
   2. Marie dit: « Je n'ai jamais vu quelque chose de si beau. »
   3. Jean promet: « Je ferai tout pour vous aider. »
   4. Ils disent: « Nous voudrions faire la connaissance de la nouvelle étudiante. »
   5. Mes parents me promettent: « Nous te donnerons une auto si tu reçois de meilleures notes. »
   6. Monsieur Leblanc dit: « Nous irons en Afrique cet été. »
   7. Claire répond: « J'ai déjà lu ce livre. »
   8. Anne dit: « J'aimerais voir ce film. »
   9. Pierre dit: « Il faisait beau hier. »
   10. Roger dit: « Il aura fini à trois heures. »
   11. Marie demande: « Ont-ils gagné le match? »
   12. Le professeur demande: « Serez-vous à la réunion? »

233. Madame Leclerc was a witness to a crime. She is being interrogated by the lawyer in a courtroom. Relate the following interview between the lawyer and Madame Leclerc, using indirect discourse.

L'avocat	Où étiez-vous à deux heures du matin le 8 octobre?
Mme Leclerc	J'étais dans la cuisine.
L'avocat	Avez-vous l'habitude d'être dans la cuisine si tard?
Mme Leclerc	Non, mais ce soir-là je ne pouvais pas dormir et donc, je suis descendue dans la cuisine pour chercher un verre de lait.
L'avocat	Avez-vous entendu ou vu quelque chose d'étrange?
Mme Leclerc	Oui, j'ai entendu des cris dans la maison de ma voisine et j'ai vu un homme attaquer ma voisine avec un couteau.
L'avocat	Pourriez-vous identifier cet homme?
Mme Leclerc	Oui, je pourrais l'identifier clairement, car la lumière était allumée dans sa maison.
L'avocat	Cet homme, est-il dans cette salle?
Mme Leclerc	Oui, c'est l'accusé.
L'avocat	Merci, vous pouvez quitter la barre des témoins.

L'avocat lui a demandé où elle était à deux heures du matin la nuit du 8 octobre. Mme Leclerc a répondu qu'elle...

Continue.

USES OF THE INFINITIVE

After Prepositions

The infinitive is used after most prepositions, such as **avant de, pour, afin de** and **sans.** The present participle is sometimes used in English.

avant de partir	*before leaving*
pour aller	*in order to go*
afin de venir	*in order to come*
sans comprendre	*without understanding*

Je lui ai parlé **avant de partir.**
I spoke to him before leaving.

En is followed by the present participle.

en parlant	*while speaking*
en sortant	*upon leaving*

En sortant, il nous a dit au revoir.
Upon leaving, he told us good-bye.
En faisant ses courses, elle a vu son ami.
While shopping, she saw her friend.

See the use of the present participle, page 134.

After the preposition **après,** the infinitive of **avoir** or **être** plus the past participle of the verb is used.

après avoir parlé	*after having spoken*
après être parti(e)(s)(es)	*after having left*
après s'être habillé(e)(s)(es)	*after having gotten dressed*

As a Noun

Vouloir c'est pouvoir.
To want to is to be able to.

Voter est un droit.
Voting is a right.

As an Imperative

Ne pas marcher sur le gazon.
Do not walk on the grass.
Laisser cuire pendant trente minutes.
Cook for thirty minutes.

In an Interrogative Phrase Expressing Deliberation

Que faire?
What shall I (we) do?
Où aller?
Where shall I (we) go?

In an Exclamatory Phrase

Oh! être jeune encore!
Oh, to be still young!

234. Substitute each indicated infinitive in the following sentences. Make all necessary changes.

1. Je lui parlerai avant de partir. (manger, chanter, danser, décider, revenir, finir, commencer)
2. Que faut-il faire afin de comprendre? (venir, réussir, finir à l'heure, savoir la leçon)
3. Il part sans dire au revoir. (manger, attendre, faire ses devoirs, parler)
4. Après avoir chanté, il est parti. (parler, finir, manger, dire au revoir)
5. Après être arrivé, il est venu me voir. (rentrer, entrer, retourner, descendre)

235. Combine the following sentences according to the model.

Il a fini la leçon. Ensuite, il est allé au théâtre.
Avant d'aller au théâtre, il a fini la leçon.
Après avoir fini la leçon, il est allé au théâtre.

1. Il a mangé. Ensuite, il est parti.
2. Nous avons déjeuné. Ensuite, nous sommes allés au musée.
3. Nous avons fait le ménage. Ensuite, nous avons joué au tennis.
4. Elle s'est habillée. Ensuite, elle a lu le journal.

236. Translate the following into French, using an infinitive.

1. before arriving
2. after arriving
3. upon arriving
4. while eating
5. after eating
6. before eating
7. Do not translate.
8. Beat three eggs.
9. What shall we do?
10. Oh, to be rich!

Faire in Causative Construction

An important use of the verb **faire** is in causative construction. In this construction, the subject causes an action to be done by someone or something else. **Faire** is followed by the infinitive.

Je fais chanter les enfants.
I have (make) the children sing.
J'ai fait réciter les élèves.
I had (made) the students recite.
Il fait faire ce travail.
He has this work done.
Il a fait faire ce travail.
He had this work done.

When there is one object, it is a direct object. If it is a noun, it follows the infinitive. If it is a pronoun, it precedes **faire** in the negative imperative and in declarative sentences.

Ne faites pas descendre les valises maintenant.
Don't have the suitcases brought down now.
Ne les faites pas descendre maintenant.
Don't have them brought down now.

Il fait chanter la fille.
He has the girl sing.
Il la fait chanter.
He has her sing.

Elle fait faire une robe.
She has a dress made.
Elle la fait faire.
She has it made.

Elle a fait construire une maison.
She had a house built.
Elle l'a fait construire.
She had it built.

In the above sentence, the object of **faire** is **construire. Faire** does not agree with the direct object pronoun.

In the affirmative imperative, the direct object noun follows the infinitive, but the direct object pronoun precedes the infinitive.

Faites laver la voiture.
Have the car washed.
Faites-la laver.
Have it washed.

When there are two noun or pronoun complements, one will be the direct object and the other will be the indirect object. The person or thing doing the action is the indirect object. Again, all pronoun objects precede **faire** except in the affirmative imperative.

Il fait réciter le poème aux étudiants.
He has the students recite the poem.
Il le fait réciter aux étudiants.
He has the students recite it.
Il leur fait réciter le poème.
He has them recite the poem.
Il le leur fait réciter.
He has them recite it.
Ne le leur fais pas réciter.
Don't have them recite it.

But:

Fais-le-leur réciter.
Have them recite it.

The past participle of **faire** is always invariable when followed by an infinitive.

La maison que nous avons fait construire
The house we had built

If necessary, review object pronouns in Chapter 8.

To avoid possible ambiguity with the indirect object, the person or thing doing the action can be introduced by **par** instead of **à**. For example, **Il fait chanter une chanson à Marie** can mean (1) *He has Mary sing a song* or (2) *He has a song sung to Mary*. If the first meaning is intended, **par** can replace **à**.

Il fait chanter une chanson par Marie.
He has Mary sing a song.

A reflexive pronoun can be used with the verb **faire** in causative construction.

Elle s'est fait faire une robe.
She had a dress made (for herself).
Je me fais couper les cheveux.
I have my hair cut.
Je me suis fait couper les cheveux.
I had my hair cut.
Je me les ai fait couper.
I had it cut.

237. Madame Dupont is having a house built. Tell who is responsible for various aspects of construction. Follow the model.

Qui construit la maison.   *la Compagnie Leclerc*
Elle fait construire la maison à la Compagnie Leclerc.

1. Qui fait les dessins? *l'architecte*
2. Qui peint les murs? *le peintre*
3. Qui installe les salles de bains? *le plombier*
4. Qui pose des fils électriques? *les électriciens*
5. Qui bâtit les étagères à livres? *le charpentier*

238. Rewrite the following sentences, substituting **par** for **à** in order to make the sentences less ambiguous.

1. Le professeur a fait écrire le devoir à la classe.
2. Elle fait chanter la chanson aux garçons.
3. Nous faisons écrire une lettre à notre ami.
4. Je fais jouer du piano à l'enfant.

239. Rewrite the following sentences, replacing the direct object by a pronoun, according to the model.

Le professeur fait expliquer la leçon.
Le professeur la fait expliquer.

1. Le professeur fera réciter les élèves.
2. La fille a fait faire la robe.
3. Nous ferons faire les portraits.
4. Il fera construire la maison.
5. Vous avez fait venir le médecin.
6. Elle s'est fait laver les cheveux.
7. Fais entrer les invités.
8. Faites venir le médecin.

240. Rewrite the following sentences, replacing the direct and indirect objects by pronouns, according to the model.

Il fait lire le poème aux étudiants.
Il le leur fait lire.

1. Il fera écrire la lettre à son fils.
2. Elle s'est fait faire un chandail.
3. Il fait écrire le résumé aux élèves.
4. Il fera faire la robe par la couturière.

5. Il fait apprendre les verbes à Marie.
6. On a fait jouer le jeu aux enfants.
7. Fais réparer le garage au charpentier.
8. Faites chanter la chanson aux enfants.

Laisser and Verbs of Perception plus the Infinitive

After the verb **laisser** and after the verbs of perception **entendre, voir, écouter, regarder** and **sentir,** the infinitive is used. Unlike in English, the infinitive precedes the noun. The pronoun precedes the main verb. These verbs function similarly to the verb **faire** in causative construction.

Je laisse Marie finir le travail.
I let Mary finish the work.
Je la (lui) laisse finir le travail.
I let her finish the work.
Je la laisse le finir.
or
Je le lui laisse finir.
I let her finish it.

Je vois coudre Hélène.
I see Helen sewing.
Je la vois coudre.
I see her sewing.

J'ai entendu chanter Marie.
I heard Mary singing.
Je l'ai entendue chanter.
I heard her singing.

J'ai entendu chanter la chanson.
I heard the song sung.
Je l'ai entendu chanter.
I heard it sung.

Note that the past participle agrees with the preceding direct object if the object performs the action expressed by the infinitive. In the expression **la femme que j'ai entendue chanter,** the woman did the singing and, therefore, the past participle agrees. However, in the expression **la chanson que j'ai entendu chanter,** the past participle does not agree since **chanson** is the object of **chanter.**

241. Translate the following sentences into French.

1. I saw Mary walking on the boulevard.
2. I see her arriving.
3. I let Peter leave.
4. I let him play.
5. I heard the baby cry.
6. I heard them (f.) sing.
7. I listen to them singing.
8. He looks at the painter's painting.

The Use of the Prepositions *à* and *de* before an Infinitive

à

The following verbs are followed by the preposition **à** before an infinitive.

aider à	continuer à (de)	se mettre à	se résigner à
aimer (à)	se décider à	obliger à (de)	se résoudre à
s'amuser à	demander à (de)	parvenir à	réussir à
apprendre à	destiner à	passer (du temps) à	servir à
arriver à	encourager à	penser à	songer à
s'attendre à	engager à	persister à	suffire à
avoir à	enseigner à	se plaire à	tarder à
chercher à	forcer à (de)	pousser à	tendre à
commencer à (de)	s'habituer à	se préparer à	tenir à
condamner à	hésiter à	recommencer à (de)	travailler à
consentir à	inviter à	renoncer à	trouver à

de

The following verbs are followed by the preposition **de** before an infinitive.

accepter de	dispenser de	inspirer de	proposer de
(s')accuser de	douter de	interdire de	refuser de
achever de	écrire de	jurer de	regretter de
s'agir de	s'efforcer de (à)	manquer de	se réjouir de
s'arrêter de	empêcher de	menacer de	remercier de
blâmer de	s'ennuyer de (à)	mériter de	se repentir de
cesser de	entreprendre de	négliger de	résoudre de
charger de	envisager de	obliger de (à)	rêver de
choisir de	essayer de	offrir de (à)	rire de
commander de	s'étonner de	ordonner de	risquer de
se contenter de	éviter de	oublier de	souhaiter de
continuer de (à)	s'excuser de	parler de	soupçonner de
convenir de	feindre de	se passer de	se souvenir de
craindre de	féliciter de	permettre de	supplier de
décider de (à)	finir de	persuader de	supporter de
défendre de	forcer de (à)	plaindre de	tâcher de
demander de (à)	se garder de	se plaindre de	tenter de
se dépêcher de	se hâter de	prier de	trembler de
dire de	s'indigner de	promettre de	venir de

Demander à is used when there is no indirect object.

Il **demande à** venir.
He asks to come.

Demander de is used when there is an indirect object.

Il **me demande de** venir.
He asks me to come.

See pages 125 and 140 for uses of **venir de.**

The following verbs have direct objects before **de.**

accuser quelqu'un de	**féliciter** quelqu'un de
avertir quelqu'un de	**menacer** quelqu'un de
blâmer quelqu'un de	**persuader** quelqu'un de
charger quelqu'un de	**prier** quelqu'un de
empêcher quelqu'un de	**remercier** quelqu'un de

The following group of verbs have an indirect object complement and are followed by **de** plus an infinitive.

commander à quelqu'un de	**ordonner** à quelqu'un de
conseiller à quelqu'un de	**permettre** à quelqu'un de
défendre à quelqu'un de	**promettre** à quelqu'un de
demander à quelqu'un de	**proposer** à quelqu'un de
dire à quelqu'un de	**refuser** à quelqu'un de
écrire à quelqu'un de	**reprocher** à quelqu'un de
interdire à quelqu'un de	**suggérer** à quelqu'un de
offrir à quelqu'un de	**téléphoner** à quelqu'un de

The following verbs are followed directly by an infinitive.

aimer	devoir	paraître	revenir
affirmer	écouter	partir	savoir
aller	entendre	penser	sembler
assurer	envoyer	pouvoir	sentir
avouer	espérer	préférer	souhaiter
compter	faire	prétendre	supposer
courir	falloir	se rappeler	valoir mieux
croire	laisser	reconnaître	venir
déclarer	mener	regarder	voir
descendre	monter	rentrer	vouloir
désirer	oser	retourner	

Some transitive verbs that are intransitive in English are not followed by a preposition.

attendre	*to wait for*	**espérer**	*to hope for*
chercher	*to look for*	**payer**	*to pay for*
demander	*to ask for*	**regarder**	*to look at*
envoyer chercher	*to send for*		

Il **a attendu** l'autobus pendant un quart d'heure.
He waited for the bus for a quarter of an hour.
Il **paie** les billets.
He pays for the tickets.

Some verbs have a thing as a direct object and a person as an indirect object.

acheter quelque chose à quelqu'un	**enseigner** quelque chose à quelqu'un
apprendre quelque chose à quelqu'un	**ôter** quelque chose à quelqu'un
arracher quelque chose à quelqu'un	**pardonner** quelque chose à quelqu'un
cacher quelque chose à quelqu'un	**prendre** quelque chose à quelqu'un
dire quelque chose à quelqu'un	**refuser** quelque chose à quelqu'un
emprunter quelque chose à quelqu'un	**souhaiter** quelque chose à quelqu'un
enlever quelque chose à quelqu'un	**voler** quelque chose à quelqu'un

For infinitives following a noun or an adjective, see Chapter 3, Prepositions, pages 78–79.

242. Complete the following sentences with the correct preposition when it is necessary.

1. Il apprend _____ chanter.
2. Elle lui a dit _____ le faire.
3. Je vous demande _____ venir me voir.
4. Nous avons essayé _____ faire du ski.
5. Savez-vous _____ jouer de la guitare?
6. Il a commencé _____ neiger.
7. Tu veux _____ parler avec moi.
8. Il refuse _____ m'aider.
9. Elle a peur _____ voir ce film.
10. Il préfère _____ rester ici.
11. Je vous prie _____ m'aider.
12. Nous espérons _____ réussir.
13. Tu réussis _____ le faire.
14. Il faut _____ commencer le travail.
15. Nous envoyons _____ chercher le médecin.
16. Elle m'a empêché _____ venir.
17. Je vous invite _____ aller au cinéma.
18. Venez _____ voir le spectacle!
19. Je dois _____ rentrer à la maison.
20. Il vous permet _____ l'aider.
21. Je le persuade _____ ne pas partir.
22. Il me promet _____ être sage.
23. J'espère _____ voir ce film bientôt.
24. Regardez _____ ce beau tableau.

PASSIVE VOICE

Forms of the Passive Voice

Infinitive	**être aimé (avoir été aimé)**
Present participle	**étant aimé(e)**
Past participle	**aimé(e) (ayant été aimé)**
Present	**je suis aimé(e)**
Present subjunctive	**que je sois aimé(e)**
Imperfect	**j'étais aimé(e)**
Future	**je serai aimé(e)**
Conditional	**je serais aimé(e)**
Imperative	**sois aimé(e), soyons aimé(e)s, soyez aimé(e)(s)(es)**
Passé composé	**j'ai été aimé(e)**
Pluperfect	**j'avais été aimé(e)**
Conditional past	**j'aurais été aimé(e)**
Past subjunctive	**que j'aie été aimé(e)**
Literary past	**je fus aimé(e)**
Imperfect subjunctive	**que je fusse aimé(e)**
Past anterior	**j'eus été aimé(e)**
Pluperfect subjunctive	**que j'eusse été aimé(e)**
Passé surcomposé	**j'ai eu été aimé(e)**

True Passive with *être*

The passive voice is used less frequently in French than in English. When the true passive voice is used, however, it is formed by using a form of the verb **être** plus the past participle.

Passive: **Les lettres ont été distribuées par le facteur.**
             The letters were delivered by the mailman.
Active: **Le facteur a distribué les lettres.**
             The mailman delivered the letters.

The agent or person who performed the action is usually introduced by the preposition **par.**

Cette lettre a été envoyée par Marie.
This letter was sent by Mary.

De is used with verbs expressing condition or emotion.

Le professeur est aimé de ses étudiants.
The teacher is liked by his students.
La montagne est couverte de neige.
The mountain is covered with snow.

The passive voice should be avoided, if possible. If the agent is expressed, simply rewrite the sentence actively.

Passive: **Ce livre sera écrit par un grand auteur.**
Active: **Un grand auteur écrira ce livre.**

When the agent is not expressed, the passive voice can be replaced by **on** and an active verb.

Passive: **La lettre a été envoyée.**
Active: **On a envoyé la lettre.**
Passive: **J'ai été admiré.**
Active: **On m'a admiré.**

The passive voice cannot be used with intransitive verbs. In English we can say:

The letter was answered.

But in French, we must say:

On a répondu à la lettre.

In English, an indirect object can be the subject of a passive verb. This cannot be done in French.

English: *John was given a present.*
French: **Un cadeau a été donné à Jean.**
             On a donné un cadeau à Jean.

243. Rewrite the following sentences in the active voice, according to the models.

La carte a été envoyée par Marie.
Marie a envoyé la carte.

La carte a été envoyée.
On a envoyé la carte.

1. Le roman a été écrit par Balzac.
2. Ce monument a été construit par les Romains.

3. Le bâtiment a été détruit par un incendie.
4. Le repas a été préparé par la bonne.
5. Cette maison sera construite par un grand architecte.
6. J'ai été aimé.
7. Le travail a été fini.
8. Cette ville a été détruite pendant la guerre.

The Passive Voice with *se*

A common way to form the passive voice in French is by using the reflexive pronoun **se** with the third person singular or plural form of the verb. This construction is most common when the action is habitual or normal or when the person by whom the action is carried out (the agent) is unimportant.

Les cravates se vendent ici.
Ties are sold here.
Le gouvernement se compose de trois parties.
The government is composed of three parts.
Le français se parle ici.
French is spoken here.
Cela ne se fait pas.
That is not done.

244. Rewrite the following sentences in the passive voice, using the reflexive form.

1. On parle français au Québec.
2. On n'écrit pas ce mot sans *s*.
3. On verra le plus beau monument au centre de la ville.
4. Autrefois, on faisait cela à la main.
5. On a modernisé la ville.
6. On ouvrira les portes à huit heures.
7. On fabriquait ces autos dans cette usine.
8. On ne dit pas cela.

Chapter 6

Interrogative Words and Constructions

FORMING QUESTIONS

Questions are formed in French in the following ways:

1. by changing the period of a statement to a question mark and using a rising intonation.

Statement	*Question*
Marie parle français.	**Marie parle français?**
Vous avez bien dormi.	**Vous avez bien dormi?**
Il se réveille.	**Il se réveille?**

2. by adding **n'est-ce pas?** to an affirmative sentence.

Statement	*Question*
Tu vas au musée.	**Tu vas au musée, n'est-ce pas?**
Il est arrivé.	**Il est arrivé, n'est-ce pas?**
Elle se débrouille.	**Elle se débrouille, n'est-ce pas?**

3. by adding **est-ce que** or **est-ce qu'** (before vowels) at the beginning of the statement and changing the period to a question mark.

Statement	*Question*
Pierre nous parlera.	**Est-ce-que Pierre nous parlera?**
Il se rase.	**Est-ce qu'il se rase?**
Elle s'est bien habillée.	**Est-ce qu'elle s'est bien habillée?**

1. Form questions according to the model.

Elle parle français.
Elle parle français, n'est-ce pas?
Est-ce qu'elle parle français?

1. Marie travaille bien.
2. Il écrit une lettre.

3. Pierre se couche.
4. Elle s'habillait bien.
5. Ils viendront à l'heure.
6. Ils sont allés au cinéma hier soir.
7. Ces étudiants ont lu ce livre.
8. Pierre s'est reposé.

INTERROGATIVE FORMS BY INVERSION — SIMPLE TENSES

Questions may be formed by inverting a pronoun subject and the verb of declarative sentences. The subject is connected to the verb with a hyphen.

Statement	*Question*
Tu vas à Londres.	**Vas-tu à Londres?**
Vous parlez français.	**Parlez-vous français?**
Nous nous levons.	**Nous levons-nous?**
Vous vous débrouillez bien.	**Vous débrouillez-vous bien?**

When inverting a third person singular subject and a verb, a **t** must be inserted between the inverted verb and the subject if the verb ends in a vowel.

Statement	*Question*
Il parle français.	**Parle-t-il français?**
Il se lève.	**Se lève-t-il?**
But:	
Il écrit.	**Écrit-il?**

Inversion is usually not used with **je.** Instead, use **est-ce que.**

Est-ce que je suis content?

Inversion with **je** is permitted with certain often-used verbs.

Suis-je
Ai-je
Puis-je

Note that **peux** becomes **puis** in inversion with **je.**

When inverting with a noun subject, state the noun, then the verb, then the pronoun.

Statement	*Question*
Marie parle français.	**Marie parle-t-elle français?**
Pierre s'habille.	**Pierre s'habille-t-il?**

After interrogative adverbs, either simple or complex inversion can be used.

Quand viendront les invités?
Quand les invités viendront-ils?

Complex inversion is obligatory

1. after **pourquoi** when the subject is a noun.

Pourquoi les élèves font-ils du bruit?

2. when the verb is followed by an adjective or direct object.

Pourquoi Pierre est-il paresseux?
À qui la fille doit-elle donner l'argent?

2. Form questions according to the model.

Tu regardes le film.
Regardes-tu le film?

1. Tu regardes la peinture.
2. Vous allez à Paris.
3. Nous savons la réponse.
4. Ils écoutent la radio.
5. Elle court.
6. Tu te dépêches.
7. Nous nous lèverons de bonne heure.
8. Elles se couchent à dix heures.
9. Je suis amusant.
10. Je peux le faire.

3. Form questions according to the model.

Il parle français.
Parle-t-il français?

1. Elle pleure beaucoup.
2. Il ouvre la porte.
3. Elle rencontre une amie au café.
4. Il se dépêche.
5. Elle se lave la figure.
6. Elle s'amuse bien.

4. Form questions according to the model.

Marie parle français.
Marie parle-t-elle français?

1. Les enfants prennent des bonbons.
2. Marie aime la peinture moderne.
3. Hélène lit un roman.
4. Les invités viendront à l'heure.
5. Pierre se rase.
6. Hélène se reposera dimanche.
7. Ces hommes se débrouillent bien.
8. Marc et Pierre se retrouvent à l'école tous les jours.

INTERROGATIVE FORMS BY INVERSION — COMPOUND TENSES

In compound tenses, the subject pronoun and the auxiliary verb are inverted.

Statement	*Question*
Il a travaillé.	**A-t-il travaillé?**
Vous êtes arrivé.	**Êtes-vous arrivé?**
Ils se sont rasés.	**Se sont-ils rasés?**
Elle s'est couchée.	**S'est-elle couchée?**

5. Rewrite the following in the interrogative form, according to the model.

Il a chanté.
A-t-il chanté?

1. Nous avons fait nos devoirs.
2. Elle a dit la vérité.
3. Louise est vite montée.
4. Nous sommes arrivés à l'heure.
5. Ils se sont couchés.
6. Elles se sont moquées de vous.
7. Nous nous sommes dépêchées.
8. Hélène s'est lavée.

INTERROGATIVE ADVERBS AND ADVERBIAL EXPRESSIONS

Following are common interrogative words used to introduce questions.

Où?	*Where?*	**Combien?**	*How many?*
Quand?	*When?*	**Pourquoi?**	*Why?*
Comment?	*How?*	**À quelle heure?**	*At what time?*

Study the following.

Où va-t-elle?	*Where is she going?*
Quand arrive-t-elle?	*When is she arriving?*
Comment va-t-il?	*How is he?*
Combien de livres y a-t-il sur la table?	*How many books are there on the table?*
Combien coûte le bifteck?	*How much does the steak cost?*
Pourquoi pleure-t-elle?	*Why is she crying?*
À quelle heure vient-il?	*At what time is he coming?*

6. Complete the following with an appropriate question word.

1. Elles partent demain. _____ partent-elles?

2. L'auto coûte deux mille dollars. _____ coûte l'auto?

3. Marie va au musée. _____ va Marie?

4. L'église est moderne. _____ est l'église?

5. Elle arrivera à trois heures. _____ arrivera-t-elle?

6. Elle met un chandail parce qu'elle a froid. _____ met-elle un chandail?

7. Elles vont à la plage en été. _____ vont-elles à la plage?

8. Elles vont à la plage en été. _____ vont-elles en été?

9. Elle a trois disques. _____ de disques a-t-elle?

10. Elle est heureuse. _____ est-elle?

INTERROGATIVE PRONOUNS

The interrogative pronouns are:

Subject

Qui?	*Who?*	**Qui** vient?	*Who is coming?*
Qui est-ce qui?		**Qui est-ce qui** vous parle?	*Who is speaking to you?*
Qu'est-ce qui?	*What?*	**Qu'est-ce qui** se passe?	*What is happening?*
		Qu'est-ce qui est arrivé?	*What happened?*

Note that there is no short form for **qu'est-ce qui.**

Object

Qui?	
Qui est-ce que?	*Whom?*
Que?	
Qu'est-ce que?	*What?*
Qui voyez-vous?	*Whom do you see?*
Qui est-ce que vous voyez?	*Whom do you see?*
Que voyez-vous?	*What do you see?*
Qu'est-ce que vous voyez?	*What do you see?*

Qui is never joined to a following word beginning with a vowel. **Que** becomes **qu'** before a word beginning with a vowel.

Qui avez-vous vu?	*Whom did you see?*
Qu'avez-vous vu?	*What did you see?*

Que can be used as a predicate.

Qu'est-il sans sa famille?
What is he without his family?
Qu'est-ce qu'un dîner sans vin?
What's a dinner without wine?

Object of a preposition

qui?   *whom?*
quoi?   *what?*

Avec qui avez-vous parlé?   *With whom did you speak?*
Avec quoi écrit-il?   *With what does he write?*

À qui, meaning *whose,* is used to denote ownership for persons.

    À qui sont ces livres?   *Whose books are these?*

De qui is used to denote relationship to someone.

    De qui est-il le fils?   *Whose son is he?*

Quoi can be used without a verb in certain idiomatic expressions.

    Quoi de neuf?
    Quoi de nouveau?   *What's new?*

Quoi can also be used alone.

    Quoi? Vous voulez me voir?
    What? You want to see me?

The third person singular form of the verb is usually used with **qui, qui est-ce qui** and **qu'est-ce qui** even when a plural answer is expected.

    Qui vient?
    Paul et Marie viennent.

When **qui** is a predicate nominative, the verb can be in the plural.

    Qui êtes-vous?

7. Complete the following with an appropriate question word.

1. Marie est venue nous voir.
    _____ est venu nous voir? (short form)
    _____ est venu nous voir? (long form)
2. Le tonnerre a fait ce bruit.
    _____ a fait ce bruit?
3. C'est Pierre que je vois.
    _____ vous voyez?
    _____ voyez-vous?
4. C'est Marie qu'il a vue.
    _____ il a vu?
    _____ a-t-il vu?

5. Elle fait une promenade.
    _____ elle fait?
    _____ fait-elle?
6. Il a cherché un hôtel.
    _____ il a cherché?
    _____ a-t-il cherché?
7. Il a parlé de Marie.
    De _____ a-t-il parlé?
8. Il a parlé de ses livres.
    De _____ a-t-il parlé?

8. Form questions, using the interrogative word that will elicit the italicized element in the response.

> *Marie* **vient.**
> **Qui vient?   Qui est-ce qui vient?**

1. *Quelqu'un* parle.
2. Elle est la sœur d'*Hélène*.
3. Il a vu *le film*.
4. Il écrit sa composition sur *l'architecture moderne*.
5. *Le vent* a fermé la porte.
6. Il parle à *Marie*.
7. *Quelque chose* se passe.
8. Elle parle de *ses peintures*.
9. Il regarde *son amie*.
10. Il fait *une promenade*.
11. Ces livres sont à *Pierre*.
12. Elle est la fille de *Madame Leblanc*.
13. *Marie et Pierre* vont à la bibliothèque.
14. *Les avions* font ce bruit.

9. Translate the following into French.

1. Whose records are these?
2. Whose son is he?
3. Whose books are these?
4. Whose mother is she?
5. What's new?

QU'EST-CE QUE C'EST

Qu'est-ce que c'est is used in explanations or definitions and means *what is*.

Qu'est-ce que c'est?	*What's that?*
Qu'est-ce que c'est que cela?	*What's that?*
Qu'est-ce que c'est que le jeu de boules?	*What's the game of boules?*

10. Translate the following into French.

1. What's the Louvre?
2. What's the *Tour de France?*
3. What's a symbol?
4. What's the Sorbonne?

INTERROGATIVE ADJECTIVE *QUEL*

The interrogative adjective **quel** (*what*) agrees with the noun it modifies.

	Masculine	Feminine
Singular	quel	quelle
Plural	quels	quelles

Quel est votre nom?	*What is your name?*
Quels livres lisez-vous?	*What books are you reading?*

Quelle heure est-il?	*What time is it?*
Quelles sont vos idées?	*What are your ideas?*

The interrogative adjective can be the subject of the verb **être** except when it refers to a person. Then **qui** is used.

Quel est votre adresse?	*What is your address?*
Qui est votre amie?	*Who is your friend?*

Quel can be used with persons when meaning *what kind of*.

Quels sont ces hommes? Ce sont des médecins.
What kind of men are they? They are doctors.
Quel est cet homme? C'est un écrivain.
What kind of man is he? He is a writer.

Quel can be used in indirect address.

Je voudrais savoir **quel** livre vous lisez.
I want to know what book you are reading.

The interrogative adjective can also mean *what a ...!*

Quel garçon!	*What a boy!*
Quelle fille!	*What a girl!*

11. Form questions, using **quel.**

1. Les robes rouges sont dans l'armoire.
2. J'aime bien ces peintures-là.
3. Le tableau au coin est grand.
4. Les restaurants là-bas sont bons.
5. Mon adresse est 15, rue de Prony.

12. Complete the following with the correct form of **quel** or **qui.**

1. _____ heure est-il?
2. _____ sont ces hommes?
   Ce sont des avocats.
3. _____ est cette fille?
4. _____ livres lisez-vous?
5. _____ est votre adresse?
6. _____ robes préférez-vous?

13. Follow the model.

Regarde le garçon!
Quel garçon!

1. Regarde le paysage!
2. Regarde la peinture!
3. Regarde les livres!
4. Regarde les animaux!
5. Regarde l'arbre!

INTERROGATIVE PRONOUN *LEQUEL*

Lequel is the interrogative word which corresponds to the English *which one*.

	Singular		*Plural*	
Masculine	**lequel**	*which one*	**lesquels**	*which ones*
Feminine	**laquelle**	*which one*	**lesquelles**	*which ones*

The forms of **lequel** must agree with the noun to which they refer.

Lequel de ces livres voulez-vous?
Which one of these books do you want?
Lesquels de ces livres voulez-vous?
Which ones of these books do you want?
Laquelle de ces peintures préférez-vous?
Which one of these paintings do you prefer?
Lesquelles de ces peintures préférez-vous?
Which ones of these paintings do you prefer?

The forms of **lequel** make the normal contractions with **à** or **de.**

à + lequel = auquel	de + lequel = duquel
à + lesquels = auxquels	de + lesquels = desquels
à + lesquelles = auxquelles	de + lesquelles = desquelles
à + laquelle do not contract.	de + laquelle do not contract.

Auquel de ces garçons parlez-vous?
To which one of these boys are you speaking?
Desquelles a-t-il parlé?
Of which ones did he speak?

14. Complete the following with the correct form of **lequel.**

1. Marie a deux livres. _____ des deux voulez-vous?
2. Hélène a deux peintures. _____ des deux voulez-vous?
3. Voilà des livres. _____ voulez-vous?   (plural)
4. Voilà des robes. _____ voulez-vous?   (plural)

15. Complete the following with the correct form of **à** plus **lequel.**

1. Il parle à une fille. _____ parle-t-il?
2. Elle parle à un garçon. _____ parle-t-elle?
3. Il parle aux filles. _____ parle-t-il?
4. Elles parlent aux garçons. _____ parlent-elles?

16. Complete the following with the correct form of **de** plus **lequel.**

1. Il a parlé d'un garçon. _____ a-t-il parlé?
2. Elle a parlé d'une fille. _____ a-t-elle parlé?
3. Il a parlé des filles. _____ a-t-il parlé?
4. Elle a parlé des garçons. _____ a-t-elle parlé?

Review

17. Complete the following questions with the appropriate expressions based on the answers given to the questions.

1. _____ de ces lettres la vedette va-t-elle répondre?
   À toutes!

2. _____ d'États y a-t-il aux États-Unis?
   Il y en a 50.

3. _____ des deux sacs à main préfères-tu?
   Je préfère celui qui est en cuir.

4. _____ a découvert le radium?
   Madame Curie.

5. _____ est-il le fils? C'est le fils de M. Dupont.

6. Des trois candidates, pour _____ as-tu voté?
   Pour la plus honnête.

7. _____ est ton film préféré?
   Casablanca.

8. _____ parle-t-il?
   De ses amis.

9. _____ a-t-on besoin pour changer le pneu?
   D'un cric, d'une manivelle et d'une clé en croix.

10. _____ part-elle en vacances?
    Le 25 juin.

11. _____ le Tour de France?
    C'est une course à bicyclette autour de la France.

12. _____ faut-il faire pour réussir?
    Il faut étudier.

13. _____ sont ces livres?
    Ils sont à Marie et à Anne.

14. _____ arrive le train de Lyon?
    À dix heures précises.

15. _____ étudie-t-elle le japonais?
    Parce qu'elle va au Japon cet été.

16. _____ s'est passé?
    Rien.

17. Vous pouvez en choisir deux. _____ voulez-vous?
    Je voudrais celui-ci et celui-là.

18. _____ va-t-elle pendant les vacances?
    En Chine.

Chapter 7

Negative Words and Constructions

NEGATION OF SIMPLE TENSES

Verbs in simple tenses are made negative by placing **ne** before the verb and **pas** after it. Note that **ne** becomes **n'** before words beginning with a vowel.

Affirmative

Il parle français.
Nous lisons beaucoup.
Elle écrira le poème.
Dans ce cas-là, elle viendrait.

Negative

Il **ne** parle **pas** français.
Nous **ne** lisons **pas** beaucoup.
Elle **n'**écrira **pas** le poème.
Dans ce cas-là, elle **ne** viendrait **pas.**

To form the negative of reflexive verbs in simple tenses, **ne** is placed before the reflexive pronoun and **pas** is placed after the reflexive verb.

Affirmative

Je me réveille.
Il s'habillera bien.
Nous nous couchions de bonne heure.

Negative

Je **ne** me réveille **pas.**
Il **ne** s'habillera **pas** bien.
Nous **ne** nous couchions **pas** de bonne heure.

In sentences with verbs followed by a complementary infinitive, **ne** is placed before and **pas** after the main verb.

Affirmative

Il veut venir.
Je vais me lever.

Negative

Il **ne** veut **pas** venir.
Je **ne** vais **pas** me lever.

See pages 132-133 for the negative imperative.

1. Rewrite the following sentences in the negative.

1. Il va au théâtre.
2. Vous lirez le roman.

3. Je crains cet homme.
4. J'écoute le professeur.
5. Tu habitais à Paris en ce temps-là.
6. Vous arriveriez en retard.
7. Je me reposerai dimanche.
8. Elles se couchaient à onze heures tous les soirs.
9. Vous vous retrouverez à la gare.
10. Ils se moquent de lui.
11. Nous nous débrouillons bien.
12. Il s'habille bien.

2. Rewrite the following sentences in the negative, according to the model.

Je veux travailler.
Je ne veux pas travailler.

1. Nous voulons partir.
2. Elle aime chanter.
3. Elle veut se lever.
4. Tu vas t'habiller.

NEGATION OF COMPOUND TENSES

Verbs in compound tenses are made negative by adding **ne** before and **pas** after the auxiliary
verb **avoir** or **être**.

Affirmative	*Negative*
J'ai fini.	Je **n'**ai **pas** fini.
Elle est venue.	Elle **n'**est **pas** venue.
Nous serons arrivés.	Nous **ne** serons **pas** arrivés.
Elles étaient venues.	Elles **n'**etaient **pas** venues.
Nous aurions fait cela.	Nous **n'**aurions **pas** fait cela.

To form the negative of reflexive verbs in compound tenses, **ne** is added before the reflexive
pronoun and **pas** is added after the auxiliary verb.

Affirmative	*Negative*
Elle s'est levée.	Elle **ne** s'est **pas** levée.
Je me serai bien habillé.	Je **ne** me serai **pas** bien habillé.

3. Rewrite the following sentences in the negative.

1. J'ai acheté la robe.
2. Vous aviez compris la situation.
3. Ils ont écrit leurs devoirs.
4. Nous sommes restés ici.
5. Elle est tombée du cheval.
6. Ils seront venus à l'heure.
7. Elle s'est bien reposée.
8. Nous nous serons dépêchées.

9. Elles se sont plaintes de tout.
10. Vous vous êtes levés de bonne heure.

4. Answer the following questions in the negative.

1. Avez-vous reçu la lettre?
2. A-t-il lu l'histoire?
3. Êtes-vous allée au cinéma hier?
4. Sont-elles parties de bonne heure?
5. Vous êtes-vous levé de bonne heure?
6. S'est-elle endormie?

THE NEGATIVE INTERROGATIVE

The negative interrogative is formed by placing **ne** before the verb and **pas** after it when using intonation, **est-ce que** or **n'est-ce pas.**

Affirmative	*Negative*
Marie travaille?	Marie **ne** travaille **pas**?
Est-ce qu'Hélène se réveille?	Est-ce qu'Hélène **ne** se réveille **pas**?
Pierre se rasera, n'est-ce pas?	Pierre **ne** se rasera **pas,** n'est-ce pas?

In compound tenses, **ne** is placed before the auxiliary verb and **pas** after it.

Affirmative	*Negative*
Est-ce qu'il a parlé?	Est-ce qu'il **n'a pas** parlé?
Elle s'est amusée, n'est-ce pas?	Elle **ne** s'est **pas** amusée, n'est-ce pas?

In interrogative sentences by inversion, **ne** is placed before the verb and **pas** is placed after the pronoun.

Affirmative	*Negative*
Travaille-t-il?	**Ne** travaille-t-il **pas**?
Georges va-t-il à Paris?	Georges **ne** va-t-il **pas** à Paris?

In compound tenses, **ne** is placed before the auxiliary verb and **pas** is placed after the subject pronoun.

Affirmative	*Negative*
A-t-il fini?	**N'**a-t-il **pas** fini?
Es-tu parti?	**N'**es-tu **pas** parti?

For reflexive verbs, **ne** precedes the reflexive pronoun and **pas** follows the subject pronoun.

Affirmative	*Negative*
Vous couchez-vous?	**Ne** vous couchez-vous **pas**?
Se lève-t-il?	**Ne** se lève-t-il **pas**?
Vous êtes-vous réveillé?	**Ne** vous êtes-vous **pas** réveillé?

5. Rewrite the following in the negative.

    1. Est-ce que Georges vous parlera?
    2. Lit-il le livre?
    3. Ouvre-t-elle la fenêtre?
    4. Se dépêche-t-il?
    5. Vous réveillez-vous?
    6. Avez-vous fini?
    7. Ont-elles craint cet homme?
    8. Sont-elles rentrées de bonne heure?
    9. Se sont-ils couchés?
   10. T'es-tu blessé?

6. Rewrite the following sentences in the inverted interrogative form.

    1. Tu ne vis pas bien ici.
    2. Il ne saura pas la vérité.
    3. Nous ne nous dépêchons pas.
    4. Vous ne vous levez pas de bonne heure.
    5. Elle n'a pas cru l'histoire.
    6. Elles ne sont pas revenues de bonne heure.
    7. Il ne s'est pas rasé.
    8. Vous ne vous êtes pas bien débrouillé.

SI IN ANSWER TO A NEGATIVE QUESTION

When answering a negative question in the affirmative, **si** is used instead of **oui.**

Ne parles-tu pas français?	*Don't you speak French?*
Si, je parle français.	*Yes, I speak French.*
Tu ne viendras pas, n'est-ce pas?	*You won't come, will you?*
Si, je viendrai.	*Yes, I will come.*

If the answer is affirmative to an affirmative question, **oui** is used.

Parles-tu français?	*Do you speak French?*
Oui, je parle français.	*Yes, I speak French*

7. Answer the following questions, using **si** or **oui.**

    1. Parlez-vous français?
    2. Ne parlez-vous pas français?
    3. Viendront-ils à l'heure?
    4. Ne viendront-ils pas à l'heure?
    5. A-t-il fini?
    6. Il n'a pas fini, n'est-ce pas?
    7. Se réveille-t-elle?
    8. Elle ne se réveille pas, n'est-ce pas?

8. Answer the following questions, using **si** or **oui.**

    1. Vit-il bien ici?
    2. Ne sont-ils pas venus?
    3. Elle ne prendra pas le déjeuner ici?
    4. A-t-il lu ce roman?
    5. N'ont-ils pas craint le criminel?

OMISSION OF *PAS*

Pas may be omitted in the negative after **savoir, pouvoir, oser** and **cesser** when they are accompanied by an infinitive.

Il ne sait que faire.	*He doesn't know what to do.*
Il ne peut la comprendre.	*He can't understand her.*
Il n'ose le faire.	*He doesn't dare do it.*
Il ne cesse de neiger.	*It doesn't stop snowing.*

9. Rewrite the following sentences, putting the first verb in the negative, omitting **pas.**

    1. Il sait ce qu'il veut.
    2. Il cesse de pleuvoir.
    3. Elle ose le dire.
    4. Elle peut le faire.

NEGATION OF THE INFINITIVE

To make an infinitive negative, place **ne pas** before the infinitive.

Il me dit de **ne pas pleurer.**	*He tells me not to cry.*

When there is a pronoun, **ne pas** precedes the pronoun.

Il m'a dit de **ne pas le faire.**	*He told me not to do it.*
Il m'a dit de **ne pas me coucher.**	*He told me not to go to bed.*
Il m'a dit de **ne pas y aller.**	*He told me not to go there.*

With the past infinitive, **pas** can come before or after the auxiliary.

Elle affirme **ne pas** avoir fait ses devoirs.
Elle affirme **n'**avoir **pas** fait ses devoirs.
Elle affirme **ne pas** les avoir faits.
Elle affirme **ne** les avoir **pas** faits.

10. Rewrite the following sentences, making the infinitive negative.

    1. Il vous dit d'avoir peur.
    2. Elle vous demande de venir.
    3. Elle vous dit d'être heureux.

4. Je vous demande de leur parler.
5. Elle vous dit de le faire.
6. Elle affirme avoir vu ce film.

NEGATIVE WORDS AND PHRASES

Many negative expressions function like **ne ... pas.**

1. **ne ... pas du tout**   *not at all*

   Il **n'**est **pas du tout** bête.
   He is not at all stupid.

2. **ne ... point**   *not* (emphatic)

   Il **ne** le **dit** point.
   He does not say it.

3. **ne ... plus**   *no longer, no more*

   Je **ne** travaille **plus.**
   I am no longer working.
   Je **n'**ai **plus** de livres.
   I have no more books.

4. **ne ... jamais**   *never*

   Il **n'**oubliera **jamais** ce film.
   He will never forget this film.

   Jamais without **ne** means *ever.*

   Êtes-vous **jamais** allé ici?
   Did you ever go here?

   It can also stand alone, meaning *never.*

   Avez-vous vu ce film?   **Jamais!**
   Have you ever seen this film?   Never!

5. **ne ... guère**   *hardly*

   Il **n'**a **guère** le temps.
   He hardly has the time.

6. **ne ... aucun(e)**   *not any*

   Il **n'**a **aucun** livre.
   He hasn't a single book.

7. **Aucun(e) ... ne**   *none*

   Aucun n'est vrai.
   None is true.

8. **ne ... plus aucun(e)**   *no longer any*

   Il **n'**a **plus aucun** livre.
   He no longer has any books.

9. **ne ... que**   *only*

   Il **n'**a **que** deux chambres.
   He has only two rooms.

Il **n'**a lu **que** des journaux.
He reads only newspapers.

Note that **que** follows the past participle in compound tenses.

10. **ne ... rien**   *nothing, anything*

Il **ne** voit **rien.**
He sees nothing.   (He doesn't see anything.)
Qu'est-ce qu'il voit?   **Rien.**
What does he see?   Nothing.
Il **n'**a **rien** vu.
He saw nothing.   (He didn't see anything.)

Note that **rien** precedes the past participle in compound tenses.

11. **Rien ne ...**   *nothing*

Rien ne peut m'aider.
Nothing can help me.

12. **ne ... personne**   *no one, anyone*

Elle **ne** regarde **personne.**
She is not looking at anyone.   (She is looking at no one.)
Elle **n'**a vu **personne.**
She saw no one.   (She didn't see anyone.)

Note that **personne** follows the past participle in compound tenses.

13. **Personne ne ...**   *No one*

Personne n'est venu.
No one came.
Qui est arrivé?   **Personne.**
Who arrived?   No one.

Note that **personne** and **rien** can stand alone.

14. **nul (nulle) ne ...**   *no one*

Nul ne sait la vérité.
No one knows the truth.

15. **ne ... ni ... ni**   *neither ... nor*

Il **n'**a **ni** père **ni** mère.
He has neither a father nor a mother.
Il **n'**a écrit **ni** à son père **ni** à sa mère.
He wrote neither to his father nor to his mother.

Ni may be used more than twice.

Il **ne** veut **ni** lire, **ni** écrire, **ni** étudier.
He wants neither to read, nor to write, nor to study.

16. **ni l'un(e) ni l'autre ne ...**   *neither one*

Ni l'un ni l'autre n'est venu.
Neither one came.

When used as a direct object, **ni l'un ni l'autre** means *either one.*

Il **ne** veut **ni l'un ni l'autre.**
He doesn't want either one.

17. **non plus**   *neither, either*

Non plus is the negative expression which replaces **aussi.**

> Il le sait. Je le sais **aussi.**
> *He knows it. I know it too.*
> Il ne le sait pas. Je ne le sais pas **non plus.**
> *He doesn't know it. I don't know it either.*
>
> Elle travaille beaucoup. **Moi aussi.**
> *She works a lot. Me too (also). (So do I.)*
> Elle ne travaille pas beaucoup. **Ni moi non plus.**
> *She doesn't work much. Neither do I.*

Note that the pronoun used is the disjunctive pronoun.

> **Ni lui non plus.**
> *Nor he either.*

Note that **de** is used instead of the partitive after **ne ... pas, ne ... plus** and **ne ... jamais.**

> Je **n'ai pas de** livres.
> *I don't have any books.*
> Elle **n'a plus** d'argent.
> *She doesn't have any more money.*
> Il **ne** mange **jamais de** tomates.
> *He never eats tomatoes.*

The partitive is used after **ne ... que.**

> Je **n'ai que des** livres.
> *I have only books.*

No article or partitive is used after **ne ... ni ... ni.**

> Il **n'a ni** frères **ni** sœurs.
> *He has neither brothers nor sisters.*

When **jamais** and **personne** are in conditional or interrogative sentences, they may appear without the **ne. Jamais** then means *ever* and **personne** means *anyone.*

> A-t-elle **jamais** fait du ski?
> *Has she ever skied?*
> Y a-t-il **personne** d'intéressant ici?
> *Is there anyone interesting here?*

Study the following:

Affirmative	*Negative*
Elle y va **toujours.**	Elle n'y va **jamais.**
Toujours, je le ferai.	**Jamais,** je ne le ferai.
Il a **quelque** problème.	Il **n'a aucun** problème.
Je vois **quelque chose.**	Je **ne** vois **rien.**
Quelque chose arrive.	**Rien n'**arrive.
Je vois **quelqu'un.**	Je **ne** vois **personne.**
Quelqu'un est venu.	**Personne n'**est venu.

Avez-vous **un** dictionnaire ou **un** roman?   Je n'ai **ni** dictionnaire **ni** roman.
Tous les deux sont venus.   **Ni l'un ni l'autre** n'est venu.

Unlike English, many negative words can be used in the same sentence.

Il **ne** dit **jamais rien** à **personne.**
He never says anything to anyone.

11. Rewrite the following sentences, replacing the italicized word with a negative phrase.

    1. Elle dit *toujours* la même chose.
    2. *Toujours,* elle le fait.
    3. Elle a *toujours* chanté.
    4. J'ai *quelque* espoir.
    5. Marie trouve *quelque chose.*
    6. Marie a perdu *quelque chose.*
    7. *Quelque chose* est dans la cuisine.
    8. *Quelque chose* s'est passé.
    9. Il y a *quelqu'un* dans la boutique.
    10. Il a vu *quelqu'un.*
    11. *Quelqu'un* frappe à la porte.
    12. *Quelqu'un* est arrivé.
    13. J'ai *un* crayon et *un* stylo.
    14. Il parle à son père et à sa mère.
    15. Elle veut *du* pain et *du* beurre.
    16. *Tous les deux* sont partis.
    17. Pierre parle *toujours* de *quelque chose à quelqu'un.*

12. Rewrite the following sentences, adding the French equivalent of the English words.

    1. J'ai vu ce film. *never*
    2. Nous avons dansé. *not at all*
    3. Il oubliera cette leçon. *never*
    4. Il prend du vin. *hardly*
    5. Est-ce qu'il va étudier? *ever*
    6. Il a un disque. *no longer any*
    7. Elle a des amis et des ennemis. *neither ... nor*
    8. Il a écrit des poèmes. *only*
    9. Il a du temps. *hardly*
    10. Elle a deux frères. *only*
    11. Elle chante des chansons. *no longer*

13. Answer the following questions, using the cue provided.

    1. Est-ce qu'il y a quelque chose d'intéressant à faire? *ne ... rien*
    2. Va-t-elle travailler? *ne ... jamais*
    3. Y a-t-il quelqu'un ici? *ne ... personne*
    4. Qui est venu? *Personne ne ...*
    5. A-t-il des livres? *ne... aucun*
    6. A-t-il des livres ou des journaux? *ne ... ni ... ni*
    7. Avez-vous le temps de le faire? *ne ... guère*
    8. Est-elle riche? *pas du tout*

14. Replace **aussi** with **non plus** in the following sentences and make necessary changes.

    1. Il est riche aussi.
    2. Elles aussi, elles ont beaucoup d'argent.
    3. Marie le sait aussi.
    4. Moi aussi, je viens.
    5. Lui aussi, il la verra.
    6. Elles mangent ici aussi.
    7. Il l'a fait aussi.

Review

15. Say that John never does what Peter does. Follow the models.

Pierre boit du lait.
Jean *ne* boit *pas* de lait.

Pierre va *toujours* au cinéma.
Jean *ne* va *jamais* au cinéma.

    1. Pierre mange des épinards.
    2. Pierre aime jouer au tennis.
    3. Pierre sait quoi faire.
    4. Pierre se lève *toujours* de bonne heure.
    5. Pierre est allé au cinéma hier.
    6. Pierre s'est couché de bonne heure hier soir.
    7. Pierre a *une* auto et *une* bicyclette.
    8. Pierre a acheté *quelques* disques hier.
    9. Pierre achète *toujours quelque chose* quand il est en vacances.
    10. Pierre parle à *tout le monde*.

Chapter 8

Pronouns

SUBJECT PRONOUNS

The subject pronouns in French are as follows.

je	*I*		**nous**	*we*
tu	*you*		**vous**	*you*
il	*he*		**ils**	*they*
elle	*she*		**elles**	*they*
on	*one, they, people, we*			

There are three ways to express *you* in French. **Tu** is used to address a friend, relative or close associate. **Vous** is used to address someone you do not know well or someone older than yourself. To address two or more people, whatever their relation to you, **vous** is used.

    Tu es gentil, **Pierre.**
    Vous êtes gentil, **Monsieur Leclerc.**
    Vous êtes gentils, **Pierre et Marie.**
    Vous êtes gentils, **Monsieur et Madame Leclerc.**

When referring to two people, one male and one female, the pronoun **ils** is used.

    Pierre et Marie vont au cinéma.
    Ils vont au cinéma.

The pronoun **on** is used with the **il/elle** form of the verb and can mean *one, people, you, they.*

    Si on étudie, on reçoit de bonnes notes.
    If one (people, you, they) studies (study), one (people, you, they) gets (get) good grades.

In spoken language, the pronoun **on** can replace the pronoun **nous.** When **on** replaces **nous,** the adjective is usually in the plural.

    Nous sommes contents ici.
    On est contents ici.

See page 216 for the uses of **on** to replace a passive voice.

1. Change the italicized words to a pronoun.

    1. *Marie* parle français.
    2. *Pierre* chante bien.
    3. *Georges et André* jouent de la guitare.
    4. *Hélène et Anne* étudient à la Faculté de Médecine.
    5. *Yvonne et Georges* vont en vacances.

2. Follow the model. Use **tu** or **vous.**

heureux / Pierre
Es-tu heureux, Pierre?

    1. content / Monsieur
    2. malheureuse / Marie
    3. paresseux / Jean et Georges
    4. fatigué / Jean
    5. contents / Monsieur et Madame Leblanc

3. **Qu'est-ce qu'on fait samedi soir?** Tell what you and your friends do and how you feel on Saturdays. Follow the model.

regarder la télévision
On regarde la télévision.

    1. aller au cinéma
    2. manger une pizza
    3. discuter politique
    4. écouter des disques
    5. être content
    6. s'amuser bien

DIRECT OBJECT PRONOUNS

Le, la, l', les

    The third person direct object pronouns in French are **le** (*it, him*), **la** (*it, her*), **l'** (*it, him, her*) and **les** (*them*). The direct object pronoun **le** replaces masculine singular nouns; **la** replaces feminine singular nouns; **l'** is used before verbs beginning with a vowel; **les** replaces plural nouns. **Les** connects with a **z** sound to a word beginning with a vowel. Note that the pronouns can refer to either persons or things and that they immediately precede the conjugated form of the verb.

Jean lit **le livre.**	*John reads the book.*
Jean **le** lit.	*John reads it.*
Pierre regarde **les nuages.**	*Peter looks at the clouds.*
Pierre **les** regarde.	*Peter looks at them.*
Marie voit **Pierre.**	*Mary sees Peter.*
Marie **le** voit.	*Mary sees him.*
Le garçon voit **l'arbre.**	*The boy sees the tree.*
Le garçon **le** voit.	*The boy sees it.*

Pierre regarde **les enfants.**	*Peter looks at the children.*
Pierre **les** regarde.	*Peter looks at them.*
André écoute **le disque.**	*Andrew listens to the record.*
André **l'**écoute.	*Andrew listens to it.*
Hélène achète **les disques.**	*Helen buys the records.*
Hélène **les** achète.	*Helen buys them.*
Jacques cherche **la photo.**	*James looks for the photo.*
Jacques **la** cherche.	*James looks for it.*
Georges regarde **les peintures.**	*George looks at the paintings.*
Georges **les** regarde.	*George looks at them.*
Nous lisons **l'histoire.**	*We are reading the story.*
Nous **la** lisons.	*We are reading it.*
Jean regarde **Marie.**	*John is looking at Mary.*
Jean **la** regarde.	*John is looking at her.*
Pierre regarde **les peintures.**	*Peter is looking at the paintings.*
Pierre **les** regarde.	*Peter is looking at them.*
Claire achète **la voiture.**	*Claire buys the car.*
Claire **l'**achète.	*Claire buys it.*
Pierre aide **les filles.**	*Peter helps the girls.*
Pierre **les** aide.	*Peter helps them.*

4. What do the people do with the following? Complete the following sentences with the appropriate object pronoun. Follow the model.

La radio?   Je _____ écoute.
La radio?   Je *l*'écoute.

1. La télévision. Je _____ regarde deux heures par jour.
2. Les élèves? Le professeur _____ enseigne.
3. Le maillot de bain? Elle _____ porte en été.
4. Les disques? Ils _____ écoutent.
5. Les pommes? Je _____ mange.
6. Le journal? Elle _____ achète chaque matin.
7. Les romans policiers? Nous _____ lisons.
8. La lettre? Il _____ écrit à son amie.
9. L'argent? Elle _____ met à la banque.
10. L'histoire? Nous _____ croyons.

5. The following people are good students. Rewrite the following sentences, substituting the italicized object with a pronoun.

1. Pierre résout *les problèmes de mathématiques.*
2. J'écris *la composition.*
3. Anne lit *le livre.*
4. Ils font *les devoirs* chaque soir.
5. Nous aimons *nos cours.*
6. Tu comprends *la leçon.*
7. Vous aidez *les autres élèves.*
8. Tu étudies *le français* cinq fois par semaine.

9. Anne et Marie préparent bien *les examens*.
10. Elles reçoivent *le prix d'honneur*.

Special Use of the Pronoun *le*

Le can be used to replace a complete idea.

Croyez-vous qu'il arrive ce soir?
Oui, je **le** crois. *Yes, I think so.*

Je suis content et elle **l**'est aussi.
I am happy and she is (happy) too.

Le can also replace an adjective in the second part of a comparison.

Il est moins intelligent que je **ne** le pensais.

6. Answer the following questions according to the model.

Pensez-vous qu'il va inviter Marie? *Oui*
Oui, je le pense.

1. Pensez-vous qu'il aime l'art moderne?   *Oui*
2. Croyez-vous qu'il fasse le travail?   *Non*
3. Pensez-vous qu'il arrive à l'heure?   *Oui*
4. Croyez-vous qu'il vienne?   *Non*
5. Savez-vous qu'il pleut?   *Oui*

7. Complete the following sentences with the correct object pronoun.

1. Pierre est content et Marie _____ est aussi.
2. Je suis fatigué et elles _____ sont aussi.
3. Elle est heureuse et il _____ est aussi.
4. Je suis triste et ils _____ sont aussi.

DIRECT AND INDIRECT OBJECT PRONOUNS

Me, te, nous, vous

The pronouns **me** (*me*), **te** (*you*, familiar), **nous** (*us*) and **vous** (*you*, formal, singular and plural) can be used as both direct and indirect object pronouns. The position is the same as for the object pronouns **le, la, l'** and **les.**

Direct:	Il **me** voit.	*He sees me.*
Indirect:	Il **me** parle.	*He speaks to me.*
Direct:	Elle **te** regarde.	*She looks at you.*
Indirect:	Elle **te** répond.	*She answers you.*
Direct:	Elle **nous** comprend.	*She understands us.*
Indirect:	Elle **nous** donne le livre.	*She gives us the book.*
Direct:	Je **vous** regarde.	*I am looking at you.*
Indirect:	Je **vous** parle.	*I am speaking to you.*

Me becomes **m'** and **te** becomes **t'** before a vowel.

Il **m**'aime.
Il **t**'écoute.

There is a liaison between **nous** or **vous** and a word beginning with a vowel.

Il nous‿écoute.
Il vous‿aime.

8. Answer the following questions in the affirmative.

1. Est-ce que Paul te parle?
2. Est-ce que Jean t'écoute?
3. Est-ce qu'il me dit bonjour?
4. Est-ce qu'il m'invite?
5. Est-ce qu'elle nous voit?
6. Est-ce qu'elle nous appelle?
7. Pierre, est-ce qu'elle vous répond?
8. Hélène, est-ce qu'il vous écoute?
9. Pierre et André, est-ce qu'ils vous regardent?
10. Marie et Anne, est-ce qu'ils vous écrivent?

9. Follow the model.

Pierre est gentil.

répondre gentiment / toi et moi
Il *nous* répond gentiment.

1. apporter des fleurs / moi
2. inviter à dîner / ma mère et moi
3. aider / toi et ton fils
4. donner des cadeaux / toi
5. respecter / mes amies et moi
6. téléphoner souvent / moi
7. prêter ses outils / toi et ton père
8. écouter toujours / toi

INDIRECT OBJECT PRONOUNS

Lui, leur

The third person indirect object pronouns are **lui** (*him, her*) in the singular and **leur** (*them*) in the plural. They refer only to people. Note that in the third person there is a difference between the direct and indirect object pronouns. The direct object pronouns are **le (l'), la (l')** and **les.** With the indirect object pronouns, there is no gender differentiation.

Je parle **à Pierre.**	*I speak to Peter.*
Je **lui** parle.	*I speak to him.*
Je donne le livre **à Marie.**	*I give the book to Mary.*
Je **lui** donne le livre.	*I give the book to her. (I give her the book.)*
Je parle **aux garçons.**	*I speak to the boys.*
Je **leur** parle.	*I speak to them.*
Je donne la lettre **aux filles.**	*I give the letter to the girls.*
Je **leur** donne la lettre.	*I give the letter to them. (I give them the letter.)*

10. Follow the model.

> **Qu'est-ce que Nicole donne comme cadeaux?**
> **à ses amis / des biscuits**
> **Elle *leur* donne des biscuits.**

1. à son frère / un livre
2. à ses parents / des photos
3. à sa sœur / un collier
4. à Georges et André / des cravates
5. à son amie / un bracelet
6. à Pierre / des disques

11. Complete the following sentences with the appropriate direct or indirect object pronoun.

1. Marie visite son amie. Marie _____ visite.
2. Le père lit le conte à son fils. Le père _____ lit le conte.
3. Marie voit Charles à la plage. Marie _____ voit à la plage.
4. La fille sait les verbes. La fille _____ sait.
5. L'enfant répond à ses parents. L'enfant _____ répond.
6. Pierre dit bonjour à Marie. Pierre _____ dit bonjour.
7. Le garçon voit son amie et il donne la main à son amie. Le garçon _____ voit et il _____ donne la main.

THE PRONOUN *Y*

The pronoun **y** can replace a prepositional phrase beginning with any preposition other than **de** when the object of the preposition is a thing. When **y** replaces a phrase telling the name of a place, it means *there*.

Je vais **à la gare.**	*I am going to the railroad station.*
J'**y** vais.	*I am going there.*
Elle est **dans le salon.**	*She is in the living room.*
Elle **y** est.	*She is there.*
Elle met l'argent **sur la table.**	*She puts the money on the table.*
Elle **y** met l'argent.	*She puts the money there.*

When **y** stands for a thing or idea and follows a verb which requires **à,** it is translated by *it* or *them.*

Il répond **à la lettre.**	*He answers the letter.*
Il **y** répond.	*He answers it.*
Il obéit **aux lois.**	*He obeys the laws.*
Il **y** obéit.	*He obeys them.*

Remember that **lui** and **leur** are used when the object of the preposition is a person.

> Elle dit bonjour **à Marie.**
> Elle **lui** dit bonjour.

12. Rewrite the following sentences, replacing the italicized words by a pronoun.

1. Il va *à la gare.*
2. Le livre est *sur l'étagère.*
3. Elle sera *devant le cinéma.*

4. Il montera *dans le train.*
5. Il répond *à la lettre.*
6. Il obéit *aux lois.*

13. Complete the following sentences with **y, lui** or **leur.**

1. Il répond à l'invitation. Il _____ répond.
2. Elle obéit à ses parents. Elle _____ obéit.
3. Il obéit aux lois. Il _____ obéit.
4. Elle répond au professeur. Elle _____ répond.
5. Nous réfléchissons aux problèmes. Nous _____ réfléchissons.

THE PRONOUN *EN*

The pronoun **en** replaces a prepositional phrase introduced by **de.** It means *of it, of them, from it, from them, from there, some* or *any.* It is used:

1. in a prepositional sense.

Nous venons **de New York.**	*We come from New York.*
Nous **en** venons.	*We come from there.*

2. in the partitive sense.

J'ai **du pain.**	*I have some bread.*
J'**en** ai.	*I have some.*

3. with expressions followed by **de.**

Elle parle **de ce livre.**	*She speaks about this book.*
Elle **en** parle.	*She speaks about it.*

Elle est fière **de sa robe.**	*She is proud of her dress.*
Elle **en** est fière.	*She is proud of it.*

4. with expressions of quantity.

Il a **beaucoup d'argent.**	*He has a lot of money.*
Il **en** a **beaucoup.**	*He has a lot of it.*

Elle a **trop de livres.**	*She has too many books.*
Elle **en** a **trop.**	*She has too many of them.*

Elle a **dix livres.**	*She has ten books.*
Elle **en** a **dix.**	*She has ten of them.*

Elle a **plusieurs amis.**	*She has several friends.*
Elle **en** a **plusieurs.**	*She has several (of them).*

J'ai **quelques disques.**	*I have several (a few) records.*
J'**en** ai **quelques-uns.**	*I have several (a few) (of them).*

| J'ai **quelques peintures.** | *I have several (a few) paintings.* |
| J'**en** ai **quelques-unes.** | *I have several (of them).* |

14. Rewrite the following sentences, replacing the italicized words by a pronoun.

1. Nous sortons *du théâtre*.
2. Elle vient *de Paris*.
3. Ils sortiront *de ce restaurant*.
4. Il a *du pain*.
5. Elle choisit *des fleurs*.
6. Elle achète *de la viande*.
7. Il parle *de son travail*.
8. Il est fier *de son appartement*.
9. Elles ont beaucoup *de livres*.
10. Il a un peu *d'argent*.
11. Elle achète une douzaine *de poires*.
12. Il prend quatre *billets*.
13. Il a plusieurs *amis*.
14. Elle a quelques *livres*.
15. Il a quelques *cravates*.

15. Rewrite the following sentences, replacing the italicized objects with the correct pronoun, **y, en, lui** or **leur.**

1. Nous allons *à l'aéroport*.
2. Il répond *à ses amis*.
3. Nous avons besoin *de ces journaux*.
4. Les valises sont *sous le lit*.
5. Elle répond *aux questions*.
6. J'ai plusieurs *robes*.
7. Il parle *au professeur*.
8. Elle a quelques *fleurs*.
9. Il y a beaucoup *de peintures* ici.

DOUBLE OBJECT PRONOUNS

When two pronouns are used, both precede the verb in the following order except in the affirmative command.

me					
te		le		**lui**	
se	precede	la	precede	**leur**	precede **y** precede **en**
nous		les			
vous					

Il **me le** donne.	*He gives it to me.*
Il **te la** dit.	*He tells it to you.*
Elle **se le** rappelle.	*She remembers it.*
Elle **se le** fait faire.	*She has it made.*
Il **nous les** montre.	*He shows them to us.*

Je **vous** l'écris.	*I write it to you.*
Je **le lui** donne.	*I give it to him.*
Elle **la leur** apporte.	*She brings it to them.*
Il **m'en** donne.	*He gives some to me.*
Elle **lui en** donne.	*She gives some to him.*
Il **nous y** rencontre.	*He meets us there.*
Il **y en** a beaucoup.	*There are a lot of them.*

16. Rewrite the following sentences, substituting the direct object with a pronoun.

1. Elle me montre les photos.
2. Il nous sert le déjeuner.
3. Elle t'envoie la lettre.
4. Il nous dit la vérité.
5. Il vous apporte le bifteck.
6. Il lui envoie le cadeau.
7. Elle leur donne les billets.
8. Elle te donne du pain.
9. Il vous pose des questions.
10. Il lui donne plusieurs livres.
11. Il m'apporte de la soupe.
12. Elle m'attend sur le boulevard.
13. Il nous rencontre au théâtre.
14. Il y a quatre livres.

17. Rewrite the following sentences, substituting noun objects with pronouns.

1. Elle se rappelle la leçon.
2. Il se brosse les dents.
3. Vous vous lavez la figure.
4. Elles se lavent les cheveux.
5. Elle se souvient du concert.
6. Il se fait faire la chemise.

18. Rewrite the following sentences, replacing noun objects with object pronouns.

Qu'est-ce que ces gens font dans leur travail?

1. Le médecin me donne des piqûres chaque semaine.
2. Le vendeur rencontre le client devant la maison.
3. Le professeur explique la leçon aux étudiants.
4. Le banquier prête de l'argent au fermier.
5. Le bijoutier te vend ce bracelet en or.
6. Le garçon apporte trois cafés à nos amis.
7. L'avocat donne les contrats aux clients.
8. Le biologiste fait des recherches dans un laboratoire.
9. Le facteur nous apporte le courrier chaque matin.
10. Le pharmacien donne le médicament au malade.
11. L'épicier vous vend des provisions.
12. Le marchand de fruits vend les pommes à Madame Durand.
13. Le chauffeur de taxi rencontre les touristes à l'aéroport.
14. Le conducteur vend les billets aux voyageurs.

POSITION OF OBJECT PRONOUNS

With Conjugated Verbs

The object pronouns always precede the conjugated form of the verb. If the sentence is negative, **ne** precedes the object pronoun and **pas** follows the verb or auxiliary. In compound tenses the pronoun precedes the auxiliary verb.

Affirmative sentence:	Je **la** regarde.
	Je **le lui** dis.
	Il **l'**a regardé.
Negative sentence:	Je ne **l'**écoute pas.
	Je ne **le lui** donne pas.
	Je ne **le lui** ai pas donné.
Affirmative question:	**Les** voyez-vous? Est-ce que vous **les** voyez?
	Leur en parlez-vous? Est-ce que vous **leur en** parlez?
	Leur en avez-vous parlé? Est-ce que vous **leur en** avez parlé?
Negative question:	Ne **l'**entendez-vous pas? Est-ce que vous ne **l'**entendez pas?
	Ne **l'**avez-vous pas attendu? Est-ce que vous ne **l'**avez pas attendu?
	Ne **la lui** apportez-vous pas? Est-ce que vous ne **la lui** apportez pas?
	Ne **la lui** avez-vous pas apportée? Est-ce que vous ne **la lui** avez pas apportée?
Negative command:	Ne **le** regarde pas!
	Ne **la lui** donne pas!

With semiauxiliary verbs and verbs of perception followed by an infinitive, object pronouns are placed before the verb.

Je **l'**ai fait venir.
Nous ne **les** entendons pas chanter.

The pronouns always precede **voici** and **voilà.**

Les voici.
Le voilà.

Remember that when a direct object precedes the verb in compound tenses, the past participle agrees with the preceding direct object. See pages 146–147.

Il a écrit la lettre.
Il **l'**a écrit**e.**

The past participle does not agree with **en.**

Il a regardé des peintures.
Il **en** a regardé.

19. Rewrite the following sentences, substituting pronouns for the direct and indirect objects.

1. Il ne fait pas le travail.
2. Cherchez-vous vos amis à la gare?
3. N'entend-il pas ce bruit?
4. Ne mange pas la pomme dans le salon!
5. Voilà les livres.
6. Elle m'expliquera la situation.
7. Il ne nous répète pas la question.
8. J'avais donné des disques à Jean.
9. N'a-t-elle pas attendu son ami devant le cinéma?
10. Elle écrivait des cartes à ses parents.

11. Il n'aurait pas lu ce roman.
12. Il a cru l'histoire.
13. As-tu écrit les devoirs?
14. Elles ont pris les photos devant la statue.
15. Elle aura dit la vérité au professeur.
16. Il a écouté le chanteur chanter.
17. J'ai fait venir le médecin.

With an Infinitive

When a pronoun is the direct or indirect object of the infinitive, it always precedes the infinitive.

Je vais acheter **le disque.**
Je vais l'acheter.

Je vais parler **de cela à Jean.**
Je vais **lui en** parler.

Il me dit d'acheter **le disque.**
Il me dit de l'acheter.

Il me demande de ne pas faire **le travail.**
Il me demande de ne pas **le** faire.

20. Rewrite the following, substituting pronouns for the direct and indirect objects.

1. Je voudrais acheter la peinture.
2. Je voudrais donner le cadeau à Marie.
3. Je vais parler aux bouquinistes.
4. Je vais mettre les livres sur l'étagère.
5. Elle va avoir honte de ses actions.
6. Il me dit de ne pas acheter cette robe.
7. Il me demande de ne pas parler de cela à Georges.

With Affirmative Commands

In affirmative commands, the pronouns follow the verb and are attached to it and to each other with a hyphen. **Le, la, les** precede **me, te, nous, vous, lui** and **leur.** All precede **en.**

Donne-lui-en!
Donne-le-lui!
Vas-y!

Note that **me** becomes **moi** and **te** becomes **toi** in an affirmative command.

Donne-la-moi!   *But:*   **Donnez-m'en!**
Achète-le-toi!   *But:*   **Achète-t'en!**

Note that all commands that end in a vowel add **s** when followed by the pronouns **y** or **en.**

Donne du pain. **Donnes-en.**
Va au parc. **Vas-y.**

21. Rewrite the following in the affirmative.

1. Ne me parlez pas!
2. Ne la lisez pas!

    3. Ne le lui donne pas!
    4. Ne lui en parle pas!
    5. N'y allez pas!
    6. Ne te l'achète pas!

22. Rewrite the following, substituting pronouns for direct and indirect objects.

    1. Lisez l'histoire!
    2. Parlez-nous de ce sujet!
    3. Écrivez les lettres à Pierre!
    4. Réponds à la lettre!
    5. Va au parc!
    6. Parle de ce sujet!
    7. Donnez-moi des livres!

Review

23. Rewrite the following sentences, replacing the italicized words with pronouns.

    1. Il n'obéit pas *à sa mère*.
    2. Il a trop *de livres*.
    3. Elle est allée *à l'aéroport*.
    4. Elle a mis *les livres sur la table*.
    5. Il ne dit pas *la vérité à ses parents*.
    6. Elle ne répond pas *à la lettre*.
    7. N'écoute pas *cet homme*!
    8. Il se rappelle *le film*.
    9. Il y a beaucoup *de gens*.
   10. Elle a mis douze *pommes dans son panier*.
   11. Donnez-moi *du beurre*!
   12. Parlez-vous *de cela à votre ami*?
   13. Je vais donner *les livres à Marie*.
   14. Donnez *les jouets aux enfants*.
   15. As-tu donné *la montre à Marie*?
   16. Ne parle-t-elle pas *de son voyage à Jean*?

24. Say that the Leblanc family members are procrastinators. Use object pronouns. Follow the model.

Pierre / réparer la voiture
Pierre ne l'a pas réparée.
Il ne la répare pas maintenant.
Il va la réparer plus tard.

    1. Pierre / laver les voitures
    2. Anne / écrire la lettre à sa grand-mère
    3. M. Leblanc / peindre la maison
    4. M. et Mme Leblanc / acheter des provisions au supermarché
    5. Anne et Pierre / ranger la vaisselle dans les placards
    6. Mme Leblanc / jeter les ordures dans la poubelle
    7. Marie / donner de la nourriture aux chiens
    8. Mme Leblanc / planter les fleurs dans le jardin

REFLEXIVE PRONOUNS

Reflexive pronouns are used when the action in the sentence is both executed and received by the subject. For a complete review of reflexive verbs, see Chapter 5.

The reflexive pronouns are:

Singular	Plural
me	nous
te	vous
se	se

Reflexive pronouns can be direct or indirect objects.

Direct: Je **me** lève.
Indirect: Je **me** lave les cheveux.

Me, te and **se** become **m', t'** and **s'** before verbs beginning with a vowel. There is a liaison between **nous** or **vous** and a word beginning with a vowel.

Il **se** lève.
Il **s'**habille.
Nous **nous** débrouillons.
Nous **nous** habillons.

25. Complete the following sentences with the appropriate reflexive pronoun.

1. Je _____ appelle Marie.
2. Nous _____ lavons la figure.
3. À quelle heure _____ lèves-tu?
4. Pourquoi est-ce qu'elle ne _____ peigne pas?
5. Elles _____ débrouillent bien.
6. Vous _____ asseyez ici.
7. Je _____ dépêche pour arriver à l'heure.
8. Nous _____ couchons tard.
9. Elle _____ habille bien.
10. Tu _____ arrêtes un moment.

DISJUNCTIVE PRONOUNS

The disjunctive pronouns or stress pronouns are the same as the subject pronouns **elle, elles, nous** and **vous.** The other forms change.

Singular		Plural	
Subject	Disjunctive	Subject	Disjunctive
je	moi	nous	nous
tu	toi	vous	vous
il	lui	ils	eux
elle	elle	elles	elles
on	soi		

The pronouns occur:

1. after **c'est** and **ce sont.**

C'est is used with all the disjunctive pronouns except **eux** and **elles,** which can use **ce sont.** Note that the verb in the **qui** clause must agree with the subject.

C'est moi. C'est moi qui parle.
It is I. It is I who am speaking.

C'est nous. C'est nous qui l'avons fait.
It is we. It is we who did it.
C'est (Ce sont) eux. C'est (Ce sont) eux qui mentent.
It is they. It is they who are lying.
C'est (Ce sont) elles. C'est (Ce sont) elles qui arrivent.
It is they. It is they who are arriving.

2. after a preposition.

Elle parle **de lui.**	*She speaks about him.*
Nous allons **avec elle.**	*We are going with her.*

Remember that when the object of a preposition is a thing rather than a person, **y** or **en** must be used.

Je pense **à Marie.** Je pense **à elle.**
I am thinking about Mary. I am thinking about her.
Je pense **aux examens.** J'**y** pense.
I am thinking about the examinations. I am thinking about them.
Je parle **de Pierre.** Je parle **de lui.**
I am speaking about Peter. I am speaking about him.
Je parle **de ce livre.** J'**en** parle.
I am speaking about this book. I am speaking about it.

When the direct object pronoun is **me, te, se, nous** or **vous,** the indirect object is expressed by **à** plus a disjunctive pronoun.

Il **se** présente **à elle.**
He presents himself to her.
Vous **me** recommandez **à lui.**
You recommend me to him.

3. after a comparison.

Elle est **plus** intelligente **que lui.**
She is more intelligent than he.
Il est **plus** beau **que moi.**
He is more handsome than I.

4. alone for emphasis.

Qui est là? **Moi.**	*Who's there? I am.*
Qui regarde-t-elle? **Lui.**	*Whom is she looking at? Him.*

5. to add emphasis to a non-accentuated pronoun.

Moi, je prépare la salade, **toi,** tu prépares les sandwiches.

6. after **ne ... que.**

Elle **n'**aime **que lui.**	*She likes only him.*

7. as a part of a compound subject.

Vous et moi, nous le ferons.	*You and I will do it.*
Pierre et lui, ils arrivent.	*Peter and he arrive.*

8. in combination with **même**.

moi-même	*myself*	**nous-mêmes**	*ourselves*
toi-même	*yourself*	**vous-même(s)**	*yourself, yourselves*
lui-même	*himself*	**eux-mêmes**	*themselves*
elle-même	*herself*	**elles-mêmes**	*themselves*

Je le ferai **moi-même.**   *I'll do it myself.*

Soi is used when the subject is general: **on, chacun, nul, personne.**

Chacun pour **soi.**   *Each one for himself.*

26. Complete the following paragraph with the appropriate disjunctive pronoun.

Nous aimons tous les sports différents!

_____ , je préfère jouer au tennis mais _____ , tu préfères jouer au badminton. Et Phil-
          (1)   (2)
lippe? _____ et _____ , nous préférons jouer au soccer, mais Pierre, _____ , il préfère jouer
          (3)   (4)   (5)
au football. André et Marc, _____ , ils préfèrent jouer au hockey. Hélène et _____ deux,
                              (6)   (7)
vous préférez nager. Martine et Anne, _____ , elles préfèrent faire du ski nautique.
                                        (8)

27. Everyone helps prepare for a birthday party for Nicole. Follow the model.

Qui fera le menu?   *Marie, je*
C'est nous qui ferons le menu.
Elle et moi, nous ferons le menu.

1. Qui a envoyé les invitations? *je*
2. Qui a acheté le cadeau? *Martine, je*
3. Qui s'occupe de la musique? *Nicole et Jeannette*
4. Qui prépare les sandwichs? *Georges et André*
5. Qui va faire le gâteau? *il*
6. Qui va chercher les boissons? *il, tu*
7. Qui va faire les décorations? *Anne*
8. Qui va faire la présentation du cadeau? *tu*

28. Translate the following sentences into French.

1. I'll do it myself.
2. He'll do it himself.
3. The boys will do it themselves.
4. We'll do it ourselves.
5. Each one for himself.

29. Answer the following questions with the disjunctive pronoun **y** or **en**.

1. Pensez-vous à ce livre?
2. Avez-vous peur de cet homme?
3. Partirez-vous sans vos camarades?
4. Avez-vous honte de vos actions?
5. Pensez-vous à Hélène?
6. Allez-vous à la gare?
7. Est-ce que ce sont Hélène et Marie qui parlent?
8. Vont-ils chez Marianne?

9. Va-t-elle avec Pierre?
10. Avez-vous besoin de votre argent?
11. Je me présente à Pierre.

POSSESSIVE PRONOUNS

A possessive pronoun is used to replace a possessive adjective plus a noun. The possessive pronoun must agree with the noun it replaces and is accompanied by the appropriate definite article or one of its contracted forms, **au, aux, du, des.**

	Masculine		*Feminine*	
	Singular	*Plural*	*Singular*	*Plural*
mine	**le mien**	**les miens**	**la mienne**	**les miennes**
yours (fam.)	**le tien**	**les tiens**	**la tienne**	**les tiennes**
his, hers, its	**le sien**	**les siens**	**la sienne**	**les siennes**
ours	**le nôtre**	**les nôtres**	**la nôtre**	**les nôtres**
yours	**le vôtre**	**les vôtres**	**la vôtre**	**les vôtres**
theirs	**le leur**	**les leurs**	**la leur**	**les leurs**

J'ai **mon livre** et non pas **le tien.**
I have my book and not yours.
J'aime **ma blouse** et non pas **la tienne.**
I like my blouse and not yours.
Voici **tes billets.** Où sont **les miens**?
Here are your tickets. Where are mine?
Voici **vos valises.** Où sont **les miennes**?
Here are your suitcases. Where are mine?
Je préfère **mon livre au tien.**
I prefer my book to yours.
J'ai expliqué la situation **à ma mère.** As-tu expliqué la situation **à la tienne**?
I explained the situation to my mother. Did you explain the situation to yours?
J'ai besoin **de mes livres.** Ont-ils besoin **des leurs**?
I need my books. Do they need theirs?
Je parle **de mon professeur.** Parle-t-il **du sien**?
I am speaking about my teacher. Is he speaking about his?

When the possessor is an indefinite pronoun subject such as **on, personne, tout le monde, chacun,** the pronouns **le sien, la sienne, les siens, les siennes** are used.

On aime sa **famille. On** aime **la sienne.**
Tout le monde a **ses valises. Tout le monde** a **les siennes.**

If a plural subject is modified by **chacun,** the possessive pronoun agrees with the subject.

Nous avons apporté **chacun les nôtres.**

In the masculine plural, the possessive pronoun designates relatives, friends, allies, etc.

Il est **des nôtres.**
He's one of us.

30. Replace the italicized phrase with the appropriate possessive pronoun.

1. Ce son *mes livres.* Où sont *tes livres*?
2. Je n'aime pas *ma voiture.* Aimez-vous *votre voiture*?

3. Il a pensé à *ses amis* et elles ont pensé à *leurs amis.*
4. J'ai besoin de *mes livres* et vous avez besoin de *vos livres.*
5. *Notre piscine* est plus petite que *ta piscine.*
6. Nous avons *nos billets.* Avez-vous *vos billets?*
7. Il a parlé de *sa situation* et tu as parlé de *ta situation.*
8. J'ai besoin de *leur voiture.*
9. Pierre va chercher *ses valises* et *mes valises.*
10. Vous mettez *votre manteau* et je mets *mon manteau.*
11. Nous sommes fiers de *notre pays* et ils sont fiers de *leur pays.*
12. Elle préfère *nos meubles* à *vos meubles.*
13. Il a cherché *son passeport* et les filles ont cherché *leur passeport.*
14. *Ton appareil photographique* est meilleur que *mon appareil photographique.*
15. Il a téléphoné à *sa mère* et nous avons téléphoné à *notre mère.*

31. Follow the model.

À qui sont ces livres?   *à moi*
Ce sont les miens.

1. À qui sont ces disques?   *à vous*
2. À qui est ce livre?   *à moi*
3. À qui est cette bicyclette?   *à toi*
4. À qui est cette maison?   *à nous*
5. À qui est cette pomme?   *à lui*
6. À qui est ce parapluie?   *à elle*
7. À qui sont ces robes?   *à moi*
8. À qui sont ces peintures?   *à eux*

DEMONSTRATIVE PRONOUNS

The French forms of demonstrative pronouns *this one, that one, these, those* are as follows:

	Singular	*Plural*
Masculine	**celui**	**ceux**
Feminine	**celle**	**celles**

When followed by a relative pronoun, the demonstrative pronouns mean *the one, the ones, he (she) who, these* or *those.*

Celui qui travaille ici est mon ami.
The one who works here is my friend.

The demonstrative pronouns followed by **de** can indicate possession.

La bicyclette de Pierre et **celle** de Marie
Peter's bicycle and Mary's

To distinguish between *this one* and *that one* and between *these* and *those*, the suffixes **-ci** (*this*) and **-là** (*that*) are added.

J'aime **celui-ci.**   *I like this one.*
J'aime **celle-là.**   *I like that one.*

When two things are mentioned, **celui-ci** means *the latter* and **celui-là** means *the former.*

> J'ai parlé avec M. Dupont et M. Leclerc.
> **Celui-ci** (Leclerc) est médecin et **celui-là** (M. Dupont) est homme d'affaires.
> *The latter is a doctor and the former is a businessman.*

Celui-ci can be replaced by **ce dernier** and **celui-là** by **le premier.**

> **Ce dernier** est médecin et **le premier** est homme d'affaires.

32. Answer the following questions, using a demonstrative pronoun according to the model.

> **C'est ton livre? *mon frère***
> **Non, c'est celui de mon frère.**

> 1. C'est ta bicyclette? *ma sœur*
> 2. C'est ton chien? *mon ami*
> 3. Ce sont tes livres? *mon frère*
> 4. Ce sont tes fleurs? *ma mère*
> 5. C'est ton cahier? *mon amie*
> 6. C'est ta maison? *mon oncle*

33. Complete the following sentences with the appropriate demonstrative pronoun, according to the model.

> **Les légumes? _____ sont plus frais que _____ .**
> **Les légumes? *Ceux-ci* sont plus frais que *ceux-là*.**

> **Au supermarché**

> 1. Les tomates? _____ sont plus rouges que _____ .
> 2. Le bifteck? _____ est plus tendre que _____ .
> 3. Les oranges? _____ sont plus sucrées que _____ .
> 4. Le fromage? _____ est plus crémeux que _____ .
> 5. La pomme? _____ est meilleure que _____ .
> 6. Les haricots verts? _____ sont plus frais que _____ .
> 7. Le vin? _____ est plus sec que _____ .
> 8. La crème? _____ est plus douce que _____ .

INDEFINITE DEMONSTRATIVE PRONOUNS

Ce, ceci, cela (ça)

Ce

Ce (c') is used mainly with the verb **être** and sometimes with the verbs **aller, devoir** and **pouvoir.** Sometimes **ce** may be replaced by **cela.**
It is used with the verb **être:**

1. before a noun that is modified.

> Regardez cet homme. **C'**est un grand pianiste.
> *Look at this man. He's a great pianist.*
> Qui est cette fille? **C'**est ma sœur.
> *Who is this girl? She's my sister.*

2. before a proper noun.

> Voilà un jeune homme. **C'**est André Pierron.
> *There is a young man. It is Andrew Pierron.*

3. before a pronoun.

> J'ai trouvé ce paquet. Est-**ce** le vôtre?
> *I found this package. Is it yours?*

4. before a superlative.

> **Ce** sont les meilleures cerises de la ville.
> *These are the best cherries in the city.*

5. before an infinitive.

> Le problème **c'**est de savoir où commencer.
> *The problem is to know where to begin.*

6. before an adverb.

> **C'**est aujourd'hui un jour de congé.
> *Today is a holiday.*
> **C'**est maintenant ou jamais.
> *It's now or never.*

7. as a neuter subject.

> **Il** est vrai que deux et deux font quatre. Oui, **c'**est vrai.
> *It is true that two and two are four. Yes, it's true.*

Note that **ce** is used to represent something that has preceded. The pronoun **il** is used to announce something that follows.

34. Complete the following sentences with **ce (c')**, **il** or **elle.**

1. _____ est inutile de me parler.
2. Manger _____ est vivre.
3. Voilà mon amie. _____ est intelligente.
4. Voilà mon amie. _____ est une grande artiste.
5. Ne me parlez pas. _____ est inutile.
6. _____ sont les meilleurs peintures de l'artiste.

Ceci, cela (ça)

When the demonstrative pronoun replaces an indefinite expression or an idea, **ceci** or **cela** is used. **Ça** is used in familiar style. **Cela** is used when the expression has already been mentioned. **Ceci** is used to introduce the expression.

> **Ceci** est bon. Vous avez bien réussi.
> *This is good. You have succeeded well.*
> Vous avez réussi. **Cela** est bon.
> *You have succeeded. That is good.*

Like **celui-ci** and **celui-là, ceci** refers to the closest thing mentioned and **cela** to the farthest thing.

> Du cinéma ou du théâtre, **ceci** me plaît plus que **cela.**

35. Complete the following sentences with **ce, c', ceci** or **cela.**

1. _____ est bon. Vous avez bien fait.
2. Vous avez bien fait. _____ est bon.
3. _____ est mon ami.
4. J'ai un gant. Est- _____ le vôtre?
5. _____ m'est égal.
6. Ne touchez pas au feu! _____ ne se fait pas.
7. Retenez bien _____ .

RELATIVE PRONOUNS

The relative pronoun is used to introduce a clause that modifies a noun.

Qui   Who, which, that

Qui functions as the subject of the clause and may refer to either a person or a thing.

La femme **qui** parle est ma mère.
The woman who is speaking is my mother.
Le livre **qui** est sur la table est bon.
The book which is on the table is good.

Qui is used in proverbs to replace **celui qui.**

Qui aime bien châtie bien.
He (The one) who loves punishes well.

Qui can also be used in certain archaic idiomatic expressions to replace **ce qui.**

Qui plus est	*What's more is*
Qui pis est	*What's worse is*
Qui mieux est	*What's better is*

Il est désagréable et **qui pis est** méchant.
He is disagreeable and what's worse is he's naughty.

Que   Whom, which, that

Que functions as the direct object of a clause and may refer to either persons or things. Note that **que** becomes **qu'** before a vowel.

Le garçon **que** nous avons vu hier est mon frère.
The boy whom we saw yesterday is my brother.
Les livres **qu'**elle écrit sont intéressants.
The books she writes are interesting.

Que is sometimes used to replace **où** after certain expressions of time.

L'année **que** je reviendrai
The year when I will return

36. Complete the following sentences with **qui** or **que.**

1. La fille _____ parle est intelligente.
2. Le film _____ j'ai vu est merveilleux.

3. Les livres _____ il regarde sont les miens.
4. Le restaurant _____ est au coin de la rue est excellent.
5. L'homme _____ nous avons vu hier est avocat.
6. Les garçons _____ viennent d'entrer sont mes amis.
7. Les poèmes _____ elle a écrits sont beaux.
8. Les tableaux _____ sont dans le salon sont jolis.

37. Combine the following pairs of sentences, according to the model.

L'homme fait un discours. Il est avocat.
L'homme qui fait un discours est avocat.

1. Voilà un garçon. Il est sportif.
2. La dame entre. Elle est la femme de mon professeur.
3. L'église est au centre de la ville. Elle est grande.
4. La jeune fille danse. Elle est très intelligente.
5. Je connais cette femme. Elle donne de bons discours.

38. Combine the following pairs of sentences, according to the model.

Il écrit les livres. Les livres sont intéressants.
Les livres qu'il écrit sont intéressants.

1. Voilà le restaurant. Pierre préfère le restaurant.
2. Je lis le journal. Le journal est parisien.
3. Elle a acheté cette robe. La robe est très chère.
4. Nous avons vu le film. Le film est américain.
5. C'est un médecin. Je connais ce médecin.

Ce qui and ce que

Ce qui   *What, that which*

Ce qui is used as the subject of the clause when there is no antecedent.

Comprenez-vous **ce qui** se passe?
Do you understand what is happening?
Ce qui est arrivé est presque impossible.
What happened is almost impossible.

Ce que   *What, that which*

Ce que is used as the object of a verb in a relative clause when there is no antecedent.

Je ne comprends pas **ce que** vous dites.
I don't understand what you are saying.
Ce qu'il écrit est difficile à comprendre.
What he writes is difficult to understand.

Ce qui and **ce que** can be combined with **tout**.

Tout ce qui est bon est beau.
All that is good is beautiful.
Tout ce qu'elle fait est bon.
All that she does is good.

39. Complete the following sentences with **ce qui** or **ce que.**

    1. Je ne comprends pas _____ il dit.
    2. Je ne comprends pas _____ se passe.
    3. Je ne sais pas _____ va avoir lieu.
    4. Je ne sais pas _____ Pierre fait.
    5. Je ne comprends pas _____ est arrivé.
    6. Je ne comprends pas _____ on lit.

Relative Pronouns with Prepositions Other than *de: qui, lequel*

Qui

Qui as object of a preposition refers to persons only.

> La fille **à qui** vous parlez est gentille.
> *The girl to whom you are speaking is nice.*
> La femme **pour qui** je travaille est intelligente.
> *The woman for whom I work is intelligent.*

Lequel, laquelle, lesquels, lesquelles   *Which*

Lequel is the relative pronoun used after a preposition and refers to things or to persons. **Lequel** must agree with the antecedent.

> La maison **dans laquelle** Pierre habite est grande.
> *The house in which Peter lives is big.*
> Le restaurant **devant lequel** j'ai attendu mon ami est merveilleux.
> *The restaurant in front of which I waited for my friend is marvelous.*
> Les raisons **pour lesquelles** je fais cela sont évidentes.
> *The reasons why I do that are evident.*

After **parmi** and **entre,** the forms of **lequel** are obligatory when referring to persons. The pronoun **qui** cannot be used.

> Les gens **parmi lesquels** il vit sont gentils.
> *The people among whom he lives are nice.*
> Les femmes **entre lesquelles** elle se tient debout sont ses amies.
> *The women between whom she stands are her friends.*

When preceded by the preposition **à, lequel** contracts with it to form **auquel, auxquels, auxquelles. À** plus **laquelle** do not contract.

> Le concert **auquel** il a assisté a été bon.
> *The concert which he attended was good.*
> L'école **à laquelle** elle va est vieille.
> *The school where (to which) she goes is old.*
> Les garçons **auxquels** nous parlons sont gentils.
> *The boys to whom we are speaking are nice.*
> Les filles **auxquelles** nous parlons sont intelligentes.
> *The girls to whom we are speaking are intelligent.*

40. Complete the following sentences with the correct relative pronoun.

    1. La fille à _____ je parle est une bonne artiste.
    2. L'homme avec _____ je sors est intelligent.
    3. La boutique derrière _____ se trouve un arbre est une boutique moderne.

4. Le bâtiment dans _____ je travaille est un gratte-ciel.
5. Les villes vers _____ nous nous dirigeons sont de véritables musées.
6. Voilà les pinceaux avec _____ il a peint ce tableau.
7. Les garçons entre _____ il est assis sont gentils.

41. Combine the two sentences into one, according to the models.

J'ai parlé à l'homme. Il est intéressant.
L'homme à qui j'ai parlé est intéressant.

Je pense à ce travail. Il est difficile.
Le travail auquel je pense est difficile.

1. Voilà le garçon. Je suis sorti avec le garçon.
2. Voilà la maison. J'ai habité dans cette maison.
3. J'ai écrit à ces hommes. Ils sont mes anciens professeurs.
4. C'est le pinceau. L'artiste travaille avec le pinceau.
5. Voilà un morceau de papier. Il a dessiné sur ce morceau de papier.
6. Paul entre dans le restaurant. Le restaurant est très petit.
7. Nous allons chez cette fille. Elle est gentille.
8. Voilà les tables. Marie a mis des fleurs sur les tables.
9. Il attend son ami devant le musée. Le musée est formidable.
10. Nous sommes allés au théâtre. Le théâtre est très vieux.
11. Elle a assisté à la conférence. La conférence était intéressante.
12. Il a répondu à ces lettres. Elles étaient urgentes.
13. Il a écrit à ces hommes. Ces hommes sont avocats.
14. Je suis allée aux musées. Les musées sont grands.

Où

A relative clause referring to a place or time is usually introduced by **où** to avoid using a preposition plus a form of **lequel.**

Voilà la maison **dans laquelle** Georges habite.
Voilà la maison **où** habite Georges.
There is the house where George lives.
Le siècle **pendant lequel** il vécut était intéressant.
Le siècle **où** il vécut était intéressant.
The century in which he lived was interesting.

42. Rewrite the following sentences according to the model.

L'école à laquelle nous allons est vieille.
L'école où nous allons est vieille.

1. L'appartement dans lequel j'habite est très petit.
2. La boulangerie dans laquelle j'entre est bonne.
3. Le bureau auquel je vais se trouve au centre de la ville.
4. Les restaurants dans lesquels nous dînons ne sont pas chers.
5. Les églises auxquelles nous allons sont vieilles.

Relative Pronouns with the Preposition *de: dont, lequel*

While the forms **de qui,** referring to persons, and **duquel, desquels, de laquelle, desquelles,** referring to things do occur, most French-speakers use **dont.**

Dont may refer to persons or things and means *whose, of (about) which, of (about) whom.*

La femme **de qui** nous parlons est Marie Dupont.
La femme **dont** nous parlons est Marie Dupont.
The woman about whom we are speaking is Marie Dupont.

Le film **duquel** nous parlons est bon.
Le film **dont** nous parlons est bon.
The movie of which we are speaking is good.

Je connais une fille **dont** la mère est médecin.
I know a girl whose mother is a doctor.
L'homme **dont** le fils parle est avocat.
The man whose son is speaking is a lawyer.
Voilà un tableau **dont** j'admire la beauté.
There is a painting whose beauty I admire.

Dont cannot be followed by a possessive adjective.

Voilà la fille. Je connais **ses** parents.
Voilà la fille **dont** je connais **les** parents.

Dont can be used only when it immediately follows the noun to which it refers. If the noun is followed by a prepositional phrase, the appropriate form of **de** plus **lequel** must be used.

C'est le garçon avec la sœur **duquel** je suis sorti.
He is the boy whose sister I went out with.
Voilà la fille à la mère **de laquelle (de qui)** vous avez parlé.
There is the girl whose mother you spoke to.

43. Rewrite the following sentences, replacing **de qui** and the forms of **duquel** by **dont**.

    1. Le garçon de qui le père est mort est mon ami.
    2. Le musée duquel le nom m'échappe est célèbre.
    3. La dame de qui nous cherchons le chien est une amie de ma mère.
    4. L'homme de qui les usines sont à Lyon habite à Paris.
    5. J'aime ce jardin duquel les fleurs l'embellissent.
    6. Le crayon duquel vous vous servez n'est pas bon.
    7. Les livres desquels vous m'avez parlé sont intéressants.
    8. La peinture de laquelle vous avez envie est très chère.

44. Follow the model.

    Voilà le garçon. Je connais ses parents.
    Voilà le garçon dont je connais les parents.

    1. Voilà une fille. Son père est médecin.
    2. Voilà le mannequin. Ses robes sont jolies.
    3. Voilà les garçons. Vous connaissez leur sœur.
    4. Voilà un professeur. Sa fille est chimiste.
    5. Voilà un garçon. Son père est mort.
    6. Voilà une femme. J'admire la beauté de cette femme.
    7. Voilà un peintre. Le tableau de ce peintre est cher.
    8. C'est un beau tableau. Nous avons parlé de ce tableau.
    9. C'est un livre. Vous avez envie de ce livre.
    10. As-tu étudié le poème? Il a parlé du poème.
    11. C'est un livre. J'ai besoin de ce livre.

12. J'ai vu la jeune fille. Ils ont parlé de cette jeune fille.
13. C'est un beau poème. Nous avons lu quelques passages de ce poème.

45. Follow the model.

C'est le garçon. Je suis sorti avec sa sœur.
C'est le garçon avec la sœur duquel je suis sorti.

1. C'est la fille. J'ai parlé avec sa mère.
2. C'est un homme. Je suis sorti avec sa fille.
3. Il y a une boutique ici. Près de la boutique se trouve un bureau de tabac.
4. Il a fait un discours. À cause de ce discours j'ai pleuré.
5. Voilà les jeunes filles. Je suis sortie avec leur frère.

Quoi, ce dont

Quoi (*what*) is used after a preposition.

Je sais de **quoi** il s'agit.
I know what it is about.
Je sais **à quoi** vous avez pensé.
I know what you thought about.
Je sais **sur quoi** il écrit.
I know what he is writing about.

Ce dont (*what*) can be used before expressions requiring the preposition **de**.

Il sait **ce dont** vous avez besoin.
He knows what you need.

46. Complete the following sentences with **quoi, à quoi** or **ce dont**.

1. Elle comprend _____ je m'étonne.
2. Il sait de _____ il parle.
3. Je sais _____ vous pensez.
4. Elles savent de _____ il s'agit.
5. Elle comprend _____ vous avez peur.

Review

47. Complete the following sentences with the appropriate relative pronoun. Include prepositions when necessary.

1. _____ vous voulez est impossible à avoir.
2. Voilà un homme _____ est avocat.
3. C'est une fille _____ je connais le frère.
4. Voilà la maison _____ nous demeurons.
5. Voilà les livres _____ Pierre cherche.
6. Avez-vous trouvé la lettre _____ j'ai besoin?
7. Savez-vous _____ est dans le tiroir?
8. Dites-moi _____ il vous a dit.
9. C'est l'homme avec la fille _____ je suis sorti.
10. Les femmes _____ ils parlent sont jolies.
11. Je comprends de _____ il s'agit.

12. Un boucher est un homme _____ vend de la viande.
13. C'est un politicien _____ je suis d'accord.
14. Ce sont des idées _____ je suis d'accord.

INDEFINITE PRONOUNS

Following are some indefinite pronouns.

1. **aucun(e)**   *anyone, none*
   aucun(e) … ne   *none*

> **Aucun** d'eux **n'**est arrivé.
> *None of them arrived.*
> **Aucune** d'elles **n'**est arrivée.
> *None of them arrived.*
> Y a-t-il **aucun** de vous qui puisse le faire?
> *Is there anyone of you who can do it?*
> Avez-vous des peintures? **Aucune.**
> *Do you have any paintings?   None*

2. **l'autre**   *the other, the other one*
   les autres   *the others, the other ones*

> Deux filles sont restées. **Les autres** sont parties.
> *Two girls stayed. The others left.*
> J'ai perdu un foulard, mais j'en ai **d'autres.**
> *I lost a scarf, but I have others (other ones).*
> Il a quelque chose **d'autre.**
> *He has something else.*

Note that **d'autre** means *else* in the above sentence.

3. **l'un (l'une) … l'autre**   *the one … the other*
   les uns (les unes) … les autres   *the ones (some) … the others*

> **Les uns** dansaient; **les autres** bavardaient.
> *Some danced; others talked.*

4. **l'un (l'une) et l'autre**   *both, both of them*
   l'un (l'une) ou l'autre   *either one*
   ni l'un (l'une) ni l'autre   *neither one*
   l'un (l'une) à l'autre   *to each other*
   l'un (l'une) pour l'autre   *one for the other*

> Elles sont venues **l'une et l'autre.**
> *Both of them came.*
> Vous avez deux livres. Donnez-moi **l'un ou l'autre.**
> *You have two books. Give me either one. (It makes no difference)*
> **Ni l'un ni l'autre n'**est venu.
> *Neither one came.*
> Ils s'écrivent **l'un à l'autre.**
> *They write to each other.*
> Elles travaillent **l'une pour l'autre.**
> *They work for each other.*

5. **autre(s)**   *other(s)*

> Voici deux livres: je prends celui-ci; prenez **l'autre.**
> *Here are two books: I'll take this one; take the other.*

6. **autre chose**   *something else*

> Je voudrais **autre chose** de sucré.
> *I would like something else sweet.*

When an adjective modifies **autre chose,** the adjective is always masculine and is always preceded by **de.**

7. **autrui**   *others, other people*

> Il ne faut pas convoiter le bien d'**autrui.**
> *You must not covet the well-being of others.*

8. **certain, certaine**   *a certain one*
   certains, certaines   *certain ones, some*

> **Certains** d'entre eux voulaient danser.
> *Some of them wanted to dance.*

9. **chacun, chacune**   *each one, everyone*

> **Chacun** à son goût.
> *Everyone to his own taste.*
> **Chacun** des garçons apportera un cadeau.
> *Each one of the boys will bring a gift.*

10. **grand-chose**   *much*

> Il n'a pas **grand-chose** à me dire.
> *He does not have much to say to me.*

Grand-chose is always used in the negative.

11. **Je ne sais qui**   *I don't know who*
    Je ne sais quoi   *I don't know what*

> **Je ne sais qui** a téléphoné.
> *I don't know who telephoned.*
> Elle a **je ne sais quoi** d'élégant.
> *She has somewhat of an elegant air.*

12. **le même, la même**   *the same (one)*
    les mêmes   *the same (ones)*

> C'est **la même.**
> *It's the same one.*

13. **n'importe qui**   *anyone*

> **N'importe qui** pourra le faire.
> *Anyone will be able to do it.*
> Je parlerai à **n'importe qui.**
> *I will speak to anyone.*

14. **n'importe quoi**   *anything*

> Il peut faire **n'importe quoi.**
> *He can do anything.*

15. **nul**   *no one*

> **Nul** ne sait la réponse.
> *No one knows the answer.*

Nul is used in the sense of **personne**.

16. **on**   *one, they, people*

> **On** a construit ce pont.
> *They built this bridge.*
> **On** n'emploie pas le passé simple dans la langue parlée.
> *One doesn't use the* passé simple *in spoken language.*

On can be replaced by **l'on** after **et, ou, où, que, qui, quoi** and **si.**

> Si **l'on** veut, on peut tout faire.
> *If one wants, one can do anything.*

17. **Personne ne ...**   *no one*
    ne ... personne   *anyone*

> **Personne n'**est venu.
> *No one came.*
> Je **ne** vois **personne**.
> *I don't see anyone.*

18. **plusieurs**   *several*

> Il en a **plusieurs**.
> *He has several.*
> **Plusieurs** d'entre eux sont gentils.
> *Several of them are nice.*

19. **qui que**   *whoever, whomever*
    qui que ce soit qui   *whoever*
    quoi que   *whatever*
    quoi que ce soit que   *whatever*

> **Qui que** vous voyiez, ne me trahissez pas.
> *Whomever you see, don't betray me.*
> **Qui que ce soit qui** vous parle, ne dites rien.
> *Whoever speaks to you, don't say anything.*
> **Quoi que** vous disiez, je ne vous croirai pas.
> *Whatever you say, I won't believe you.*

Note that these expressions are followed by the subjunctive.

20. **quelqu'un**   *someone*

> **Quelqu'un** frappe à la porte.
> *Someone is knocking at the door.*

Quelqu'un does not have a feminine form.

21. **quelqu'un d'autre**   *someone else*

> **Quelqu'un d'autre** peut le faire.
> *Someone else can do it.*

22. **quelques-uns, quelques-unes**   *some*

> Avez-vous des livres? Oui, j'en ai **quelques-uns**.
> *Do you have any books? Yes, I have some.*

Avez-vous acheté des pommes? Oui, j'en ai acheté **quelques-unes.**
Did you buy any apples? Yes, I bought some.

Note that **en** is used when **quelques-uns** and **quelques-unes** are used as direct objects.

23. **quelque chose**   *something*

Voulez-vous **quelque chose?**
Do you want something?
Je voudrais **quelque chose** de joli.
I want something pretty.

Note that **de** precedes the adjective which refers to **quelque chose.** The adjective is always masculine.

24. **quiconque**   *anyone*

Quiconque travaille mangera.
Anyone who works will eat.

25. **Rien ne ...**   *nothing*
ne ... rien   *anything*

Rien ne se passe.
Nothing is happening.
Je **ne** vois **rien.**
I don't see anything.

26. **tel, telle**   (designates an undetermined person)

M. **un tel**   *Mr. So-and-so*
Mme **une telle**   *Mrs. So-and-so*
Mlle **une telle**   *Miss So-and-so*

The form **un tel** is used when one doesn't want to or is unable to name the person.

Tel qui rit vendredi dimanche pleurera.
He who laughs today cries tomorrow.

27. **tout, toute, tous, toutes**   *all, everything*

Tout est bien ici.
Everything is fine here.
J'ai tous les billets. Je les ai **tous.**
I have all the tickets. I have all of them.
Il a vu toutes les peintures. Il les a **toutes** vues.
He saw all the paintings. He saw all of them.

Note that **de** is never used with **tout,** although in English we say *all of them* or *all*. Note too that the **s** is pronounced in the pronoun form **tous.** Also, the pronoun **tout** precedes the past participle in compound tenses.

Il les a **tous** lus.
He read them all.

28. **tout ce qui, tout ce qui**   *everything, all that*

On a vu **tout ce qui** est dans cette ville.
We saw everything in this city.
Tout ce que nous faisons est intéressant.
Everything we do is interesting.

Tout ce qu'elle dit est intéressant.
Everything she says is interesting.

29. **tout le monde**   *everyone*

Tout le monde est ici.
Everyone is here.

Tout le monde is used with a singular verb.

See Chapter 7 for more study on negative indefinite pronouns.

48. Complete the following sentences with the correct French words for the English words in parentheses.

1. _____ (Anyone) peut le faire.
2. _____ (Someone) le fera.
3. _____ (Everyone) aime la beauté.
4. _____ (One) peut venir ici.
5. Voudriez-vous _____ (something) de bon?
6. Il a _____ (everything) compris.
7. _____ (The others) viendront plus tard.
8. Je comprends les verbes. Je les comprends _____ (all).
9. As-tu des disques? Oui, j'en ai _____ (some).
10. Elles viendront _____ (both of them).
11. Je n'aime _____ (either one).
12. _____ (Certain ones) d'entre elles voudraient bavarder.
13. Il dira _____ (anything).
14. Voudriez-vous _____ (something else)?
15. _____ (All that) Pierre fait est intéressant.
16. Il en a _____ (several).
17. Avez-vous des blouses? Oui, j'en ai _____ (some).
18. _____ (Each one) des mères apportera quelque chose.
19. _____ (Someone else) pourra le faire.
20. _____ (Some) voulaient danser; _____ (the others) voulaient aller au cinéma.
21. Ils parlent _____ (to each other).
22. Vous avez deux robes. Donnez-moi _____ (either one).
23. _____ (Anyone) le dira.
24. Est-ce que c'est une autre robe? Non, c'est _____ (the same).
25. _____ (None) d'elles ne viendra.
26. _____ (No one) ne sait la réponse.
27. _____ (Everything) est bien ici.
28. _____ (Nothing) n'est arrivé.
29. Allez voir _____ (Mr. So-and-so).
30. _____ (Whoever) essaiera, réussira.
31. Il ne faut pas dire du mal d' _____ (anyone).
32. Avez-vous _____ (something else)?

Chapter 9

Special Meanings of Certain Verbs

EXPRESSIONS WITH *ALLER*

Some idiomatic expressions with the verb **aller** are:

aller à la pêche   *to go fishing*
aller à la chasse   *to go hunting*
aller à pied   *to go on foot, to walk*
aller à bicyclette   *to go by bicycle*
aller en voiture, en avion, par le train   *to go by car, by plane, by train*
aller loin   *to succeed*
    Elle est intelligente. Elle ira loin.
aller trop loin   *to go too far*
    Il va trop loin. Je suis très fâché.
aller bien, mal, mieux   *to feel (be) well (fine), bad, better*
    Je vais bien.
aller à quelqu'un   *to suit, to become*
    Cette robe vous va très bien.
Allez-y! *Go ahead!*
Comment allez-vous?
Comment vas-tu?   } *How are you?*
Comment ça va? (fam.)
Comment va-t-il?   *How is he?*
Ça va? (informal)   *How are you?*

1. Translate the following sentences into French, using the verb **aller.**

    1. He is going by car.
    2. He will succeed.
    3. I feel bad.
    4. He feels better today.
    5. This hat is becoming to you.
    6. How are you?
    7. I am fine.
    8. He is going fishing.

EXPRESSIONS WITH *AVOIR*

The verb **avoir** is used in many idiomatic expressions.

avoir chaud   *to be warm*
  Elle a chaud en été.
avoir froid   *to be cold*
  Il a froid en hiver.
avoir faim   *to be hungry*
  J'ai très faim.
avoir soif   *to be thirsty*
  Elle a très soif.
avoir sommeil   *to be sleepy*
  Elle va se coucher. Elle a sommeil.
avoir peur de   *to be afraid*
  Il a peur du lion.
avoir honte de   *to be ashamed of*
  Il a honte de ses actions.
avoir raison   *to be right*
  Elle a raison.
avoir tort   *to be wrong*
  Cet élève a tort.
avoir mal à   *to have an ache in*
  Elle a mal à la tête.
  Elle a mal aux dents.
avoir lieu   *to take place*
  L'action a eu lieu dans une grande ville.
avoir beau   *to do something in vain*
  Il avait beau étudier; il n'a pas réussi à l'examen.
  He studied in vain; he didn't pass the exam.
avoir l'air ...   *to look, to seem*
  Elle a l'air contente.
avoir de la chance   *to be lucky*
  Marie a de la chance.
avoir de la patience   *to be patient*
  Les mères ont de la patience.
avoir ... de retard   *to be late by ...*
  L'avion a quinze minutes de retard.
avoir ... d'avance   *to be early by ...*
  Ils ont dix minutes d'avance.
avoir envie de   *to want to*
  Il a envie d'aller au cinéma.
avoir besoin de   *to need*
  Il a besoin d'étudier.
avoir l'habitude de   *to be in the habit of*
  Elle a l'habitude de prendre du thé à quatre heures.
avoir l'occasion de   *to have the chance to*
  Il a l'occasion d'aller à Paris.
avoir l'intention de   *to intend to*
  J'ai l'intention d'étudier davantage.
avoir le temps de   *to have the time to*
  J'ai le temps de le faire.
avoir quelque chose   *to have something wrong*
  Vous avez quelque chose?

avoir ... ans   *to be ... years old*
    Quel âge avez-vous?
    J'ai vingt ans.
avoir à   *to have to*
    J'ai à faire ce travail.
avoir ... de longueur, de hauteur, d'épaisseur   *to be ... long, tall, thick*
    La boîte a dix mètres de longueur.
    La tour a cent mètres de hauteur.
    Le mur a trente centimètres d'épaisseur.

2. Follow the model. Use an expression with the verb **avoir** in your answer.

   Je voudrais un sandwich.
   J'ai faim.

   1. Je voudrais boire.
   2. Je voudrais manger.
   3. Je voudrais dormir.
   4. Je vais porter un manteau.
   5. J'ouvre la fenêtre.
   6. Je prends de l'aspirine.
   7. Je vais chez le dentiste.
   8. Je demande pardon.
   9. Je pense que Tokio est la capitale du Japon.
   10. Je pense qu'il y a 52 États aux États-Unis.

3. Translate the following sentences into French, using the verb **avoir**.

   1. I came in vain. No one was there.
   2. She is afraid of this man.
   3. He is ashamed of his work.
   4. We were right.
   5. I have a headache.
   6. The girls look tired.
   7. Peter is lucky.
   8. The train is a half hour late.
   9. The plane is ten minutes early.
   10. He has the chance to go to Martinique.
   11. What's wrong with you?
   12. How old are you?
   13. He is fifty years old.
   14. She needs the book.
   15. The house is twenty meters high.
   16. We are warm.
   17. The children are sleepy.

EXPRESSIONS WITH *ÊTRE*

être en train de   *to be in the act of*
    Je suis en train de travailler.
être à   *to belong to*
    Ces disques sont à moi.
être de   *to be from*
    Elle est de New York.

être égal à   *to make no difference to*
Cela m'est égal.
être de retour   *to be back*
Elle sera de retour lundi.
Ça y est   *It's all right. It's done.*
Vous avez terminé? Oui, ça y est.

4. Translate the following sentences into French, using the verb **être**.

1. She's in the act of studying.
2. The boys are from Paris.
3. It makes no difference to me.
4. We will be back tomorrow.
5. These books belong to her.
6. It's all right.

EXPRESSIONS WITH *FAIRE*

The verb **faire** is used in many weather expressions.

Il fait chaud.   *It is warm.*
Il fait froid.   *It is cold.*
Il fait frais.   *It is cool.*
Il fait mauvais.   *The weather is bad.*
Il fait bon (beau).   *The weather is good (nice).*
Il fait du soleil.   *The sun is shining.*
Il fait du vent.   *It is windy.*
Il fait du brouillard.   *It is foggy.*

Some other idiomatic expressions with the verb **faire** are:

Il fait nuit.   *It is night.*
Il fait jour.   *It is daylight.*

faire l'impossible   *to do the impossible*
faire de son mieux   *to do one's best*
faire son possible   *to do one's best*

faire du bien   *to produce a good effect*
Le soleil vous fera du bien.
faire fortune   *to become rich*
faire des économies   *to save money*
faire plaisir   *to give pleasure*
faire mal   *to hurt*
Ma jambe me fait mal.   *My leg hurts.*
faire mal à   *to harm*
se faire du mal   *to hurt oneself*
Elle s'est fait du mal.   *She hurt herself.*
Elle s'est fait mal au bras.   *She hurt her arm.*
faire attention   *to pay attention*
faire peur à   *to scare*
Le tigre leur fait peur.   *The tiger scares them.*
faire confiance à   *to trust*
Faites-moi confiance.   *Trust me.*
faire la connaissance de quelqu'un   *to meet someone*
faire ses courses   *to run errands*

faire le ménage　　*to do housework*
faire la queue　　*to wait in line*
faire un voyage　　*to take a trip*
faire une promenade　　*to take a walk*
faire exprès　　*to do something on purpose*
　　Je ne l'ai pas fait exprès.
faire semblant　　*to pretend*
　　Elle fait semblant de dormir.
Ça ne fait rien.　　*It doesn't matter.*

5. Complete each sentence with an expression using **faire**.

Le soleil brille, le ciel est bleu et la température est de 25° Celsius. Il...
Il fait beau.

　1. Elle ne dépense pas d'argent. Elle...
　2. Nous écoutons bien en classe. Nous...
　3. Il donne un coup de chiffon aux meubles et il balaye le plancher. Il...
　4. J'aime marcher. Je ... tous les jours.
　5. Tu deviens riche. Tu...
　6. Ils vont chez le boulanger, chez le boucher, chez l'épicier. Ils...

6. Translate the following sentences into French, using the verb **faire**.

　1. It is warm.
　2. The weather is cool.
　3. The sun is shining.
　4. It is foggy.
　5. It is night.
　6. He does his best.
　7. This medicine will do you good.
　8. I hurt my arm.
　9. We waited in line for an hour.
　10. I did it on purpose.
　11. It doesn't matter.
　12. They pretended not to hear.

SPECIAL USES OF OTHER VERBS

Devoir, pouvoir, savoir, vouloir

　　The verbs **devoir, pouvoir, savoir** and **vouloir** have special meanings in different tenses.

Devoir

　　present tense　　*to owe*
　　je dois　　*I owe*

　　　Je **dois** dix francs à Jean.　　*I owe John ten francs.*

　　devoir plus infinitive　　*must, to have to*
　　je dois　　*I must, I have to*

　　　Il **doit** travailler.　　　*He must work.*
　　　Je **devrai** travailler.　　*I shall have to work.*
　　　Elle **a dû** travailler.　　*She had to work.*

present and imperfect tenses   *to be supposed to, to be scheduled to*

> Elle **doit** partir demain.
> *She is supposed to (is scheduled to) leave tomorrow.*
> Il **devrait** partir lundi.
> *He was supposed to leave on Monday.*

present, *passé composé* and imperfect tenses — to express probability — *must be*

> Il **doit** être malade.
> *He must be (is probably) sick.*
> Il **a dû** être malade.
> *He must have been (was probably) sick.*
> Le film **devait** être bon.
> *The movie was probably good.*

conditional tense to express an advice or reproach—*should, ought to*
je devrais   *I should, I ought to*
j'aurais dû   *I should have, I ought to have*

> Vous **devriez** travailler.
> *You should (ought to) work.*
> Vous **auriez dû** travailler.
> *You should have (ought to have) worked.*

Pouvoir

present tense   *to be able to*
je peux   *I can, I am able*

> **Pouvez-vous** jouer du violon?   *Can you play the violin?*

passé composé
j'ai pu   *I was able, I could (I succeeded)*

> J'**ai pu** m'échapper.   *I was able to escape (succeeded in escaping).*
> Je **n'ai pas pu** le faire.   *I couldn't do it. (But I tried.)*

conditional tense
je pourrais   *I could, I would be able*

> Je **pourrais** vous aider.   *I could help you.*

conditional perfect
j'aurais pu   *I could have, I would have been able*

> Elle **aurait pu** le faire.   *She could have done it (would have been able to do it).*

Savoir

present　　　*to know, to know how to, to be able to*
je sais　　*I know, I know how, I can*

Je **sais** jouer du piano.　　　　*I know how to play the piano.*
　　　　　　　　　　　　　　　　I can play the piano.

passé composé
j'ai su　　*I knew, I found out*

J'**ai su** la vérité.　　　　*I found out the truth.*

conditional
je saurais　　*I would be able to, I can*

Je ne **saurais** pas cacher ma colère.　　*I wouldn't be able to hide my anger.*

Vouloir

present　　　*to want*
je veux　　*I want*

Je **veux** ce livre.　　　　*I want this book.*

passé composé
j'ai voulu　　*I tried*

J'**ai voulu** le faire.　　　　*I tried to do it.*

je n'ai pas voulu　　*I refused*

Je **n'ai pas voulu** le faire.　　　　*I refused to do it.*

conditional tense
je voudrais　　*I want, I would like*

Je **voudrais** du beurre.　　　　*I want some butter.*
Je **voudrais** aller au cinéma.　　　*I would like to go to the movies.*

7. Translate the following sentences into French, using **devoir, pouvoir, savoir** or **vouloir.**

1. I owe Mary five dollars.
2. He must come.
3. She was supposed to leave for New York.
4. He must be sick.
5. You should have come.
6. He ought to study.
7. I can do it.
8. We couldn't finish. (But we tried.)
9. I could have helped you.
10. He succeeded in doing it.
11. We found out the truth.
12. She tried to open the door.
13. He refused to go there.

Habiter, demeurer, vivre

Habiter, demeurer and **vivre** all mean *to live*. **Habiter** and **demeurer** mean *to live, to dwell* and are used with names of places.

Il **demeure** à Paris.	*He lives in Paris.*
Elle **habite** à Paris.	*She lives in Paris.*

Habiter is sometimes used without a preposition.

Il **habite l'Angleterre.**	*He lives in England.*
Il **habite Paris.**	*He lives in Paris.*

Vivre means *to live, to be alive*.

Il **vivra** longtemps.	*He'll live a long time.*

8. Complete the following sentences with the correct form of the present tense of **demeurer** or **vivre.**

   1. Elle _____ bien.
   2. Nous _____ en Suisse.
   3. Mon père _____ toujours.
   4. Vous _____ en Espagne.
   5. Ils _____ longtemps.

9. Rewrite the following sentences according to the model.

Ils habitent en Angleterre.
Ils habitent l'Angleterre.

   1. Elle habite à Paris.
   2. Ils habitent en Suisse.
   3. Vous habitez à New York.
   4. Nous habitons au Mexique.

Jouer, jouer à, jouer de

Jouer means *to play*. **Jouer à** means *to play (a game)*. **Jouer de** means *to play (a musical instrument)*.

   Ils **jouent** dans le jardin.
   They are playing in the garden.
   Elle **joue** un morceau de Beethoven.
   She is playing a piece by Beethoven.
   Il **joue au** football.
   He plays soccer.
   Elle **joue du** piano.
   She plays the piano.

10. Complete the following sentences with the correct form of the present tense of **jouer, jouer à** or **jouer de.**

   1. Il _____ le rôle de Rodrigue.
   2. Nous _____ violon.
   3. Ils _____ cartes.
   4. Vous _____ la clarinette.
   5. Ils _____ dans le parc.
   6. Vous _____ football.

Manquer, manquer à, manquer de

The verb **manquer** means *to miss*. **Manquer de** means *to be lacking*. Study the following:

Il a **manqué** son train.	*He missed his train.*
André **manque à** Marie.	*Mary misses Andrew.*
André **lui manque.**	*She misses Andrew.*
Il **lui manque.**	*She misses him.*
Cette ville **me manque.**	*I miss this city.*
Nous **manquons d'**argent.	*We are lacking money.*
Il **manque d'**intelligence.	*He is lacking in intelligence.*

11. Complete the following sentences with the correct form of the present tense of **manquer,** **manquer à** or **manquer de.**

   1. Il _____ l'autobus.
   2. Marie _____ Paul.
   3. Vous _____ patience.
   4. Elles _____ le concert.
   5. Les cafés _____ ces étudiants.

12. Translate the following sentences into French.

   1. He missed the train.
   2. I miss her.
   3. She misses me.
   4. They are lacking in patience.

Penser à, penser de

Penser à and **penser de** both mean *to think about*. **Penser de** is used when *to think about* means *to have an opinion about something or someone*.

Elle **pense à** ses amis.
She is thinking about her friends.
Que **pensez-vous de** mes amis?
What do you think about (What is your opinion about) my friends?

After **penser à,** a stress pronoun is used when talking about a person. When the object is a thing, **y** is used to replace **à** plus the noun.

Il pense **à sa mère.**
Il pense **à elle.**

Il pense **à cette lettre.**
Il **y** pense.

After **penser de,** a stress pronoun is used when talking about a person. When talking about a thing, **en** replaces **de** plus the noun.

Que pensez-vous **de Pierre?**
Que pensez-vous **de lui?**

Que pensez-vous **du tableau?**
Qu'**en** pensez-vous?

13. Complete the following sentences with the correct form of the preposition **à** or **de.**

1. Que pensez-vous _____ projet?
2. Il pense toujours _____ Marie.
3. Que pense-t-elle _____ ce roman?
4. Elle pense _____ examens.
5. Nous pensons _____ cette fille.

14. Rewrite the following sentences, replacing the nouns with pronouns.

1. Je pense à Hélène.
2. Que pense-t-il du film?
3. Elle pense à Georges.
4. Que pense-t-elle de l'auteur?
5. Nous pensons à ces problèmes.
6. Que pensent-elles de mes amis?

Partir, sortir, s'en aller, laisser, quitter

Partir, sortir, s'en aller, laisser and **quitter** all mean *to leave.*

Partir means *to leave, to go away.*

Nous **partons** pour Paris.	*We are leaving for Paris.*
Nous **partons** de Paris.	*We are leaving Paris.*

Note that **de** is used with **partir** in the above sentence.

Sortir means *to leave, to go out, to go out of a place, to come out, to go out with someone, to take out.*

Elle **sort** souvent.	*She goes out often.*
Elle **sort** de la salle.	*She leaves (goes out of) the room.*
Elle **sort** avec Pierre.	*She goes out with Peter.*
Elle **sort** du sucre.	*She takes out some sugar.*

S'en aller means *to leave, to go away.*

Je **m'en vais.**	*I'm going away.*

Laisser means *to leave, to leave a thing or person behind.*

Elle **a laissé** le livre à la bibliothèque.
She left the book in the library.
Elle **a laissé** sa sœur au cinéma.
She left her sister at the movies.

Quitter means *to leave, to leave a place or person.*

Elle **quitte** la maison à huit heures.
She leaves the house at eight o'clock.
Je vous **quitte** maintenant.
I am leaving you now.

15. Complete the following sentences, choosing the correct form of the present tense of one of the indicated verbs.

1. Paul _____ avec Hélène.   *sortir / quitter*
2. Il _____ ce soir.   *s'en aller / laisser*
3. Elle _____ ses livres dans le tiroir.   *sortir / laisser*
4. Je _____ . Je suis fatigué.   *s'en aller / quitter*

5. Il _____ son appartement à sept heures.   *quitter/laisser*
6. Il _____ de la salle.   *s'en aller/sortir*
7. Je _____ pour New York.   *partir/quitter*

Passer, se passer, se passer de

Passer means *to pass, to spend (time).*

Il **a passé** deux semaines à Paris.
He spent two weeks in Paris.

Se passer means *to take place, to happen.*

L'action **s'est passée** dans une rue déserte.
The action took place in a deserted street.
Qu'est-ce qui **se passe**?
What is happening?

Se passer de means *to do without.*

Il **s'est passé de** viande.
He did without meat.

16. Complete the following sentences with the correct form of the *passé composé* of **passer, se passer** or **se passer de.**

    1. Il _____ trois semaines
       dans le Midi.
    2. Qu'est-ce qui _____ ?
    3. Nous _____ dessert.
    4. D'étranges choses _____ ici.
    5. Elle _____ la nuit chez Hélène.
    6. L'accident _____ au coin de la rue.
    7. Il _____ beurre.

Plaire

When **plaire** is used in place of **aimer,** an indirect object is used. Note the following.

Paris me plaît.
I like Paris. (Paris is pleasing to me.)
Les disques me plaisent.
I like the records. (The records are pleasing to me.)

17. Rewrite the following sentences according to the model.

Elle aime le concert.
Le concert lui plaît.

    1. J'aime le film.
    2. Elle aime les peintures modernes.
    3. Il aime le cinéma.
    4. Elles aiment la pièce.
    5. Tu aimes le livre.

Se rappeler, se souvenir de

Both **se rappeler** and **se souvenir de** mean *to remember.*

Il **se rappelle** la leçon.   *He remembers the lesson.*
Il **se la rappelle.**   *He remembers it.*

Il **se souvient de** la leçon.   *He remembers the lesson.*
Il **s'**en **souvient.**   *He remembers it.*

Note that when the direct object is replaced by a pronoun, the direct object pronouns are used with **se rappeler** while **en** is used with **se souvenir de.**

18. Rewrite the following sentences, substituting **se souvenir de** for **se rappeler.**

1. Je me rappelle cette occasion.
2. Je me rappelle cette fille.
3. Ils se rappellent cette soirée.
4. Vous vous rappelez la guerre.
5. Nous nous le rappelons.

Servir, se servir de

Servir means *to serve, to serve as, to be of use as.*

Elle **sert** le déjeuner.   *She serves lunch.*
Elle nous **sert** de guide.   *She serves as a guide for us.*

Se servir de means *to use.*

Je **me sers d'**un stylo pour écrire.
I use a pen to write with.

19. Complete the following sentences with the appropriate form of the present tense of **servir** or **se servir de.**

1. Ce papier _____ à écrire.
2. Le petit _____ une petite cuiller.
3. Il _____ le dîner.
4. Elle ne lui _____ à rien.
5. Elle _____ ce livre.

Savoir versus Connaître

Savoir and **connaître** both mean *to know.*

Savoir means *to know a fact, a reason* or *a learning discipline.* Used with an infinitive, it means *to know how to.*

Il **sait** les résultats.   *He knows the results.*
Il **sait** jouer du piano.   *He knows how to play the piano.*

Connaître is used with persons, places, works of art, literature, countries, etc. It has the meaning of *to be acquainted with.*

Je **connais** Marie.   *I know Mary.*
Nous **connaissons** ce poème.   *We know this poem.*

Study the meanings of **savoir** and **connaître** in the imperfect and the *passé composé.*

Elle **connaissait** cet homme.   *She knew this man.*
Elle **a connu** cet homme.   *She met the man.*

Elle **savait** la réponse.   *She knew the answer.*
Elle **a su** la réponse.   *She found out the answer.*

20. Complete the following sentences with the correct form of the present tense of the verb **savoir** or **connaître.**

    1. Nous _____ jouer du piano.
    2. Elle _____ Robert.
    3. Je _____ que vous avez raison.
    4. _____ -vous l'heure?
    5. Ils _____ cette partie de la ville.
    6. Elle _____ son adresse.
    7. Vous _____ la littérature canadienne.
    8. _____ -tu cette maison? Oui, je _____ qu'elle est en bon état.

21. Translate the following sentences using **savoir** or **connaître** in the *passé composé* or the imperfect tense as necessary.

    1. He found out the truth.
    2. He has met this woman.
    3. She knew the truth.
    4. She knew these children.

Venir de

The present tense of **venir de** followed by an infinitive means *to have just (done something).* The imperfect tense of **venir de** followed by an infinitive means *had just (done something).*

Il **vient d'**arriver.
He has just arrived.
Il **venait d'**arriver quand nous sommes sortis.
He had just arrived when we left.

22. Complete the following sentences with the correct form of **venir de** in the present tense.

    1. Je _____ chanter cette chanson.
    2. Elles _____ sortir.
    3. Vous _____ arriver.
    4. Nous _____ rentrer d'Espagne.
    5. Tu _____ manger.
    6. Il _____ entrer.

23. Rewrite the sentences of the above exercise in the imperfect tense.

Answers to Exercises

Chapter 1

1. 1. Le, la, le
2. Le, le, la
3. Le, l', l', la, la
4. L', la
5. La, le, la
6. L', le
7. L, la
8. La, la, le
9. L', le, le
10. La, la, le

2. 1. La, l' (f.), l' (f.)
2. le, le, le, la
3. la, la
4. l' (m.), la
5. la, la
6. Le, le
7. La, la
8. Le, le

3. 1. Le, la
2. le, la
3. le, la
4. Le, La
5. Le, la
6. la
7. La
8. le, la
9. La, Le
10. le

4. 1. tables
2. vers
3. noyaux
4. sous
5. poux
6. festivals
7. Mesdames, mesdemoiselles
8. genoux
9. feux
10. amis
11. nez
12. vœux
13. animaux
14. vitraux
15. choux
16. éventails

5. 1. Les lois sont justes.
2. Les voix sont jolies.
3. Regardez les feux!
4. Les trous sont grands.
5. Les repas sont bons.
6. Les journaux expliquent les travaux.
7. Les écoles sont modernes.
8. Les châteaux sont jolis.
9. Les détails des dessins sur les chandails sont magnifiques.
10. Les prix sont élevés.
11. Les jeux sont amusants.
12. Voilà les clous.
13. Les bijoux sont jolis.
14. Les cailloux sont petits.
15. Les bateaux sont grands.
16. Les musées sont grands.
17. Les yeux sont grands.
18. Les chevaux sont les animaux que vous aimez.
19. Les messieurs sont grands.
20. Les bals ont lieu samedi.
21. Les gentilshommes sont grands.
22. Voici des bonshommes de neige.

6. 1. Le roi habite dans le château.
2. Le nez est grand.
3. Le joujou est intéressant.
4. Le carnaval est amusant.
5. Le ciel est bleu.
6. L'ami est aimable.
7. La peau de vison est chère.
8. Le journal est intéressant.
9. L'aïeul est célèbre.
10. L'œil est brun.
11. Le bras est fort.
12. Le clou est long.
13. Le vitrail est joli.
14. Le vœu est compréhensible.
15. Le chandail est chaud.
16. Le hibou est noir.
17. La voix du chanteur est jolie.
18. Le jeu de cartes est intéressant.

7. 1. Les après-midi les grands-pères dorment.
2. Les réveille-matin sonnent à huit heures du matin.
3. Les grands-mères mettent les choux-fleurs dans les paniers pour les pique-niques.
4. Il lit les chefs-d'œuvre de Racine.
5. Il y a des gratte-ciel à New York.
6. Les timbres-poste sont dans les coffres-forts.
7. Mets tes plumes dans les porte-plume.
8. Pour ouvrir les bouteilles de vin, prenez des tire-bouchons.
9. Les beaux-frères mangent les hors-d'œuvre.
10. Les belles-sœurs aiment les arcs-en-ciel.

8. 1. Les
2. La
3. La
4. Les

5. Les   9. les
6. Les   10. les
7. L'   11. La
8. Le   12. Les

9. 1. Le   6. —
      2. Le   7. —
      3. —   8. le
      4. —   9. Le
      5. —   10. La

10. 1. —   5. —
      2. le   6. —
      3. la   7. —
      4. Le

11. 1. —   7. le
      2. le   8. —
      3. L'   9. —
      4. le (—)   10. Le
      5. —   11. le
      6. —   12. le, l'

12. 1. La   5. —
      2. L'   6. La
      3. Les   7. le
      4. Le   8. L'

13. 1. Les, la   3. Les, la
      2. le   4. Le, le

14. 1. les   4. la
      2. la   5. les
      3. la

15. 1. au, du
      2. à la, de la
      3. à l', de l'
      4. à la, de la, aux, des

16. 1. un, un, des
      2. un, une
      3. une, un, une, des
      4. une, des, un
      5. un, un
      6. un, un, un, des, des
      7. un, un
      8. une, une, un

17. 1. —, un   5. —
      2. —   6. —
      3. un   7. un
      4. une   8. un

18. 1. —   5. —
      2. —   6. des
      3. un   7. —
      4. —   8. —,—

19. 1. du   3. des
      2. de la   4. des

5. du   12. du
6. du   13. du
7. du   14. du
8. du   15. des
9. de la   16. du
10. de la   17. de l'
11. de la   18. du

20. 1. Il aime beaucoup l'eau minérale et il va prendre de l'eau minérale maintenant.
      2. Il aime beaucoup la soupe aux pois et il va prendre de la soupe aux pois maintenant.
      3. Il aime beaucoup les artichauts et il va prendre des artichauts maintenant.
      4. Il aime beaucoup la salade et il va prendre de la salade maintenant.
      5. Il aime beaucoup le pain italien et il va prendre du pain italien maintenant.
      6. Il aime beaucoup le thé et il va prendre du thé maintenant.

21. 1. le, du, du, Le
      2. La, la, la, la, une
      3. le, le, un, du
      4. du, le, le, un

22. 1. Il n'a pas de courage.
      2. Il n'y a pas de soupe.
      3. Je n'ai pas de bonbons.
      4. Je ne bois pas d'eau.
      5. Elle ne fume pas de cigarettes.

23. 1. Il y a de belles peintures ici.
      2. Nous lisons des livres intéressants.
      3. Ce sont de grandes villes.
      4. Elle mange des petits pains et des petits pois.
      5. Ce sont des jeunes filles.
      6. J'ai de grandes armoires.

24. 1. d'   7. des
      2. d'   8. de
      3. de   9. de
      4. —   10. d'
      5. de   11. de
      6. —   12. du

25. 1. Le, au   7. La, à la
      2. l'   8. L', le
      3. La, la   9. le, du
      4. Les, la   10. Les, à l'
      5. La   11. les, aux
      6. La, des   12. Le, de l', les

26. 1. Les repas sont bons.
      2. Les chevaux sont des animaux.
      3. J'aime les carnavals.
      4. Ouvrez vos yeux.
      5. Les bateaux sont petits.

6. Les prix des clous ne sont pas chers.
7. Les choux sont dans les trous.
8. Les eaux entourent les châteaux.
9. Les jeux sont intéressants.
10. Les après-midi, il prépare les hors-d'œuvre et les choux-fleurs pour les pique-niques.
11. Messieurs, ne prenez pas ces bijoux.
12. Les grands-pères vont acheter des abat-jour.

27.
1. —, une, une, la, Les, un,—
2. —, un,—, une
3. —, un, un, La, une
4. un, un, l',—, le, le, le, le, le,—

28.
1. À la, de la, du, du, une, d', du, le, un
2. de la, à la, de la, du, du, de l'
3. À la, de, de, Le, le, le
4. Au, d',—, des, de la, du, du, de la, d', des
5. de, du, de, à l', de, de la, la, une, une, des, de la (une)

29.
1. Il attend l'arrivée du professeur.
2. Il entend les cris de l'enfant.
3. Il parle à l'ami de Jean.
4. Elle aime la voix du chanteur.
5. Il cherche les jouets des enfants.
6. Il va au supermarché du village.
7. Il aime le vitrail de l'église.
8. Il regarde les peintures du musée.
9. Elle veut aller à la bibliothèque de la ville.
10. Il achète du sucre, des gâteaux et de la glace.

Chapter 2

1.
1. L'idée est mauvaise.
2. La cathédrale est grande.
3. La tour est haute.
4. La cuisine est parfaite.
5. La sorcière est laide.
6. La peinture est jolie.
7. La femme est honnête.
8. La chemise est rouge.
9. La pierre est dure.
10. La réponse est claire.

2.
1. mauvais
2. française
3. grand
4. poli
5. noir
6. faible
7. noire
8. fantastique
9. formidable
10. compliquée

3.
1. cruelle
2. parisienne
3. bonne
4. muette
5. épaisse
6. discrète
7. prête
8. sotte
9. chère
10. fière

4.
1. Le film est sensationnel.
2. La peinture est ancienne.
3. Ce paquet est gros.
4. Cette étudiante est lasse.
5. Cette histoire est secrète.
6. L'homme est inquiet.
7. Madame Leclerc est étrangère.
8. Pierre est premier en math.
9. Cette phrase est pareille.

5.
1. heureuse
2. sérieuse
3. furieux
4. doux
5. douce
6. rousse
7. fausse
8. menteuse
9. protectrice
10. meilleure
11. créatrice
12. majeure

6.
1. actif
2. attentive
3. neuf
4. neuve
5. brève
6. blanche
7. franc
8. sèche
9. grecque
10. publique

7.
1. aiguë
2. longue
3. favorite
4. maligne
5. malin
6. fraîche

8.
1. nouveau
2. belle
3. vieil
4. nouvelle
5. nouvel
6. vieux
7. belle
8. vieille
9. bel
10. beau
11. beau
12. vieux
13. nouveau

9.
1. Les films sont incroyables.
2. Les films sont merveilleux.
3. Les robes sont bleues.
4. Les notes sont mauvaises.
5. Les lois sont légales.
6. Les châteaux sont beaux.
7. Les chandails sont bleus.
8. Les hommes sont gros.
9. Les coups sont fatals.
10. Les maisons sont nouvelles.
11. Les tomates sont parfaites.
12. Les mots sont finals.

10.
1. intéressants
2. merveilleuses
3. médiévaux
4. nouveaux
5. finals
6. grands
7. bleus
8. frais
9. fatals
10. épais
11. royaux
12. belles
13. légales
14. intelligentes
15. bleues
16. heureux
17. beaux

11.
1. nu
2. vieilles
3. demie
4. demi
5. nue
6. mi
7. ci-jointes
8. demi
9. Haut
10. âgés
11. marron
12. brun foncé

12.
1. tragi-comique
2. sourde-muette
3. nouveau-nés
4. sud-américains
5. sous-développés
6. grandes ouvertes

13.
1. Il y a un joli tableau.
2. Il y a une vieille chaise.
3. Il y a une peinture intéressante.
4. Il y a un bon livre.
5. Il y a un gros divan-lit.
6. Il y a une petite lampe.
7. Il y a un fauteuil confortable.
8. Il y a une grande cheminée.
9. Il y a un tapis oriental.
10. Il y a une chaise rouge.

14.
1. Ce sont des livres intéressants.
2. Ce sont des films formidables.
3. Ce sont des conférences importantes.
4. Ce sont de bons amis.
5. Ce sont d'autres histoires.
6. Ce sont de bonnes écoles.
7. Ce sont de vieux amis.
8. Ce sont de beaux écrivains.
9. Ce sont de vieilles amies.
10. Ce sont de grandes maisons.
11. Ce sont de nouveaux hôtels.
12. Ce sont des jeunes filles.
13. Ce sont des petits pois.

15.
1. Elle achète un grand stéreo japonais.
2. Elle achète une longue robe bleue.
3. Elle achète un gentil petit chien amusant.
4. Elle achète de beaux meubles français.
5. Elle achète de nouvelles chaussures italiennes.
6. Elle achète de beaux gants noirs.
7. Elle achète un nouvel appareil photographique fantastique.
8. Elle achète un gros diamant brillant.
9. Elle achète un petit jeune chat.
10. Elle achète de jolies vieilles peintures.

16.
1. C'est un monument ancien.
   Monsieur Dupont est (C'est) mon ancien professeur.
2. C'est un homme brave.
   C'est un brave homme.
3. C'est un chandail cher.
   C'est un cher ami.
4. La semaine dernière il est allé au cinéma.
   C'est la dernière semaine du trimestre.
5. Différentes personnes sont venues.
   Des personnes différentes sont venues.
6. C'est un grand écrivain.
   C'est un écrivain grand.
7. C'est une pauvre garçon.
   C'est un garçon pauvre.
8. C'est une chambre propre.
   C'est ma propre chambre.

17.
1. Cette femme qui assiste à l'accouchement est une sage femme.
   Une femme qui sait tout est une femme sage.
2. Tu vas sûrement tout perdre. C'est un risque certain.
   Si tu joues à la Bourse, tu vas courir un certain risque.
3. Elle est arrivée le jour même comme prévu.
   Même le professeur va être d'accord avec vous.
   Marcher et *aller à pied* sont presque la même chose.
4. Je viens d'acheter cette robe; c'est une nouvelle robe.
   Au printemps, les maisons de haute couture vont présenter une collection de robes nouvelles.
5. Une personne seule ne peut pas tout faire.
   Mon seul souci, c'est ma famille.
6. Ce garçon est désagréable. C'est un vilain garçon.
   Ce garçon n'est pas beau. C'est un garçon vilain.
7. Le piano ne marche pas bien. J'entends une fausse note.
   Il faut chanter la note b, pas la note c. C'est une note fausse.
8. C'est un manteau sale.
   Cet homme n'est pas gentil. C'est un sale homme.
9. Cette histoire ne vaut rien. C'est une triste histoire.
   Cette histoire me fait pleurer. C'est une histoire triste.
10. Un homme qui extorque de l'argent aux autres est un malhonnête homme.
    Un homme qui dit des grossièretés est un homme malhonnête.
11. Je vous verrai la semaine prochaine.
    La prochaine fois, dites la vérité.

12. Diverses personnes discutent des
circonstances diverses.

18. 1. Elle chante doucement.
    2. Il a prononcé parfaitement.
    3. Elle étudie sérieusement.
    4. Elle danse naturellement.
    5. Il a compris finalement.
    6. Il est parti soudainement.
    7. Il agit dangereusement.
    8. Il parle rapidement.
    9. Elle répond franchement.
    10. Il écoute attentivement.

19. 1. Il agit hardiment.
    2. Elle agit résolument.
    3. Elles chantent gaîment (gaiement).
    4. Il parle continûment.
    5. Il parle crûment.

20. 1. confusément
    2. profondément
    3. exquisément
    4. aveuglément
    5. précisément
    6. opportunément

21. 1. couramment
    2. fréquemment
    3. patiemment
    4. brillamment
    5. décemment
    6. Évidemment
    7. prudemment
    8. patiemment
    9. constamment
    10. lentement
    11. véhémentement
    12. abondamment

22. 1. brièvement   7. bas
    2. gentiment   8. cher
    3. bien   9. dur
    4. mal   10. bien
    5. peu   11. court
    6. clair   12. fort

23. 1. Il court rapidement.
    2. La situation est absolument
       impossible.
    3. Elle a beacoup voyagé.
    4. Il a bien étudié.
    5. Nous avons déjà mangé.
    6. Nous y sommes souvent allés.
    7. Elle est arrivée hier.
    8. Elle a travaillé patiemment.
    9. Elle va trop travailler
       (Elle va travailler trop.)
    10. J'ai assez mangé.

24. 1. Naturellement, je suis content.
    2. Certainement, il va être à l'heure.
    3. Évidemment, il est triste.
    4. Finalement, elle est arrivée.
    5. Heureusement, elle est arrivée à l'heure.

25. 1. Anne est plus intelligente que sa sœur.
    2. Cet enfant est aussi poli que sa sœur.
    3. Elle est moins patiente que sa sœur.
    4. Annette est plus sérieuse que sa sœur.
    5. Il est aussi gentil que sa sœur.
    6. Hélène parle plus intelligemment que sa
       sœur.
    7. Cet homme conduit aussi
       dangereusement que sa sœur.
    8. Vous chantez moins doucement que
       votre (sa) sœur.
    9. Judith attend plus patiemment que sa
       sœur.
    10. Vous agissez aussi poliment que votre
       (sa) sœur.
    11. Il a mangé plus de tartes que sa sœur.
    12. Elle a pris moins de livres que sa sœur.

26. 1. Georges est plus grand que lui.
    2. Pierre est plus intelligent que moi.
    3. Les autres travaillent plus patiemment
       que nous.
    4. Hélène danse aussi gaiement qu'elle.
    5. Pierre écoute aussi attentivement
       qu'eux.
    6. Marc est moins intelligent qu'elles.

27. 1. Il ne parle pas plus vite que moi.
    2. Il ne répond pas si (aussi) intelligemment
       que Georges.
    3. Il ne chante pas moins doucement que
       Pierre.
    4. Elle n'est pas plus belle que Babeth.
    5. Elle n'est pas si (aussi) gentille que sa
       sœur.

28. 1. Il est moins bête que vous ne le croyez.
    2. Elle est plus intelligente que vous ne le
       trouvez.
    3. Il est moins drôle que vous ne le pensez.
    4. Il est plus méchant qu'il n'en a l'air.
    5. Cette chanson est moins compliquée
       qu'elle n'en a l'air.

29. 1. Anne a autant d'argent que moi.
    2. Elle a moins de robes que moi.
    3. Il a plus d'autos que moi.
    4. Elle a autant de gâteaux que moi.
    5. Vous avez plus de peintures que moi.
    6. Vous avez autant de disques que moi.

30. 1. Oui, c'est la fille la plus intéressante du
       village.

2. Oui, c'est la plus petite rue du village.
3. Oui, ce sont les enfants les plus amusants du village.
4. Oui, c'est le plus joli jardin du village.
5. Oui, c'est le garçon le plus honnête du village.
6. Oui, c'est le professeur le plus exigeant du village.
7. Oui, c'est la plus vieille église du village.
8. Oui, ce sont les filles les plus intelligentes du village.
9. Oui, c'est le plus grand musée du village.
10. Oui, c'est la plus belle peinture du village.

31.
1. Oui, il chante le plus fort de tous.
2. Oui, elle travaille le plus sérieusement de toutes.
3. Oui, elle danse le plus exquisément de toutes.
4. Oui, il parle le plus profondément de tous.
5. Oui, elle chante le plus brillamment de toutes.

32.
1. meilleur
2. mieux
3. meilleure
4. mieux
5. pire (plus mauvais)
6. plus mal (pis)
7. plus
8. moins
9. les meilleures
10. le plus mal
11. la plus petite
12. la moindre

33.
1. Ce gâteau-ci est aussi bon que ce gâteau-là.
   Ce gâteau-ci est moins bon que ce gâteau-là.
   Ce gâteau-ci est meilleur que ce gâteau-là.
   Ce gâteau-ci est le meilleur de tous.
2. Ces fromages-ci sont aussi bons que ces fromages-là.
   Ces fromages-ci sont moins bons que ces fromages-là.
   Ces fromages-ci sont meilleurs que ces fromages-là.
   Ces fromages-ci sont les meilleurs de tous.
3. Cette orange-ci est aussi bonne que cette orange-là.
   Cette orange-ci est moins bonne que cette orange-là.
   Cette orange-ci est meilleure que cette orange-là.

Cette orange-ci est la meilleure de toutes.
4. Ces tomates-ci sont aussi bonnes que ces tomates-là.
   Ces tomates-ci sont moins bonnes que ces tomates-là.
   Ces tomates-ci sont meilleures que ces tomates-là.
   Ces tomates-ci sont les meilleures de toutes.
5. Ce beurre-ci est aussi mauvais que ce beurre-là.
   Ce beurre-ci est moins mauvais que ce beurre-là.
   Ce beurre-ci est plus mauvais (pire) que ce beurre-là.
   Ce beurre-ci est le plus mauvais (le pire) de tous.
6. Cette tarte-ci est aussi mauvaise que cette tarte-là.
   Cette tarte-ci est moins mauvaise que cette tarte-là.
   Cette tarte-ci est plus mauvaise que cette tarte-là.
   Cette tarte-ci est la plus mauvaise (la pire) de toutes.
7. Elle chante aussi bien que vous.
   Elle chante moins bien que vous.
   Elle chante mieux que vous.
   Elle chante le mieux de toutes.
8. Il écrit aussi bien que vous.
   Il écrit moins bien que vous.
   Il écrit mieux que vous.
   Il écrit le mieux de tous.
9. Il travaille aussi mal que vous.
   Il travaille moins mal que vous.
   Il travaille plus mal (pis) que vous.
   Il travaille le plus mal de tous.

34.
1. L'enfant parle de plus en plus chaque jour.
2. Plus il travaille, plus il comprend.
3. Tant mieux!
4. L'économie va de mal en pis.
5. Il est d'autant plus heureux qu'il habite à la campagne.
6. Le malade mange de mieux en mieux.
7. Marie est ma sœur aînée.

35.
1. ma, mes, mon
2. ton, ta, tes
3. sa, son, ses
4. notre, nos
5. vos, votre
6. leurs, leur

36.
1. C'est son cahier.
2. C'est son livre.
3. C'est sa photo.

4. Ce sont ses amies.
5. C'est son amie.
6. Ce sont ses lettres.
7. C'est leur école.
8. C'est son adresse.
9. Ce sont ses livres.
10. C'est leur auto.
11. Ce sont leurs amis.
12. Ce sont leurs livres.

37.
1. nos	9. mes
2. son	10. tes
3. mon	11. leur
4. leurs	12. ma
5. ta	13. ses
6. sa	14. ton
7. notre	15. vos
8. votre	

38.
1. Mon	14. ta
2. Ton	15. Votre
3. ma	16. Mes
4. sa	17. ses
5. son	18. ses
6. leur	19. notre
7. son	20. les
8. leurs	21. la
9. son	22. ses
10. sa	23. tes
11. son	24. la
12. nos	25. vos
13. vos	26. son

39.
1. C'est son père à elle.
2. C'est sa sœur à lui.
3. C'est mon livre à moi.
4. C'est leur propriété à eux.
5. Ce sont ses stylos à elle.
6. C'est ton chien à toi.
7. Ce sont nos enfants à nous.
8. C'est votre bicyclette à vous.

40.
1. ce	6. cet
2. cette	7. Cette
3. Cet	8. Ces
4. ces	9. ce
5. Ces	10. Cette

41.
1. Je voudrais cette orange-ci, pas cette orange-là.
2. Je voudrais cet abricot-ci, pas cet abricot-là.
3. Je voudrais ces cerises-ci, pas ces cerises-là.
4. Je voudrais cette pomme-ci, pas cette pomme-là.
5. Je voudrais ce pamplemousse-ci, pas ce pamplemousse-là.
6. Je voudrais ces raisins-ci, pas ces raisins-là.

42.
1. quelque
2. quelques (plusieurs)
3. plusieurs (quelques)
4. certaines
5. diverses
6. Chaque (Tout)
7. Chaque
8. Tous
9. autre
10. aucune
11. Même
12. même
13. même
14. une telle
15. Telle, telle
16. Tel
17. Quelle que
18. quelconque
19. Autres, autres
20. toute, tout
21. Quelques
22. quelconque
23. si
24. quelque
25. même
26. d'autres
27. Nul

43.
1. Marie est intelligente aussi.
2. Marie est forte aussi.
3. Marie est sûre d'elle-même aussi.
4. Marie est honnête aussi.
5. Marie est gentille aussi.
6. Marie est bonne aussi.
7. Marie n'est pas sotte non plus.
8. Marie n'est pas grosse non plus.
9. Marie est discrète aussi.
10. Marie est fière aussi.
11. Marie est sérieuse aussi.
12. Marie est rousse aussi.
13. Marie est créatrice aussi.
14. Marie est sportive aussi.
15. Marie est franche aussi.
16. Marie n'est pas maligne non plus.

44.
1. une grande maison blanche, aux volets bleu foncé
2. un très joli jardin, aux couleurs vives
3. de beaux vieux meubles, une belle chaise noir et blanc, une vieille lampe marron, un vieil abat-jour marron
4. des fleurs fraîches cueillies, une belle petite photo
5. une petite jeune fille rousse, aux yeux bleu clair, aux joues ivoire, un bel homme blond (et) sérieux, aux cheveux châtains, des gens royaux, ma photo favorite

6. une autre table, une grande statue
merveilleuse, une grosse chatte maligne,
aux longues griffes
7. de grosses peintures, de nos villages
natals (et) nord-africains
8. une grande cuisine, un vieil évier, une
vieille poêle, un vieux réfrigérateur,
l'odeur douce, fenêtres grandes-ouvertes
9. une grande table ancienne, de style
français
10. de nouveaux meubles élégants, une belle
armoire nouvelle (une belle nouvelle
armoire), un bon lit, une grande
commode nouvelle (une grande nouvelle
commode)

45. 1. C'est une chaise chère.
2. C'est un homme brave.
3. C'est une fille pauvre.
4. C'est une robe propre.
5. Il est parti le jour même.
6. Ce sont de nouvelles bottes.

46. 1. Il parle résolument.
2. Il vient fréquemment.
5. Il parle couramment.
4. Elle travaille continûment.
5. Il a bien dormi.
6. Il est parti tard.
7. Finalement, il a fini.
(Il a fini finalement.)
8. Heureusement, il a bien mangé.
(Il a bien mangé, heureusement.)
9. Elle a fini hier.
10. Elle chante bien.
11. Il parle haut.
12. Il voit clair.
13. Il crie fort.

47. 1. Pierre est sérieux.
Il travaille sérieusement.
2. Anne est précise.
Elle parle précisément.
3. Yvette est attentive.
Elle écoute attentivement.
4. Jean est franc.
Il répond franchement.
5. Jacques et Charles sont intelligents.
Ils répondent intelligemment.
6. Marie et Jeanne sont gentilles.
Elles agissent gentiment.
7. André et Marc sont patients.
Ils écoutent patiemment.
8. Diane est brillante.
Elle résout le problème brillamment.
9. Paul et Philippe sont véhéments.
Ils agissent véhémentement.
10. David et Georges sont loyaux.
Ils agissent loyalement.

11. Éric et Roger sont lents.
Ils marchent lentement.
12. Nicole est naturelle.
Elle agit naturellement.

48. 1. Les attractions de la ville A sont aussi
bonnes que les attractions de la ville B.
Les attractions de la ville A sont moins
bonnes que les attractions de la ville C.
Les attractions de la ville A ne sont pas
si bonnes que les attractions de la ville C.
Les attractions de la ville A sont
meilleures que les attractions de la ville D.
Les attractions de la ville C sont les
meilleures de toutes.
2. Les restaurants de la ville A sont aussi
bons que les restaurants de la ville B.
Les restaurants de la ville A sont moins
bons que les restaurants de la ville C.
Les restaurants de la ville A ne sont pas
si bons que les restaurants de la ville C.
Les restaurants de la ville A sont
meilleurs que les restaurants de la ville D.
Les restaurants de la ville C sont les
meilleurs de tous.
3. Les magasins de la ville A sont aussi
chics que les magasins de la ville B.
Les magasins de la ville A sont moins
chics que les magasins de la ville C.
Les magasins de la ville A ne sont pas si
chics que les magasins de la ville C.
Les magasins de la ville A sont plus
chics que les magasins de la ville D.
Les magasins de la ville C sont les plus
chics de tous.
4. La pollution de la ville A est aussi
mauvaise que la pollution de la ville B.
La pollution de la ville A est moins
mauvaise que la pollution de la ville C.
La pollution de la ville A n'est pas si
mauvaise que la pollution de la ville C.
La pollution de la ville A est pire (plus
mauvaise) que la pollution de la ville D.
La pollution de la ville C est la pire (la
plus mauvaise) de toutes.
5. Les habitants de la ville A marchent
aussi vite que les habitants de la ville B.
Les habitants de la ville A marchent
moins vite que les habitants de la ville C.
Les habitants de la ville A ne marchent
pas si vite que les habitants de la ville C.
Les habitants de la ville A marchent plus
vite que les habitants de la ville D.
Les habitants de la ville C marchent le
plus vite de tous.
6. Les habitants de la ville A vivent aussi
bien que les habitants de la ville B.
Les habitants de la ville A vivent moins

bien que les habitants de la ville C.
Les habitants de la ville A ne vivent pas si bien que les habitants de la ville C.
Les habitants de la ville A vivent mieux que les habitants de la ville D.
Les habitants de la ville C vivent le mieux de tous.

7. La ville A a plus de théâtres que la ville B.
La ville A a moins de théâtres que la ville C.
La ville A a autant de théâtres que la ville D.

8. La ville A a plus de cafés que la ville B.
La ville A a moins de cafés que la ville C.
La ville A a autant de cafés que la ville D.

49. 1. Marie est la fille la plus intelligente de la classe.
2. Hélène est la plus jolie fille de la classe.
3. Pierre est le plus bel homme de la classe.
4. Henri est le garçon le plus intéressant de la classe.

50. 1. Ce, mon
2. Ces, ses
3. Cette, ta
4. Cette, son
5. Cette, sa
6. Ces, vos
7. Ces, nos
8. Ces, mes
9. Cet, ton
10. Ce, leur
11. Ce, votre
12. Cette, ma
13. Ces, leurs
14. Ces, tes
15. Cette, notre

51. 1. les
2. vos
3. sa
4. la

52. 1. Je veux cette robe-ci, pas cette robe-là.
2. Je veux cet appareil photographique-ci, pas cet appareil photographique-là.
3. Je veux ce disque-ci, pas ce disque-là.
4. Je veux ces cravates-ci, pas ces cravates-là.

53. 1. Marie a quelques journaux.
2. Hélène a plusieurs amis.
3. Il a quelque temps.
4. Certains problèmes sont difficiles à résoudre.
5. Nous avons parlé à diverses personnes.
6. Chaque homme veut réussir.
7. Avez-vous d'autres disques?
8. J'ai vu toutes les maisons.
9. Il n'y a aucun livre ici.
10. J'ai mangé tous les gâteaux.
11. Même son ennemi le croit.
12. Je n'ai jamais vu une telle pièce.
13. Tel est mon choix.

14. Tout homme veut être heureux.
15. D'autres livres sont intéressants.
16. Il a couru quelque cent mètres.
17. Elle est toute grande.
18. Prenez un livre quelconque.

Chapter 3

1. 1. au, dans la
2. à l', en, dans la
3. dans
4. chez
5. dans
6. au, chez
7. dans
8. du, à la
9. sur
10. en

2. 1. en
2. en, à la
3. à (de), de
4. en, dans l'
5. à
6. au, dans l'
7. pour, par
8. en, en
9. en, dans le, au
10. aux
11. du, d'
12. au, à
13. à, en
14. d'(pour l'), de (pour le)

3. 1. à
2. en, en
3. en
4. à
5. par le
6. en
7. en
8. en
9. à (en), à (en)
10. par, par

4. 1. en, à
2. en
3. à
4. avant, après

5. 1. en
2. dans
3. dans
4. Dans
5. dans
6. dans
7. en
8. en

6. 1. à
2. de
3. de, de
4. de, de
5. aux, aux, au
6. à, à
7. d'
8. de
9. à la, aux
10. en, en, en
11. de
12. de

7. 1. avec
2. d'
3. à
4. d'
5. avec
6. à

8. 1. à
2. à
3. de
4. à, à
5. de
6. à
7. d'
8. à
9. à
10. de

9. 1. une tasse de thé
2. une tasse à thé
3. un verre d'eau
4. un verre à eau

5. une cuiller à soupe
6. une tarte aux cerises
7. de la glace au chocolat
8. une bicyclette à vendre
9. l'homme aux yeux bruns
10. la soupe aux tomates
11. une agence de voyage
12. un professeur de géographie
13. une robe en soie
14. une robe de soie

10. 1. de, en, en
2. de, à, par le
3. au, en
4. à l', à
5. par, par
6. chez le, en
7. dans, à, en
8. sur, à, au, au
9. du, en
10. de l', dans l', en
11. chez le, en
12. dans le, aux
13. en, à la
14. à, en, dans

11. 1. à l'
2. de
3. à
4. en
5. du
6. à
7. à l'
8. en
9. de
10. au
11. à
12. dans
13. à
14. à
15. à
16. à
17. à
18. à
19. dans
20. aux
21. au
22. aux
23. au
24. devant
25. en
26. à
27. d'
28. avec
29. à
30. avant
31. en
32. dans
33. dans
34. à
35. Chez
36. d'

Chapter 4

1. 1. dix
2. dix-neuf
3. vingt
4. vingt et un
5. vingt-sept
6. trente et un
7. soixante et un
8. soixante-dix
9. soixante-douze
10. quatre-vingts
11. quatre-vingt-quatre
12. quatre-vingt-dix
13. quatre-vingt-dix-neuf
14. cent
15. deux cents
16. cinq cent soixante-cinq
17. sept cent quatre-vingt-dix-huit
18. mille cent vingt-quatre (onze cent vingt-quatre)
19. un million cent quarante-cinq mille sept cent quatre-vingt-douze
20. deux mille neuf cent cinquante-quatre
21. deux à deux
22. tous les quinze jours
23. une personne sur dix
24. tous les deux ans
25. toutes les dix minutes

2. 1. premier
2. neuvième
3. cinquième
4. première
5. deuxième
6. cent et unième
7. deuxième (seconde)
8. tierce

3. 1. Napoléon premier
2. Louis quinze
3. les deux premières années
4. les deux derniers jours

4. 1. Je voudrais une dizaine de pêches.
2. Je voudrais une vingtaine de poires.
3. Je voudrais une trentaine de pommes.
4. Il y a un million de gens dans cette salle.
5. Elle gagne dans les trente mille dollars par an.

5. 1. un demi (la moitié)
2. une demi-bouteille
3. vingt et un et demi
4. un tiers
5. trois quarts
6. sept seizièmes
7. dix et un quart

6. 1. Dix plus cinq font quinze.
2. Dix-huit moins six font douze.
3. Huit fois douze font quatre-vingt-seize.
4. Cinquante divisé par cinq fait dix.
5. Cette boîte a quinze centimètres (15 cm) de long (de longueur) sur dix centimètres (10 cm) de large (de largeur) sur huit centimètres (8 cm) de haut (de hauteur).

7. 1. le lundi vingt-cinq juin
2. le mardi quatre décembre

3. au mois de janvier
4. en juin
5. le premier avril
6. Quel jour est-ce aujourd'hui? (Quel jour sommes-nous aujourd'hui?)
7. C'est aujourd'hui le vendredi onze août, mil neuf cent (dix-neuf cent) quatre-vingt-neuf.
8. au printemps
9. en été
10. en hiver

8. 1. Il est une heure.
2. Il est quatre heures moins le quart.
(Il est quatre heures moins un quart.)
3. Il est huit heures et demie.
(Il est huit heures trente.)
4. Il est midi.
5. Il est minuit.
6. Il est neuf heures et quart.
(Il est neuf heures quinze.)
7. Il est midi et demi.
8. Il est minuit et demi.
9. Il est dix heures vingt-cinq.
10. Il est dix heures moins vingt.

9. 1. Il est une heure.
2. Il est quinze heures quarante-cinq.
3. Il est huit heures trente.
4. Il est douze heures.
(Il est midi.)
5. Il est zéro heure.
(Il est minuit.)
6. Il est vingt et une heure quinze.
7. Il est douze heures trente.
(Il est midi est demi.)
8. Il est zéro heure trente.
(Il est minuit et demi.)
9. Il est vingt-deux heures vingt-cinq.
10. Il est neuf heures quarante.

10. 1. On célèbre l'Hallowe'en le 31 octobre en automne.
Octobre et le dixième mois de l'année.
2. On célèbre Noël le 25 décembre en hiver.
Décembre est le douzième mois de l'année.
3. On célèbre la fête nationale en France le 14 juillet en été.
Juillet est le septième mois de l'année.
4. On célèbre la fête du travail en France le 1er mai au printemps.
Mai est le cinquième mois de l'année.
5. On célèbre le jour de l'An le premier janvier en hiver.
Janvier est le premier mois de l'année.
6. On célèbre le jour du Saint-Patrick le 17 mars en hiver.
Mars et le troisième mois de l'année.

11. 1. Soixante-dix-huit et vingt font quatre-vingt-dix-huit.
2. Un tiers et deux tiers font un.
3. Mille et mille cinq cents (quinze cents) font deux mille cinq cents (vingt-cinq cents).
4. Trois quarts moins un demi font un quart.
5. Mille fois mille font un million.
6. Quatre-vingts pour cent de cent font quatre-vingts.
7. Mille deux cents (Douze cents) divisé par cent font douze.
8. Un milliard divisé par un million font mille.
9. Deux fois vingt-cinq font cinquante.
10. Mil (Mille) neuf cent cinquante-cinq (Dix-neuf cent cinquante-cinq) moins mil (mille) huit cent cinquante (dix-huit cent cinquante) font cent cinq.

12. 1. Elle se lève à sept heures moins le quart (six heures quarante-cinq) du matin.
2. Elle prend le petit déjeuner à sept heures du matin.
3. Elle part pour l'université à sept heures et demie (sept heures trente) du matin.
4. Elle a son cours de français à huit heures du matin.
5. Elle prend un café à neuf heures moins dix (huit heures cinquante) du matin.
6. Elle a son cours d'histoire à neuf heures et quart (neuf heures quinze) du matin.
7. Elle prend le déjeuner à la cafétéria à midi et quart (midi quinze) de l'après-midi.
8. Elle travaille dans la bibliothèque à une heure de l'après-midi.
9. Elle rentre chez elle à cinq heures moins le quart (cinq heures moins quinze, quatre heures quarante-cinq) de l'après-midi.
10. Elle prend le dîner à six heures et demie (six heures trente) du soir.
11. Elle va au cinéma à huit heures dix du soir.
12. Elle se couche à minuit.

Chapter 5

1. 1. e
2. e
3. e
4. e
5. e
6. es
7. es
8. ent
9. ent
10. ons
11. ons
12. ez
13. ez
14. ez

2.
1. loue
2. parlons
3. regardent
4. restez
5. travaille
6. tombent
7. traverses
8. raconte
9. rencontrent
10. posons
11. cherchez
12. dessine
13. chantes
14. commandons
15. dînent

3.
1. cache
2. fréquentes
3. déjeunons
4. gardent
5. fermez
6. fouille

4.
1. Elle danse à la discothèque.
2. Nous louons un appartement.
3. Ils jouent dans le parc.
4. Tu goûtes le vin.
5. Je raconte une histoire.
6. Vous fermez la fenêtre.

5.
1. J'allume la lampe.
2. J'oublie son nom.
3. J'attire une foule.
4. J'arrive en retard.
5. J'apporte le déjeuner.

6.
1. J'aime la peinture moderne.
2. Nous arrivons à l'heure.
3. Tu oublies le livre.
4. J'aide mes amis.
5. Vous enseignez le français.
6. Ils étudient l'histoire.
7. Elles habitent à Paris.
8. J'écoute des disques.
9. Le garçon apporte le bifteck.
10. Nous avouons nos défauts.

7.
1. commençons
2. recommençons
3. avançons
4. mangeons
5. changeons
6. nageons

8.
1. commence, commençons
2. voyages, voyageons
3. mangent, mangeons
4. commence, commencez
5. nage, nagez
6. lance, lancent

9.
1. Tu cèdes ta place.
2. Je considère ce poste.
3. Je célèbre la fête.
4. Tu répètes les exercices.
5. Tu préfères partir de bonne heure.

10.
1. Nous espérons le voir.
2. Nous cédons à ses demandes.

3. Vous préférez venir à huit heures.
4. Vous interprétez le poème.

11.
1. interprétez
2. complètent
3. protégeons
4. préfère
5. considèrent
6. cèdes

12.
1. Je lève le rideau.
2. Tu pèses cinquante kilos.
3. Je gèle en hiver.
4. Tu mènes une vie tranquille.
5. J'appelle un taxi.
6. Tu jettes la balle.

13.
1. Nous achetons des disques.
2. Vous levez le rideau.
3. Nous enlevons les ordures.
4. Vous emmenez le chien dans de longues promenades.
5. Nous appelons Pierre.
6. Vous jetez le livre.

14.
1. mène
2. jettent
3. jetez
4. appellent
5. enlevons
6. pèsent
7. appelles
8. menez
9. achète
10. appelons

15.
1. nettoie
2. envoies
3. paie (paye)
4. essuient
5. ennuient
6. employons
7. payez

16.
1. Je paie (paye) ces dettes.
2. Tu emploies une femme de ménage.
3. Tu essaies (essayes) de réussir.
4. J'envoie le cadeau.
5. Il nettoie les meubles.
6. Elle essaie (essaye) de le faire.

17.
1. it
2. it
3. is
4. is
5. is
6. is
7. issent
8. issent
9. issons
10. issons
11. issez
12. issez

18.
1. remplis
2. réunissons
3. obéissent
4. choisit
5. réfléchis
6. agrandissez
7. envahissent
8. punit
9. finissons
10. réussissez

19.
1. saisis
2. remplit
3. punissez
4. applaudissent
5. accomplissons
6. réussis

20.
1. Nous bâtissons une maison à la campagne.
2. Les enfants grandissent chaque année.
3. Il réussit à l'examen.

4. Vous choisissez votre programme
   d'études.
5. Je finis le travail.
6. Tu obéis aux lois.

21. 1. défend   7. fendent
      2. fond   8. répandent
      3. réponds   9. vendons
      4. descends   10. rendons
      5. pends   11. perdez
      6. entends   12. tendez

22. 1. Elles vendent l'auto.
      2. Vous descendez sur la place.
      3. Nous entendons le professeur.
      4. Ils fendent du bois.

23. 1. Il entend du bruit.
      2. Tu attends le train.
      3. Elle perd le match.
      4. Je défends cet homme.

24. 1. Vous tendez un piège pour la souris.
      2. J'entends la chanson.
      3. Elles descendent la rue.
      4. Nous perdons l'espoir.
      5. Il rend les devoirs au professeur.
      6. J'attends un copain devant le cinéma.
      7. Tu vends la maison.
      8. Ils répondent à la question.

25. 1. cueillent   6. ouvrons
      2. ouvre   7. découvre
      3. accueille   8. recouvre
      4. offrez   9. recouvrons
      5. souffres   10. souffrent

26. 1. Il rit aux éclats.
      2. Elle court vite.
      3. Il conclut l'accord.
      4. Elle sourit beaucoup.
      5. Il rompt les liens.
      6. Elle interrompt le professeur.

27. 1. court   9. rit
      2. rient   10. sourions
      3. corrompt   11. interrompons
      4. secourez   12. cours
      5. conclus   13. concluent
      6. romps   14. interrompent
      7. ris   15. riez
      8. parcourons

28. 1. Je mets les vêtements dans l'armoire.
      2. Tu bats le tapis.
      3. Il remet le travail à demain.
      4. Elle promet d'aller avec moi.

29. 1. Ils admettent le crime.
      2. Les armées soumettent les rebelles.

3. Vous mettez la nappe sur la table.
4. Nous battons le linge pour le nettoyer.

30. 1. battent   7. mets
      2. soumets   8. soumettent
      3. promet   9. admettez
      4. remettons   10. permet
      5. combattez   11. transmettons
      6. bats   12. promets

31. 1. ment   7. partent
      2. sort   8. sortent
      3. sers   9. servons
      4. pars   10. mentons
      5. dors   11. sortez
      6. sens   12. dormez

32. 1. Je pars à huit heures.
      2. Tu dors bien.
      3. Tu sers des apéritifs.
      4. Elle sert un bon repas.
      5. Il sent l'odeur fraîche.
      6. Elle dort huit heures.

33. 1. Nous sortons de la classe.
      2. Ils mentent au professeur.
      3. Elles dorment sur le divan.
      4. Vous partez de bonne heure.

34. 1. Nous vainquons le rival.
      2. Vous vainquez la difficulté.
      3. Ils convainquent le sceptique.
      4. Elles convainquent l'homme de sa
         culpabilité.

35. Je vaincs l'ennemi.
      Vous vainquez l'ennemi.
      Elles vainquent l'ennemi.
      Nous vainquons l'ennemi.
      Tu vaincs l'ennemi.

36. 1. connaissent   9. connaissons
      2. reconnaissent   10. haïssez
      3. apparaît   11. reconnaissez
      4. naît   12. connais
      5. disparaît   13. disparais
      6. hait   14. hais
      7. paraît   15. connais
      8. reconnaissons

37. 1. L'invité paraît à la porte.
      2. Je connais les Leclerc.
      3. Tu reconnais le criminel.
      4. Il hait la bureaucratie.
      5. Ils disparaît souvent.

38. 1. Nous reconnaissons cet enfant.
      2. Vous connaissez le poète.
      3. Elles haïssent l'injustice.
      4. Ces hommes paraissent malades.

5. Les chiens disparaissent derrière l'arbre.

39. 1. Il plaît à tout le monde.
2. Elle se tait pendant le concert.
3. Je plais à Marie.
4. Tu te tais pendant la conférence.

40. 1. Ils plaisent à cette femme.
2. Elles se taisent pendant le spectacle.
3. Vous plaisez à tout le monde.
4. Nous nous taisons maintenant.
5. Ces livres déplaisent à Pierre.

41. 1. La troupe détruit la ville.
2. Il élit un président.
3. Tu dis la vérité.
4. Tu traduis la phrase.
5. Je lis un roman.
6. Je conduis une Citroën.

42. 1. Elles lisent *le Monde* tous les jours.
2. Ils conduisent une Renault.
3. Nous disons la vérité.
4. Nous détruisons le livre.
5. Vous produisez un nouveau jouet.
6. Vous dites bonjour.

43. 1. lit   6. détruit
2. dites   7. traduisons
3. suffit   8. interdit
4. conduis   9. reconstruis
5. reconstruisent 10. construit

44. 1. suivent   7. suit
2. écrivent   8. écrit
3. décrivons   9. décris
4. suivons   10. poursuis
5. écrivez   11. suis
6. vivez   12. vis

45. 1. Nous vivons bien ici.
2. Vous suivez ce cours.
3. Elles écrivent un poème.
4. Ils décrivent le match.

46. 1. Elle survit à l'accident.
2. Il écrit les devoirs.
3. Je vis bien.
4. Tu suis un cours de français.

47. 1. croyons   4. croyez
2. voyons   5. croyez
3. nous enfuyons 6. voyez

48. Vous mourez de faim.
Il meurt de faim
Je meurs de faim.
Tu meurs de faim
Elles meurent de faim.

49. 1. Elle le voit.
2. Je crois en Dieu.

3. Tu fuis sa présence.
4. Il croit cette histoire.
5. Il meurt de fatigue.
6. Je meurs de peur.

50. 1. Nous voyons qu'il a tort.
2. Elles croient que vous êtes fatigué.
3. Ils s'enfuient de la salle précipitamment.
4. Vous mourez de faim.
5. Vous croyez l'histoire.

51. 1. craignent   7. craint
2. joignent   8. peint
3. éteignons   9. plains
4. atteignons   10. rejoins
5. plaignez   11. crains
6. peignez   12. peins

52. 1. Nous craignons cet homme.
2. Vous rejoignez Pierre à l'heure.
3. Ils peignent un paysage.
4. Elles se plaignent de tout.
5. Elles joignent les deux bouts.

53. 1. Elle craint de répondre.
2. Je peins le mur.
3. Tu éteins la lumière.
4. Il vous plaint.
5. Je joins les deux bouts.

54. 1. rejoignez   4. éteins
2. craignons   5. plains
3. peignent   6. atteint

55. 1. Nous prenons le déjeuner à midi.
2. Nous apprenons les verbes.
3. Vous reprenez le disque.
4. Vous surprenez l'enfant.
5. Ils comprennent le français.
6. Ces nouvelles nous surprennent.

56. 1. comprends   5. apprends
2. surprend   6. prenez
3. prenons   7. reprend
4. comprennent

57. 1. viennent   7. obtiens
2. retiennent   8. parviens
3. convient   9. revenons
4. appartient   10. tenons
5. reviens   11. maintenez
6. deviens   12. obtenez

58. 1. Il vient tout de suite.
2. Tu deviens riche.
3. Je maintiens ma position.
4. La boîte contient des papiers.
5. Je parviens à un âge avancé.

59. 1. Ils tiennent à vous voir.
2. Elles viennent tout de suite.

3. Ces livres vous appartiennent.
4. Vous obtenez le prix.
5. Nous venons maintenant.

60. 1. J'acquiers de l'expérience.
2. Je conquiers son affection.
3. Tu acquiers une maison.
4. Tu conquiers l'ennemi.

61. 1. acquiers   4. acquérez
2. conquièrent   5. conquiert
3. acquiers   6. conquérons

62. 1. peuvent   4. veut
2. veux   5. voulons
3. peux   6. pouvez

63. 1. Je peux partir maintenant.
2. Je veux revenir demain.
3. Tu peux sortir maintenant.
4. Tu veux rester ici.
5. Il peut venir ce soir.
6. Elle veut savoir la réponse.

64. 1. Nous pouvons attendre une minute.
2. Nous voulons sortir maintenant.
3. Ils veulent jouer au football samedi.
4. Elles peuvent rester ici si elles le veulent.

65. 1. boivent   8. reçois
2. reçoivent   9. aperçois
3. doivent   10. reçois
4. reçoit   11. buvons
5. doit   12. recevons
6. déçoit   13. décevez
7. bois   14. buvez

66. 1. bois, buvez
2. reçois, recevons
3. dois, devez
4. buvez, boivent
5. devons, doivent

67. 1. Nous devons de l'argent.
2. Nous recevons une carte postale.
3. Vous buvez du vin.
4. Vous recevez la lettre.
5. Ils déçoivent le professeur.
6. Elles reçoivent de l'argent.

68. 1. a   7. avons
2. a   8. avons
3. as   9. avez
4. as   10. avez
5. ai   11. ont
6. ai   12. ont

69. 1. Les amis (Ils) ont les billets aussi.
2. J'ai de l'argent aussi.

3. Vous avez vos passeports aussi.
(Nous avons nos passeports aussi.)
4. Les autres (Ils) ont les billets aussi.
5. Pierre (Il) a des cartes de crédit aussi.
6. Nous avons nos visas aussi.

70. 1. J'ai les sandwichs.
2. Vous avez le couvert.
3. Nous avons le dessert.
4. Anne a le panier.
5. Michel et André ont les boissons.
6. Pierre a les serviettes.
7. Tu as le tire-bouchon.

71. 1. est   7. sont
2. est   8. sont
3. es   9. sommes
4. es   10. sommes
5. suis   11. êtes
6. suis   12. êtes

72. 1. Je suis française.
2. Ils sont heureux.
3. Elle est malade.
4. Tu es loyal.
5. Nous sommes forts.
6. Vous êtes grands.

73. 1. Je suis de la France.
Je suis français(e).
2. Il est de l'Italie.
Il est italien.
3. Tu es des États-Unis.
Tu es américain(e).
4. Nous sommes de l'Allemagne.
Nous sommes allemand(e)s.
5. Elles sont de la Russie.
Elles sont russes.
6. Vous êtes de la Chine.
Vous êtes chinois(e)(es).

74. 1. Elle est journaliste.
2. Il est avocat.
3. Elles sont dentistes.
4. Nous sommes ingénieurs.
5. Tu es chirurgien.
6. Je suis professeur.

75. 1. va   7. vont
2. va   8. vont
3. vas   9. allons
4. vas   10. allons
5. vais   11. allez
6. vais   12. allez

76. 1. Nous allons très bien.
2. Vous allez bien.
3. Ils vont très mal.
4. Tu vas assez bien.

5. Elle va mieux.
6. Je vais mal.

77. 1. Elle va à la discothèque.
2. Tu vas à la bibliothèque.
3. Nous allons au cinéma.
4. Je vais à la piscine.
5. Vous allez au restaurant.
6. Anne et Michèle vont à la boulangerie.

78. 1. fait
2. fait
3. fais
4. fais
5. fais
6. fais
7. font
8. font
9. faisons
10. faisons
11. faites
12. faites

79. Tu fais fortune.
Nous faisons fortune.
Ils font fortune.
Elle fait fortune.
Vous faites fortune.

80. 1. fait des réparations à l'auto
2. faisons la vaisselle
3. fais le ménage
4. font une promenade
5. faites attention
6. fais du ski

81. 1. sait
2. sait
3. sais
4. sais
5. sais
6. sais
7. savent
8. savent
9. savons
10. savons
11. savez
12. savez

82. 1. Nous savons qu'elle est malade.
2. Vous savez où elle habite.
3. Ils savent faire du ski.
4. Elles savent faire la cuisine.

83. 1. Nous savons guérir les maladies.
2. Elle sait réparer les autos.
3. Je sais jouer du piano.
4. Vous savez faire la cuisine.
5. Ils savent parler espagnol.
6. Tu sais bien conduire.

84. 1. vaut
2. faut
3. valent
4. valez

85. Il faut arriver de bonne heure.
Il vaux mieux arriver de bonne heure.
Il vaut mieux venir de bonne heure.

86. 1. connaissons
2. est
3. demeure
4. apprenons
5. écrivez

87. 1. Il y a une heure que je lis ce poème.
Ça fait une heure que je lis ce poème.
Voilà une heure que je lis ce poème.

2. Il y a cinq minutes que j'attends l'autobus.
Ça fait cinq minutes que j'attends l'autobus.
Voilà cinq minutes que j'attends l'autobus.

3. Il y a deux semaines qu'elle cherche ce livre.
Ça fait deux semaines qu'elle cherche ce livre.
Voilà deux semaines qu'elle cherche ce livre.

4. Il y a cinq heures qu'ils dorment.
Ça fait cinq heures qu'ils dorment.
Voilà cinq heures qu'ils dorment.

88. 1. Je travaille (Nous travaillons) depuis une heure.
2. Il y a deux ans qu'il habite ici.
3. Ça fait 15 minutes que j'attends le train.
4. Je conduis (Nous conduisons) une auto depuis l'âge de 18 ans.
5. Voilà dix minutes que j'attends (nous attendons) un taxi.
6. Il y a longtemps qu'il étudie le français.
7. Ils lisent depuis une heure.
8. Il y a un mois que je joue (nous jouons) de la guitare.
9. Elle vient d'arriver il y a deux minutes.
10. Je viens (Nous venons) de finir le travail il y a une heure.

89. 1. préfère
2. envoies
3. commençons
4. appelle
5. choisissez
6. offres
7. rit
8. vainquent
9. croyons
10. meurt
11. connaît
12. plaît
13. mets
14. faites
15. dort
16. traduisons
17. suit
18. craignez
19. peint
20. comprenons
21. reviennent
22. peuvent
23. voulez
24. reçoit
25. devez
26. buvons
27. sait, vient
28. avons
29. êtes
30. vais
31. faut

90. 1. Vous mangez au restaurant
2. Les garçons nagent dans le lac.
3. Nous appelons la police quand nous voyons un crime.
4. Je réussis aux examens.
5. Les hommes rompent les liens.
6. Ils vendent leur maison.
7. Nous ouvrons les fenêtres quand il fait chaud.

8. Les chefs mettent du sel dans le ragoût.
9. J'attends mon ami devant le cinéma.
10. Les bébés dorment tout le temps.
11. Marie mène une vie tranquille.
12. Georges convainc cet homme de partir.
13. Nous connaissons cette chanson.
14. Vous lisez beaucoup de journaux (beaucoup de lettres).
15. Angèle apprend sa leçon (cette chanson).
16. Les Pierron viennent ici souvent.
17. Les enfants voient un bon film au cinéma.
18. Je peux le faire.
19. David reçoit beaucoup de lettres (beaucoup de journaux).
20. Nous savons toujours les réponses.

91.
1. s'
2. me
3. se
4. t'
5. nous
6. vous
7. m'
8. te
9. se
10. nous

92.
1. se réveille
2. me dépêche
3. te laves
4. nous retrouvons
5. vous débrouillez
6. se rasent
7. s'habillent
8. m'appelle
9. t'amuses
10. se marie
11. nous promenons
12. vous moquez

93.
1. Je m'appelle Marie.
2. L'action se passe dans une rue déserte.
3. La pharmacie se trouve à côté du bureau de poste.
4. Nous nous demandons si nous recevrons une bonne note.
5. Je m'ennuie (Nous nous ennuyons) parce que le film n'est pas intéressant.
6. Il s'en va parce qu'il est fatigué.
7. Elles se couchent à dix heures.
8. Oui, ils se fâchent souvent.
9. Je me porte (Nous nous portons) bien.
10. Je me souviens de mes vacances.
11. Il se tait parce que la conférence commence.
12. L'enfant s'endort sur le divan.

94.
1. s'assied
2. s'assied
3. m'assieds
4. m'assieds
5. t'assieds
6. t'assieds
7. s'asseyent
8. s'asseyent
9. nous asseyons
10. nous asseyons
11. vous asseyez
12. vous asseyez

95.
1. Ils s'asseyent devant vous.
2. Nous nous asseyons devant le feu.
3. Vous vous asseyez dans le fauteuil.
4. Elles s'asseyent au premier rang.

96.
1. Je m'assieds.
2. Tu t'assieds à table.
3. Il s'assied devant le bureau.
4. Elle s'assied sur le balcon.

97.
1. la
2. les
3. les
4. la

98.
1. me
2. —
3. —
4. se
5. nous
6. —
7. —
8. t'

99.
1. Nous nous écrivons.
2. Ils s'aiment.
3. Ils se regardent.
4. Nous nous cherchons.

100.
1. m'asseoir
2. te raser
3. nous peigner
4. se réveiller
5. s'habiller
6. vous endormir

101.
1. Parle français! Parlons français! Parlez français!
2. Écoute le professeur! Écoutons le professeur! Écoutez le professeur!
3. Choisis un livre! Choisissons un livre! Choisissez un livre!
4. Réfléchis à ces idées! Réfléchissons à ces idées! Réfléchissez à ces idées!
5. Attends le train! Attendons le train! Attendez le train!
6. Vends l'auto! Vendons l'auto! Vendez l'auto!
7. Prends le déjeuner! Prenons le déjeuner! Prenez le déjeuner!
8. Ouvre la porte! Ouvrons la porte! Ouvrez la porte!
9. Bois du lait! Buvons du lait! Buvez du lait!
10. Écris la lettre! Écrivons la lettre! Écrivez la lettre!
11. Pars maintenant! Partons maintenant! Partez maintenant!
12. Viens tout de suite! Venons tout de suite! Venez tout de suite!

102.
1. Sois toujours honnête!
2. Soyons toujours en avance!
3. Soyez toujours heureux!
4. Aie toujours de la patience!
5. Ayons toujours du courage!
6. Ayez toujours de la pitié!
7. Sache toujours la vérité!
8. Sachons toujours la réponse!

9. Sachez toujours le poème par cœur!

103. 1. Lève-toi!
2. Amusez-vous!
3. Habille-toi vite!
4. Dépêchons-nous!

104. 1. Ne parlez pas!
2. Ne travaille pas!
3. Ne soyez pas en retard!
4. Ne restons pas ici!
5. N'aie pas de courage!
6. N'écoutez pas la conversation!
7. N'arrivons pas à l'heure!

105. 1. Ne te couche pas!
2. Ne t'habille pas!
3. Ne vous dépêchez pas!
4. Ne vous amusez pas bien!
5. Ne nous réveillons pas!

106. 1. J'écoute la radio en faisant mes devoirs.
2. Pierre regarde la télévision en mangeant.
3. Anne écoute la musique en s'habillant.
4. Nous écoutons les nouvelles à la radio en conduisant.
5. Vous lisez en attendant l'autobus.
6. Le chef chante en préparant le repas.

107. 1. En se promenant, il rencontre son ami Paul.
2. En descendant la rue, elle tombe.
3. En racontant une histoire amusante, elle rit.
4. En regardant la télévision, il s'endort.
5. En se levant, les spectateurs crient bravo.

108. 1. C'est en étudiant qu'on reçoit de bonnes notes.
2. C'est en jouant du piano tous les jours qu'on apprend à bien jouer.
3. C'est en ayant de l'ambition qu'on devient chef de l'entreprise.
4. C'est en courant tous les jours qu'on reste en forme.
5. C'est en étant généreux qu'on a de bons amis.
6. C'est en sachant les verbes qu'on réussit à l'examen de français.
7. C'est en mangeant moins qu'on maigrit.
8. C'est en travaillant qu'on gagne de l'argent.

109. 1. Il se brûle la main en faisant la cuisine.
2. Elle s'ennuie en faisant ce travail.
3. Nous nous amusons (Je m'amuse) en nageant.
4. Elles entrent en courant.
5. Il parle en dormant.

6. Elle finit par dormir.
7. Il commence par remercier les invités.

110. 1. Étant chirurgien, il veut travailler à l'hôpital.
2. Ayant de l'argent, elle peut voyager partout.
3. Voulant réussir, nous travaillons.
4. Disant au revoir, il part.
5. Sachant la leçon, (maintenant) je peux jouer avec mes amis (maintenant).

111. 1. Nous travaillions beaucoup.
2. Nous prenions le déjeuner à huit heures.
3. Nous pouvions le faire.
4. Nous attendions longtemps.
5. Nous écrivions beaucoup de lettres.
6. Nous lisions des romans policiers.
7. Nous voyions clair.
8. Nous riions souvent.
9. Nous craignions de partir.
10. Nous venions souvent.
11. Nous nous débrouillions.
12. Nous nous couchions de bonne heure.

112. 1. changeais　　7. prenaient
2. vendais　　　8. voulaient
3. parlais　　　9. disions
4. préférais　　10. buvions
5. employait　　11. faisiez
6. suivait　　　12. lisiez

113. 1. J'étais content.
2. Tu étais heureux.
3. Elle était fatiguée.
4. Nous étions malades.
5. Vous étiez triste.
6. Ils étaient enfants.

114. 1. Ils pouvaient chanter.
2. Nous apprenions le français.
3. Je sortais souvent.
4. Tu avais beaucoup de temps.
5. Elle venait nous voir.
6. Vous buviez du lait.
7. Il mentait souvent.
8. Elle croyait ses amis.
9. Nous étions heureuses.
10. Elle se dépêchait.
11. Vous vous habilliez bien.
12. Ils se promenaient dans le parc.

115. 1. Chaque année, elle allait en vacances.
2. Nous lisions souvent.
3. Nous rentrions toujours à la même heure.
4. Elle faisait des courses tous les jours.
5. Chaque matin, elles achetaient des baguettes.

6. D'habitude, je mangeais des croissants au petit déjeuner.
7. Bien des fois, vous saviez comment vous débrouiller.
8. Tu voyageais fréquemment.
9. Elle allait en Europe chaque été.
10. Il craignait le tonnerre.
11. Il faisait du ski quelquefois.
12. De temps en temps, vous disiez des bêtises.

116.
1. Pas maintenant, mais en ce temps-là, je lisais souvent.
2. Pas maintenant, mais quand j'étais jeune, je riais.
3. Pas maintenant, mais autrefois je chantais bien.
4. Pas maintenant, mais quand j'étais jeune, je me couchais de bonne heure.

117.
1. Je ne voulais pas partir.
2. Vous regrettiez les jours passés.
3. Nous pouvions venir tous les samedis.
4. Il ne savait pas les réponses.
5. Elles croyaient que vous aviez raison.
6. Nous espérions recevoir de bonnes notes.
7. À quoi pensais-tu?
8. Nous étions désolés de ne pas pouvoir venir.
9. Elle préférait voyager en auto.
10. Je le désirais beaucoup.

118.
1. Il était huit heures du soir.
2. Il faisait froid.
3. Les étoiles brillaient dans le ciel.
4. Il y avait beaucoup de monde sur la patinoire.
5. Il y avait un homme qui avait à peu près soixante ans.
6. Une fille faisait du patinage avec son ami.
7. Elle était blonde et lui, il était brun.
8. Ils portaient de beaux patins.
9. Ils étaient heureux.

119.
1. Si on jouait aux cartes?
   Si nous jouions aux cartes?
2. Si on faisait du ski?
   Si nous faisions du ski?
3. Si on allait au cinéma?
   Si nous allions au cinéma?
4. Si on dînait au restaurant?
   Si nous dînions au restaurant?
5. Si on achetait une nouvelle voiture?
   Si nous achetions une nouvelle voiture?

120.
1. travailliez
2. écrivait
3. voulait
4. connaissait
5. étudiais
6. construisaient
7. savions
8. habitiez
9. veniez de
10. venait de

121.
1. J'ai oublié ma valise
2. Elle a préparé un bon repas.
3. Nous avons ramassé les papiers.
4. Vous avez sauté de joie.
5. Elles ont goûté le vin.
6. Tu as porté une nouvelle robe.
7. Le petit a frappé à la porte.
8. Ils ont appelé leurs amis.
9. J'ai payé l'addition.
10. J'ai vite mangé.
11. Elle a toujours gardé le secret.
12. Elle a déjà acheté des cadeaux pour Noël.
13. J'ai vite travaillé.
14. Le conférencier a quitté la salle.
15. Il a jeté les ordures.
16. Tu as cherché partout.
17. J'ai chassé le gibier.
18. Nous avons dîné au restaurant.
19. Vous avez fermé la porte.
20. Elles ont loué l'appartement.

122.
1. Ils ont applaudi le concert.
2. J'ai choisi un beau tapis.
3. Elle a rempli la tasse de café.
4. Nous avons réfléchi aux problèmes.
5. La police a saisi le criminel.
6. Vous avez bien dormi.
7. Tu as obéi aux lois.
8. Vous avez déjà accompli la tâche.
9. Les écoliers ont fini leurs devoirs.
10. Les ouvriers ont bâti une maison.

123.
1. Le bûcheron a fendu du bois.
2. Nous avons entendu du bruit.
3. Ils ont rompu les liens.
4. Vous avez vaincu le problème.
5. Il a battu le tapis.
6. Elle a vite répondu.
7. La marchande a vendu des légumes.
8. La glace a fondu.
9. Tu as attendu tes amis.
10. L'avocat a défendu son client.

124.
1. été
2. fait
3. souri
4. suffi
5. suivi
6. acquis
7. mis
8. pris
9. compris
10. surpris
11. conduit
12. construit
13. cuit
14. détruit
15. traduit
16. dit
17. écrit
18. décrit

125. 1. Elle a suivi un cours d'histoire.
2. L'élève a appris l'alphabet.
3. Vous avez écrit vos devoirs.
4. Nous avons fait des progrès.
5. J'ai dit la vérité.
6. Ils ont surpris leurs amis.
7. Tu as ri aux éclats.
8. Elle a suivi ce boulevard.
9. Ils ont construit un pont.
10. Elle a mis le couvert.

126. 1. apparu   10. cru
2. reconnu   11. su
3. retenu   12. pu
4. couru   13. vu
5. déplu   14. voulu
6. dû   15. valu
7. reçu   16. lu
8. bu   17. vécu
9. eu

127. 1. J'ai connu les LeBlanc.
2. Cette décision a déplu à ces gens.
3. Elle a cru le professeur.
4. Il a survécu à ses parents.
5. Tu as vu tes amis.
6. Elles ont reçu le prix.
7. Elle a retenu une chambre à l'hôtel.
8. Nous avons vite couru.
9. Ils ont maintenu un air calme.
10. Vous avez aperçu quelque chose d'étrange.
11. Tu as dû répondre.
12. Cet homme a paru étrange.
13. Elle a lu les romans de Proust.
14. Cette conférence a plu à tout le monde.
15. Il a eu de l'argent.
16. Vous avez tenu votre promesse.
17. Ils ont élu un président.
18. Nous avons reconnu cette peinture.
19. Nous avons bu du lait.
20. Il a voulu faire ce devoir.

128. 1. Il a ouvert la fenêtre.
2. Le biologiste a découvert un microbe.
3. Vous avez souffert d'un rhume.
4. Nous avons ouvert les cadeaux.
5. La mère a couvert l'enfant.
6. Il a offert un cadeau à son ami.
7. Tu as couvert le mur de peintures.
8. J'ai souffert de maux de tête.

129. 1. Il a atteint son but.
2. Elle a craint cet homme.
3. Nous avons rejoint nos amis.
4. Vous avez éteint la lumière.
5. L'artiste a peint un portrait.
6. Nous avons plaint cet homme.
7. Vous avez craint les rues désertes.

8. Nous avons joint nos amis par téléphone.

130. 1. prise   6. craints
2. pris   7. endurées
3. peinte   8. endurés
4. peint   9. vue
5. craintes   10. vu

131. 1. Quelle leçon avez-vous apprise?
2. Quel livre avez-vous compris?
3. Quels disques avez-vous mis?
4. Quels murs avez-vous couverts?
5. Quelle phrase avez-vous dite?
6. Quelle auto avez-vous conduite?
7. Quelles blouses avez-vous prises?
8. Quelles fenêtres avez-vous ouvertes?
9. Quel poème avez-vous lu?
10. Quel criminel avez-vu craint?
11. Quelles pièces avez-vous vues?
12. Quelle histoire avez-vous crue?

132. 1. es   4. —
2. —   5. —
3. —   6. es

133. 1. est allée   9. est rentrée
2. est entré   10. est sorti
3. sont arrivées   11. sont parties
4. sont montés   12. sont venus
5. est né   13. est descendue
6. est retourné   14. est revenu
7. sont tombées   15. sont devenues
8. sont restés   16. sont morts

134. 1. Elle est montée dans le wagon.
2. Nous sommes arrivées de bonne heure.
3. Monsieur, vous êtes rentré tard.
4. Pierre et Georges, vous êtes devenus ennuyeux.
5. Marie et Lucille, vous êtes revenues trop tard.
6. Nous sommes restés chez nous.
7. Vous êtes morte de faim.
8. Nous sommes parties de bonne heure.
9. Je suis rentrée chez moi.
10. Tu es descendu dans la rue.
11. Vous êtes entrées dans l'atelier.
12. Les bonnes sont venues à l'heure.
13. Les enfants sont tombés dans l'escalier.
14. Je suis allé au bureau.
15. Tu es allée au restaurant.
16. Il est parti à l'heure.

135. 1. Elle est vite montée.
2. Elle a monté l'escalier.
3. Nous sommes descendues du train.
4. Nous avons descendu la valise.
5. Elles sont sorties samedi.
6. Elles ont sorti l'argenterie du tiroir.

7. Il est monté dans sa chambre.
8. Ils ont descendu les valises.
9. Nous avons sorti de l'argent.
10. Elles sont descendues de l'autobus.

136.
1. s'est dépêchée
2. s'est rasé
3. se sont ennuyées
4. se sont souvenus
5. me suis assis
6. me suis trompée
7. t'es réveillé
8. t'es lavée
9. vous êtes amusés
10. vous êtes habillées
11. nous sommes reposés
12. nous sommes endormies

137.
1. Il s'est bien débrouillé.
2. Elle s'est levée de bonne heure.
3. Nous nous sommes bien amusées.
4. Hélène et Marie, vous vous êtes trompées.
5. Elles se sont retrouvées devant le musée.
6. Elle s'est lavé les mains.
7. Ils se sont brossé les dents.
8. Je me suis assise devant le feu.
9. Elles se sont couchées dans le lit.
10. Tu t'es réveillé à huit heures.
11. Vous vous êtes peignée.
12. Je me suis trompé.
13. Nous nous sommes dépêchés.
14. Pierre et Jean, vous vous êtes rasés.

138.
1. sommes allé(e)s
2. a bâti
3. a vu
4. sont venus
5. avez voyagé
6. s'est couchée
7. avons loué
8. a découvert
9. a dit
10. s'est rasé

139.
1. Elle venait me voir bien des fois.
2. Tu le voyais bien des fois.
3. Pierre disait cela bien des fois.
4. Nous recevions des lettres bien des fois.
5. Vous l'appeliez bien des fois.

140.
1. Elle est venue me voir l'année passée.
2. Je suis allé(e) à Paris l'année passée.
3. J'ai vu Marie l'année passée.
4. Nous avons voyagé en Europe l'année passée.
5. Elle a joué ce rôle l'année passée.

141.
1. Ils regardaient la télévision chaque soir.
2. L'autre jour il a joué au tennis.
3. Elle a répété cette phrase une fois.
4. Pierre venait ici tous les dimanches.
5. Nous sommes allé(e)s à ce restaurant samedi dernier.
6. Souvent nous discutions politique.
7. Ta mère a été malade pendant deux ans.
8. Pendant tous ses voyages, elle payait avec des chèques de voyage.
9. Nous y allions de temps en temps.
10. Ce matin, il a dormi jusqu'à sept heures.

142.
1. Oui, j'ai reçu la carte hier.
2. Oui, j'ai habité à New York l'année dernière.
3. Oui, j'allais au concert tous les dimanches.
4. Oui, en ce temps-là, je travaillais beaucoup.
5. Oui, j'ai beaucoup dormi hier soir.
6. Oui, je conduisais toujours cette auto.
7. Oui, j'ai beaucoup nagé l'été dernier.
8. Oui, je suis allé(e) à la plage la semaine dernière.

143.
1. lisais, a frappé
2. faisait, a découvert
3. mangeaient, as téléphoné
4. avons fait, étions
5. parlait, suis entré(e)
6. ai vu(e)(s)(es), sortiez
7. prenait, a entendu
8. dormais, a sonné
9. discutaient, a annoncé
10. étions, sont entrés

144.
1. a mangé, a bu
2. est entrée, est parti
3. a fait, a pris
4. a pleuré, a aboyé
5. a préparé, ai mis

145.
1. Un homme mangeait et un autre buvait du vin.
2. La police entrait et le voleur partait.
3. Pierre faisait les valises et Marie prenait les billets.
4. Le bébé pleurait et le chien aboyait.
5. Ma mère préparait le repas pendant que je mettais le couvert.

146.
1. Pierre est allé chez le médecin parce qu'il était malade.

2. Monsieur et Madame Dupont sont allés en vacances parce qu'ils avaient besoin de repos.
3. Nicole a mangé parce qu'elle avait faim.
4. Nous nous sommes dépêché(e)s parce que nous étions en retard.
5. Vous avez mis un imperméable parce qu'il pleuvait.
6. Tu as nagé parce que tu voulais être en forme.

147. C'était le sept juillet. Il était quatre heures de l'après-midi. Il faisait très chaud. Je faisais des courses. Pendant que je me promenais le long du boulevard, j'ai rencontré mon amie. Nous avons décidé d'aller chez le bijoutier. Pendant que nous regardions les bracelets et les colliers, un homme est entré dans le magasin. Il avait à peu près 25 ans. Il avait les cheveux noirs. Il portait un pantalon noir, une chemise verte et un masque au visage. Il a tiré un révolver et il a demandé de l'argent au caissier. Le caissier avait (a eu) peur et il lui a donné de l'argent. Mais heureusement, un autre employé a vu le vol et a appelé la police. La police est arrivée et a arrêté le voleur.

148. 1. Tu as beaucoup parlé.
2. Elles ont bien dormi.
3. Ils ont répondu à la question.
4. Elles ont suivi les instructions.
5. Elle a descendu l'escalier.
6. Nous nous sommes levées de bonne heure.
7. Nous sommes allées au musée.
8. Elle est monté dans le wagon.
9. Nous avons pris les billets.
10. Il a fait la leçon.
11. Elles ont monté les bagages.
12. J'ai reconnu cet homme.
13. Il est revenu tout de suite.
14. Elles ont écrit les devoirs.
15. Elles se sont promenées dans le parc.
16. Cette peinture m'a plu.
17. Vous avez reçu la lettre.
18. Tu as lu le roman.
19. Ils ont bien vécu ici.
20. Vous avez peint ce paysage.
21. Elle a ouvert la fenêtre.
22. Voilà les photos que je vous ai offertes.
23. Voilà les pièces que j'ai lues.
24. Elles se sont bien débrouillées.

149. 1. Non, mais j'ai appris cette leçon hier.
2. Non, mais il a voulu aller au cinéma hier.
3. Non, mais je l'ai comprise (nous l'avons comprise) hier.

4. Non, mais je me suis souvenu(e) [nous nous sommes souvenu(e)s] de la réponse hier.
5. Non, mais il a valu le prix hier.
6. Non, mais elle a ri hier.
7. Non, mais j'ai souffert (nous avons souffert) d'un rhume hier.
8. Non, mais vous avez dit la vérité hier.
9. Non, mais elle est revenue à huit heures hier.
10. Non, mais j'ai mis (nous avons mis) un imperméable hier.
11. Non, mais il est resté jusqu'à dix heures hier.
12. Non, mais j'ai vu Pierre hier.

150. 1. allait, assistait, voyait
2. nous sommes levé(e)s, avons travaillé, avons passé
3. allait, travaillait, rentrait
4. ont joué, ont regardé, ont écouté, se sont couchés
5. prenions, nous amusions
6. avons fait, avons vu, nous sommes amusé(e)s

151. Il était sept heures du matin. Je suis allé(e) dans les montagnes parce que je voulais faire du ski. Il faisait froid et il faisait du vent mais le soleil brillait. Je portais un beau costume de ski. Je suis arrivé(e) au chalet. J'ai acheté mon billet pour les remonte-pentes et j'ai fait la queue pour monter la montagne. J'ai remarqué qu'il y avait beaucoup de monde sur les pistes de ski. Je montais. Je descendais. J'étais très content(e). Je savais bien faire du ski. Mais malheureusement, à la quatrième descente, je suis tombé(e). Je me suis cassé la jambe. On m'a emmené(e) à l'hôpital ou on a mis ma jambe dans du plâtre. La journée qui a commencé bien a fini mal.

152. 1. On publia le livre en 1973.
2. On brûla Jeanne d'Arc en 1431 à Rouen.
3. Tu achetas ce disque.
4. Tu appelas ton père.
5. J'emmenai mes amis avec moi.
6. J'envoyai le télégramme.
7. Nous allâmes à Paris.
8. Nous trouvâmes ce livre.
9. Vous célébrâtes la fête.
10. Vous arrivâtes à l'heure.
11. Les Américains débarquèrent en Normandie en 1944.
12. Ils commencèrent la construction de la cathédrale en 1150.

153. 1. Il a cherché son père.
2. Nous avons donné de l'argent à nos amis.
3. Elles ont médité sur l'avenir.
4. J'ai frappé à la porte.
5. Vous avez deviné les résultats.
6. Tu es vite monté(e).
7. Nous avons compté notre argent.
8. Ils ont marché dans les rues désertes.
9. Je suis retourné(e) chez moi.
10. Elle est allée à l'église.

154. 1. découvrit 7. perdîmes
2. attendit 8. finîmes
3. embellis 9. réussîtes
4. défendis 10. vendîtes
5. applaudis 11. choisirent
6. partis 12. répondirent

155. 1. Ils ont découvert la vérité.
2. Nous avons réfléchi aux problèmes.
3. Il a agrandi le palais.
4. Vous avez répandu la nouvelle.
5. J'ai vendu des timbres.
6. Tu as rendu tes devoirs.
7. Elles ont fini leurs devoirs.
8. Vous avez descendu le boulevard.

156. 1. Elle suivit la route.
2. Tu partis.
3. Je sortis.
4. Nous mentîmes.
5. Vous dormîtes huit heures.
6. Ils rirent aux éclats.
7. Elle acquit les peintures.
8. Je mis le couvert.
9. Tu dis la vérité.
10. Nous prîmes le déjeuner.
11. Vous apprîtes la vérité.
12. Ils comprirent la situation.

157. 1. Nous sommes sorti(e)s ce soir-là.
2. Elle a suivi la route pour Dijon.
3. Elles ont pris les livres.
4. Vous avez mis votre manteau.
5. Tu as servi un bon repas.
6. J'ai souri en entrant.

158. 1. Elle but trop de vin.
2. Il courut vite.
3. Tu voulus venir.
4. Tu pus le faire.
5. Je crus l'histoire.
6. Je reconnus cet homme.
7. Nous lûmes *les Misérables*.
8. Nous reçûmes la lettre.
9. Vous dûtes travailler.
10. Vous eûtes des difficultés.
11. Les étoiles apparurent à l'horizon.
12. Ils vécurent à Londres.

159. 1. bûmes 5. lûtes
2. reconnurent 6. purent
3. reçus 7. plut
4. vécus 8. crûmes

160. 1. rompit 11. craignîtes
2. battîmes 12. rejoignîmes
3. offrîtes 13. fit
4. conduisit 14. fîmes
5. traduisirent 15. fus
6. convainquis 16. furent
7. écrivîmes 17. mourut
8. naquit 18. vint
9. vîtes 19. retînmes
10. peignit 20. revinrent

161. 1. Il a traduit le livre.
2. Ils ont écrit des romans.
3. Il a été roi de France.
4. Je suis venu(e) te voir.
5. Elles ont rejoint leurs amis.
6. Ils sont venus de Paris.
7. Nous avons ouvert la porte.
8. Vous avez beaucoup souffert.
9. Elle est née à Paris.
10. Nous avons vu le film.

162. 1. Samuel de Champlain a fondé Québec en 1608.
2. Pierre et Marie Curie ont découvert le radium.
3. Edgar Degas a peint des portraits et des scènes de danse.
4. Napoléon a vaincu l'ennemi dans beaucoup de batailles.
5. Albert Camus est mort dans un accident de voiture.
6. Le peuple de Paris a détruit la Bastille.
7. Charles de Gaulle a été président de la Cinquième République.
8. Le Corbusier a fait bâtir beaucoup de bâtiments célèbres.
9. Jean Anouilh a écrit *Antigone*.
10. Louis XIV est devenu roi de France en 1643.

163. 1. vais 4. allez
2. allons 5. vont
3. va 6. vas

164. 1. Nous allons faire les valises.
2. Je vais regarder la télévision.
3. Elle va parler au professeur.
4. Vous allez sortir de bonne heure.
5. Ils vont habiter à New York.
6. Tu vas venir tout de suite.
7. Nous allons boire du café.
8. Vous allez lire le journal.
9. Il va savoir les résultats.
10. Vous allez finir le travail.

165.
1. discutera
2. finira
3. vendras
4. parleras
5. mangerai
6. remplirai
7. obéirez
8. répondrez
9. voyagerons
10. suivrons
11. se réveilleront
12. rendront

166.
1. Nous regarderons la télévision.
2. Vous étudierez davantage.
3. J'écrirai des cartes postales.
4. Il plaira à cette fille.
5. Elles dormiront huit heures.
6. L'artiste peindra un portrait.
7. Tu conduiras prudemment.
8. Elle dira la vérité.
9. Elles rejoindront leurs amis.
10. Vous suivrez les instructions.
11. Je prendrai le déjeuner à midi.
12. Elle se couchera à dix heures.

167.
1. Elle nettoiera sa chambre.
2. Il paiera ses dettes.
3. Elle essaiera de partir.
4. Il ennuiera ses amis.
5. On achètera des bonbons.
6. Elle mènera une vie tranquille.
7. Elle lèvera le rideau.
8. Il appellera ses amis.
9. Elle jettera la lettre dans la corbeille.

168.
1. nettoierons
2. appellerez
3. emmèneront
4. pèserai
5. enlèveras
6. jettera
7. achètera
8. essaierons

169.
1. cueilleront
2. s'assiéront
3. irons
4. aura
5. serez
6. ferons
7. saurez
8. faudra
9. vaudra
10. voudrons
11. apercevrons
12. décevra
13. devras
14. pleuvra
15. recevra
16. courras
17. secourront
18. mourra
19. pourra
20. verront
21. enverras
22. viendront
23. retiendra
24. reviendrons

170.
1. Non, mais la prochaine fois, ils pourront finir à l'heure.
2. Non, mais la prochaine fois, je ferai (nous ferons) le voyage en avion.
3. Non, mais la prochaine fois, ils sauront la vérité.
4. Non, mais la prochaine fois, j'irai voir ce film.
5. Non, mais la prochaine fois, il aura confiance en son ami.
6. Non, mais la prochaine fois, j'enverrai la lettre par avion.
7. Non, mais la prochaine fois, elle verra Pierre.
8. Non, mais la prochaine fois, je retiendrai (nous retiendrons) une chambre.
9. Non, mais la prochaine fois, elle viendra avec André.
10. Non, mais la prochaine fois, il recevra une bonne note.
11. Non, mais la prochaine fois, je secourrai (nous secourrons) les pauvres.
12. Non, mais la prochaine fois, il vaudra la peine d'y aller.
13. Non, mais la prochaine fois, je ferai de mon mieux (nous ferons de notre mieux).
14. Non, mais la prochaine fois, je cueillerai des fleurs.
15. Non, mais la prochaine fois, ils seront à l'heure.
16. Non, mais la prochaine fois, je voudrai sortir.
17. Non, mais la prochaine fois, il faudra le faire.
18. Non, mais la prochaine fois, je devrai le faire.
19. Non, mais la prochaine fois, j'apercevrai (nous apercevrons) l'incendie.
20. Non, mais la prochaine fois, je m'assiérai (nous nous assiérons) au premier rang.
21. Non, mais la prochaine fois, il pleuvra.
22. Non, mais la prochaine fois, il mourra.
23. Non, mais la prochaine fois, nous courrons (je courrai).

171.
1. arrivera, mangerons
2. verrai, donnerai
3. finira, paierai
4. terminerons, sortirons
5. dormira, lirai
6. feront, mettront
7. pourrez
8. voudrez
9. voyagerez
10. partirons, arriveront

172.
1. Je pense qu'elle étudiera.
2. Je sais qu'il viendra.
3. J'espère que nous arriverons à l'heure.
4. Je crois qu'ils viendront.
5. Je ne sais s'il voudra y aller.
6. Je ne sais si elle pourra venir.

173. 1. Il dit qu'il sortira.
2. Elle dit qu'elle pourra le faire.
3. Elles disent qu'elles travailleront.
4. Ils disent qu'ils sauront le poème par cœur.

174. 1. sera   3. aura
2. sera   4. auront

175. 1. Elle n'est pas dans sa chambre. Elle sera avec Pierre.
2. Regardez ce qu'ils achètent. Ils auront de l'argent à jeter.
3. Comme elle court! Elle aura peur.
4. Elles viennent me voir. Elles auront besoin de moi.
5. Elle ne mange pas. Elle sera malade.

176. 1. Il aura peur.
2. Il sera chez lui.
3. Il sera malade.
4. Elle aura froid.

177. 1. attendront
2. sera
3. viendra, ferons
4. viendront, irons
5. nettoiera, paierai
6. mènerez
7. réfléchiras
8. saura
9. verront
10. pourrons
11. aura
12. faudra
13. nous assiérons
14. mourront
15. voudrez

178. 1. Pierre gagnera à la loterie et il achètera une villa.
2. Anne deviendra millionnaire et elle fera le tour du monde.
3. Nicole sera chirurgienne et elle saura guérir les gens malades.
4. Martine et Sylvie découvriront un remède contre le cancer et elles obtiendront le prix Nobel.
5. Monique se mariera et elle aura trois enfants.
6. Georges et Nicole seront astronautes et ils pourront voyager en fusée.
7. Tu courras dans le marathon et tu recevras une médaille d'or.
8. Nous pourrons voyager partout et nous verrons beaucoup de sites historiques.
9. Vous serez écrivain et vous écrirez un roman.
10. Paul ira habiter à la campagne et il mènera une ville tranquille.

179. 1. Je dînerais en ville.
2. Tu resterais à la maison.
3. Elle prendrait l'avion.
4. Nous paierions nos dettes.
5. Vous viendriez à trois heures.
6. Il serait de retour à huit heures.
7. Elle aurait faim.
8. Nous le ferions.
9. Elle enverrait la lettre par avion.
10. Il mourrait de remords.
11. Elles verraient leurs amis.
12. Vous pourriez voir ce film.
13. Ils secourraient les pauvres.
14. Nous nous assiérions devant le feu.

180. 1. nageraient   11. m'assiérais
2. écrirais   12. recevrais
3. paierait   13. pourriez
4. iriez   14. devrions
5. viendraient   15. achèteraient
6. serions   16. emploierais
7. ferait   17. verrait
8. enverrait   18. voudrais
9. saurions   19. aurions
10. vous coucheriez   20. mourrait

181. 1. À votre place, j'étudierais.
2. À votre place, je viendrais.
3. Dans ce cas-là, j'irais à Paris.
4. Dans ce cas-là, j'écrirais.

182. 1. finirait, reviendrait
2. lirait, aurait
3. comprendrait, expliqueriez
4. pourrait, donneriez
5. rentrerait
6. reviendraient

183. 1. Pourriez-vous venir tout de suite?
2. Pourriez-vous me conduire à l'aéroport?
3. Pourriez-vous me donner ce livre?
4. Pourriez-vous m'aider?
5. Voudriez-vous dîner en ville?
6. Voudriez-vous assister à la conférence?
7. Voudriez-vous aller voir ce film?
8. Voudriez-vous prendre le train?
9. Je voudrais du vin rouge.
10. Je voudrais deux billets aller et retour.
11. Je voudrais ce livre.
12. Je voudrais ces chaussures.

184. 1. Il serait huit heures. Ils sont arrivés.
2. Elle aurait bien 50 ans!
3. Comme il court! Il saurait les résultats.
4. Il ferait sa médecine à Paris maintenant.

185.
1. Il habiterait à Paris.
2. Elle aurait une peinture de Picasso.
3. Le président serait à New York.
4. Il serait deux heures.

186.
1. Il m'a dit qu'il sortirait ce soir.
2. Elle m'a assuré qu'elle serait heureuse.
3. Il m'a demandé si je mènerais une vie tranquille.
4. Elle a dit qu'elle m'écrirait.

187.
1. écrira
2. viendrais
3. fera
4. auraient
5. mettrions
6. pourra
7. serait
8. serai

188.
1. paierait
2. irions
3. boirais
4. faudrait
5. mourrais
6. ferait
7. auriez
8. sauraient
9. verrions
10. enverrais
11. pourrait
12. serait
13. viendraient
14. achèteriez

189.
1. étions, arrivées
2. avait lu
3. avais fait
4. avait cassé
5. étions, descendus
6. avaient mangé
7. étais, partie
8. étiez revenus
9. s'était couchée
10. nous étions levées

190.
1. J'étais déjà revenu quand elle est entrée.
2. Elles avaient déjà déjeuné quand je suis arrivé.
3. J'avais déjà fini mes devoirs quand le téléphone a sonné.
4. Elle avait déjà écrit la lettre quand son ami a frappé à la porte.
5. Les voleurs étaient déjà partis quand la femme a crié.
6. Nous nous étions déjà couchés quand il est revenu.

191.
1. Non, j'avais déjà regardé la télévision quand on a annoncé le dîner.
2. Non, ils avaient déjà fait leurs devoirs quand le professeur est entré.
3. Non, nous étions déjà sorti(e)s [j'étais déjà sorti(e)] quand elles sont arrivées.
4. Non, elles étaient déjà rentrées quand il a commencé à pleuvoir.
5. Non, elle avait déjà lu le journal quand il est arrivé.
6. Non, il s'était déjà rasé quand je suis parti.

7. Non, vous vous étiez déjà moqué(e)(s)(es) du politicien quand il est arrivé sur la scène.

192.
1. aurons, parlé
2. serez rentré(e)(s)(es)
3. auront fait
4. auras appris
5. aura acheté
6. sera rentrée
7. seras, parti(e)
8. aurons vu
9. aurez écrit
10. vous serez couché(e)(s)(es)
11. aurez lu
12. aurai acheté

193.
1. Je partirai quand ils seront rentrés.
2. Ils iront mieux quand ils auront pris le médicamment.
3. Vous vous coucherez quand vous aurez éteint les lumières.
4. Tu auras un diplôme quand tu auras étudié pendant quatre ans.
5. Nous résoudrons le problème quand le professeur aura expliqué une chose.
6. Elle mangera quand elle sera allée au supermarché.

194.
1. auraient fini
2. aurions mangé
3. serions rentré(e)s
4. aurait accompagné
5. aurais vu
6. auriez bu
7. aurait pris
8. aurait pu
9. me serais couché(e)
10. te serais habillé(e)

195.
1. Il se serait rasé, mais il n'avait pas de rasoir.
2. Elles auraient mangé au restaurant, mais elles n'avaient pas d'argent.
3. Vous auriez fait un voyage, mais vous n'aviez pas le temps.
4. Nous aurions écrit la lettre, mais nous n'avions pas de papier.
5. Je serais parti(e), mais je n'avais pas de parapluie.
6. Tu aurais ouvert le paquet, mais tu n'avais pas de couteau.

196.
1. Quand il a eu mangé, il est parti.
2. Lorsqu'elles ont été réunies, elles ont élu un président.
3. Lorsque le professeur a eu fini le discours, il est descendu de l'estrade.

4. À peine a-t-il eu fini que nous sommes arrivé(e)s.
5. Après qu'ils ont été guéris, ils sont retournés au travail.
6. Quand il a été arrivé, la conférence a commencé.

197.
1. Dès qu'elle eut appris la nouvelle, elle décida de partir.
2. À peine eut-elle reçu l'invitation qu'elle y répondit.
3. À peine fut-elle entrée qu'elle comprit la situation.
4. Aussitôt qu'ils furent partis, ils soupirèrent.

198.
1. ont	7. ferais
2. êtes	8. resterions
3. partirai	9. avait pris
4. ferons	10. étiez venu(e)(s)(es)
5. avaient	11. aurait mis
6. avait	12. seriez arrivé

199.
1. Si Anne a de l'argent, elle achètera une Mercedes.
Si Anne avait de l'argent, elle achèterait une Mercedes.
Si Anne avait eu de l'argent, elle aurait acheté une Mercedes.
2. Si nous avons de l'argent, nous irons en Europe.
Si nous avions de l'argent, nous irions en Europe.
Si nous avions eu de l'argent, nous serions allé(e)s en Europe.
3. Si tu as de l'argent, tu t'habilleras bien.
Si tu avais de l'argent, tu t'habillerais bien.
Si tu avais eu de l'argent, tu te serais bien habillé(e).
4. Si Marie et Nicole ont de l'argent, elles viendront nous voir plus souvent.
Si Marie et Nicole avaient de l'argent, elles viendraient nous voir plus souvent.
Si Marie et Nicole avaient eu de l'argent, elles seraient venues nous voir plus souvent.
5. Si Georges a de l'argent, il ne travaillera pas.
Si Georges avait de l'argent, il ne travaillerait pas.
Si Georges avait eu de l'argent, il n'aurait pas travaillé.
6. Si j'ai de l'argent, je ferai un long voyage.
Si j'avais de l'argent, je ferais un long voyage.
Si j'avais eu de l'argent, j'aurais fait un long voyage.
7. Si les Dupont ont de l'argent, ils vivront bien.
Si les Dupont avaient de l'argent, ils vivraient bien.
Si les Dupont avaient eu de l'argent, ils auraient bien vécu.
8. Si vous avez de l'argent, vous aurez une grande maison.
Si vous aviez de l'argent, vous auriez une grande maison.
Si vous aviez eu de l'argent, vous auriez eu une grande maison.

200.
2. Si elle se casse la jambe, elle ira à la salle d'urgence à l'hôpital.
Si elle se cassait la jambe, elle irait à la salle d'urgence à l'hôpital.
Si elle s'était cassé la jambe, elle serait allée à la salle d'urgence à l'hôpital.
3. S'il accepte ce poste, il gagnera beaucoup d'argent.
S'il acceptait ce poste, il gagnerait beaucoup d'argent.
S'il avait accepté ce poste, il aurait gagné beaucoup d'argent.
4. Si nous rentrons trop tard, nos parents se fâcheront.
Si nous rentrions trop tard, nos parents se fâcheraient.
Si nous serions rentré(e)s trop tard, nos parents se seraient fâchés.
5. Si tu vas en Egypte, tu verras les Pyramides.
Si tu allais en Egypte, tu verrais les Pyramides.
Si tu étais allé(e) en Egypte, tu aurais vu les Pyramides.
6. S'il fait beau, les enfants joueront dans le parc.
S'il faisait beau, les enfants joueraient dans le parc.
S'il avait fait beau, les enfants auraient joué dans le parc.
7. Si vous arrivez à l'aéroport à temps, vous pourrez prendre l'avion de 10 heures.
Si vous arriviez à l'aéroport à temps, vous pourriez prendre l'avion de 10 heures.
Si vous étiez arrivé(e)(s)(es) à l'aéroport à temps, vous auriez pu prendre l'avion de 10 heures.
8. Si les étudiants étudient, ils réussiront à l'examen.
Si les étudiants étudiaient, ils réussiraient à l'examen.

Si les étudiants avaient étudié, ils
auraient réussi à l'examen.

9. Si j'ai sommeil, je dormirai.
Si j'avais sommeil, je dormirais.
Si j'avais eu sommeil, j'aurais dormi.

10. Si nous sommes en retard, nous nous
dépêcherons.
Si nous étions en retard, nous nous
dépêcherions.
Si nous avions été en retard, nous nous
serions dépêché(e)s.

201. 1. parlent, entrent, finissent, réussissent,
attendent, répondent
2. parte, sorte, mente, se repente, dorme
3. rompe les liens, vainque mes passions,
craigne cet homme, peigne ce portrait.
4. écrives la lettre, suives la route, vives
ici, décrives la vue, serves le déjeuner.
5. parlions, lisions, dormions,
disparaissions, nous asseyions
6. souriiez, étudiiez, riiez, oubliiez ceci

202. 1. envoient
2. nettoyions
3. croient
4. voyiez
5. considèrent
6. cédions
7. achètent
8. levions
9. appellent
10. jetiez

203. 1. prennent
2. preniez
3. vienne
4. reteniez
5. meure
6. mouriez
7. reçoivent
8. recevions
9. boives
10. buvions

204. 1. vous soyez, ils soient, elle soit, tu sois,
je sois
2. j'aie, il ait, elles aient, nous ayons, vous
ayez
3. nous puissions, vous puissiez, ils
puissent, tu puisses, elle puisse
4. je fasse, il fasse, elles fassent, nous
fassions, vous fassiez
5. vous sachiez, nous sachions, ils sachent,
elle sache, je sache
6. nous voulions, vous vouliez, tu veuilles,
elles veuillent, je veuille
7. tu ailles, ils aillent, elle aille, nous
allions, vous alliez
8. elle vaille, nous valions, vous valiez, tu
vailles, ils vaillent

205. 1. parlent, mangent, écrivent, dorment,
viennent, sortent, conduisent
2. payions, cédions, appelions le garçon,
venions, buvions, allions, soyons ici
3. travaille, lise, vienne, finisse, sorte
4. veniez, compreniez, mangiez, attendiez

206. *A.*1. Le professeur veut que tu lises le livre.
2. Le professeur veut que vous étudiiez la
leçon.
3. Le professeur veut que nous
complétions nos devoirs.
4. Le professeur veut qu'elles sachent les
réponses.
5. Le professeur veut que je fasse
attention en classe.
6. Le professeur veut qu'il soit à l'heure.

*B.*1. Je doute que le politicien dise la vérité.
2. Je doute que tu partes à l'heure.
3. Je doute qu'il pleuve demain.
4. Je doute que vous achetiez cette
maison.
5. Je doute qu'ils meurent de faim.
6. Je doute que nous prenions nos
vacances sur la lune.

*C.*1. Pierre est heureux que ses amis puissent
aller en Europe en eté.
2. Pierre est heureux que Babeth vienne le
voir.
3. Pierre est heureux que Jeanne et Anne
reçoivent de bonne notes.
4. Pierre est heureux que Claire peigne un
beau portrait.
5. Pierre est heureux que nous
considérions son offre.
6. Pierre est heureux que vous receviez le
prix.

*D.*1. Le médecin ordonne que vous preniez
les pilules quatre fois par jour.
2. Le médecin ordonne que tu aies de la
patience.
3. Le médecin ordonne que la patiente se
repose.
4. Le médecin ordonne que nous buvions
huit verres d'eau par jour.
5. Le médecin ordonne que je suive un
régime.
6. Le médecin ordonne que vous soyez
calme.

*E.*1. Anne regrette que vous ne vouliez pas
venir à la surprise-partie.
2. Anne regrette que tu ne veuilles pas le
faire.
3. Anne regrette que son amie n'obtienne
pas la médaille d'or.
4. Anne regrette que nous ne puissions pas
aller au cinéma avec elle.
5. Anne regrette que sa sœur ne soit pas à
la maison.

207. 1. conduises
2. arriviez
3. fume
4. connaisse
5. soyez
6. fasse
7. allions
8. sachiez

9. veuillent
10. traduisions
11. rentre
12. vienne

13. comprenne
14. aille
15. sortiez

208. 1. prépare, lise, reçoive, fasse, sache, perde
2. finissions, mangions, comprenions, suivions, fassions, répétions, retenions
3. compreniez, veniez, finissiez, sortiez, sachiez la réponse
4. réussisse, comprenne, arrive, finisse, réponde

209. 1. Il est essentiel que nous recevions ces lettres.
2. Il suffit que je te le dise.
3. Il vaut mieux que tu sois ici.
4. Il est bon que vous vouliez venir.
5. Il est important qu'elle écrive ses devoirs.
6. Il faut qu'ils aillent au marché.
7. Il est temps que vous veniez.
8. C'est dommage que vous soyez malade.
9. Il vaut mieux qu'elles partent tout de suite.
10. Il est heureux que tu réussisses à l'examen.
11. Il est douteux que Paul puisse venir.
12. Il est honteux que tu mentes.
13. Il est bon qu'ils sachent la vérité.
14. Il est possible qu'on le craigne.
15. Il convient qu'ils viennent demain.

210. 1. sera
2. fasse
3. viennent
4. viendront
5. sachions
6. alliez
7. fait (fera)
8. obtienne
9. finissions
10. a
11. sache
12. croie
13. veut (voudra)
14. veuillent
15. puissions

211. 1. Non, je ne crois pas que Jean le sache.
2. Non, je ne suis pas certain que Pierre le sache.
3. Non, il n'est pas probable qu'il conduise une auto.
4. Non, il n'est pas sûr qu'ils viennent.
5. Non, je ne crois pas (nous ne croyons pas) qu'elles arrivent demain.
6. Non, il n'est pas sûr qu'elle parte tout de suite.
7. Non, il n'est pas probable qu'il vienne.
8. Non, je ne suis pas certain que Jean vienne.

212. 1. saches la leçon, fasses tes devoirs, lises le roman, écrives la composition

2. neige, fasse froid, pleuve
3. sera fatigué, arrivera, rentrera, reviendra

213. 1. parte
2. sorte
3. vienne
4. reçoive
5. reviennent
6. dise
7. compreniez
8. puisse
9. soyons
10. pleuve
11. arrivent
12. soit
13. étudient
14. neige
15. arriviez
16. fasse
17. saches

214. 1. arrivera
2. attende
3. viendra
4. compreniez
5. jouais
6. parte

215. 1. Qu'elle vienne tout de suite!
2. Qu'il conduise sagement!
3. Qu'il réponde au professeur!
4. Qu'ils obéissent à leurs parents!
5. Qu'elle apprenne la leçon!
6. Qu'elles disent la vérité!
7. Qu'il sache la réponse!
8. Qu'elles finissent leurs devoirs!

216. 1. parle français, écrit bien, sait taper à la machine
2. parle français, écrive bien, sache taper à la machine

217. 1. Je cherche un homme qui connaisse la route.
2. J'ai trouvé un homme qui connaît cette chanson.
3. Je veux acheter une blouse qui m'aille bien.
4. J'ai une blouse qui me va bien.
5. Je cherche un poste qui soit intéressant.
6. J'ai un poste qui est intéressant.

218. 1. sache
2. veuille
3. puisse
4. lit
5. puisse

219. 1. aie
2. veuille
3. connaisse
4. existe
5. comprenne

220. 1. ayez
2. soyez
3. fasse
4. allions
5. soient
6. dise
7. sois
8. agisse
9. parle
10. vienne, vienne

221. 1. Il se dépêche afin d'arriver à l'heure.
2. Il est content d'être ici.
(Il est content de sa venue.)
3. Il ordonne à son fils de partir.

4. Il permet à l'avocat de parler.
5. J'attends son arrivée.
6. Nous ferons cela avant notre départ.

222.
1. alliez
2. plaise
3. vient (viendra)
4. revenions
5. peut (pourra)
6. boive
7. puisse
8. parte
9. sait
10. connaisse
11. fassions
12. dit (dira)
13. pleuve
14. soyons
15. ayez
16. arriver

223.
1. sois arrivé(e)
2. ayons dit
3. aient reconnu(e)(s)(es)
4. soit venue
5. soyez resté(e)(s)(es)
6. ait souffert
7. aient fait
8. ait étudié
9. se soit amusée
10. se soient couchés

224.
1. Elle doute que nous ayons compris.
2. Je regrette que tu sois arrivé(e).
3. Il est possible que vous ayez fini à l'heure.
4. Je ne crois pas qu'elles soient venues.
5. Je doute qu'elle ait fait le travail.
6. Pensez-vous qu'il se soit rasé?

225.
1. Il doute que nous ayons reconnu cet homme.
2. Je ne crois pas qu'ils soient partis.
3. Il est important que vous ayez fait vos devoirs.
4. Il se peut qu'elle soit revenue de bonne heure.
5. Je doute qu'il ait su la réponse.

226.
1. vînt
2. pût
3. fût
4. finissent
5. fussions
6. sussiez
7. fissions
8. écrivît
9. vinssiez
10. rentrassent
11. devinsses
12. se couchassent

227.
1. Il voulait que nous venions.
2. J'étais heureux qu'elles soient à l'heure.
3. Il fallait qu'elle le fasse.
4. Elle était trop fatiguée pour que la soirée soit agréable.

5. Je cherchais quelqu'un qui puisse le faire.
6. Je craignais que l'équipe ne gagne pas le prix.

228.
1. eût été
2. fussent, venues
3. eussiez su
4. fût parti
5. eût écrit
6. eusses réussi
7. eussent su
8. eusse eu
9. fussent revenus
10. eût, fini
11. eussions fait
12. nous fussions débrouillé(e)s

229.
1. Je regrettais qu'elle ne soit pas venue à l'heure.
2. Bien qu'elles aient déjà compris, ils continuaient à leur expliquer.
3. J'étais contente qu'il ait connu mon ami.
4. Il fallait que vous ayez dit cela.
5. Il semblait que nous ayons fait des efforts.
6. Il avait peur que le pain ne soit devenu trop dur.

230.
1. S'il eût eu assez d'argent, il fût allé au cinéma.
2. Si vous fussiez venu, vous eussiez vu Paul.
3. S'il eût été prêt, il fût parti.
4. Si vous fussiez venu, vous eussiez appris la nouvelle.
5. S'il eût fait beau, nous fussions partis.
6. Si elle fût revenue, elle fût venue nous revoir.

231.
1. Le nez de Cléopâtre s'il avait été plus court, toute la face de la terre aurait changé.
2. Si elle avait eu assez d'argent, elle serait venue nous voir.
3. Si nous avions su cela, nous l'aurions dit.
4. S'il avait fait beau, elle serait partie.
5. S'il avait plu, elles ne seraient pas venues.
6. Si j'avais su cela, je ne vous aurais pas répondu.

232.
1. André dit qu'il ne peut pas le faire.
   André a dit qu'il ne pouvait pas le faire.
2. Marie dit qu'elle n'a jamais vu quelque chose de si beau.
   Marie a dit qu'elle n'avait jamais vu quelque chose de si beau.

3. Jean promet qu'il fera tout pour nous aider.
   Jean a promis qu'il ferait tout pour nous aider.
4. Ils disent qu'ils voudraient faire la connaissance de la nouvelle étudiante.
   Ils ont dit qu'ils auraient voulu faire la connaissance de la nouvelle étudiante.
5. Mes parents me promettent qu'ils me donneront une auto si je reçois de meilleures notes.
   Mes parents m'ont promis qu'ils me donneraient une auto si je reçois de meilleures notes.
6. Monsieur Leblanc dit qu'ils iront en Afrique cet été.
   Monsieur Leblanc a dit qu'ils iraient en Afrique cet été.
7. Claire répond qu'elle a déjà lu ce livre.
   Claire a répondu qu'elle avait déjà lu ce livre.
8. Anne dit qu'elle aimerait voir ce film.
   Anne a dit qu'elle aurait aimé voir ce film.
9. Pierre dit qu'il faisait beau hier.
   Pierre a dit qu'il avait fait beau hier.
10. Roger dit qu'il aura fini à trois heures.
    Roger dit qu'il aurait fini à trois heures.
11. Marie demande s'ils ont gagné le match.
    Marie a demandé s'ils avaient gagné le match.
12. Le professeur demande si nous serons à la réunion.
    Le professeur a demandé si nous serions à la réunion.

233.   L'avocat lui a demandé où elle était à deux heures du matin le 8 octobre.
Mme Leclerc a répondu qu'elle était dans la cuisine.
L'avocat lui a demandé si elle avait l'habitude d'être dans la cuisine si tard.
Mme Leclerc a répondu que non, mais que ce soir-là elle ne pouvait pas dormir et donc, elle était descendue dans la cuisine pour chercher un verre de lait.
L'avocat lui a demandé si elle avait entendu ou vu quelque chose d'étrange.
Mme Leclerc lui a répondu que oui, qu'elle avait entendu des cris dans la maison de sa voisine et qu'elle avait vu un homme attaquer sa voisine avec un couteau.
L'avocat lui a demandé si elle pourrait identifier cet homme.
Mme Leclerc lui a répondu que oui, qu'elle pourrait l'identifier clairement, car la lumière était allumée dans sa

maison.
L'avocat lui a demandé si cet homme était dans la salle.
Mme Leclerc a répondu que oui que c'était l'accusé.
L'avocat lui a dit qu'elle pouvait quitter la barre des témoins.

234. 1. Je lui parlerai avant de manger.
Je lui parlerai avant de chanter.
Je lui parlerai avant de danser.
Je lui parlerai avant de décider.
Je lui parlerai avant de revenir.
Je lui parlerai avant de finir.
Je lui parlerai avant de commencer.
2. Que faut-il faire afin de venir?
Que faut-il faire afin de réussir?
Que faut-il faire afin de finir à l'heure?
Que faut-il faire afin de savoir la leçon?
3. Il part sans manger.
Il part sans attendre.
Il part sans faire ses devoirs.
Il part sans parler.
4. Après avoir parlé, il est parti.
Après avoir fini, il est parti.
Après avoir mangé, il est parti.
Après avoir dit au revoir, il est parti.
5. Après être rentré, il est venu me voir.
Après être entré, il est venu me voir.
Après être retourné, il est venu me voir.
Après être descendu, il est venu me voir.

235. 1. Avant de partir, il a mangé.
Après avoir mangé, il est parti.
2. Avant d'aller au musée, nous avons déjeuné.
Après avoir déjeuné, nous sommes allés au musée.
3. Avant de jouer au tennis, nous avons fait le ménage.
Après avoir fait le ménage, nous avons joué au tennis.
4. Avant de lire le journal, elle s'est habillée.
Après s'être habillée, elle a lu le journal.

236. 1. avant d'arriver
2. après être arrivé(e)(s)(es)
3. en arrivant
4. en mangeant
5. après avoir mangé
6. avant de manger
7. Ne pas traduire.
8. Battre trois œufs.
9. Que faire!
10. Oh! être riche!

237. 1. Elle fait faire les dessins à l'architecte.
2. Elle fait peindre les murs au peintre.
3. Elle fait installer les salles de bains au plombier.
4. Elle fait poser des fils électriques aux électriciens.
5. Elle fait bâtir les étagères à livres au charpentier.

238. 1. Le professeur a fait écrire le devoir par la classe.
2. Elle fait chanter la chanson par les garçons.
3. Nous faisons écrire une lettre par notre ami.
4. Je fais jouer du piano par l'enfant.

239. 1. Le professeur les fera réciter.
2. La fille l'a fait faire.
3. Nous les ferons faire.
4. Il la fera construire.
5. Vous l'avez fait venir.
6. Elle se les ai fait laver.
7. Fais-les entrer.
8. Faites-le venir.

240. 1. Il la lui fera écrire.
2. Elle se l'est fait faire.
3. Il le leur fait écrire.
4. Il la lui fera faire.
5. Il les lui fait apprendre.
6. On le leur a fait jouer.
7. Fais-le-lui réparer.
8. Faites-la-leur chanter.

241. 1. J'ai vu Marie marcher sur le boulevard.
2. Je la vois arriver.
3. Je laisse (J'ai laissé) partir Pierre.
4. Je le laisse jouer.
(Je l'ai laissé jouer.)
5. J'ai entendu pleurer le bébé.
6. Je les ai entendues chanter.
7. Je les écoute chanter.
8. Il regarde les peintres peindre.

242.

1. à		13. à
2. de		14. —
3. de		15. —
4. de		16. de
5. —		17. à
6. à		18. —
7. —		19. —
8. de		20. de
9. de		21. de
10. —		22. d'
11. de		23. —
12. —		24. —

243. 1. Balzac a écrit le roman.

2. Les Romains ont construit ce monument.
3. Un incendie a détruit le bâtiment.
4. La bonne a préparé le repas.
5. Un grand architecte construira cette maison.
6. On m'a aimé.
7. On a fini le travail.
8. On a détruit cette ville pendant la guerre.

244. 1. Le français se parle au Québec.
2. Ce mot ne s'écrit pas sans s.
3. Le plus beau monument se verra au centre de la ville.
4. Autrefois, cela se faisait à la main.
5. La ville s'est modernisée.
6. Le portes s'ouvriront à huit heures.
7. Ces autos se fabriquaient dans cette usine.
8. Cela ne se dit pas.

Chapter 6

1. 1. Marie travaille bien, n'est-ce pas?
Est-ce que Marie travaille bien?
2. Il écrit une lettre, n'est-ce pas?
Est-ce qu'il écrit une lettre?
3. Pierre se couche, n'est-ce pas?
Est-ce que Pierre se couche?
4. Elle s'habillait bien, n'est-ce pas?
Est-ce qu'elle s'habillait bien?
5. Ils viendront à l'heure, n'est-ce pas?
Est-ce qu'ils viendront à l'heure?
6. Ils sont allés au cinéma hier soir, n'est-ce pas?
Est-ce qu'ils sont allés au cinéma hier soir?
7. Ces étudiants ont lu ce livre, n'est-ce pas?
Est-ce que ces étudiants ont lu ce livre?
8. Pierre s'est reposé, n'est-ce pas?
Est-ce que Pierre s'est reposé?

2. 1. Regardes-tu la peinture?
2. Allez-vous à Paris?
3. Savons-nous la réponse?
4. Écoutent-ils la radio?
5. Court-elle?
6. Te dépêches-tu?
7. Nous lèverons-nous de bonne heure?
8. Se couchent-elles à dix heures?
9. Suis-je amusant?
10. Puis-je le faire?

3. 1. Pleure-t-elle beaucoup?
2. Ouvre-t-il la porte?
3. Rencontre-t-elle une amie au café?

4. Se dépêche-t-il?
5. Se lave-t-elle la figure?
6. S'amuse-t-elle bien?

4. 1. Les enfants prennent-ils des bonbons?
2. Marie aime-t-elle la peinture moderne?
3. Hélène lit-elle un roman?
4. Les invités viendront-ils à l'heure?
5. Pierre se rase-t-il?
6. Hélène se reposera-t-elle dimanche?
7. Ces hommes se débrouillent-ils bien?
8. Marc et Pierre se retrouvent-ils à l'école tous les jours?

5. 1. Avons-nous fait nos devoirs?
2. A-t-elle dit la vérité?
3. Louise est-elle vite montée?
4. Sommes-nous arrivés à l'heure?
5. Se sont-ils couchés?
6. Se sont-elles moquées de vous?
7. Nous sommes-nous dépêchées?
8. Hélène s'est-elle lavée?

6. 1. Quand
2. Combien
3. Où
4. Comment
5. À quelle heure (Quand)
6. Pourquoi
7. Quand
8. Où
9. Combien
10. Comment

7. 1. Qui
   Qui est-ce qui
2. Qu'est-ce qui
3. Qui est-ce que
   Qui
4. Qui est-ce qu'
   Qui
5. Qu'est-ce qu'
   Que
6. Qu'est-ce qu'
   Qu'
7. qui
8. quoi

8. 1. Qui parle? (Qui est-ce qui parle?)
2. De qui est-elle la sœur?
3. Qu'est-ce qu'il a vu? (Qu'a-t-il vu?)
4. Sur quoi est-ce qu'il écrit (écrit-il) sa composition?
5. Qu'est-ce qui a fermé la porte?
6. À qui est-ce qu'il parle (parle-t-il)?
7. Qu'est-ce qui se passe?
8. De quoi est-ce qu'elle parle? (De quoi parle-t-elle?)

9. Qui est-ce qu'il regarde? (Qui regarde-t-il?)
10. Qu'est-ce qu'il fait? (Que fait-il?)
11. À qui sont ces livres?
12. De qui est-elle la fille?
13. Qui va à la bibliothèque? (Qui est-ce qui va à la bibliothèque?)
14. Qu'est qui fait ce bruit?

9. 1. À qui sont ces disques?
2. De qui est-il le fils?
3. À qui sont ces livres?
4. De qui est-elle la mère?
5. Quoi de neuf (nouveau)?

10. 1. Qu'est-ce que c'est que le Louvre?
2. Qu'est-ce que c'est que le Tour de France?
3. Qu'est-ce que c'est qu'un symbole?
4. Qu'est-ce que c'est que la Sorbonne?

11. 1. Quelles robes sont dans l'armoire?
2. Quelles peintures aimez-vous? (aimes-tu?)
3. Quel tableau est grand?
4. Quels restaurants sont bons?
5. Quelle est votre (ton) adresse?

12. 1. Quelle   4. Quels
2. Quels (Qui)   5. Quelle
3. Qui   6. Quelles

13. 1. Quel paysage!
2. Quelle peinture!
3. Quels livres!
4. Quels animaux!
5. Quel arbre!

14. 1. Lequel   3. Lesquels
2. Laquelle   4. Lesquelles

15. 1. À laquelle   3. Auxquelles
2. Auquel   4. Auxquels

16. 1. Duquel   3. Desquelles
2. De laquelle 4. Desquels

17. 1. Auxquelles
2. Combien
3. Lequel
4. Qui (Qui est-ce qui)
5. De qui
6. laquelle
7. Quel
8. De qui
9. De quoi
10. Quand
11. Qu'est-ce que c'est que
12. Que
13. À qui

14. À quelle heure (Quand)
15. Pourquoi
16. Qu'est-ce qui
17. Lesquels
18. Où

Chapter 7

1. 1. Il ne va pas au théâtre.
2. Vous ne lirez pas le roman.
3. Je ne crains pas cet homme.
4. Je n'écoute pas le professeur.
5. Tu n'habitais pas à Paris en ce temps-là.
6. Vous n'arriveriez pas en retard.
7. Je ne me reposerai pas dimanche.
8. Elles ne se couchaient pas à onze heures tous les soirs.
9. Vous ne vous retrouverez pas à la gare.
10. Ils ne se moquent pas de lui.
11. Nous ne nous débrouillons pas bien.
12. Il ne s'habille pas bien.

2. 1. Nous ne voulons pas partir.
2. Elle n'aime pas chanter.
3. Elle ne veut pas se lever.
4. Tu ne vas pas t'habiller.

3. 1. Je n'ai pas acheté la robe.
2. Vous n'aviez pas compris la situation.
3. Ils n'ont pas écrit leurs devoirs.
4. Nous ne sommes pas restés ici.
5. Elle n'est pas tombée du cheval.
6. Ils ne seront pas venus à l'heure.
7. Elle ne s'est pas bien reposée.
8. Nous ne nous serons pas dépêchées.
9. Elles ne se sont pas plaintes de tout.
10. Vous ne vous êtes pas levés de bonne heure.

4. 1. Non, je n'ai pas (nous n'avons pas) reçu la lettre.
2. Non, il n'a pas lu l'histoire.
3. Non, je ne suis pas allée au cinéma hier.
4. Non, elles ne sont pas parties de bonne heure.
5. Non, je ne me suis pas levé de bonne heure.
6. Non, elle ne s'est pas endormie.

5. 1. Est-ce que Georges ne vous parlera pas?
2. Ne lit-il pas le livre?
3. N'ouvre-t-elle pas la fenêtre?
4. Ne se dépêche-t-il pas?
5. Ne vous réveillez-vous pas?
6. N'avez-vous pas fini?
7. N'ont-elles pas craint cet homme?
8. Ne sont-elles pas rentrées de bonne heure?

9. Ne se sont-ils pas couchés?
10. Ne t'es-tu pas blessé?

6. 1. Ne vis-tu pas bien ici?
2. Ne saura-t-il pas la vérité?
3. Ne nous dépêchons-nous pas?
4. Ne vous levez-vous pas de bonne heure?
5. N'a-t-elle pas cru l'histoire?
6. Ne sont-elles pas revenues de bonne heure?
7. Ne s'est-il pas rasé?
8. Ne vous êtes-vous pas bien débrouillé?

7. 1. Oui, je parle (nous parlons) français.
2. Si, je parle (nous parlons) français.
3. Oui, ils viendront à l'heure.
4. Si, ils viendront à l'heure.
5. Oui, il a fini.
6. Si, il a fini.
7. Oui, elle se réveille.
8. Si, elle se réveille.

8. 1. Oui, il vit bien ici.
2. Si, ils sont venus.
3. Si, elle prendra le déjeuner ici.
4. Oui, il a lu ce roman.
5. Si, ils ont craint le criminel.

9. 1. Il ne sait ce qu'il veut.
2. Il ne cesse de pleuvoir.
3. Elle n'ose le dire.
4. Elle ne peut le faire.

10. 1. Il vous dit de ne pas avoir peur.
2. Elle vous demande de ne pas venir.
3. Elle vous dit ne ne pas être heureux.
4. Je vous demande de ne pas leur parler.
5. Elle vous dit de ne pas le faire.
6. Elle affirme ne pas avoir vu ce film. (Elle affirme n'avoir pas vu ce film.)

11. 1. Elle ne dit jamais la même chose.
2. Jamais, elle ne le fait.
3. Elle n'a jamais chanté.
4. Je n'ai aucun espoir.
5. Marie ne trouve rien.
6. Marie n'a rien perdu.
7. Rien n'est dans la cuisine.
8. Rien ne s'est passé.
9. Il n'y a personne dans la boutique.
10. Il n'a vu personne.
11. Personne ne frappe à la porte.
12. Personne n'est arrivé.
13. Je n'ai ni crayon ni stylo.
14. Il ne parle ni à son père ni à sa mère.
15. Elle ne veut ni pain ni beurre.
16. Ni l'un ni l'autre n'est parti.
17. Pierre ne parle jamais de rien à personne.

12.
1. Je n'ai jamais vu ce film.
2. Nous n'avons pas du tout dansé.
3. Il n'oubliera jamais cette leçon.
4. Il ne prend guère de vin.
5. Est-ce qu'il va jamais étudier?
6. Il n'a plus aucun disque.
7. Elle n'a ni amis ni ennemis.
8. Il n'a écrit que des poèmes.
9. Il n'a guère de temps.
10. Elle n'a que deux frères.
11. Elle ne chante plus de chansons.

13.
1. Non, il n'y a rien d'intéressant à faire.
2. Non, elle ne va jamais travailler.
3. Non, il n'y a personne ici.
4. Personne n'est venu.
5. Non, il n'a aucun livre.
6. Non, il n'a ni livres ni journaux.
7. Non, je n'ai guère le temps de le faire.
8. Non, elle n'est pas du tout riche.

14.
1. Il n'est pas riche non plus.
2. Ni elles non plus, elles n'ont pas beaucoup d'argent.
3. Marie ne le sait pas non plus.
4. Ni moi non plus, je ne viens pas.
5. Ni lui non plus, il ne la verra pas.
6. Elles ne mangent pas ici non plus.
7. Il ne l'a pas fait non plus.

15.
1. Jean ne mange pas d'épinards.
2. Jean n'aime pas jouer au tennis.
3. Jean ne sait (pas) quoi faire.
4. Jean ne se lève jamais de bonne heure.
5. Jean n'est pas allé au cinéma hier.
6. Jean ne s'est pas couché de bonne heure hier soir.
7. Jean n'a ni auto ni bicyclette.
8. Jean n'a acheté aucun disque hier.
9. Jean n'achète jamais rien quand il est en vacances.
10. Jean ne parle à personne.

Chapter 8

1.
1. Elle parle français.
2. Il chante bien.
3. Ils jouent de la guitare.
4. Elles étudient à la Faculté de Médecine.
5. Ils vont en vacances.

2.
1. Êtes-vous content, Monsieur?
2. Es-tu malheureuse, Marie?
3. Êtes-vous paresseux, Jean et Georges?
4. Es-tu fatigué, Jean?
5. Êtes-vous contents, Monsieur et Madame Leblanc?

3.
1. On va au cinéma.
2. On mange une pizza.
3. On discute politique.
4. On écoute des disques.
5. On est content(s).
6. On s'amuse bien.

4.
1. la	6. l'
2. les	7. les
3. le	8. l'
4. les	9. le
5. les	10. la

5.
1. Pierre les résout.
2. Je l'écris.
3. Anne le lit.
4. Ils les font chaque soir.
5. Nous les aimons.
6. Tu la comprends.
7. Vous les aidez.
8. Tu l'étudies cinq fois par semaine.
9. Anne et Marie les préparent bien.
10. Elles le reçoivent.

6.
1. Oui, je le pense.
2. Non, je ne le crois pas.
3. Oui, je le pense.
4. Non, je ne le crois pas.
5. Oui, je le sais.

7.
1. l'	3. l'
2. le	4. le

8.
1. Oui, Paul me parle.
2. Oui, Jean m'écoute.
3. Oui, il vous (te) dit bonjour.
4. Oui, il t'invite (vous invite).
5. Oui, elle vous (nous) voit.
6. Oui, elle vous (nous) appelle.
7. Oui, elle me répond.
8. Oui, il m'écoute.
9. Oui, ils nous regardent.
10. Oui, ils nous écrivent.

9.
1. Il m'apporte des fleurs.
2. Il nous invite à dîner.
3. Il vous aide.
4. Il te donne des cadeaux.
5. Il nous respecte.
6. Il me téléphone souvent.
7. Il vous prête ses outils.
8. Il t'écoute toujours.

10.
1. Elle lui donne un livre.
2. Elle leur donne des photos.
3. Elle lui donne un collier.

4. Elle leur donne des cravates.
5. Elle lui donne un bracelet.
6. Elle lui donne des disques.

11.
1. la
2. lui
3. le
4. les
5. leur
6. lui
7. la, lui

12.
1. Il y va.
2. Le livre y est.
3. Elle y sera.
4. Il y montera.
5. Il y répond.
6. Il y obéit.

13.
1. y
2. leur
3. y
4. lui
5. y

14.
1. Nous en sortons.
2. Elle en vient.
3. Ils en sortiront.
4. Il en a.
5. Elle en choisit.
6. Elle en achète.
7. Il en parle.
8. Il en est fier.
9. Elles en ont beaucoup.
10. Il en a un peu.
11. Elle en achète une douzaine.
12. Il en prend quatre.
13. Il en a plusieurs.
14. Elle en a quelques-uns.
15. Il en a quelques-unes.

15.
1. Nous y allons.
2. Il leur répond.
3. Nous en avons besoin.
4. Les valises y sont.
5. Elle y répond.
6. J'en ai plusieurs.
7. Il lui parle.
8. Elle en a quelques-unes.
9. Il y en a beaucoup ici.

16.
1. Elle me les montre.
2. Il nous le sert.
3. Elle te l'envoie.
4. Il nous la dit.
5. Il vous l'apporte.
6. Il le lui envoie.
7. Elle les leur donne.
8. Elle t'en donne.
9. Il vous en pose.
10. Il lui en donne plusieurs.
11. Il m'en apporte.
12. Elle m'y attend.
13. Il nous y rencontre.
14. Il y a en a quatre.

17.
1. Elle se la rappelle.
2. Il se les brosse.
3. Vous vous la lavez.
4. Elles se les lavent.
5. Elle s'en souvient.
6. Il se la fait faire.

18.
1. Le médecin m'en donne chaque semaine.
2. Le vendeur l'y rencontre.
3. Le professeur la leur explique.
4. Le banquier lui en prête.
5. Le bijoutier te le vend.
6. Le garçon leur en apporte trois.
7. L'avocat les leur donne.
8. Le biologiste y en fait.
9. Le facteur nous l'apporte.
10. Le pharmacien le lui donne.
11. L'épicier vous en vend.
12. Le marchand de fruits les lui vend.
13. Le chauffeur de taxi les y rencontre.
14. Le conducteur les leur vend.

19.
1. Il ne le fait pas.
2. Les y cherchez-vous?
3. Ne l'entend-il pas?
4. Ne l'y mange pas!
5. Les voilà.
6. Elle me l'expliquera.
7. Il ne nous la répète pas.
8. Je lui en avais donné.
9. Ne l'y a-t-elle pas attendu?
10. Elle leur en écrivait.
11. Il ne l'aurait pas lu.
12. Il l'a crue.
13. Les as-tu écrits?
14. Elles les y ont prises.
15. Elle la lui aura dite.
16. Il l'a écouté chanter.
17. Je l'ai fait venir.

20.
1. Je voudrais l'acheter.
2. Je voudrais le lui donner.
3. Je vais leur parler.
4. Je vais les y mettre.
5. Elle va en avoir honte.
6. Il me dit de ne pas l'acheter.
7. Il me demande de ne pas lui en parler.

21.
1. Parlez-moi!
2. Lisez-la!
3. Donne-le-lui!
4. Parle-lui-en!
5. Allez-y!
6. Achète-le-toi!

22.
1. Lisez-la!
2. Parlez-nous-en!
3. Écrivez-les-lui!
4. Réponds-y!
5. Vas-y!
6. Parles-en!

7. Donnez-m'en!

23. 1. Il ne lui obéit pas.
2. Il en a trop.
3. Elle y est allée.
4. Elle les y a mis.
5. Il ne la leur dit pas.
6. Elle n'y répond pas.
7. Ne l'écoute pas!
8. Il se le rappelle.
9. Il y en a beaucoup.
10. Elle y en a mis douze.
11. Donnez-m'en!
12. Lui en parlez-vous?
13. Je vais les lui donner.
14. Donnez-les-leur.
15. La lui as-tu donnée?
16. Ne lui en parle-t-elle pas?

24. 1. Pierre ne les a pas lavées.
Il ne les lave pas maintenant.
Il va les laver plus tard.
2. Anne ne la lui a pas écrite.
Elle ne la lui écrit pas maintenant.
Elle va la lui écrire plus tard.
3. M Leblanc ne l'a pas peinte.
Il ne la peint pas maintenant.
Il va la peindre plus tard.
4. M et Mme Leblanc n'y en ont pas acheté.
Ils n'y en achètent pas maintenant.
Ils vont y en acheter plus tard.
5. Anne et Pierre ne l'y ont pas rangée.
Ils ne l'y rangent pas maintenant.
Ils vont l'y ranger plus tard.
6. Mme Leblanc ne les y a pas jetées.
Elle ne les y jette pas maintenant.
Elle va les y jeter plus tard.
7. Marie ne leur en a pas donné.
Elle ne leur en donne pas maintenant.
Elle va leur en donner plus tard.
8. Mme Leblanc ne les y a pas plantées.
Elle ne les y plante pas maintenant.
Elle va les y planter plus tard.

25. 1. m'   6. vous
2. nous   7. me
3. te   8. nous
4. se   9. s'
5. se   10. t'

26. 1. Moi   5. lui
2. toi   6. eux
3. Lui   7. vous
4. moi   8. elles

27. 1. C'est moi qui ai envoyé les invitations.
Moi, j'ai envoyé les invitations.

2. C'est nous qui avons acheté le cadeau.
Elle et moi, nous avons acheté le cadeau.
3. Ce sont elles qui s'occupent de la musique.
Elles, elles s'occupent de la musique.
4. Ce sont eux qui préparent les sandwichs.
Eux, ils préparent les sandwichs.
5. C'est lui qui va faire le gâteau.
Lui, il va faire le gâteau.
6. C'est vous qui allez chercher les boissons.
Lui et toi, vous allez chercher les boissons.
7. C'est elle qui va faire les décorations.
Elle, elle va faire les décorations.
8. C'est toi qui vas faire la présentation du cadeau.
Toi, tu vas faire la présentation du cadeau.

28. 1. Je le ferai moi-même.
2. Il le fera lui-même.
3. Les garçons le feront eux-mêmes.
4. Nous le ferons nous-mêmes.
5. Chacun pour soi.

29. 1. Oui, j'y pense (nous y pensons).
2. Oui, j'ai (nous avons) peur de lui.
3. Oui, je partirai (nous partirons) sans eux.
4. Oui, j'en ai (nous en avons) honte.
5. Oui, je pense (nous pensons) à elle.
6. Oui, j'y vais (nous y allons).
7. Oui, c'est elles (ce sont elles) qui parlent.
8. Oui, ils vont chez elle.
9. Oui, elle va avec lui.
10. Oui, j'en ai (nous en avons) besoin.
11. Je me présente à lui.

30. 1. Ce sont les miens. Où sont les tiens?
2. Je n'aime pas la mienne. Aimez-vous la vôtre?
3. Il a pensé aux siens et elles ont pensé aux leurs.
4. J'ai besoin des miens et vous avez besoin des vôtres.
5. La nôtre est plus petite que la tienne.
6. Nous avons les nôtres. Avez-vous les vôtres?
7. Il a parlé de la sienne et tu as parlé de la tienne.
8. J'ai besoin de la leur.
9. Pierre va chercher les siennes et les miennes.
10. Vous mettez le vôtre et je mets le mien.

11. Nous sommes fiers du nôtre et ils sont fiers du leur.
12. Elle préfère les nôtres aux vôtres.
13. Il a cherché le sien et les filles ont cherché le leur.
14. Le tien est meilleur que le mien.
15. Il a téléphoné à la sienne et nous avons téléphoné à la nôtre.

31.
1. Ce sont les vôtres.
2. C'est le mien.
3. C'est la tienne.
4. C'est la nôtre.
5. C'est la sienne.
6. C'est le sien.
7. Ce sont les miennes.
8. Ce sont les leurs.

32.
1. Non, c'est celle de ma sœur.
2. Non, c'est celui de mon ami.
3. Non, ce sont ceux de mon frère.
4. Non, ce sont celles de ma mère.
5. Non, c'est celui de mon amie.
6. Non, c'est celle de mon oncle.

33.
1. Celles-ci, celles-là
2. Celui-ci, celui-là
3. Celles-ci, celles-là
4. Celui-ci, celui-là
5. Celle-ci, celle-là
6. Ceux-ci, ceux-là
7. Celui-ci, celui-là
8. Celle-ci, celle-là

34.
1. Il
2. c'
3. Elle
4. C'
5. C'
6. Ce

35.
1. Ceci
2. Cela
3. C'
4. ce
5. Cela
6. Cela (Ça)
7. ceci (cela)

36.
1. qui
2. que
3. qu'
4. qui
5. que
6. qui
7. qu'
8. qui

37.
1. Voilà un garçon qui est sportif.
2. La dame qui entre est la femme de mon professeur.
3. L'église qui est au centre de la ville est grande.
4. La jeune fille qui danse est très intelligente.
5. Je connais cette femme qui donne de bons discours.

38.
1. Voilà le restaurant que Pierre préfère.
2. Le journal que je lis est parisien.
3. La robe qu'elle a achetée est très chère.
4. Le film que nous avons vu est américain.
5. C'est un médecin que je connais.

39.
1. ce qu'
2. ce qui
3. ce qui
4. ce que
5. ce qui
6. ce qu'

40.
1. qui
2. qui
3. laquelle
4. lequel
5. lesquelles
6. lesquels
7. lesquels

41.
1. Voilà le garçon avec qui je suis sorti.
2. Voilà la maison dans laquelle j'ai habité.
3. Les hommes à qui j'ai écrit sont mes anciens professeurs.
4. C'est le pinceau avec lequel l'artiste travaille.
5. Voilà un morceau de papier sur lequel il a dessiné.
6. Le restaurant dans lequel Paul entre est très petit.
7. La fille chez qui nous allons est gentille.
8. Voilà les tables sur lesquelles Marie a mis des fleurs.
9. Le musée devant lequel il attend son ami est formidable.
10. Le théâtre auquel nous sommes allés est très vieux.
11. La conférence à laquelle elle a assisté était intéressante.
12. Les lettres auxquelles il a répondu étaient urgentes.
13. Les hommes à qui il a écrit sont avocats.
14. Les musées auxquels je suis allée sont grands.

42.
1. L'appartement où j'habite est très petit.
2. La boulangerie où j'entre est bonne.
3. Le bureau où je vais se trouve au centre de la ville.
4. Les restaurants où nous dînons ne sont pas chers.
5. Les églises où nous allons sont vieilles.

43.
1. Le garçon dont le père est mort est mon ami.
2. Le musée dont le nom m'échappe est célèbre.
3. La dame dont nous cherchons le chien est une amie de ma mère.
4. L'homme dont les usines sont à Lyon habite à Paris.
5. J'aime ce jardin dont les fleurs l'embellissent.

6. Le crayon dont vous vous servez n'est pas bon.
7. Les livres dont vous m'avez parlé sont intéressants.
8. La peinture dont vous avez envie est très chère.

44.
1. Voilà une fille dont le père est médecin.
2. Voilà le mannequin dont les robes sont jolies.
3. Voilà les garçons dont vous connaissez la sœur.
4. Voilà un professeur dont la fille est chimiste.
5. Voilà un garçon dont le père est mort.
6. Voilà une femme dont j'admire la beauté.
7. Voilà un peintre dont le tableau est cher.
8. C'est un beau tableau dont nous avons parlé.
9. C'est un livre dont vous avez envie.
10. As-tu étudié le poème dont il a parlé?
11. C'est un livre dont j'ai besoin.
12. J'ai vu la jeune fille dont ils ont parlé.
13. C'est un beau poème dont nous avons lu quelques passages.

45.
1. C'est la fille avec la mère de laquelle j'ai parlé.
2. C'est un homme avec la fille duquel je suis sorti.
3. Il y a une boutique ici près de laquelle se trouve un bureau de tabac.
4. Il a fait un discours à cause duquel j'ai pleuré.
5. Voilà les jeunes filles avec le frère desquelles je suis sortie.

46.
1. ce dont
2. quoi
3. à quoi
4. quoi
5. ce dont

47.
1. Ce que
2. qui
3. dont
4. où (dans laquelle)
5. que
6. dont
7. ce qui
8. ce qu'
9. duquel
10. dont (de qui)
11. quoi
12. qui
13. avec qui
14. avec lesquelles

48.
1. N'importe qui
2. Quelqu'un

3. Tout le monde (Chacun)
4. On
5. quelque chose
6. tout
7. Les autres
8. tous
9. quelques-uns
10. l'une et l'autre
11. ni l'un(e) ni l'autre
12. Certaines
13. n'importe quoi
14. autre chose
15. Tout ce que
16. plusieurs
17. quelques-unes
18. Chacune
19. Quelqu'un d'autre
20. Les un(e)s, les autres
21. l'un à l'autre
22. l'une ou l'autre
23. N'importe qui
24. la même
25. Aucune
26. Personne (Nul)
27. Tout
28. Rien
29. M un tel
30. Quiconque
31. autrui
32. autre chose

Chapter 9

1.
1. Il va en voiture.
2. Il ira loin.
3. Je vais mal.
4. Il va mieux aujourd'hui.
5. Ce chapeau vous (te) va bien.
6. Comment allez-vous? (Comment vas-tu? Comment ça va? Ça va?)
7. Je vais bien.
8. Il va à la pêche.

2.
1. J'ai soif.
2. J'ai faim.
3. J'ai sommeil.
4. J'ai froid.
5. J'ai chaud.
6. J'ai mal à la tête.
7. J'ai mal aux dents.
8. J'ai tort. (J'ai honte.)
9. J'ai raison.
10. J'ai tort.

3.
1. J'avais beau venir. Personne n'était ici.
2. Elle a peur de cet homme.
3. Il a honte de son travail.
4. Nous avions raison.

5. J'ai mal à la tête.
6. Les filles ont l'air fatiguées.
7. Pierre a de la chance.
8. Le train a une demi-heure de retard.
9. L'avion a dix minutes d'avance.
10. Il a l'occasion d'aller à la Martinique.
11. Qu'avez-vous? (Qu'as-tu?)
12. Quel âge avez-vous? (Quel âge as-tu?)
13. Il a cinquante ans.
14. Elle a besoin du livre.
15. La maison a vingt mètres de hauteur.
16. Nous avons chaud.
17. Les enfants ont sommeil.

4. 1. Elle est en train d'étudier.
    2. Les garçons sont de Paris.
    3. Cela m'est égal.
    4. Nous serons de retour demain.
    5. Ces livres sont à elles.
    6. Ça y est.

5. 1. Elle fait des économies.
    2. Nous faisons attention.
    3. Il fait le ménage.
    4. Je fais une promenade
    5. Tu fais fortune.
    6. Ils font leurs courses.

6. 1. Il fait chaud.
    2. Il fait frais.
    3. Il fait du soleil.
    4. Il fait du brouillard.
    5. Il fait nuit.
    6. Il fait de son mieux.
    7. Ce médicament vous (te) fera du bien.
    8. Je me suis fait mal au bras.
    9. Nous avons fait la queue pendant une heure.
    10. Je l'ai fait exprès.
    11. Ça ne fait rien.
    12. Ils ont fait semblant de ne pas entendre.

7. 1. Je dois cinq dollars à Marie.
    2. Il doit venir.
    3. Elle devait partir pour New York.
    4. Il doit être malade.
    5. Vous auriez (Tu aurais) dû venir.
    6. Il devrait étudier.
    7. Je peux le faire.
    8. Nous n'avons pas pu finir.
    9. J'aurais pu vous aider (t'aider).
    10. Il a pu le faire.
    11. Nous avons su la vérité.
    12. Elle a voulu ouvrir la porte.
    13. Il n'a pas voulu y aller.

8. 1. vit   4. demeurez
    2. demeurons   5. vivent
    3. vit

9. 1. Elle habite Paris.
    2. Ils habitent la Suisse.
    3. Vous habitez New York.
    4. Nous habitons le Mexique.

10. 1. joue   4. jouez de
    2. jouons du   5. jouent
    3. jouent aux   6. jouez au

11. 1. manque   4. manquent
    2. manque à   5. manquent à
    3. manquez de

12. 1. Il a manqué le train.
    2. Elle me manque.
    3. Je lui manque.
    4. Ils manquent de patience.

13. 1. du   4. aux
    2. à   5. à
    3. de

14. 1. Je pense à elle.
    2. Qu'en pense-t-il?
    3. Elle pense à lui.
    4. Que pense-t-elle de lui?
    5. Nous y pensons.
    6. Que pensent-elles d'eux?

15. 1. sort   5. quitte
    2. s'en va   6. sort
    3. laisse   7. pars
    4. m'en vais

16. 1. a passé
    2. s'est passé
    3. nous sommes passé(e)s de
    4. se sont passées
    5. a passé
    6. s'est passé
    7. s'est passé de

17. 1. Le film me plaît.
    2. Les peintures modernes lui plaisent.
    3. Le cinéma lui plaît.
    4. La pièce leur plaît.
    5. Le livre te plaît.

18. 1. Je me souviens de cette occasion.
    2. Je me souviens de cette fille.
    3. Ils se souviennent de cette soirée.
    4. Vous vous souvenez de la guerre.
    5. Nous nous en souvenons.

19. 1. sert   4. sert
    2. se sert d'   5. se sert d'
    3. sert

20.
1. savons
2. connaît
3. sais
4. Savez
5. connaissent
6. sait
7. connaissez
8. Connais, sais

21.
1. Il a su la vérité.
2. Il a connu cette femme.
3. Elle savait la vérité.
4. Elle connaissait ces enfants.

22.
1. viens de
2. viennent de
3. venez d'
4. venons de
5. viens de
6. vient d'

23.
1. Je venais de chanter cette chanson.
2. Elles venaient de sortir.
3. Vous veniez d'arriver.
4. Nous venions de rentrer d'Espagne.
5. Tu venais de manger.
6. Il venait d'entrer.

Verb Charts

REGULAR VERBS

Infinitive	**parler**	**finir**	**répondre**
Present participle	parlant	finissant	répondant
Past participle	parlé	fini	répondu
Present	je parle	je finis	je réponds
	tu parles	tu finis	tu réponds
	il parle	il finit	il répond
	nous parlons	nous finissons	nous répondons
	vous parlez	vous finissez	vous répondez
	ils parlent	ils finissent	ils répondent
Present subjunctive	je parle	je finisse	je réponde
	tu parles	tu finisses	tu répondes
	il parle	il finisse	il réponde
	nous parlions	nous finissions	nous répondions
	vous parliez	vous finissiez	vous répondiez
	ils parlent	ils finissent	ils répondent
Imperfect	je parlais	je finissais	je répondais
	tu parlais	tu finissais	tu répondais
	il parlait	il finissait	il répondait
	nous parlions	nous finissions	nous répondions
	vous parliez	vous finissiez	vous répondiez
	ils parlaient	ils finissaient	ils répondaient
Future	je parlerai	je finirai	je répondrai
	tu parleras	tu finiras	tu répondras
	il parlera	il finira	il répondra
	nous parlerons	nous finirons	nous répondrons
	vous parlerez	vous finirez	vous répondrez
	ils parleront	ils finiront	ils répondront
Conditional	je parlerais	je finirais	je répondrais
	tu parlerais	tu finirais	tu répondrais
	il parlerait	il finirait	il répondrait
	nous parlerions	nous finirions	nous répondrions
	vous parleriez	vous finiriez	vous répondriez
	ils parleraient	ils finiraient	ils répondraient

Imperative	parle	finis	réponds
	parlons	finissons	répondons
	parlez	finissez	répondez
Conversational past **(Passé composé)**	j'ai parlé	j'ai fini	j'ai répondu
	tu as parlé	tu as fini	tu as répondu
	il a parlé	il a fini	il a répondu
	nous avons parlé	nous avons fini	nous avons répondu
	vous avez parlé	vous avez fini	vous avez répondu
	ils ont parlé	ils ont fini	ils ont répondu
Pluperfect	j'avais parlé	j'avais fini	j'avais répondu
	tu avais parlé	tu avais fini	tu avais répondu
	il avait parlé	il avait fini	il avait répondu
	nous avions parlé	nous avions fini	nous avions répondu
	vous aviez parlé	vous aviez fini	vous aviez répondu
	ils avaient parlé	ils avaient fini	ils avaient répondu
Future perfect	j'aurai parlé	j'aurai fini	j'aurai répondu
	tu auras parlé	tu auras fini	tu auras répondu
	il aura parlé	il aura fini	il aura répondu
	nous aurons parlé	nous aurons fini	nous aurons répondu
	vous aurez parlé	vous aurez fini	vous aurez répondu
	ils auront parlé	ils auront fini	ils auront répondu
Conditional past	j'aurais parlé	j'aurais fini	j'aurais répondu
	tu aurais parlé	tu aurais fini	tu aurais répondu
	il aurait parlé	il aurait fini	il aurait répondu
	nous aurions parlé	nous aurions fini	nous aurions répondu
	vous auriez parlé	vous auriez fini	vous auriez répondu
	ils auraient parlé	ils auraient fini	ils auraient répondu
Past subjunctive	j'aie parlé	j'aie fini	j'aie répondu
	tu aies parlé	tu aies fini	tu aies répondu
	il ait parlé	il ait fini	il ait répondu
	nous ayons parlé	nous ayons fini	nous ayons répondu
	vous ayez parlé	vous ayez fini	vous ayez répondu
	ils aient parlé	ils aient fini	ils aient répondu
Literary past **(Passé simple)**	je parlai	je finis	je répondis
	tu parlas	tu finis	tu répondis
	il parla	il finit	il répondit
	nous parlâmes	nous finîmes	nous répondîmes
	vous parlâtes	vous finîtes	vous répondîtes
	ils parlèrent	ils finirent	ils répondirent
Imperfect subjunctive	je parlasse	je finisse	je répondisse
	tu parlasses	tu finisses	tu répondisses
	il parlât	il finît	il répondît
	nous parlassions	nous finissions	nous répondissions
	vous parlassiez	vous finissiez	vous répondissiez
	ils parlassent	ils finissent	ils répondissent
Past anterior **(Passé antérieur)**	j'eus parlé	j'eus fini	j'eus répondu
	tu eus parlé	tu eus fini	tu eus répondu
	il eut parlé	il eut fini	il eut répondu
	nous eûmes parlé	vous eûmes fini	nous eûmes répondu
	vous eûtes parlé	vous eûtes fini	vous eûtes répondu
	ils eurent parlé	ils eurent fini	ils eurent répondu

Pluperfect subjunctive	j'eusse parlé	j'eusse fini	j'eusse répondu
	tu eusses parlé	tu eusses fini	tu eusses répondu
	il eût parlé	il eût fini	il eût répondu
	nous eussions parlé	nous eussions fini	nous eussions répondu
	vous eussiez parlé	vous eussiez fini	vous eussiez répondu
	ils eussent parlé	ils eussent fini	ils eussent répondu
Passé surcomposé	j'ai eu parlé	j'ai eu fini	j'ai eu répondu
	tu as eu parlé	tu as eu fini	tu as eu répondu
	il a eu parlé	il a eu fini	il a eu répondu
	nous avons eu parlé	nous avons eu fini	nous avons eu répondu
	vous avez eu parlé	vous avez eu fini	vous avez eu répondu
	ils ont eu parlé	ils ont eu fini	ils ont eu répondu

VERBS WITH SPELLING CHANGES

acheter

Present	j'achète, tu achètes, il achète, nous achetons, vous achetez, ils achètent
Present subjunctive	j'achète, tu achètes, il achète, nous achetions, vous achetiez, ils achètent
Future	il achètera, nous achèterons, ils achèteront

appeler

Present	j'appelle, tu appelles, il appelle, nous appelons, vous appelez, ils appellent
Present subjunctive	j'appelle, tu appelles, il appelle, nous appelions, vous appeliez, ils appellent
Future	il appellera, nous appellerons, ils appelleront

commencer (and all verbs ending in **-cer**)

Present	je commence, tu commences, il commence, nous commençons, vous commencez, ils commencent
Imperfect	il commençait, nous commencions, ils commençaient
Passé simple	il commença, nous commençâmes, ils commencèrent

espérer (préférer, répéter, protéger, etc.)

Present	j'espère, tu espères, il espère, nous espérons, vous espérez, ils espèrent
Present subjunctive	j'espère, tu espères, il espère, nous espérions, vous espériez, ils espèrent

essayer (and all verbs ending in **-ayer, oyer, uyer**)
(Note also alternate forms: **j'essaye, j'essayerai,** etc., for verbs ending in **-ayer.**)

Present	j'essaie, tu essaies, il essaie, nous essayons, vous essayez, ils essaient
Present subjunctive	j'essaie, tu essaies, il essaie, nous essayions, vous essayiez, ils essaient
Future	il essaiera, nous essaierons, ils essaieront

jeter

Present	je jette, tu jettes, il jette, nous jetons, vous jetez, ils jettent
Present subjunctive	je jette, tu jettes, il jette, nous jetions, vous jetiez, ils jettent
Future	il jettera, nous jetterons, ils jetteront

lever (mener, emmener, geler, etc.)

Present	je lève, tu lèves, il lève, nous levons, vous levez, ils lèvent
Present subjunctive	je lève, tu lèves, il lève, nous levions, vous leviez, ils lèvent
Future	il lèvera, nous lèverons, ils lèveront

manger (and other verbs ending in **-ger**)

Present	je mange, tu manges, il mange, nous mangeons, vous mangez, ils mangent
Present subjunctive	je mange, tu manges, il mange, nous mangions, vous mangiez, ils mangent
Imperfect	il mangeait, nous mangions, ils mangeaient
Passé simple	il mangea, nous mangeâmes, ils mangèrent

In this list, the number at the right of each verb corresponds to the number of the verb, or of a similarly conjugated verb, in the table which follows. An asterisk (*) indicates that **être** is used as the auxiliary verb in the compound tenses. A dash plus an asterisk (—*) indicates that the verb is conjugated with **avoir** or **être** in compound tenses.

acquérir	1	croire	11	offrir	25	revoir	41
accueillir	12	cueillir	12	ouvrir	25	rire	32
admettre	22	découvrir	25	paraître	8	rompre	33
*aller	2	décrire	15	parcourir	9	savoir	34
*s'en aller	2	détruire	7	*partir	26	secourir	9
apercevoir	31	*devenir	39	*parvenir	39	sentir	26
—*apparaître	8	devoir	13	peindre	10	*se sentir	26
appartenir	39	dire	14	permettre	22	servir	26
apprendre	30	—*disparaître	8	plaindre	10	*se servir de	26
*s'asseoir	3	dormir	26	*se plaindre	10	*sortir	26
atteindre	10	écrire	15	plaire	27	souffrir	25
avoir	4	élire	21	pleuvoir	28	soumettre	22
battre	5	*s'endormir	26	poursuivre	36	sourire	32
*se battre	5	envoyer	16	pouvoir	29	*se souvenir de	39
boire	6	être	17	prendre	30	suffire	35
combattre	5	faire	18	prévoir	41	suivre	36
comprendre	30	falloir	19	produire	7	surprendre	30
conduire	7	interdire	14	promettre	22	survivre	40
connaître	8	interrompre	33	recevoir	31	*se taire	27
conquérir	1	haïr	20	reconnaître	8	tenir	39
construire	7	joindre	10	reconstruire	7	traduire	7
contenir	39	lire	21	recouvrir	25	transmettre	22
convaincre	37	maintenir	39	*redevenir	39	vaincre	37
convenir	39	mentir	26	rejoindre	10	valoir	38
corrompre	33	mettre	22	remettre	22	*venir	39
courir	9	*mourir	23	reprendre	30	vivre	40
couvrir	25	*naître	24	retenir	39	voir	41
craindre	10	obtenir	39	*revenir	39	vouloir	42

IRREGULAR VERBS

Note: Only irregular forms are given for the following verbs. The conditional tense is always formed by adding the regular endings to the future stem. An asterisk (*) indicates that the verb is conjugated with **être** in auxiliary tenses.

[1]**acquérir**

Past participle	acquis
Present	j'acquiers, tu acquiers, il acquiert, nous acquérons, vous acquérez, ils acquièrent

Present subjunctive	j'acquière, tu acquières, il acquière, nous acquérions, vous acquériez, ils acquièrent
Future	il acquerra
Passé simple	il acquit, ils acquirent

[2]*aller

Present	je vais, tu vas, il va, nous allons, vous allez, ils vont
Present subjunctive	j'aille, tu ailles, il aille, nous allions, vous alliez, ils aillent
Future	il ira
Imperative	va, allons, allez

[3]*s'asseoir

(There is another, less used conjugation for this verb:
je m'assois, nous nous assoyons, il s'assoira, etc.)

Past participle	assis
Present	je m'assieds, tu t'assieds, il s'assied, nous nous asseyons, vous vous asseyez, ils s'asseyent
Present subjunctive	je m'asseye, tu t'asseyes, il s'asseye, nous nous asseyions, vous vous asseyiez, ils s'asseyent
Future	il s'assiéra
Imperative	assieds-toi, asseyons-nous, asseyez-vous
Passé simple	il s'assit, ils s'assirent

[4]avoir

Present participle	ayant
Past participle	eu
Present	j'ai, tu as, il a, nous avons, vous avez, ils ont
Present subjunctive	j'aie, tu aies, il ait, nous ayons, vous ayez, ils aient
Future	il aura
Imperative	aie, ayons, ayez
Passé simple	il eut, ils eurent

[5]battre

Present	je bats, tu bats, il bat, nous battons, vous battez, ils battent

[6]boire

Past participle	bu
Present	je bois, tu bois, il boit, nous buvons, vous buvez, ils boivent
Present subjunctive	je boive, tu boives, il boive, nous buvions, vous buviez, ils boivent
Passé simple	il but, ils burent

[7]conduire

Past participle	conduit
Present	je conduis, tu conduis, il conduit, nous conduisons, vous conduisez, ils conduisent
Passé simple	il conduisit, ils conduisirent

[8]connaître

Past participle	connu
Present	je connais, tu connais, il connaît, nous connaissons, vous connaissez, ils connaissent
Passé simple	il connut, ils connurent

[9]**courir**

Past participle	couru
Present	je cours, tu cours, il court, nous courons, vous courez, ils courent
Future	il courra
Passé simple	il courut, ils coururent

[10]**craindre** (and other verbs ending in **-indre**)

Past participle	craint
Present	je crains, tu crains, il craint, nous craignons, vous craignez, ils craignent
Passé simple	il craignit, ils craignirent

[11]**croire**

Past participle	cru
Present	je crois, tu crois, il croit, nous croyons, vous croyez, ils croient
Present subjunctive	je croie, tu croies, il croie, nous croyions, vous croyiez, ils croient
Passé simple	il crut, ils crurent

[12]**cueillir**

Present	je cueille, tu cueilles, il cueille, nous cueillons, vous cueillez, ils cueillent
Future	il cueillera

[13]**devoir**

Past participle	dû (*fem.* due)
Present	je dois, tu dois, il doit, nous devons, vous devez, ils doivent
Present subjunctive	je doive, tu doives, il doive, nous devions, vous deviez, ils doivent
Future	il devra
Passé simple	il dut, ils durent

[14]**dire**

Past participle	dit
Present	je dis, tu dis, il dit, nous disons, vous dites, ils disent
Passé simple	il dit, ils dirent

[15]**écrire**

Past participle	écrit
Present	j'écris, tu écris, il écrit, nous écrivons, vous écrivez, ils écrivent
Passé simple	il écrivit, ils écrivirent

[16]**envoyer**

Present	j'envoie, tu envoies, il envoie, nous envoyons, vous envoyez, ils envoient
Present subjunctive	j'envoie, tu envoies, il envoie, nous envoyions, vous envoyiez, ils envoient
Future	il enverra

[17]**être**

Present participle	étant
Past participle	été
Present	je suis, tu es, il est, nous sommes, vous êtes, ils sont
Present subjunctive	je sois, tu sois, il soit, nous soyons, vous soyez, ils soient
Imperfect	il était
Future	il sera

| **Imperative** | sois, soyons, soyez |
| **Passé simple** | il fut, ils furent |

[18]faire

Past participle	fait
Present	je fais, tu fais, il fait, nous faisons, vous faites, ils font
Present subjunctive	je fasse, tu fasses, il fasse, nous fassions, vous fassiez, ils fassent
Future	il fera
Passé simple	il fit, ils firent

[19]falloir

Past participle	fallu
Present	il faut
Present subjunctive	il faille
Future	il faudra
Passé simple	il fallut

[20]haïr

Past participle	haï
Present	je hais, tu hais, il hait, nous haïssons, vous haïssez, ils haïssent
Passé simple	il haït, ils haïrent

[21]lire

Past participle	lu
Present	je lis, tu lis, il lit, nous lisons, vous lisez, ils lisent
Passé simple	il lut, ils lurent

[22]mettre

Past participle	mis
Present	je mets, tu mets, il met, nous mettons, vous mettez, ils mettent
Passé simple	il mit, ils mirent

[23]*mourir

Past participle	mort
Present	je meurs, tu meurs, il meurt, nous mourons, vous mourez, ils meurent
Present subjunctive	je meure, tu meures, il meure, nous mourions, vous mouriez, ils meurent
Future	il mourra
Passé simple	il mourut, ils moururent

[24]*naître

Past participle	né
Present	je nais, tu nais, il naît, nous naissons, vous naissez, ils naissent
Passé simple	il naquit, ils naquirent

[25]ouvrir

| **Past participle** | ouvert |
| **Present** | j'ouvre, tu ouvres, il ouvre, nous ouvrons, vous ouvrez, ils ouvrent |

[26]*partir

| **Present** | je pars, tu pars, il part, nous partons, vous partez, ils partent |
| **Passé simple** | il partit, ils partirent |

[27]**plaire** (**se taire**: present, **il se tait**)

Past participle	plu
Present	je plais, tu plais, il plaît, nous plaisons, vous plaisez, ils plaisent
Passé simple	il plut, ils plurent

[28]**pleuvoir**

Present participle	pleuvant
Past participle	plu
Present	il pleut
Present subjunctive	il pleuve
Future	il pleuvra
Passé simple	il plut

[29]**pouvoir**

Past participle	pu
Present	je peux, tu peux, il peut, nous pouvons, vous pouvez, ils peuvent
Present subjunctive	je puisse, tu puisses, il puisse, nous puissions, vous puissiez, ils puissent
Future	il pourra
Passé simple·	il put, ils purent

[30]**prendre**

Past participle	pris
Present	je prends, tu prends, il prend, nous prenons, vous prenez, ils prennent
Present subjunctive	je prenne, tu prennes, il prenne, nous prenions, vous preniez, ils prennent
Passé simple	il prit, ils prirent

[31]**recevoir**

Past participle	reçu
Present	je reçois, tu reçois, il reçoit, nous recevons, vous recevez, ils reçoivent
Present subjunctive	je reçoive, tu reçoives, il reçoive, nous recevions, vous receviez, ils reçoivent
Future	il recevra
Passé simple	il reçut, ils reçurent

[32]**rire**

Past participle	ri
Present	je ris, tu ris, il rit, nous rions, vous riez, ils rient
Passé simple	il rit, ils rirent

[33]**rompre**

Present	je romps, tu romps, il rompt, nous rompons, vous rompez, ils rompent
Passé simple	il rompit, ils rompirent

[34]**savoir**

Present participle	sachant
Past participle	su
Present	je sais, tu sais, il sait, nous savons, vous savez, ils savent
Present subjunctive	je sache, tu saches, il sache, nous sachions, vous sachiez, ils sachent
Future	il saura
Imperative	sache, sachons, sachez
Passé simple	il sut, ils surent

[35]suffire

Past participle	suffi
Present	je suffis, tu suffis, il suffit, nous suffisons, vous suffisez, ils suffisent
Passé simple	il suffit, ils suffirent

[36]suivre

Past participle	suivi
Present	je suis, tu suis, il suit, nous suivons, vous suivez, ils suivent
Passé simple	il suivit, ils suivirent

[37]vaincre

Present	je vaincs, tu vaincs, il vainc, nous vainquons, vous vainquez, ils vainquent
Passé simple	il vainquit, ils vainquirent

[38]valoir

Past participle	valu
Present	je vaux, tu vaux, il vaut, nous valons, vous valez, ils valent
Present subjunctive	je vaille, tu vailles, il vaille, nous valions, vous valiez, ils vaillent
Future	il vaudra
Passé simple	il valut, ils valurent

[39]*venir

Past participle	venu
Present	je viens, tu viens, il vient, nous venons, vous venez, ils viennent
Present subjunctive	je vienne, tu viennes, il vienne, nous venions, vous veniez, ils viennent
Future	il viendra
Passé simple	il vint, ils vinrent

[40]vivre

Past participle	vécu
Present	je vis, tu vis, il vit, nous vivons, vous vivez, ils vivent
Passé simple	il vécut, ils vécurent

[41]voir

Past participle	vu
Present	je vois, tu vois, il voit, nous voyons, vous voyez, ils voient
Present subjunctive	je voie, tu voies, il voie, nous voyions, vous voyiez, ils voient
Future	il verra
Passé simple	il vit, ils virent

[42]vouloir

Past participle	voulu
Present	je veux, tu veux, il veut, nous voulons, vous voulez, ils veulent
Present subjunctive	je veuille, tu veuilles, il veuille, nous voulions, vous vouliez, ils veuillent
Future	il voudra
Imperative	veuille, veuillons, veuillez
Passé simple	il voulut, ils voulurent

INDEX